ASPEN PUBL

M000273112

CONSTITUTIONAL LAW

4TH EDITION

NEIL C. BLOND

Third edition revised by

Professor William D. Araiza

Loyola Law School Los Angeles

Wolters Kluwer
Law & Business

AUSTIN   BOSTON   CHICAGO   NEW YORK   THE NETHERLANDS

To contact Customer Care, e-mail customer.care@aspenpublishers.com, call 1-800-234-1660, fax 1-800-901-9075, or mail correspondence to:

> Aspen Publishers
> Attn: Order Department
> PO Box 990
> Frederick, MD 21705

Printed in the United States of America.
1 2 3 4 5 6 7 8 9 0

ISBN 978-0-7355-8612-3

About Wolters Kluwer Law & Business

Wolters Kluwer Law & Business is a leading provider of research information and workflow solutions in key specialty areas. The strengths of the individual brands of Aspen Publishers, CCH, Kluwer Law International and Loislaw are aligned within Wolters Kluwer Law & Business to provide comprehensive, in-depth solutions and expert-authored content for the legal, professional and education markets.

CCH was founded in 1913 and has served more than four generations of business professionals and their clients. The CCH products in the Wolters Kluwer Law & Business group are highly regarded electronic and print resources for legal, securities, antitrust and trade regulation, government contracting, banking, pension, payroll, employment and labor, and healthcare reimbursement and compliance professionals.

Aspen Publishers is a leading information provider for attorneys, business professionals and law students. Written by preeminent authorities, Aspen products offer analytical and practical information in a range of specialty practice areas from securities law and intellectual property to mergers and acquisitions and pension/benefits. Aspen's trusted legal education resources provide professors and students with high-quality, up-to-date and effective resources for successful instruction and study in all areas of the law.

Kluwer Law International supplies the global business community with comprehensive English-language international legal information. Legal practitioners, corporate counsel and business executives around the world rely on the Kluwer Law International journals, loose-leafs, books and electronic products for authoritative information in many areas of international legal practice.

Loislaw is a premier provider of digitized legal content to small law firm practitioners of various specializations. Loislaw provides attorneys with the ability to quickly and efficiently find the necessary legal information they need, when and where they need it, by facilitating access to primary law as well as state-specific law, records, forms and treatises.

Wolters Kluwer Law & Business, a unit of Wolters Kluwer, is headquartered in New York and Riverwoods, Illinois. Wolters Kluwer is a leading multinational publisher and information services company.

Check Out These Other Great Titles:

BLOND'S LAW GUIDES

Comprehensive, Yet Concise . . . JUST RIGHT!

Each Blond's Law Guide book contains: Black Letter Law Outline · EasyFlow™ Charts · Case Clips · Mnemonics

Available titles in this series include:

Blond's Civil Procedure

Blond's Constitutional Law

Blond's Contracts

Blond's Criminal Law

Blond's Criminal Procedure

Blond's Evidence

Blond's Property

Blond's Torts

Law school is very different from your previous educational experiences. In the past, course material was presented in a straightforward manner both in lectures and texts. You did well by memorizing and regurgitating. In law school, your fat casebooks are stuffed with material, most of which will be useless when finals arrive. Your professors ask a lot of questions but don't seem to be teaching you either the law or how to think. Sifting through voluminous material seeking out the important concepts is a hard, time-consuming chore. We've done that job for you. This book will help you study effectively. We hope to teach you the law and how to think.

Preparing for Class

Most students start their first year by reading and briefing all their cases. They spend too much time copying unimportant details. After finals they realize they wasted time on facts that were useless on the exam.

Case Clips

Case Clips help you focus on what your professor wants you to get out of your cases. Facts, Issues, and Rules are carefully and succinctly stated. Left out are details irrelevant to what you need to learn from the case. In general, we skip procedural matters in lower courts. We don't care which party is the appellant or petitioner because the trivia is not relevant to the law. Case Clips should be read before you read the actual case. You will have a good idea what to look for in the case, and appreciate the significance of what you are reading. Inevitably you will not have time to read all your cases before class. Case Clips allow you to prepare for class in about five minutes. You will be able to follow the discussion and listen without fear of being called upon.

"Should I read all the cases even if they aren't from my casebook?"

Yes, if you feel you have the time. Most major cases from other texts will be covered at least as a note case in your book. The principles of these cases are universal and the fact patterns should help your understanding. The Case Clips are written in a way that should provide a tremendous amount of understanding in a relatively short period of time.

EasyFlow™ Charts

A very common complaint among law students is that they "can't put it all together." When you are reading 400 pages a week it is difficult to remember how the last case relates to the first and how November's read-ings relate to September's. It's hard to understand the relationship between different torts topics when you have read cases for three or four other classes in between. Our EasyFlow™ Charts will help you put the whole course together. They are designed to help you memorize fundamentals. They reinforce your learning by showing you the material from another perspective.

Outlines

More than one hundred lawyers and law students were interviewed as part of the development of this series. Most complained that their casebooks did not teach them the law and were far too voluminous to be useful before an exam. They also told us that the commercial outlines they purchased were excellent when used as hornbooks to explain the law, but were too wordy and redundant to be effective during the weeks before finals. Few students can read four 500-page outlines during the last month of classes. It is virtually impossible to memorize that much material and even harder to decide what is important. Almost every student interviewed said he or she studied from homemade outlines. We've written the outline you should use to study.

"But writing my own outline will be a learning experience."

True, but unfortunately many students spend so much time outlining they don't leave time to learn and memorize. Many students told us they spent six weeks outlining, and only one day studying before each final!

Mnemonics

Most law students spend too much time reading, and not enough time memorizing. Mnemonics are included to help you organize your essays and spot issues. They highlight what is important and which areas deserve your time.

CONTENTS

EASYFLOW™ CHARTS

CHAPTER 1

The Supreme Court's Authority

I. INTRODUCTION

The nature and source of the Supreme Court's authority is an evolving area of judicial debate. Although *Marbury v. Madison* will constitute the basis of discussion, other areas will also be explored. These include Supreme Court review of congressional actions and state court judgments; Congress' authority to limit federal court jurisdiction; and the jurisdiction and practice of the Supreme Court.

II. REVIEW OF CONGRESSIONAL ACTS

A. *Marbury v. Madison* established the doctrine of judicial review: the Supreme Court is the ultimate interpreter of the Constitution for the coordinate branches of government.

B. The Judiciary Act of 1789 authorized the Supreme Court to issue writs of mandamus (an order to compel an official to perform a duty) to persons holding office under U.S. authority. According to Chief Justice Marshall (the first Chief Justice), this statute was at odds with Article III, §2 of the Constitution, which only granted the Supreme Court original jurisdiction in certain types of cases. The federal statute was therefore unconstitutional because the issuance of writs of mandamus in this type of case fell outside the purview of Article III.

C. As a species of law, the Constitution is within the province of the Judiciary. The Constitution is also the supreme law of the land, and the Supreme Court Justices, like other judges, are constitutionally bound to protect that supremacy. Any statute at variance with the Constitution is therefore null and void (Article VI).

D. The judicial branch of government has the duty and power to declare what the law is. *Marbury v. Madison*. The Supreme Court has the authority to declare a statute unconstitutional and to refuse to apply it.

III. REVIEW OF STATE LAWS

A. Article VI establishes that the "Constitution, and the Laws of the United States . . . made in Pursuance thereof; and all Treaties made . . . under the Authority of the United States, shall be the supreme Law of the Land; and the Judges in every State shall be bound thereby. . . ." Thus, state court judges must follow the U.S. Constitution, even when state laws conflict with it. The Supreme Court's power to assess the constitutionality of state legislation logically extends from its role as the ultimate arbiter of the Constitution.

B. The Supreme Court contends that review of state law is essential to the development of uniform constitutional principles. The Constitution would have little effect if each state were free to apply the document as it saw fit.

IV. REVIEW OF STATE COURT JUDGMENTS

The Supreme Court can only review a state court's decision under the Court's appellate jurisdiction. Article III, §2 states that the Supreme Court has "appellate Jurisdiction, both as to Law and Fact, with such Exceptions, and under such Regulations as the Congress shall make." Such review is limited, however, to federal questions decided in state courts.

V. CONGRESS' AUTHORITY TO LIMIT FEDERAL COURT JURISDICTION

The Constitution specifically prescribes the Supreme Court's original jurisdiction. Congress may not add to or take away from that jurisdiction. The Supreme Court exercises its *appellate jurisdiction*, however, at Congress' discretion. *Ex Parte McCardle*. Although Congress can alter the scope of that appellate jurisdiction, it may not prescribe the rules by which the Court arrives at its decisions. *United States v. Klein*.

A. Article III, §1 established the federal court system by providing that judicial power "shall be vested in one supreme Court, and in such inferior Courts as the Congress may from time to time ordain and establish."

B. Article III, §2 states that the Supreme Court's and the lower federal courts' appellate jurisdiction is subject to congressional exceptions and regulations.

VI. SUPREME COURT JURISDICTION AND PRACTICE

Prior to 1988, the Supreme Court would hear a case either by appeal or by certiorari.

A. Appeal

Prior to 1988, the Court was compelled to hear cases that came before it on appeal. In 1988, however, Congress all but eliminated the mandatory appeal process. Now, nearly every case reaches the Supreme Court by a grant of certiorari.

B. Certiorari

Certiorari is the process by which the Supreme Court determines which cases it will hear. Because the Court has full discretion in granting or denying certiorari, the Court now has full control of the nature and number of cases it hears.

C. Standards for Granting Certiorari

The Court will grant certiorari in any of the following instances:

1. Conflicts between different federal courts of appeal.
2. Conflicts between the highest courts of two states.
3. Conflicts between a state's highest court and a federal court of appeals.
4. A state court or federal court of appeals decision involving an important question not yet settled by the Supreme Court.

D. Further Requirements for Certiorari

1. The case must be based on federal law.
2. The "four vote" requirement: four of the nine Justices must cast votes approving a grant of certiorari.

VII. REQUIRED CONDITIONS FOR CONSTITUTIONAL ADJUDICATION

A. The Supreme Court and lower federal courts will only hear justiciable cases, i.e., cases appropriate for federal adjudication on the merits.

B. Sources of Justiciability Standards

The conditions necessary for justiciability are derived either from interpretations of the Article III, §2 requirement that there be a "case or controversy," or from general Supreme Court policies developed apart from the Constitution.

C. Requirements for Justiciability

A suit is justiciable when certain conditions are present.

Mnemonic: **SCRIMPS**
1. **S**tanding (*Allen v. Wright*)
   A plaintiff must have standing to invoke the adjudicatory power of the federal courts. Standing is created when the plaintiff has a personal stake in the suit's outcome. The "personal stake" requirement is met where:
   a. There is distinct and palpable (not speculative) injury to the plaintiff;
   b. A fairly traceable causal connection exists between the claimed injury and the challenged conduct; and
   c. There is a substantial likelihood that the relief requested will prevent or redress the claimed injury.
   d. Taxpayer Standing
      A taxpayer will have standing to challenge a congressional expenditure only if it meets the dual-nexus test established in *Flast v. Cohen*.
      i. The expenditure must be an exercise of power under the Taxing and Spending Clause.
      ii. The expenditure must violate a specific constitutional provision that limits the taxing and spending power, such as the prohibition against an established religion.
   In reviewing a suit that requests more than one type of relief, the Supreme Court will impose a separate standing test for each.
2. **C**ase or Controversy (*Warth v. Seldin*)
   The issues must arise out of an actual and current case or controversy between adverse litigants. Adjudication of hypothetical or removed disputes would result in advisory opinions, which federal courts may not issue.
3. **R**ipeness (*United Public Workers v. Mitchell*)
   The case must be ripe for review, i.e., the issues must be fully crystallized and the controversy concrete. Ripeness is established when litigants claim actual interference with their rights. Hypothetical threats to those rights do not invoke federal adjudicatory power.
4. **M**ootness (*DeFunis v. Odegaard*)
   A federal case must involve controversies that are active and ongoing at the time of adjudication. A case becomes moot, and thus ineligible for judgment on the merits, once the controversy between the parties ceases to be definite and concrete and when a court's decision would no longer affect the litigants' rights.
5. **P**olitical Question (*Goldwater v. Carter*)
   A suit is a nonjusticiable political question if:
   a. The issues involve resolution of questions committed by the Constitution's text to a coordinate governmental branch;

   b. There is a lack of judicially discoverable and manageable stan-
      dards for resolving the case, or if a decision would require a
      policy determination clearly outside judicial discretion; and
   c. Judicial intervention would produce an embarrassing diver-
      sity of pronouncements on the issue by various governmen-
      tal departments.
6. **Self-restraint/Discretion** (*Barrows v. Jackson*)
   There must not be a risk that federal adjudication would
   breach principles of judicial self-restraint and discretion. For
   example, federal courts and the Supreme Court avoid suits that
   would entail interfering with:
   a. State courts' ability to resolve federal question cases;
   b. Pending state court proceedings; or
   c. Execution of state court judgments.
   Judicial self-restraint recognizes the importance of preserving
   the balance between state and federal interests. Such restraint
   also prevents the unwarranted federal constitutional decisions
   that may result when federal courts interpret state statutes.
D. The Problem of "Jus Tertii"
   The Supreme Court and lower federal courts do not recognize the
   standing of a plaintiff who represents the constitutional rights of
   third parties ("jus tertii"), i.e., those not parties to the case. This
   rule is not constitutionally based; it is founded on policies of
   judicial self-restraint.
   1. The Court hesitates to permit assertions of "jus tertii"
      (third-party rights) because:
      a. Non-parties may not want to assert their own rights;
      b. Non-party rights may be unaffected by the outcome of the
         litigation; and
      c. Third parties are often the best proponents of their own
         interests.
   2. Federal courts may recognize "jus tertii" standing when:
      a. A non-party's rights are inextricably bound up with the
         activity the litigant wishes to pursue;
      b. The plaintiff is as effective a proponent of the third party's
         rights as the third party would be; and
      c. There is a genuine obstacle to the non-party representing its
         own interests.

VIII. STATE SOVEREIGN IMMUNITY

Generally, states are sovereign and cannot be sued in federal court
without their consent. There are several exceptions to this rule,
however.

A. The Supreme Court may hear a case against a state appealed from the state court system.
B. Federal courts can hear cases against a state brought by the federal government or by another state.
C. Federal courts can hear cases against a state where the relief requested is prospective (such as an injunction), rather than retrospective (such as damages), and where the relief ostensibly runs against a state official rather than the state itself.
D. Congress can abrogate a state's sovereign immunity when legislating pursuant to its power to enforce the Fourteenth Amendment or its power under the Bankruptcy Clause of Article I.

CASE CLIPS

Marbury v. Madison (S. Ct. 803)

Facts: Marbury was a justice of the peace whom President Adams, on his last day in office, appointed for the District of Columbia. Although Acting Secretary of State Marshall sealed the commissions, several (including Marbury's) were not delivered on time. Jefferson, President Adams' successor, ordered Madison, the new Secretary of State, not to deliver the commissions. Marbury argued that (a) he and the other appointees were entitled to the commissions and (b) Madison's failure to deliver the commissions entitled the appointees to a writ of mandamus.

Issue: Does the Supreme Court have the right to review acts of Congress and decide their constitutionality?

Rule: (Marshall, C.J.) Implicitly, Article VI, §2 of the Constitution gives the Supreme Court the authority to review acts of Congress and determine their constitutionality.

Note: As a result of this rule, the Court denied the requested writ of mandamus. Although generally authorized by the Judiciary Act of 1789, such a writ could not be granted because the Court lacked original jurisdiction over this type of proceeding. The provisions of the Judiciary Act that expanded the Court's original jurisdiction beyond the scope of Article III, and under which Marbury sought the writ, were deemed unconstitutional.

Ex Parte McCardle (S. Ct. 1869)

Facts: After the Civil War, Congress imposed military government upon several former Confederate states. The Congressional Act of 1867 authorized federal courts to grant writs to those detained in violation of their constitutional rights and gave appellate authority to the circuit courts and to the Supreme Court. D, held in custody for publishing libelous and incendiary articles, brought a writ of habeas corpus under the Act. Before the case reached the Court, Congress repealed the Act under which D applied for the writ.

Issue: May Congress withdraw certain cases from the Supreme Court's appellate jurisdiction by rescinding a statute that initially granted such jurisdiction?

Rule: (Chase, C.J.) The appellate jurisdiction of the Supreme Court is conferred by the Constitution but with such exceptions and under such regulations as Congress shall make. Congress may therefore pass and rescind a statute altering the scope of the Supreme Court's appellate jurisdiction.

Valley Forge Christian College v. Americans United for Separation of Church and State, Inc. (S. Ct. 1982)

Facts: Exercising its power under the Constitution's Property Clause (Art. IV, §3), Congress leased surplus government land to D at no cost. Ps brought a federal suit, as taxpayers, claiming that the government's transfer of land to a religious institution violated the First Amendment's Establishment Clause.

Issue: Under what circumstances may federal courts recognize the standing of plaintiff taxpayers who claim an allegedly unconstitutional use of federal tax funds?

Rule: (Rehnquist, J.) Standing requires both *actual injury* to the plaintiff and the probability that the requested relief will cure the alleged wrong. Taxpayers, however, cannot attain standing to sue on the allegedly unconstitutional expenditure of public funds to which they contribute as taxpayers unless (1) the complaint is directed at an exercise of Congress' taxing and spending power and (2) the complaint is based on an alleged breach by Congress of a specific constitutional limitation imposed upon the exercise of that power.

Dissent: (Brennan, J.) The majority risks deciding difficult questions of substantive law obliquely in the course of opinions purporting to do nothing more than determine what the Court labels "standing." The Court's opinion is a stark example of the unfortunate trend of resolving cases at the "threshold" while obscuring the nature of the underlying rights and interests at stake.

Dissent: (Stevens, J.) For the Court to hold that standing depends on one constitutional clause, rather than on another, is to trivialize the standing doctrine.

Warth v. Seldin (S. Ct. 1975)

Facts: Ps brought a class action challenging strict land-use and building requirements of a residential zoning ordinance. They claimed the ordinance resulted in costlier housing and effectively excluded low- and moderate-income residents. Ps did not show they would have purchased a home "but for" the statute.

Issue: May one have standing to challenge a statute when he is unable to show that the statute directly affected him?

Rule: (Powell, J.) A party will not have standing to challenge a statute unless there is a "substantial probability" that he will be directly affected if relief is granted.

Dissent: (Douglas, J.) The technicalities of standing have become a barrier to full development of a case's merits and to people's access to justice.

Dissent: (Brennan, J.) The majority opinion, purporting to turn on "standing," really involves outmoded notions of pleading and justiciability. While the Court asserts that standing is independent of a complaint's merits, the opinion can only be explained by a hostility to those merits. Courts cannot refuse to hear a case on the merits just because they prefer not to.

Baker v. Carr (S. Ct. 1962)

Facts: The Tennessee Assembly had not been reapportioned between 1901 and 1961, despite population's growth and changing demographics. The state constitution required that representation be on the basis of population. P's suit claimed that the failure to periodically reapportion voting districts, as required by the state constitution, resulted in unequal representation.

Issue: Is a challenge to the apportionment of voting districts a political question and therefore beyond the authority of the Supreme Court?

Rule: (Brennan, J.) The Supreme Court may not entertain "political question" cases. Apportionment suits and other disputes involving political rights and issues are not necessarily political and thus nonjusticiable. Factors to be weighed in distinguishing "political question" cases include: (1) whether the issue is committed to another governmental branch; (2) whether judicial standards exist for handling the issue; and (3) whether there is great need for uniform pronouncement on the issue.

Dissent: (Frankfurter, J.) This case involves a Guaranty Clause claim masquerading under a different label. The claim that votes have been diluted by malapportionment cannot be adjudicated without the Court first determining what a vote should be worth. This would improperly require the Court to choose among competing theories of political philosophy. Federal courts should only examine whether there is a rational legislative policy for retaining an existing apportionment.

Martin v. Hunter's Lessee (S. Ct. 1816)

Facts: D, a British citizen, claimed title to a parcel of land in Virginia, which he obtained through a familial will. P claimed the land under state laws that confiscated the property of British citizens. D supported his claim with the anti-confiscation provisions of treaties between the United States and England.

Issue: Does the Supreme Court have appellate jurisdiction to overturn state court decisions involving interpretations of federal law?

Rule: (Story, J.) The Supreme Court's appellate jurisdiction extends to state court judgments that involve federal law.

McCulloch v. Maryland (S. Ct. 1819)

Facts: Congress chartered a bank that established an active branch in Maryland. Because the bank was not chartered by the Maryland legislature, it was subject to a Maryland state tax levied on all banks operating without that state's authority. McCulloch failed to comply with the tax law, arguing that the tax constituted a wrongful interference with Congress' lawmaking powers.

Issue: May the Supreme Court broadly interpret the Constitution to determine the scope of authority of the other governmental branches and the relation between federal and state governmental authority?

Rule: (Marshall, C.J.) The Supreme Court, as the ultimate interpreter of the Constitution, is fit to speak both on the relative powers of the three branches of government and on the supremacy of federal over state government.

Allen v. Wright (S. Ct. 1984)

Facts: Ps challenged the tax-exempt status of private schools that practiced racial discrimination. They argued that (a) they were harmed directly by the mere fact of government financial aid to discriminatory private schools and (b) federal tax exemptions to such institutions thwarted efforts to integrate public schools.

Issue: May federal courts hear cases where an alleged injury is not personal, not fairly traceable to the defendant's unlawful conduct, and not likely to be cured by the relief sought?

Rule: (O'Connor, J.) A litigant must have "standing" to invoke the power of a federal court. Standing is established when the plaintiff alleges personal injury that is fairly traceable to the defendant's allegedly unlawful conduct and that is likely to be redressed by the requested relief. In a suit against a government agency not to enforce specific legal obligations whose violation works a direct harm, but to seek a restructuring of the apparatus established by the executive branch to fulfill its duties, the separation of powers doctrine counsels against the recognition of standing.

Dissent: (Brennan, J.) The Court relies on generalities about the separation of governmental powers and ignores the real issues and the nature of the injuries suffered. The Court's denial of standing reflects an insensitivity to the historical role of federal courts in eradicating public school segregation. Requirements of causation and direct injury are met. Ps have identified communities containing enough racially discriminatory tax-exempt schools to make an appreciable difference in public school integration.

Dissent: (Stevens, J.) This case meets the causation requirement for "standing." When a subsidy makes a given activity more or less expensive, resulting in an increase or decrease in the ability to engage in the activity, injury can be fairly traced to the subsidy for the purposes of determining "standing." Considerations of tax policy, economics, and pure logic all confirm the conclusion that Ps' injury in fact is fairly traceable to the government's allegedly wrongful conduct.

Cooper v. Aaron (S. Ct. 1958)

Facts: An Arkansas federal court ordered desegregation of the public schools in Little Rock. In an attempt to thwart the desegregation process, the governor and the state legislature claimed that state officials had no duty to obey federal court orders, even when those orders were based on the Supreme Court's interpretation of the Constitution.

Issue: Do state officials have the right to disobey federal court orders?

Rule: (Warren, C.J.) State officials may not disobey federal court orders that are based on the Supreme Court's interpretation of the Constitution. "The federal judiciary is supreme in the exposition of the law of the Constitution."

Muskrat v. United States (S. Ct. 1911)

Facts: Congress passed legislation allocating certain lands to specified members of the Cherokee Nation. Congress later enacted a statute that increased the number of Native Americans entitled to share in the final distribution of Cherokee lands and funds, but it gave the original grantees the right to challenge the increase.

Issue: May the federal courts review the constitutionality of legislative acts when such review is sought outside the context of actual litigation?

Rule: (Day, J.) Federal courts may not issue advisory opinions. All judicial determinations of the constitutional validity of legislative acts must arise out of actual cases and controversies between adverse litigants, duly instituted in courts of proper jurisdiction.

Note: The term "cases" encompasses all types of suits. "Controversies" refers to civil suits only.

Powell v. McCormack (S. Ct. 1969)

Facts: P was excluded from his seat in Congress due to allegations of misconduct, despite having met the requirements for congressional membership as stipulated in Article I, §2. P brought an action seeking declaratory judgment and back pay. Ds argued that this case was nonjusticiable because (1) the Constitution explicitly granted the House the power to determine the qualifications of its members and (2) judicial resolution would produce a potentially embarrassing confrontation between coordinate branches of the federal government.

Issue: May the federal courts properly hear a case challenging Congress' exercise of power to control its membership?

Rule: (Warren, C.J.) The federal courts may interpret the scope of the Constitution's grant of authority and responsibilities to coordinate branches of government. That includes the authority to hear cases involving explication of Congress' constitutional power to control its membership. Such cases do not involve "political questions."

International Longshoremen's and Warehousemen's Union v. Boyd (S. Ct. 1954)

Facts: An immigration law required all aliens seeking entry into the United States via Alaska (then a U.S. territory) to submit to a structured immigration procedure before admission. The law applied to aliens who had previously been living in the United States as legal, resident aliens. Because P's union workers traveled annually from the continental United States to Alaska for summer work, P sought a ruling that the statute, if enforced, should not apply to those of its members who were legal aliens.

Issue: May the Supreme Court rule on a statute's validity based only on the law's hypothetical infringement of constitutional rights?

Rule: (Frankfurter, J.) A statute may not be challenged by a party who will not be affected by the statute until a later date.

Dissent: (Black, J.) Judicial action is essential here to save P from irreparable harm resulting from alleged unlawful enforcement of a federal statute. This suit is not based on a hypothetical abridgment of rights because the statute, to P's detriment, has already been applied.

DeFunis v. Odegaard (S. Ct. 1974)

Facts: P was denied admission to law school. He sued in state court, asserting that the school's admissions procedures and criteria discriminated against him on the basis of race in violation of the Fourteenth Amendment's Equal Protection Clause. The trial court granted the requested mandatory injunction, under which the school then admitted P. Eventually the case was appealed to the Supreme Court, by which time P was near completion of the law program, with no risk of denial of registration.

Issue: May federal courts adjudicate cases when the circumstances have changed, rendering the litigated issues obsolete?

Rule: (Burger, C.J.) Federal courts will only entertain cases involving controversies that are active and ongoing at the time of adjudication. A case becomes moot, and thus ineligible for judgment on the merits, once the controversy between the parties ceases to be definite and concrete and when a court's decision would no longer affect the litigants' rights.

Dissent: (Brennan, J.) Disposal of this case as moot disserves the public interest; the suit involves constitutional issues that deserve adjudication because they concern vast numbers of people and organizations. Dismissal of the case will also result in undesirable repetition of litigation. Finally, the majority is merely transforming principles of avoidance of constitutional decisions into devices for sidestepping resolution of difficult cases.

Note: The prohibition against adjudicating moot cases is a natural extension of the requirement that a suit arise from an actual case or controversy (see Article III).

Massachusetts v. Mellon Frothingham v. Mellon (S. Ct. 1923)

Facts: In two cases joined by the Court, Ps challenged the 1921 Maternity Act, which offered matching federal grants to states that provided funds for social services aimed at protecting mothers' and infants' health.

Issue 1: May the Supreme Court exercise jurisdiction over a case in which a state, suing on its own behalf or on behalf of its citizens, challenges a federal statute as violative of the state's powers of local government reserved to the states?

Rule 1: (Sutherland, J.) Insofar as a case depends upon the assertion of a right on the part of a state to sue on its own behalf, the Court is without jurisdiction because the question presented for adjudication is not about rights of persons or property, or rights actually invaded or threatened, but abstract questions of political power, of sovereignty, of government. Further, state citizens are also federal citizens, and when representation on behalf of citizens becomes appropriate, it is not a state's duty or power to enforce the citizens' rights in respect of their relations with the federal government.

Issue 2: May the Supreme Court exercise jurisdiction over a case in which a taxpayer challenges the administration of a federal appropriation statute as violative of due process?

Rule 2: (Sutherland, J.) Because a taxpayer's interest in the moneys of the Treasury — partly realized from taxation and partly from other sources — is shared with millions of others, is comparatively minute and indeterminable, and because the effect upon future taxation uncertain, the administration of a statute likely to affect a vast number of taxpayers is essentially a matter of public and not of individual concern. Therefore, a suit of this character cannot be maintained.

Flast v. Cohen (S. Ct. 1968)

Facts: P sued to prevent the disbursal of monies established by a congressional act to fund religious school education. P asserted that use of federal taxes for this funding violated the First Amendment's Establishment and Free Exercise Clauses.

Issue: Does an ordinary taxpayer have standing to challenge the constitutionality of a federal appropriation law?

Rule: (Warren, C.J.) A taxpayer has standing to challenge the constitutionality of federal law only if there is a "logical nexus" between the status of the taxpayer and the challenged statute. To satisfy that requirement, the statute must be an exercise of power under the Taxing and Spending Clause, and the alleged violation must be a breach of the constitutional limitations imposed upon that power. Additionally, the dispute must be presented in an adversarial context and in a form historically viewed as capable of judicial resolution.

Dissent: (Harlan, J.) Standing requires the representation of an infringed private interest. P's case, however, represents the public interest. Individual litigants have standing to speak for the public interest only if Congress has personally authorized such suits.

Duke Power Co. v. Carolina Environmental Study Group, Inc. (S. Ct. 1978)

Facts: Ps sued D, a public utility. The suit alleged the unconstitutionality of the Price-Anderson Act, a federal law limiting utility companies' liability for nuclear power accidents. Ps claimed the Act violated the Fifth Amendment by (1) not assuring adequate compensation to nuclear accident victims and (2) forcing such victims to pay the human price (in injuries) for the societal benefits of nuclear energy.

Issue: How does the Court decide that the party seeking to invoke the Court's jurisdiction has sufficiently demonstrated a "personal stake" in the outcome of the controversy?

Rule: (Burger, C.J.) The Supreme Court acknowledges a plaintiff's standing to sue when he or she has a "personal stake" in the outcome of the suit. The "personal stake" requirement is met where (1) there is distinct and palpable injury to the plaintiff; (2) a fairly traceable causal connection exists between the claimed injury and the challenged conduct; and (3) there is a substantial likelihood that the relief requested will prevent or redress the claimed injury. Standing will not be allowed when the asserted harm is merely a generalized grievance shared equally by a large number of people.

Singleton v. Wulff (S. Ct. 1976)

Facts: Ps, a group of physicians, challenged a Missouri statute that denied Medicaid benefits for abortions that were not medically necessary. Although they had a direct interest in the case's outcome, Ps did not claim they had a constitutional right to perform abortions, but argued that their patients had a right to terminate pregnancy.

Issue: Under what circumstances may the Supreme Court grant standing to those asserting third-party rights?

Rule: (Blackmun, J.) Access to Supreme Court review traditionally requires direct injury to the plaintiff; the litigant may not ordinarily claim standing to vindicate third-party rights. The Court hesitates to permit assertions of "jus tertii" (third-party rights) because non-parties may not want to assert those rights, non-party rights may be unaffected by the litigation's outcome, and third parties are often the best proponents of their own interests. "Jus tertii" standing may be granted, however, if (1) the non-parties' rights are inextricably bound up with the activity the litigant wishes to pursue; (2) the plaintiff is no less effective a proponent of third-party rights than the third parties themselves; and (3) there is a genuine obstacle to the non-parties' representing their own interests.

Concurrence/Dissent: (Powell, J.) A party may not attack governmental action on the ground that it infringes third-party rights. The factors to be weighed in making exceptions to this rule do not justify allowing physicians to assert their patients' rights.

Maryland v. Baltimore Radio Show, Inc. (S. Ct. 1950)

Facts: Omitted.
Issue: Omitted.
Rule: Omitted.
Note: (Frankfurter, J.) (Opinion respecting the denial of the petition for writ of certiorari.) The Court's denial of a petition of writ of certiorari . . . merely means that fewer than four members of the Court deemed it desirable to review a decision of the lower court as a matter of "sound judicial discretion." Narrowly technical reasons may lead to denials. A decision may satisfy all the technical requirements, yet may not commend itself for review to four members of the Court. The Court has rigorously insisted that such a denial of a petition for a writ of certiorari is no indication of the Court's views on the merits of a case.

Barrows v. Jackson (S. Ct. 1953)

Facts: P filed suit in state court when D violated a racially restrictive covenant. An earlier case held that enforcement of such covenants against African-American purchasers was a denial of equal protection.

Issue: May federal courts recognize standing for a party asserting a third party's rights when (1) a state court adjudication might result in denial of the third party's constitutional rights and (2) the third party would have no opportunity to present his or her grievances?

Rule: (Minton, J.) One who asserts the rights of non-parties when challenging a state action's constitutionality will ordinarily not be granted standing. However, standing may be conferred if a state court suit might deny the non-party's constitutional rights and where that third party has little, if any, means of asserting his or her rights. In that case, the rule denying standing to raise another's rights is outweighed by the need to protect the fundamental rights of those without the opportunity to represent their own interests.

Laird v. Tatum (S. Ct. 1972)

Facts: Ps filed a class action in federal court, claiming their constitutional rights were being invaded by the U.S. Army's alleged systematic surveillance of civilian political activity.

Issue: May a plaintiff challenge the constitutionality of government activity when the harm to the plaintiff is indirect or speculative?

Rule: (Burger, C.J.) A plaintiff must show that he or she has sustained or is immediately in danger of sustaining direct injury from the defendant's activity to invoke standing.

Dissent: (Douglas, J.) The Court's forbearance in refusing to adjudge the constitutionality of an act can inhibit freedom of speech. Here, to withhold standing to sue until one suffers actual harm immunizes all surveillance activities from judicial scrutiny, regardless of their misuses and deterrent effect.

Poe v. Ullman (S. Ct. 1961)

Facts: Ps sued in state court to challenge the constitutionality of state laws that prohibited use of contraceptives and medical advice on how to use such devices.

Issue: Does a plaintiff who challenges a law in advance of its enforcement against him or her have standing?

Rule: (Frankfurter, J.) A plaintiff lacks standing to invoke Supreme Court review when challenging a law simply because it exists. Federal judicial power may strike down legislation only at the instance of one who is himself immediately harmed, or immediately threatened with harm, by the challenged action.

Dissent: (Black, J.) The Court should grant standing so that it can decide the case's constitutional issues.

Dissent: (Douglas, J.) The Court should not deny standing by relying on the conclusion that the statutes will not be enforced.

Dissent: (Harlan, J.) There is no lack of "ripeness" when plaintiffs have stated that they intend to disobey the law. There is no circumstance except detection or prosecution to make remote the particular controversy. This is not a feigned, hypothetical, or friendly suit such as lacks an adversarial nature.

Younger v. Harris (S. Ct. 1971)

Facts: P filed for a federal court injunction to enjoin a pending state action.
Issue: May a federal court stay or enjoin a pending state action?
Rule: (Black, J.) Federal courts may not stay or enjoin a pending state court proceeding, except under special circumstances.

Fletcher v. Peck (S. Ct. 1810)

Facts: In 1795, the Georgia legislature, induced by bribery, conveyed 35 million acres of state lands to private companies. In 1796, the legislature moved to rescind the grant, even though the land had been sold to private northern investors.
Issue: May the Supreme Court act to prevent a state legislature from rescinding a state statute, passed by a prior legislature, that would divest certain property owners of their legal rights to land acquired in the state?
Rule: (Marshall, C.J.) States are constitutionally barred from passing ex post facto laws, issuing bills of attainder, and impairing contractual obligations. If the rescission of a state law has the effect of any of the foregoing, it is unconstitutional, and the Supreme Court may act to protect the vested rights of individuals affected.

The Antelope (S. Ct. 1825)

Facts: The Antelope, a slave ship transporting slaves to the United States in violation of several federal statutes, was apprehended and its cargo confiscated. Spain and Portugal claimed that the African slaves were the property of their citizens.
Issue: Do federal statutes prohibiting the importation of African slaves into the country apply to slave ships owned by foreign nationals and confiscated by U.S. federal authorities?
Rule: (Marshall, C.J.) No nation can prescribe a rule for other nations. Therefore, the slave trade remains lawful to those whose governments have not forbidden it. Consequently, a foreign vessel engaged in the African slave trade and captured on the high seas in time of peace by an American ship must be restored to its rightful foreign owner.

Cherokee Nation v. Georgia (S. Ct. 1831)

Facts: The Cherokees had been granted four million acres of land within Georgia's borders through various treaties with the United States. In 1827 they declared themselves an independent nation and adopted a constitution, in part to protect their claims to recently discovered gold deposits. The Georgia legislature responded by passing "Indian laws" that annulled all Cherokee "laws, usages, and customs." The Cherokee Nation, describing itself as a foreign state, attempted to invoke the original jurisdiction of the Supreme Court.

Issue: May the Supreme Court assume original jurisdiction over the claims of Native American tribes?

Rule: (Marshall, C.J.) The Native American tribes are properly viewed as domestic dependent nations, completely under the sovereignty and dominion of the United States. Thus, they do not constitute foreign states under the Constitution and cannot maintain actions in the federal courts.

Concurrence: (Johnson, J.) It is clear that the Constitution does not speak of the Native American tribes as states or foreign states. In addition, the claim of the Cherokee Nation is of a political character — they wish to contest the jurisdiction of a sovereign over its land. Such disputes are not properly redressed by the judicial department.

Dissent: (Thompson, J.) Whether the Cherokee Nation is "foreign" for jurisdictional purposes depends not upon international law or the language of the Constitution, but upon their political condition. The distinct culture and government of the Cherokee Nation demonstrates that they have never relinquished their separate existence, and thus they should be treated as a foreign nation in this instance.

United Public Workers v. Mitchell (S. Ct. 1947)

Facts: Ps sought an injunction and declaratory judgment in federal court against Ds, to prohibit enforcement of a statutory clause that forbade officers and employees in the federal government's executive branch to "take any active part in political management or in political campaigns."

Issue: May federal courts adjudicate cases involving only hypothetical injury, i.e., cases lacking "ripeness"?

Rule: (Reed, J.) A case must be "ripe" for federal court adjudication and injunctive relief. Thus, concrete legal issues, not abstractions, are required, and actual interference with litigants' rights must be at issue. Hypothetical threats to those rights do not invoke this power.

Dissent: (Douglas, J.) Federal courts may only adjudicate actual controversies. There is an actual controversy here. The threat to Ps is real and immediate, not fanciful and remote.

Eakin v. Raub (S. Ct. 1825)

Facts: Omitted, except to indicate that the case involved the power of the Pennsylvania Supreme Court to invalidate a state law.
Issue: Is the scope of the Judiciary's authority to judge the constitutionality of legislative acts necessarily broad?
Rule: Omitted.
Dissent: (Gibson, J.) Although laws in direct collision with the Constitution are necessarily void, it is beyond the scope of the Judiciary's authority to annul legislative acts as unconstitutional when such judgments are rendered outside of a case or controversy. It is not the role of the Judiciary to determine the validity of a legislature's construction of the Constitution. The Judiciary should interpret the laws, not scan legislatures' authority. Construction of the Constitution belongs to the legislature, which ought to have superior capacity to judge the constitutionality of its own acts. Finally, it is the people's job to correct legislative abuses by instructing their representatives to repeal wrongful legislation.
Note: This case is relevant for Justice Gibson's dissent, expressing a view he reversed 20 years later.

Rogers v. Missouri Pacific Railroad Co. (S. Ct. 1957)

Facts: The Supreme Court granted certiorari to review three Federal Employer's Liability Act cases and one Jones Act case involving workers' compensation for merchant marines. The Court reviewed the evidence in all four cases to determine sufficiency for submission to a jury.
Issue: Should the Supreme Court review cases not involving constitutional or national issues, such as cases that only turn on questions of facts or sufficiency of evidence?
Rule: Omitted.
Dissent: (Frankfurter, J.) The Supreme Court should restrict its reviewing power to the adjudication of constitutional issues or other questions of national importance. The Court's resources are misspent granting certiorari for cases solely involving review of sufficiency of evidence. Granting certiorari in these cases encourages the filing of certiorari petitions in other cases that likewise have no business being brought before the Court.

Burns Baking Co. v. Bryan (S. Ct. 1924)

Facts: P challenged a 1921 Nebraska act that prohibited the sale of bread loaves that exceeded a prescribed weight. The Nebraska Supreme Court upheld the statute, but the U.S. Supreme Court held that the act violated the Fourteenth Amendment by abridging certain economic freedoms without due process.

Issue: In assessing a statute's constitutionality, should the Supreme Court examine (a) the legislative intent behind a statute; (b) the circumstances the act was meant to address; and (c) the statute's effectiveness in meeting legislative goals?

Rule: Omitted.

Dissent: (Brandeis, J.) The Supreme Court is not to decide questions of fact when assessing a statute's constitutionality. Such assessment requires an inappropriate inquiry into legislative intent, the circumstances the statute addresses, and the act's effectiveness in fulfilling its intended purpose.

Note: The dissent's advocacy of examination of the circumstances and legislative intent behind a statute conflicts with *Fletcher v. Peck*'s implicit disregard of such matters in reviewing a statute's validity.

West Virginia State Board of Educ. v. Barnette (S. Ct. 1943)

Facts: P sought to prevent enforcement of a mandate that required all West Virginia public school children to salute the American flag. A majority of the Supreme Court found the directive unconstitutional.

Issue: What limits should the Supreme Court place on itself in reviewing the constitutionality of validly enacted statutes?

Rule: Omitted.

Dissent: (Frankfurter, J.) In reviewing a law's constitutionality, the Supreme Court should defer to the legislature and limit its inquiry to a determination as to whether, within a legislature's broad authority, the lawmakers have reasonable justification for the statute in question.

Thomas v. Collins (S. Ct. 1945)

Facts: D violated a Texas law requiring labor organizers to obtain a state permit before engaging in labor union activity.

Issue: How deferential to the legislature should the Supreme Court be when reviewing the constitutionality of a state statute that represents a direct collision between state interests and powers and fundamental constitutional rights?

Rule: (Rutledge, J.) The usual deference to the legislature is balanced by the preferred place given to the great, indispensable, democratic freedoms secured by the First Amendment. First Amendment rights, for example, cannot be abridged unless there is a clear and present danger that such abridgment seeks to curb, or public safety, health, morality, or the like, is at stake.

Michigan v. Long (S. Ct. 1983)

Facts: Marijuana was found by police in the passenger compartment and trunk of D's car. The police searched the compartment because they had reason to believe it contained weapons potentially dangerous to the officers. In ruling that the drugs taken from D's car were the product of an illegal search, the Michigan Supreme Court referred to the state constitution twice, but otherwise relied upon federal law.

Issue: What are the parameters of the Supreme Court's review of state court decisions that rest on grounds of both state and federal law?

Rule: (O'Connor, J.) The Supreme Court will not review state court decisions that clearly and expressly rest on independent state grounds. However, the Court will review state court decisions that fairly appear to rest primarily on federal law or that appear to be interwoven with the federal law.

Dissent: (Stevens, J.) The Court should not hear suits in which a state court has upheld a citizen's rights under both state and federal law. In reviewing state court decisions, this Court's primary role is to ensure that persons seeking to vindicate federal rights have been fairly heard. This case falls outside these parameters, since the state court simply provided greater protection to one of its citizens than some other state or the Supreme Court might require.

Pennhurst State School & Hospital v. Halderman (S. Ct. 1984)

Facts: P represented a class that filed suit in federal court against a state-run institution. The case involved both state and federal causes of action, including alleged violations of the Eighth and Fourteenth Amendments.

Issue: May federal courts recognize suits brought against a state by its own or another state's citizens?

Rule: (Powell, J.) The Eleventh Amendment prohibits federal courts from recognizing suits brought against a state by its own or another state's citizens, unless the defendant state expressly consents to jurisdiction. However, a suit challenging the constitutionality of a state official's *actions* is not a suit against the state and, thus, can be heard in federal court.

Dissent: (Brennan, J.) The Eleventh Amendment bars those federal court suits brought against states by citizens of *other* states. In addition, a defendant state may not claim sovereign immunity when its conduct contravenes its own laws.

Dissent: (Stevens, J.) The majority's opinion will require the federal courts to decide federal constitutional questions despite the availability of state-law grounds for decision. The Court's prohibition of pendent jurisdiction over state law claims against a state thwarts the goal of avoiding both duplicative litigation and unnecessary decision of federal constitutional questions. The majority prevents federal courts from implementing state policies through equitable enforcement of state law. Instead, federal courts are required to resolve cases on federal grounds that no state authority can undo.

Fitzpatrick v. Bitzer (S. Ct. 1976)

Facts: Ps sued Connecticut in federal court, asserting that provisions in that state's statutory retirement plan discriminated against them because of their sex and therefore contravened Title VII of the 1964 Civil Rights Act.
Issue: Are there instances where federal courts may recognize private suits against states or state officials?
Rule: (Rehnquist, J.) Federal courts may recognize private suits against states or state officials when Congress, for the purpose of enforcing provisions of the Fourteenth Amendment, so permits, even though such suits would be constitutionally impermissible in other contexts.

Pennzoil v. Texaco, Inc. (S. Ct. 1987)

Facts: P filed suit in Texas state court, alleging that D tortiously had induced Getty to breach a contract to sell its shares to P. A jury found for P and awarded multi-billion dollar damages. Because D could not afford to post the bond that Texas law's lien and bond provisions required for suspension of the judgment's execution, D filed suit in federal district court, alleging that the Texas proceedings violated both the Fourteenth Amendment and various federal statutes. The district court issued a preliminary injunction against the Texas court, and the Court of Appeals affirmed.
Issue: May federal courts interfere with pending or executable state court decisions?
Rule: (Powell, J.) Preservation of comity and avoidance of unwarranted determination of federal constitutional questions justify a mandate that federal courts not interfere with (1) state courts' ability to resolve federal question cases; (2) pending state court proceedings; or (3) execution of state court judgments. Comity refers to the sensitivity to, and balance between, the legitimate interests of both state and national governments, such that the national government protects federal rights without unduly interfering with legitimate state activities.
Concurrence: (Brennan, J.) Texaco invokes a remedy, enforceable in federal court, that could be frustrated if the federal court were not empowered to enjoin a state court proceeding. Precedent forbids federal courts to engage in appellate review of state court decisions.

Concurrence: (Marshall, J.) Only the Supreme Court has appellate review of state court judgments. The district court's assumption of subject matter jurisdiction over this case is therefore unwarranted. It fails to distinguish between review of the substance of a state court judgment and a "mere" constitutional challenge to that state court's procedures.

Craig v. Boren (S. Ct. 1976)

Facts: Ps, a beer vendor and a male between the ages of 18 and 21, brought an equal protection suit challenging a statute proscribing the sale of beer to males under age 21 and females under 18. The vendor claimed standing as a third party asserting the rights of males aged 18 to 21.

Issue: When may federal courts recognize the standing of one who asserts the rights of third parties?

Rule: (Brennan, J.) Federal courts will not recognize the standing of a plaintiff who represents the constitutional rights of third parties ("jus tertii"), unless (1) there would be a clear, adverse impact on the third parties' rights if the plaintiff were not granted standing, and (2) the relation between plaintiff and third party is such that the plaintiff adequately represents the third party's interests. Under this test the Court held that the vendor had standing.

Dissent: (Burger, J.) The Court should not veer from the rule that a litigant may only assert his or her own constitutional rights or immunities. Third-party standing is limited to cases where the relationship between the claimant and third party was not simply the fortuitous connection between vendor and potential vendees but the relationship between one who acted to protect the rights of a minority and the minority itself.

Lujan v. Defenders of Wildlife (S. Ct. 1992)

Facts: P sued the U.S. government, alleging that it was violating a statutory requirement that there be consultation before funding any government project that might lead to the extinction of species.

Issue: Did P have standing, either because they had studied endangered species in the past, because of their status as experts on those species, or because of the statute's provision that "any person" could sue to enforce the statute's provisions?

Rule: (Scalia, J.) In order for a P to have standing to sue, it must have suffered a past injury or one that is imminent; a generalized interest in having the government obey the law is insufficient.

Concurrence: (Kennedy, J.) Congress can create rights by the statute, the deprivation of which constitutes injury for Article III standing purposes.

Dissent: (Blackmun, J.) Congress should be able to deputize courts to watch over how the executive administers laws by granting citizens standing to sue.

City of Los Angeles v. Lyons (S. Ct. 1983)

Facts: P sought damages and injunctive and declaratory relief in a suit claiming excessive force by police.
Issue: Do the federal courts require that each form of relief requested in a suit meet standing requirements?
Rule: (White, J.) In reviewing a suit that requests more than one type of relief, federal courts will impose a separate standing test for each relief sought. Even though a claim for damages may meet standing requirements, standing for injunctive and declaratory relief will not be conferred unless the threat to a plaintiff is sufficiently real and immediate.
Dissent: (Marshall, J.) The majority fragments the standing inquiry and imposes a separate standing hurdle with respect to each form of relief sought. In doing so, it immunizes from prospective equitable relief any perceived threat of future impairment of rights, as long as no individual can establish with substantial certainty that he or she will be injured in the future.

Goldwater v. Carter (S. Ct. 1979)

Facts: D, the President of the United States, terminated a treaty with Taiwan. Several Congressmen claimed that D deprived them of their constitutional role with respect to a change in the supreme law of the land.
Issue: May the Judiciary question the allocation of power between the President and Congress before those two government branches reach an impasse?
Rule: Omitted.
Concurrence: (Powell, J.) The Court should not decide cases that are not ripe for review, i.e., where the issues are not fully crystallized and the controversy is not concrete. Similarly, the Court will not address political question cases (although this case falls outside that category). A suit is nonjusticiable as a political question if (1) the issues involve resolution of questions committed by the Constitution's text to a coordinate governmental branch; (2) there is a lack of judicially discoverable and manageable standards for resolving the case, or if a decision would require a policy determination clearly outside judicial discretion; and (3) judicial intervention would produce an embarrassing diversity of pronouncements on the issue by various governmental departments.

Concurrence: (Rehnquist, J.) This case is "political" because it involves both the President's authority in foreign affairs and Congress' authority to negate presidential actions.

Dissent: (Brennan, J.) Whether a government branch is constitutionally designated for political decision-making power is not a political question.

Robertson v. Seattle Audubon Ass'n (S. Ct. 1992)

Facts: Congress enacted a compromise between logging interests and environmentalists by imposing new restrictions on government management of national forests, and enacting that compliance with those new restrictions satisfied other requirements of federal forest management law.

Issue: Does the statute prescribe a rule of decision, in violation of *United States v. Klein?*

Rule: (Thomas, J.) The statute is simply an amendment of preexisting forest management laws, even though it is written in a manner that ostensibly retains previous statutory requirements and deems those requirements to be satisfied under certain conditions.

Plaut v. Spendthrift Farm (S. Ct. 1995)

Facts: P's securities fraud suit was dismissed as untimely, but after the dismissal became final, Congress enacted a law retroactively extending the limitations period for that class of cases.

Issue: Can Congress reopen final judgments by retroactively extending limitations periods?

Rule: (Scalia, J.) Once a judgment is final, it represents the final word of the Article III courts on the case, and a statute cannot authorize its reopening.

Concurrence: (Breyer, J.) There should be no absolute rule against reopening judgments, but this case was correctly decided because the reopening statute was directed at a discrete and closed class of defendants, and thus reflects inappropriate singling out by Congress.

Dissent: (Stevens, J.) Congress needs flexibility to correct situations where courts misunderstand statutory requirements.

Seminole Tribe v. Florida (S. Ct. 1995)

Facts: A federal statute provides that in certain situations states can be sued by Indian tribes when the state and the tribe fail to agree on Indian gaming in that state.

Issue: Can Congress subject states to suit when legislating under its Article I powers?

Rule: (Rehnquist, C.J.) The Eleventh Amendment prohibits Congress from making states liable for retrospective relief (such as damages) when legislating under its Article I power, and *Ex parte Young* relief is not available here because the remedial scheme in the statute reflects an implicit congressional wish to preclude other types of relief.

Dissent: (Souter, J.) Congress' Article I powers provide it with the authority to abrogate state sovereign immunity, and in many instances Congress has prescribed the kind of relief that can be had in an *Ex parte Young* — type suit.

Note: This case overturned *Pennsylvania v. Union Gas* (S. Ct. 1989).

College Savings Bank v. Florida Prepaid (S. Ct. 1999)

Facts: Florida operated a college savings plan that was sued for violating federal unfair advertising laws.

Issue: Did Florida's voluntary participation in interstate commerce, with the knowledge that federal unfair advertising laws existed, constitute a waiver of the state's sovereign immunity from lawsuit?

Rule: (Scalia, J.) State waivers of sovereign immunity must be explicit rather than implied; thus, mere participation in interstate commerce does not constitute a waiver of its sovereign immunity from any claims arising out of federal regulation of interstate commerce.

Dissent: (Stevens, J.) By protecting property interests, unfair advertising laws reflect valid congressional abrogation of states' sovereign immunity.

Dissent: (Breyer, J.) States' participation in interstate commerce is best understood as a waiver of their sovereign immunity.

Note: This case overruled *Parden v. Terminal Railway* (S. Ct. 1964), where the Court had held that a state's participation in interstate commerce constituted a waiver of its sovereign immunity.

Idaho v. Coeur d'Alene Tribe of Idaho (S. Ct. 1997)

Facts: P Indian tribe sued the state, claiming that under a federal treaty it had sovereignty over certain lands, and requesting as relief an injunction against the state exercising sovereignty over those lands.

Rule: (Kennedy, J.) (plurality) (with O'Connor, J., concurring in the judgment) Such relief would violate the state's sovereignty, in violation of the Eleventh Amendment.

Concurrence: (O'Connor, J.) Such relief implicates the state's sovereignty too much, and thus falls outside the bounds of appropriate *Young* relief.

Dissent: (Souter, J.) The tribe's relief satisfies the requirements of *Ex parte Young*, and thus is appropriate.

Bennett v. Spear (S. Ct. 1997)

Facts: P farmers sued under the Endangered Species Act, which allowed "any person" to sue to enforce it.

Issue: Were the farmers within the "zone of interests" such that Congress could be said to have eliminated any prudential bars to standing?

Rule: (Scalia, J.) Congress can eliminate whatever prudential barriers to standing exist, as long as the requirements of Article III standing are satisfied.

Lance v. Coffman (S. Ct. 2007)

Facts: Colorado voters sue state, alleging that district lines were being drawn in an unconstitutional manner.

Issue: Do the plaintiffs have standing?

Rule: (per curiam) There is no standing where, as here, the plaintiffs' only injury lies in the fact that the government has allegedly violated the law. Such generalized grievances do not provide the injury required for Article III standing.

Massachusetts v. EPA (S. Ct. 2007)

Facts: The Clean Air Act requires the U.S. Environmental Protection Agency (EPA) to regulate air "pollutants." The State of Massachusetts requested EPA to issue regulations dealing with greenhouse gases, which the state alleged were causing global warming that put its land at risk of flooding from rising sea levels. The EPA refused, and Massachusetts sued.

Issue: Does the state have standing to sue?

Rule: (Stevens, J.) The state has standing. It has a concrete interest in protecting its lands that are threatened by sea level rises, and a ruling requiring the EPA to regulate greenhouse gases would redress injury to that interest. The fact that the plaintiff is a sovereign state also counsels in favor of finding standing, given that its sovereign control over its property is at stake.

Dissent: (Roberts, C.J.) There is no special standing rule for states. The state's interest in preserving its land turns on a change in the world's environment, and thus the relief requested focuses not on the state particularly but on the world as a whole. Any current land-loss alleged by the state is too speculative, and the state never shows that the amount of emissions that could be regulated by the EPA would redress any land loss.

Dissent: (Scalia, J.) I join the Chief Justice's dissent, and also dissent from the holding on the merits that the EPA violated the statute when refusing to regulate greenhouse gases.

Sprint Communications v. APCC Services (S. Ct. 2008)

Facts: Under contractual agreements payphone operators charge long-distance carriers for long-distance calls made from payphones. The payphone operators assign their collection rights to a third party, who sues the carriers for unpaid charges.

Issue: Do the third parties have standing?

Rule: (Breyer, J.) They do. There is a long tradition of assignees being able to sue, and there is no reason to change that rule with regard to assignees for collection, even though successful plaintiff-assignees pass back all the litigation proceeds in return for a fee. Nor is there any prudential reason to limit such assignees' standing.

Dissent: (Roberts, C.J.) The assignees must turn over the proceeds of the litigation to the payphone operators; thus, they do not have a personal stake in the litigation and therefore do not have standing.

Summers v. Earth Island Institute (S. Ct. 2009)

Facts: Environmental group sues the Forest Service over the Service's plans to dispose of certain woodlands. The parties settle the case, but the court nevertheless adjudicated the legal claims raised by the plaintiff-environmental group.

Issue: Did the plaintiff retain standing to sue after the settlement?

Rule: (Scalia, J.) No. The plaintiff has lost the personal stake in the dispute, and has not alleged facts suggesting that its members would be harmed by further Service action. The claim of purely procedural injury does not suffice to establish standing, under *Lujan v. Defenders of Wildlife*, 504 U.S. 555 (1992).

Concurrence: (Kennedy, J.) This case would be different if the statute provided some redress for a concrete injury, but the statute does not do so.

Dissent: (Breyer, J.) The plaintiffs have alleged all they should have to allege to prove that they will likely use the areas subject to the Service's regulations that remain in force even after the settlement. Thus, they should satisfy the requirement that the plaintiff show imminent injury.

DaimlerChrysler v. Cuno (S. Ct. 2006)

Facts: State and city taxpayers challenged state tax credits given to company to induce it to remain in the city.

Issue: Do taxpayers have standing to challenge state government tax credits on the theory that the credits reduce the amount of money available for other state purposes and thus injure them?

Rule: (Roberts, C.J.) They have no standing. The Court rejected a similar claim for federal taxpayers in *Frothingham v. Mellon*, 262 U.S. 447 (1923). A contrary rule would make federal courts the constant monitors of state government spending decisions. This case is also not analogous to the limited taxpayer standing to challenge government expenditures for religious purposes as allowed in *Flast v. Cohen*, 392 U.S. 83 (1968), as the underlying claim here is very different from the one that citizens have a right not to have to support religion through their tax money.

Concurrence: (Ginsburg, J.) While I agree with the Court's analysis, one does not have to agree with subsequent limitations on standing imposed by the Court.

Kowalski v. Tesmer (S. Ct. 2004)

Facts: Ps, attorneys who had performed indigent criminal defense work in the past, sued to challenge state law rule limiting the ability of criminal defendants to appeal guilty and *nolo contendere* pleas, alleging the rule violated the due process rights of those defendants.

Issue: Did attorneys have standing to assert the due process rights of the criminal defendants?

Rule: (Rehnquist, C.J.) Attorneys did not have third-party standing. There was an insufficiently close relationship between the attorneys and the defendants, as they had no current attorney-client relationship, which distinguished the case from others where attorneys have been held to have standing to assert the rights of their clients. Moreover, the defendants themselves were not hindered in their ability to assert their own rights.

Concurrence: (Thomas, J.) The Court's third-party standing jurisprudence has gone too far in calling certain relationships sufficiently "special" as to allow an exception to the normal prohibition on the assertion of third-party rights.

Dissent: (Ginsburg, J.) The earlier cases allowing attorney standing did not turn on whether there was an existing attorney-client relationship at the time of the suit. The defendants may be hindered from asserting their own rights given the complexity of litigation and the low educational level many inmates have.

Hein v. Freedom from Religion Foundation (S. Ct. 2007)

Facts: Plaintiff challenges a federal agency's expenditure of money to fund conferences to consider "faith-based initiatives," alleging standing based on the holding in *Flast v. Cohen*, 392 U.S. 83 (1968).

Issue: Does *Flast*'s exception to the general rule against taxpayer standing allow challenges to executive branch action that allegedly violates the Establishment Clause?

Rule: (Alito, J.) (plurality) *Flast*, which dealt with standing to challenge a specific congressional authorization of expenditures alleged to violate the Establishment Clause, does not cover this case. *Flast* has been construed narrowly, and extending it to cover executive action would open up every executive action touching on religion to a taxpayer suit, in violation of the general rule against taxpayer standing.

Concurrence: (Kennedy, J.) I join the plurality opinion, which explains that without limiting *Flast* as held today there would be a boundless expansion of the judiciary's supervision over the executive branch.

Concurrence: (Scalia, J.) *Flast* should be overruled as inconsistent with Article III.

Dissent: (Souter, J.) There is no principled basis for distinguishing between allegations of congressional violation of the Establishment Clause and allegations of executive branch violations, for purposes of standing.

Central Virginia Community College v. Katz (S. Ct. 2006)

Facts: Person transferred assets to various debtors, including a state-run community college, just before declaring bankruptcy. The trustee of the bankruptcy estate sued the college to recover the funds, which the trustee alleged were fraudulently transferred in violation of federal bankruptcy law.

Issue: Is the college, as an arm of the state, immune from suit in federal court because of the Eleventh Amendment?

Rule: (O'Connor, J.) Congress' Article I power to enact bankruptcy laws gives it the authority to make state entities such as the college suable for retrospective relief such as recovery of funds fraudulently transferred by a party on the verge of declaring bankruptcy. The history of the Bankruptcy Clause reveals an intent to make states suable in these instances.

Dissent: (Thomas, J.) Today's result is inconsistent with *Seminole Tribe v. Florida*, 517 U.S. 44 (1996), which holds that no Article I regulatory power gives Congress the power to make states liable for such retrospective relief.

CHAPTER 2

National Power and Commerce Power

I. NATIONAL POWER

A. Introduction
   1. The Federalism Concept
      Our federal system is a dual system of government: a national government and state government. This reflects the philosophy that there are two levels of concern of government — national and local — and that each should be addressed by national and local governments respectively.
   2. Constitutionality of Federal Action
      Every law passed by Congress must meet two criteria to be constitutional:
      a. Enumerated Powers
         All laws passed by Congress must be pursuant to the powers granted to it by the Constitution, or "necessary and proper" to the execution of those powers. Congress does not possess a general police power. The Tenth Amendment reserves to the states those powers not granted to the federal government.
      b. Even if a law is within one of Congress' enumerated powers, it must be within constitutional limitations to be held valid.
B. Historical Background — Pre-1789: Articles of Confederation
   The Articles of Confederation granted the national government very limited powers, reserving most powers to the states. This resulted in conflict among the states, and it was decided that a new national government with expanded powers had to be formed. The Constitution was drafted with that purpose. The limits of the expanded powers remained a subject of debate.

C. Federalists vs. Antifederalists
   1. Federalists
      The Federalists of the late eighteenth century believed that a strong centralized government would be more advantageous to the nation's economy and security by unifying the states. This philosophy fostered the broad interpretation of the enumerated powers concept to include powers implied in the Constitution.
   2. Antifederalists
      The Antifederalists believed that the individual states should retain most lawmaking power and that the people should be governed locally, except in cases of national concern, where the Constitution explicitly granted Congress the power to act.
   3. Tenth Amendment Interpretation
      The Tenth Amendment of the Constitution states that "the powers not delegated to the United States by the Constitution, nor prohibited by it to the States, are reserved to the States respectively, or to the people." This was the focal point of the Antifederalists' argument. Any enlargement of the federal power not specifically granted in the Constitution was deemed a usurpation of state sovereignty. The Federalists argued that the Tenth Amendment was a reminder that the fact that the federal government is one of enumerated powers does not preclude the concept of a strong centralized government.
D. Doctrine of Implied Powers — *McCulloch v. Maryland*
   In *McCulloch v. Maryland,* Chief Justice Marshall established that Congress had powers implied in the Constitution in addition to those specifically enumerated. He based his view partly on a broad reading of the "necessary and proper" clause of the Constitution (stating that Congress may make laws that are necessary and proper for carrying out Congress' powers), and partly on a basically Federalist view, emphasizing the need for a strong centralized government capable of effectuating policies of national concern.
E. The Supremacy Clause (Article VI, §2)
   The Supremacy Clause states that U.S. laws are the supreme law of the land and that no state may enact laws contrary to them. Marshall also used this Clause to support his view of the purpose and intent of the Framers of the Constitution.
F. Limits on National Authority
   Although Congress has broad powers, they are still limited by other provisions of the Constitution, e.g., the Bill of Rights.

II. COMMERCE POWER

Article I, §8 of the Constitution grants Congress the power to regulate commerce among the several states. The scope of federal commerce power has been the subject of debate for many years and has gone through historical cycles. There was always a tension as to whether a particular activity was considered interstate commerce or sufficiently affected interstate commerce such that it fell within the federal commerce power.

A. Defined

There is no legislative history to tell us what exactly was meant by "interstate commerce" when the Constitution was drafted. We do know that the Constitution was intended to remedy the economic situation as it stood under the Articles of Confederation where the national government did not have power to regulate commerce between the states. The commerce power can be read broadly, because much of the activity that takes place within the country relates to economic issues that eventually affect interstate commerce *per se*.

B. Purpose

The commerce power was designed to promote the economic welfare of citizens throughout the country by preventing destructive state-by-state regulation of interstate commerce, which often attempted to benefit local production and trade at the expense of production and trade from other states.

C. Pre-1888 Cases

1. Congress may regulate any activity engaged in to achieve a commercial end if the activity concerns more than one state. *Gibbons v. Ogden.*

2. There are no judicial limitations on Congress' commerce power other than the ones prescribed in the Constitution. *Id.*

3. Activities completely within a state are outside federal commerce power. *Id.* However, if a completely internal activity is linked to activities engaged outside the state, it would be within the commerce power. *The Daniel Ball.*

D. 1888-1933

1. Courts began to use the Tenth Amendment to limit the use of federal commerce power that infringed on states' sovereignty. With this application, the courts began to separate different activities as being either intrastate or interstate.

   Example: While transportation between states was considered an interstate activity, manufacturing was identified as an intrastate activity. *United States v. E.C. Knight.*

2. Directness Test

   The courts distinguished between interstate and intrastate activities by employing a test that measured whether the activity in question had a direct connection to interstate commerce.

   a. All forms of interstate transportation are considered interstate commerce. *Id.*

   b. Even though a particular activity is directly connected to inter-
      state commerce, a police regulation has to prevent some harm-
      ful effect on interstate commerce itself. *Hammer v. Dagenhart.*
      The majority ruling in *Champion*, as well as Holmes' dissent in
      Hammer, rest on the fundamental policies of national commerce
      power. Essentially, the Framers of the Constitution wanted to
      avoid situations where states would impose tariffs and close off
      borders in order to bar access by people and products from other
      states, as had occurred under the Articles of Confederation. Such
      actions led to the breakdown of relations among the states and
      adversely affected the economy. The Commerce Clause of the
      Constitution effectively gave Congress the power to act on behalf
      of states and to protect them against the intrusive activities of
      other states. To meet these goals, it is necessary to interpret the
      Commerce Clause to include the interstate transportation of
      anything because it is the Commerce Clause that essentially
      bars the states from regulating what is brought inside its borders.
      Therefore, the Commerce Clause must vest this power in some
      other governmental body — namely, Congress.
3. Impact Test
   During this period, the Supreme Court relaxed the directness test
   in areas of national economic interest and allowed the regulation
   of intrastate activities, if Congress found the particular activity to
   have a real, if not direct, impact on interstate commerce. *Houston,
   East & West Texas Railway Co. v. United States.*
4. Stream of Commerce
   Additionally, the Court found certain activities to be regulable
   because, although they were, by themselves, intrastate, they
   were nevertheless sufficiently a part of the stream of interstate
   commerce and directly connected to the interstate movement of
   goods. E.g., stockyard activities, see *Stafford v. Wallace.*
E. The New Deal: 1933-1936
   1. Broader interpretation was applied to Tenth Amendment restric-
      tions, in response to unprecedented national legislation regulat-
      ing local activities such as manufacturing and mining.
   2. The directness test was applied in all cases — even those where
      the regulated activity had a substantial effect on interstate
      commerce. *Schechter; Carter v. Carter Coal Co.*
F. 1937-1995
   1. This period marked a return to pre-1888 views of federal
      commerce power, including:
      a. A narrow reading of the Tenth Amendment. "[T]he Tenth
         Amendment [is] but a truism that all is retained which has
         not been surrendered." *United States v. Darby.*
      b. No more applications of any directness tests. *Wickard v. Filburn.*

      c. Elimination of intra/interstate and production/commerce distinctions. *NLRB v. Jones & Laughlin Steel Corp.*

      d. The obsolescence of the stream of commerce theory.

      e. The regulability of any activity that in some way affects interstate commerce. *Jones & Laughlin.*

      f. The idea that the determination of whether a particular activity sufficiently affects interstate commerce should be left to the discretion of the Congress, as long as a rational basis for a relation between a regulation and interstate commerce can be found. *United States v. Darby.*

  2. 1976-1985

    In 1976, the Supreme Court used the Tenth Amendment to impose a check on Congress' ability to regulate state and local governments and agencies. *National League of Cities v. Usery.* In 1985, the Court reversed itself. *Garcia v. San Antonio Metropolitan Transit Authority.*

  3. Congress' motive in regulating a particular activity under the commerce power is irrelevant as long as the necessary tests are met and there are no constitutional limitations. Congress has passed laws under the commerce power covering criminal statutes, *Perez v. United States*, and civil rights legislation (*Heart of Atlanta Motel v. United States, Katzenbach v. McClung*).

G. 1995-Present

  In 1995 the Supreme Court decided *United States v. Lopez*, which marked the first time in 60 years that the Supreme Court had struck down a federal law as exceeding Congress' Commerce Clause powers. *Lopez* introduced a new era where the Court will consider the constitutionality of federal commerce regulation more carefully.

  1. The federal commerce power may be exercised under three broad categories.

      a. regulation of the channels of interstate commerce, i.e., the activities that themselves constitute interstate commerce;

      b. regulation of the instrumentalities of interstate commerce, e.g., railroads, trucking companies and airlines; and

      c. regulation of activities, such as intrastate transactions, that substantially affect interstate commerce.

  2. The "substantial effects" test potentially allows regulation of non-economic activity, but the Court will scrutinize very carefully whether such activity does in fact substantially affect interstate commerce. By contrast, regulation of intrastate economic activity can be much more easily justified under the substantial effects test; in that situation, courts can aggregate the effects of individual instances of the regulated activity, and courts will give deferential scrutiny to Congress' implied determination that there was a substantial effect on interstate commerce.

CASE CLIPS

McCulloch v. Maryland (S. Ct. 1819)

Facts: Congress chartered a bank that established an active branch in Maryland. Because the bank was not chartered by the Maryland legislature, it was subject to a Maryland state tax that applied to all banks operating without that state's authority. The bank failed to comply with the tax law, arguing that the tax constituted a wrongful interference with Congress' lawmaking powers.

Issue 1: Does the exercise of federal power predominate over a state's claims to power?

Rule 1: (Marshall, C.J.) The federal government emanates from the people, not from the states. Therefore, the states may not limit the powers granted to Congress by the Constitution.

Issue 2: To what extent has the Constitution granted Congress the power to make laws?

Rule 2: (Marshall, C.J.) Although the federal government is one of enumerated powers, i.e., having only the powers granted to it, the powers are not limited to those *explicitly* stated in the Constitution, but also include those powers that are *implied* in the nature and spirit of the Constitution. In granting specific powers to Congress to achieve certain national goals, the Framers of the Constitution intended that the federal government have the means available to achieve those goals, although not expressly stated. An example would be Congress' power to punish for the violation of its laws. Although not expressly granted, such a power is *implied* for Congress successfully to bring about the desired goals of its lawmaking.

The Necessary and Proper Clause of the Constitution is an explicit grant to Congress to enact laws that are necessary to carry out its objectives.

(a) The Supreme Court defines "necessary" as something that is convenient, useful, or essential to achieving a desired purpose. It does not mean indispensable.

(b) The decision of whether a law is necessary should be left to the Congress to determine and should not be invalidated by the Court unless it is clear that the law is not within Congress' powers.

Issue 3: May a state tax federal entities located within its jurisdiction?

Rule 3: (Marshall, C.J.) The power to tax is the power to destroy. Therefore, a state tax statute that interferes with Congress' power to make laws is invalid.

Gibbons v. Ogden (S. Ct. 1824)

Facts: P was granted a monopoly by the State of New York to operate steamboats in New York waters. D, licensed for coastal trade under a federal statute, began a competing service.

Issue: What kinds of commerce may be regulated by the federal government under the Commerce Clause?

Rule: (Marshall, C.J.) The Supremacy Clause gives the federal government supreme power to regulate commerce between the states. Commerce is not limited to buying and selling but includes all commercial intercourse.

Note: Justice Marshall is consistent in this opinion with his belief in a strong centralized national government. Based on his ruling, the federal statute was found to be valid and thereby invalidated the New York monopoly.

Champion v. Ames [The Lottery Case] (S. Ct. 1903)

Facts: D challenged the constitutionality of the Federal Lottery Act of 1895, which prohibited, *inter alia,* the interstate transportation of lottery tickets.

Issue: Does the congressional power to regulate interstate commerce include the power to regulate interstate transportation?

Rule: (Harlan, J.) To protect public morals, Congress may regulate interstate transportation under its power to regulate interstate commerce.

Dissent: (Fuller, J.) Although commercial items may be prohibited as part of congressional regulatory power of interstate commerce, lottery tickets should not be considered articles of commerce just because they are being transported. The underlying purpose of the Federal Lottery Act is to execute a general police power (suppression of lotteries), and not to regulate commerce among the several states. General police power is not one of the federal government's enumerated powers.

Hammer v. Dagenhart [The Child Labor Case] (S. Ct. 1918)

Facts: Congress enacted a law prohibiting the interstate shipment of goods produced by children under certain ages.

Issue: May the federal government prohibit the interstate transportation of goods in order to regulate the conditions under which the goods are manufactured?

Rule: (Day, J.) The federal government may not regulate interstate transportation of harmless goods to regulate the employment conditions where the goods were manufactured.

Dissent: (Holmes, J.) If an act is within the scope of congressional authority (i.e., regulation of interstate commerce), it cannot be pronounced unconstitutional because of its indirect effect on state power. The child labor statute confines itself to prohibiting the transportation of certain goods. It is within the scope of congressional authority. The majority opinion's distinction of the transportation being necessary to the accomplishment of harmful results is tenuous at best. It is enough that in the opinion of Congress the transportation encourages the evil.

Note: Compare this case to the previous case. In *Champion*, the goods themselves were tainted; hence, transportation could be regulated. In *Hammer*, the goods were fine, but the conditions of their manufacture were improper. The holding in *Hammer* has subsequently been overruled in *United States v. Darby, infra*, and Justice Holmes' dissenting opinion has been followed.

Carter v. Carter Coal Co. (S. Ct. 1936)

Facts: The Bituminous Coal Conservation Act of 1935 included minimum wage and maximum hour requirements for coal miners.

Issue: Do employment/labor relationships involving "production" of goods have a sufficiently direct effect on interstate commerce so as to fall within congressional authority?

Rule: (Sutherland, J.) Production is a purely local activity and may not be regulated as interstate commerce, even if the goods to be produced are eventually moved between states.

Dissent: (Cardozo, J.) The *degree* of the effect of certain types of local activity on interstate commerce should also be considered when determining the scope of commerce power granted to Congress.

Note: The Bituminous Coal Conservation Act was an example of Congress' attempt to address problems of national concern. Congress felt that it was the only governmental body that could adequately deal with the national economic problems of the time. This case was overruled by *Darby*.

NLRB v. Jones & Laughlin Steel Corp. (S. Ct. 1937)

Facts: The National Labor Relations Act of 1935 prohibited certain types of unfair labor practices, such as terminating employees for participating in union activity.

Issue: May the operations of a large corporation be regulated under the Commerce Clause when the company operates factories in several states and exports 75% of its goods out of state?

Rule: (Hughes, C.J.) Activity that has a "substantial effect" upon interstate commerce may be regulated under the Commerce Clause.

Dissent: (McReynolds, J.) The chain of causation linking unfair labor practices and their effect on interstate commerce is too remote.

Note: This case vastly expanded the federal government's power to regulate interstate commerce.

Wickard v. Filburn (S. Ct. 1942)

Facts: A federal marketing quota limited the amount of wheat that individual farmers were allowed to raise.

Issue: May the activities of one farmer be regulated as interstate commerce?

Rule: (Jackson, J.) When an individual's small act combines with the many small acts of others, and all these acts belong to the same "class," each small act may be federally regulated if the entire "class" of acts combines to affect interstate commerce.

Note: This case substantially expanded federal regulation.

United States v. Darby (S. Ct. 1941)

Facts: The Fair Labor Standards Act of 1938 prescribed minimum wages and maximum hours for employees engaged in the production of goods for interstate commerce. It also prohibited the interstate shipment of goods manufactured in violation of those wage and hour regulations.

Issue: May the federal government regulate goods destined for interstate commerce to achieve policy objectives?

Rule: (Stone, J.) Congress, following its own conceptions of public policy, is free to exclude articles from commerce when their use in the states for which they are destined is perceived to be injurious to the public health, morals, or welfare.

Note: Both *Hammer v. Dagenhart* and *Carter v. Carter Coal Co.* were over-ruled by the *Darby* decision.

Perez v. United States (S. Ct. 1971)

Facts: D was convicted of loansharking, pursuant to Title II of the Consumer Credit Protection Act.

Issue: May the criminal activity of one offender, by itself not affecting interstate commerce, warrant conviction for a federal offense because the activity belongs to a "class of activities" that affect interstate commerce?

Rule: (Douglas, J.) A class of activities may be properly regulated by Congress without proof that the particular activity against which a sanction was laid had an effect on interstate commerce.

Dissent: (Stewart, J.) There is no discernible difference between loan-sharking and other crimes. All classes of criminal activity may affect interstate commerce, but what must be judged is the individual activity with which the defendant is charged.

Note: This case extended Commerce Clause powers to criminal statutes.

Heart of Atlanta Motel v. United States (S. Ct. 1964)

Facts: Title II of the Civil Rights Act of 1964 prohibited racially based inequality in access to public establishments. P owned a hotel near two interstate highways. The hotel, frequented by out-of-state guests and advertised nationally, refused to allow African Americans as guests.

Issue: May the federal government use its commerce powers to guarantee equal access to public places?

Rule: (Clark, J.) Congress may use its commerce power to regulate interstate transactions and transportation, even if the transactions are not commercial in nature but affect interstate commerce. Therefore, Congress may exercise the commerce power to enact a statute that guarantees equal access to public places. Congress need only have a rational basis for finding that enactment of the statute was sufficiently connected to interstate commerce.

Katzenbach v. McClung (S. Ct. 1964)

Facts: P's restaurant engaged in interstate activity that was limited to the purchase of meat originating outside the state. When P was held in violation of Title II of the Civil Rights Act for refusing to serve African Americans, P challenged the Act's constitutionality.

Issue: May federal civil rights laws be imposed on a restaurant whose interstate activities are limited to purchasing out-of-state meat?

Rule: (Clark, J.) The decreased spending arising from a refusal to serve African Americans has a close connection to interstate commerce. Moreover, there is testimony that discrimination has a direct effect on African Americans' interstate travel.

Note: Civil rights legislation can also be based on the Fourteenth Amendment.

National League of Cities v. Usery (S. Ct. 1976)

Facts: An amendment to the Federal Labor Standards Act of 1938 required state and local governments to meet federal minimum wage and maximum hour requirements.

Issue: May the federal government regulate state and local governments and their agencies?

Rule: (Rehnquist, J.) Although Congress has the plenary authority to regulate the commerce of private entities, it is limited by the Tenth Amendment in that it may not exercise its authority over state and local governments and agencies if such regulation affects a "traditional government function."

Concurrence: (Blackmun, J.) In order to determine properly whether or not to allow federal regulation of state and local governments and agencies, a balancing test must be applied. Where a federal interest outweighs a state interest, a federal statute should be upheld.

Dissent: (Brennan, J.) The Tenth Amendment only reserves to the states powers not delegated to the federal government. Otherwise, there is nothing in the Constitution that grants sovereignty to the states. Moreover, the resulting displacement of state policies by a challenged federal statute is no greater than when the federal government chooses to ouster state laws (which is clearly within federal authority). The *Gibbons* doctrine, which looks to the political (not judicial) process for restraints on commerce power, should not be disregarded. Justice Blackmun's balancing approach amounts to a policy judgment not within judicial authority. Judicial intervention serves only to tie Congress' hands.

Dissent: (Stevens, J.) The challenged amendments are no different than other federally imposed regulations on state activities that all would agree are permissible.

Garcia v. San Antonio Metropolitan Transit Authority (S. Ct. 1985)

Facts: An amendment to the Federal Labor Standards Act of 1938 required state and local governments to meet federal minimum wage and maximum hour requirements.

Issue: May the federal government regulate state and local governments and their agencies?

Rule: (Blackmun, J.) Although in *National League of Cities v. Usery* it was ruled that a state or local government may be federally regulated in relation to a "nontraditional governmental function," subsequent history has shown that the distinction between "traditional" and "nontraditional" is unworkable. Since a distinction cannot be made, a state or local government or agency may be federally regulated.

Dissent: (Powell, J.) The Tenth Amendment was intended to maintain complete state sovereignty as part of a dual system of independent governments. Federal regulation of state governments effectively destroys state sovereignty.

Dissent: (O'Connor, J.) By overruling *National League of Cities*, all that stands between state sovereignty and Congress is the latter's underdeveloped capacity for self-restraint.

Dissent: (Rehnquist, J.) The balancing test mentioned in *National League of Cities*, that the federal interest must be demonstrably greater than the state interest in order for the state government to be regulable, is a sufficient test for this case and should have been applied in favor of state sovereignty.

Note: This case explicitly overruled *National League of Cities v. Usery*.

A.L.A. Schechter Poultry Corp v. United States (S. Ct. 1935)

Facts: Ds were slaughterhouse operators who bought poultry for slaughter and resale in the New York metropolitan area. All their transactions were intrastate, except that they purchased live poultry from other states. Ds were convicted of violating the wage and hour provisions of the Federal Live Poultry Code.

Issue: May Congress extend its commerce power to activities that are mostly intrastate?

Rule: (Hughes, C.J.) Congress may not regulate activities that indirectly affect interstate commerce.

Concurrence: (Cardozo, J.) Activities local in their immediacy do not become interstate and national because of distant repercussions.

The Daniel Ball (S. Ct. 1871)

Facts: The Daniel Ball was a steamship that was fined $500 for not being licensed or inspected for safety under U.S. laws.

Issue: May an intrastate ferry operator be federally regulated on the grounds that its passengers are transferred to another transporter engaged in interstate commerce?

Rule: (Field, J.) A ship is considered to be participating in interstate commerce when it participates in movements of goods or persons between two states, even if the participation is limited to activities within one state.

United States v. E.C. Knight Co. (S. Ct. 1895)

Facts: D purchased four refineries, thereby acquiring complete control of the manufacture of refined sugar within the United States. The government claimed that the acquisition amounted to a monopoly, and was therefore in violation of federal antitrust statutes.

Issue: Does the commerce power extend to intrastate commercial activities such as manufacturing?

Rule: (Fuller, C.J.) Where interstate commerce is indirectly affected by intrastate commercial activity such as manufacturing, the federal government has no power to regulate the intrastate activity, lest state sovereignty break down.

Houston, East & West Texas Railway Co. v. United States [The Shreveport Rate Case] (S. Ct. 1914)

Facts: The Interstate Commerce Commission ordered railroad companies to change their rates for intrastate freight so that they would be comparable with interstate rates.

Issue: May intrastate activity be regulated to protect interstate commerce?
Rule: (Hughes, J.) Congress may prevent the common instrumentalities of interstate and intrastate commercial intercourse from being used in their intrastate operations to the injury of interstate commerce.

Stafford v. Wallace (S. Ct. 1922)

Facts: In 1921, Congress enacted the Packers and Stockyards Act in an effort to regulate the wholesale meat market and to control the proliferation of unfair business practices.
Issue: Are intrastate activities that affect interstate transactions subject to federal commerce regulation?
Rule: (Taft, C.J.) If activities are part of the flow of interstate commerce, they are subject to federal commerce power, even if those activities are solely intrastate.

New York v. United States (S. Ct. 1992)

Facts: The Low-Level Radioactive Waste Policy Amendments Act required states to provide for the disposal of radioactive waste generated within their borders or to take title and possession of the waste and assume liability for certain consequential damages. The Act was based on a proposal submitted by the National Governors' Association.
Issue: May Congress compel states to enact and enforce federal regulatory programs?
Rule: (O'Connor, J.) The Commerce Clause authorizes Congress to pre-empt state regulation and regulate interstate commerce directly, and to provide incentives by attaching conditions to receipt of federal funds. However, the Tenth Amendment forbids Congress from regulating the state government's regulation of interstate commerce, no matter how powerful the federal interest involved. Requiring states to either take ownership of waste or regulate according to the instructions of Congress exceeds congressional authority.
Dissent: (White, J.) The action by the federal government is the result of agreements among the states and is thus a permissible ratification of an interstate compact. Moreover, the majority opinion is not supported by recent Tenth Amendment cases.

Flood v. Kuhn (S. Ct. 1972)

Facts: P challenged previous Supreme Court rulings exempting baseball from antitrust laws on the grounds that the rulings had no rational basis.

Issue: May the Judiciary overturn irrational decisions, even if it is clear that Congress had the opportunity to clarify and remedy the issues but chose not to, indicating its approval of the current rulings?

Rule: (Blackmun, J.) Congress can use legislation to counter the effect of seemingly irrational court decisions. In light of this, the Judiciary must uphold previous decisions, even though they seem irrational.

Dissent: (Douglas, J.) Congressional inaction should not be used to broaden an explicit act of Congress. It was the Supreme Court that decided to exempt baseball from federal antitrust laws, and the Supreme Court should now overrule those decisions.

Dissent: (Marshall, J.) The previous cases involving federal antitrust law should be overruled. However, since the reserve system is based on a collective bargaining agreement, federal labor statutes should apply.

Cooley v. Board of Wardens of the Port of Philadelphia (S. Ct. 1851)

Facts: D was sued for violating a Pennsylvania statute governing the hiring of ship pilots. There was no conflicting federal statute respecting the issue.

Issue: Does the grant of commercial power to Congress *per se* deprive the states of all power to regulate interstate commerce?

Rule: (Curtis, J.) The grant of the commerce power to Congress is not exclusive. The states may therefore regulate certain subjects of interstate commerce that do not require a uniform system of regulation.

Coe v. Town of Errol (S. Ct. 1886)

Facts: The town of Errol assessed a property tax on goods prepared for interstate shipment.

Issue: When do goods become part of interstate commerce?

Rule: (Bradley, J.) Goods do not become part of interstate commerce until actually launched on their way to another state.

Russell v. United States (S. Ct. 1985)

Facts: D was convicted of arson under 18 U.S.C. §844, which made it a federal offense to maliciously destroy any building used in interstate commerce or in any activity affecting interstate commerce.

Issue: Does a two-family residential rental building affect interstate commerce?

Rule: (Stevens, J.) The local rental of an apartment unit is part of interstate commerce, since it is merely an element of a much broader commercial market in rental properties. The congressional power to regulate the class of activities that constitutes the real estate rental market includes the power to regulate individual activity within that class.

Printz v. United States (S. Ct. 1997)

Facts: P sheriff challenged federal gun control law requiring local law enforcement authorities to investigate would-be gun purchasers before sale license would be issued.

Issue: Does the federal mandate to local law enforcement violate principles of federalism?

Rule: (Scalia, J.) The federal government may not commandeer state law enforcement apparatus to enforce federal law, any more than it could commandeer the state legislature in *New York v. United States*. There is no history of such federal mandates until recently, suggesting that earlier Congresses did not believe they possessed this authority.

Dissent: (Stevens, J.) The Court's rule makes federal intrusion more likely, as now more federal law enforcement will be necessary in order to enforce federal law. The federal government must have flexibility to operate effectively.

United States v. Lopez (S. Ct. 1995)

Facts: D was convicted under a federal law criminalizing possession of a gun in a school zone.

Issue: May the federal government use its commerce power to regulate the possession of a gun in a school zone, absent any requirement that the gun have traveled in interstate commerce?

Rule: (Rehnquist, C.J.) The commerce power is not limitless, and does not extend to a non-economic activity when there are no contemporaneous congressional findings of the link to interstate commerce and the activity.

Concurrence: (Kennedy, J.) Education has historically been a state matter and federal regulation of education under the Commerce Clause makes it difficult for states to experiment with different solutions to problems.

Dissent: (Souter, J.) Congress has broad power to determine when an activity affects interstate commerce, and could rationally have reached that conclusion here.

Dissent: (Breyer, J.) Gun possession affects interstate commerce because of the costs associated with crime and the effect gun possession in schools has on educational attainment and therefore the nation's economic competitiveness.

Note: This was the first time in 60 years that the Court had struck a statute down as exceeding Congress' interstate commerce power.

United States v. Morrison (S. Ct. 2000)

Facts: D was sued under the Violence Against Women Act, which gave victims of gender-motivated violence a federal cause of action against their attackers.

Issue: Is the Violence Against Women Act a valid statute under either the commerce power or Congress' power to enforce the Fourteenth Amendment?

Rule: (Rehnquist, C.J.) Congress exceeded its powers under the Commerce Clause because gender-motivated violence is a non-economic activity; thus, congressional findings on the impact it has on interstate commerce are by themselves insufficient to uphold the statute.

Concurrence: (Thomas, J.) The commerce power should be reexamined to determine whether even the substantial effects test is too broad a reading.

Dissent: (Souter, J.) The majority opinion takes too narrow a view of congressional power, especially where, as here, Congress supplied findings linking the regulated activity to interstate commerce.

Dissent: (Breyer, J.) Determinations of the substantiality of the effect a transaction has on interstate commerce should be left to Congress, which is better suited to make them, especially given the interconnectedness of modern American society.

Note: The Violence Against Women Act, unlike the statute struck down in *Lopez*, contained findings linking the regulated activity to interstate commerce; thus, the Court's striking down of the statute restricts congressional power beyond that in *Lopez*.

Gonzalez v. Raich (S. Ct. 2005)

Facts: Federal prosecutors charge D with possession of marijuana that she grew herself and possesses for personal consumption under a license from the State of California allowing for the use of marijuana for medical purposes.

Issue: Does federal regulatory power extend to the possession of home-grown marijuana intended for personal consumption under a state license for medical use?

Rule: (Stevens, J.) Congress could have rationally concluded that possession of marijuana for personal consumption might leak into the interstate market for marijuana that Congress was trying to stamp out in the Controlled Substances Act; given that possession of a commodity is an economic activity, such possession is not governed by the more restrictive rules in *United States v. Lopez* (1995) or *United States v. Morrison* (2001), but rather by the more generous rules governing federal power from *Wickard v. Fillburn* (1942).

Concurrence: (Scalia, J.) Even if this conduct may not be economic activity, Congress may nevertheless reach it as it is an activity the regulation of which is essential to the effective regulation of the interstate commerce in marijuana.

Dissent: (O'Connor, J.) The majority's broad definition of "economic activity" brings nearly any activity at all within congressional authority, and destroys the role of states as laboratories for policy experimentation.

Dissent: (Thomas, J.) The majority's approach demonstrates the flaws in the Court's Commerce Clause jurisprudence, by expanding federal power far beyond anything the drafters intended.

CHAPTER 3

Other National Powers

I. THE TAXING POWER

Article I, §8 of the U.S. Constitution provides, "the Congress shall have power to lay and collect taxes, duties, imposts, and excises." Like its other powers (e.g., the commerce power), Congress has utilized its taxing power to regulate certain sectors of society and even invoked this power in areas where other powers could not directly reach. Congress has also resorted to its taxing power when other forms of regulations seemed constitutionally suspect.

A. Restraints on the Taxing Power

The taxing power as granted by the Constitution has to be exercised within certain limits.

  1. Uniformity

    Article I, §8 mandates that "all duties, imposts, and excises shall be uniform throughout the United States."

    a. This does not require that all individuals must be taxed uniformly; it only forbids discriminatory taxation among the states.

    b. The provision only affects indirect taxes, i.e., those that tax activities.

  2. Apportionment

    Article I, §2 requires that "direct taxes shall be apportioned among the several states which may be included within this Union." Hence, direct taxes must be so apportioned that each state would raise an amount in proportion to its share of the national population.

  3. Exports

    Article I, §9 also imposes a restriction on Congress' taxing power. It provides, "No tax or duty shall be laid on articles exported from any state."

II. THE SPENDING POWER

The spending power (Article I, §8) grants Congress the power "to pay the debts and provide for the common defense and general welfare of the United States." Hence, the power to tax and the power to spend are interrelated.

The scope of the spending power is far-reaching. It involves payment to individuals, as in the case of Social Security, as well as grants to states for education and welfare. Moreover, this power is not limited to the enumerated powers of Article I, §8. Theoretically, Congress may utilize this power for whatever purpose it chooses.

Congress has also utilized this power to regulate activities that could not be easily reached under its other powers. Example: Congress has used highway funding to enforce the 55 miles per hour speed limit.

III. WAR, TREATY, AND FOREIGN AFFAIRS POWERS

The war, treaty, and foreign affairs powers are not as frequently utilized as the commerce, taxing, and spending powers; nonetheless, they are important sources of power for Congress.

A. The War Power

Article I, §8 gives Congress the power to declare war, raise and support armies, provide for and maintain a navy, and tax and spend for the national defense. Article II, §2 makes the President the Commander-in-Chief of the armed forces.

B. The Treaty and Foreign Affairs Powers

The power to make treaties calls for a united effort between the President and the Senate. Article II, §2 provides that the President "shall have power, by and with the advice and consent of the Senate, to make treaties, provided two thirds of the Senate concur." Article II, §2 gives the President unilateral power to "appoint Ambassadors and other public Ministers and Consuls . . . and all other officers of the United States." Since Article I, §10 forbids the states from making treaties, it is clear that foreign affairs is an area reserved solely for the federal government.

IV. CONGRESSIONAL AND JUDICIAL POWERS

A. Judicial Powers

The federal judicial powers are outlined in Article III, §2. They permit the Judiciary to decide cases:

1. Arising under the Constitution and under federal law;
2. Involving ambassadors and diplomats;
3. Involving admiralty and maritime matters;

    4. In which the United States is a party;

    5. Between a state and another state, between a state and a citizen of another state, or between citizens of different states; and

    6. Between a state or its citizens and foreign states or citizens;

B. Congressional Powers

    Article I, §8 grants Congress the power to:

    1. Coin and regulate the value of money;

    2. Establish laws governing bankruptcy;

    3. Establish post offices;

    4. Control copyrights and patents;

    5. Govern the District of Columbia and all other federal properties; and

    6. Control immigration and naturalization of aliens.

    The Thirteenth, Fourteenth, and Fifteenth Amendments all have "enforcement" provisions (Section 2 of the Thirteenth Amendment, Section 5 of the Fourteenth Amendment and Section 2 of the Fifteenth Amendment) that authorize Congress to enforce the provisions of those Amendments.

CASE CLIPS

Bailey v. Drexel Furniture Co. (Child Labor Tax Case) (S. Ct. 1922)

Facts: Congress enacted the Child Labor Tax Law of 1919, which imposed a 10% excise tax on the annual net profits of employers utilizing child labor.
Issue: May Congress, pursuant to its taxing power, enact laws that are primarily regulatory rather than revenue-producing?
Rule: (Taft, C.J.) Congress may not use its taxing power to regulate areas within a state's regulatory power.

United States v. Kahriger (S. Ct. 1953)

Facts: The Revenue Act of 1951 required bookmakers to pay an occupational tax and register with the Internal Revenue Service. D was charged with violation of the Act.
Issue: May Congress, pursuant to its taxing power, enact laws to regulate conduct that falls within the regulatory responsibility of the states?
Rule: (Reed, J.) Although a federal excise tax has regulatory effects, it is still revenue-producing and thus a valid exercise of federal power.
Dissent: (Frankfurter, J.) The Act is an inadmissible intrusion into a domain of legislation reserved to the states. Further, the enforcement provision of the Act is designed for the systematic confession of crimes with a view to prosecution.
Note: *Marchetti v. United States* (1968) overruled *Kahriger*.

United States v. Butler (S. Ct. 1936)

Facts: Congress sought to raise farm prices by curtailing agricultural production. The Agricultural Adjustment Act of 1933 authorized the Secretary of Agriculture to make contracts with farmers to reduce production acreage in exchange for benefit payments. A processing tax was imposed upon producing farmers to raise funds for payments made to farmers curtailing production.
Issue: May Congress, pursuant to its taxing power, regulate agricultural production among the states, under the guise of providing for the general welfare?
Rule: (Roberts, J.) The taxing power rests on its own authority, and does not require that Congress tax only the activities that it could otherwise regulate under Article I. However, Congress may not use the guise of providing for the general welfare to regulate areas that are traditionally within local control. Here, the tax is such a guise, and as such is an

unconstitutional attempt to regulate activities that are reserved to state regulation.

Dissent: (Stone, J.) The Constitution requires that public funds shall be spent for the promotion of the general welfare. Thus, it is a contradiction in terms to say that there is power to spend for the national welfare, while rejecting any power to impose conditions reasonably suited to achieve that end.

Woods v. Cloyd W. Miller Co. (S. Ct. 1948)

Facts: Congress enacted the Housing and Rent Act of 1947 as a means of addressing the housing shortage that persisted after World War II. The Act was challenged on the grounds that federal authority to regulate rent under the War Powers Act had ended with the Presidential Proclamation, which terminated wartime hostilities.

Issue: May Congress, pursuant to its War Powers, promulgate a regulation to address a deficit caused by the war, even after hostilities have ceased?

Rule: (Douglas, J.) Congress may, pursuant to its War Powers, impose regulations aimed at remedying conditions that are the direct result of war, even if the war has ended.

Missouri v. Holland (S. Ct. 1920)

Facts: In 1916, the United States and Great Britain entered into the Migratory Bird Treaty to protect species of birds that annually migrated to certain areas of the United States and Canada.

Issue: May Congress, pursuant to its treaty power, enact federal statutes to regulate a subject area otherwise regulated by the states?

Rule: (Holmes, J.) Federal statutes enacted within the scope of the Treaty Power are "necessary and proper means" of executing an enumerated power of the national government. Therefore, such action does not violate the Tenth Amendment.

Steward Machine Co. v. Davis (S. Ct. 1937)

Facts: Congress, through the Social Security Act, required employers with eight or more employees to pay a payroll tax to the U.S. Treasury. Employers who made contributions to state unemployment funds received a credit against their federal tax.

Issue: Does Congress' adoption of measures conditioning the receipt of benefits upon participation in a state program violate the Tenth Amendment, which reserves undelegated national powers to the states?

Rule: (Cardozo, J.) Congress may adopt measures to alleviate a national unemployment crisis as long as those measures do not infringe on a state's quasi-sovereign powers.

United States v. Sonzinsky (S. Ct. 1937)

Facts: Section 2 of the National Firearms Act of 1934 required the registration of dealers with the Collector of Internal Revenue and imposed varying annual taxes to be paid by dealers, manufacturers, importers, and transferors of firearms.

Issue: To what extent does the regulatory effect of a tax render it not a tax but instead a regulation to be tested for conformance with Congress' Article I regulatory powers?

Rule: (Stone, J.) Any tax has some regulatory effect. As long as the tax produces some revenue the Court will not examine whether in reality it is an attempt to regulate the taxed activity. Here it does produce revenue, is not tied to regulatory provisions and the subject of the tax is not treated as criminal. Thus, the Court concludes it is a tax.

Katzenbach v. Morgan (S. Ct. 1966)

Facts: Section 4(e) of the Voting Rights Act of 1965 provided that no person who had completed the sixth grade in a Puerto Rican school where instruction was in Spanish could be denied voting privileges because of illiteracy in English. A New York voting statute required literacy in English.

Issue: May Congress, pursuant to §5 of the Fourteenth Amendment (empowering Congress to enact appropriate legislation to effect the Amendment's equal protection guarantees), constitutionally override a state's voting requirement?

Rule: (Brennan, J.) Section 5 of the Fourteenth Amendment gives Congress the authority to enforce the Amendment's equal protection guarantees. Therefore, Congress may enact legislation to counteract state laws violative of equal protection.

Dissent: (Harlan, J.) Congress does have the authority to enact appropriate remedial legislation. However, the determination of an equal protection infringement is initially and ultimately a judicial question.

National League of Cities v. Usery (S. Ct. 1976)

Facts: An amendment to the Federal Labor Standards Act of 1938 required state and local governments to meet federal minimum wage and maximum hour requirements.

Issue: May the federal government regulate state and local governments and their agencies?

Rule: (Rehnquist, J.) While Congress has the plenary authority to regulate the commerce of private entities, it is limited by the Tenth Amendment in that it may not exercise its authority over state and local governments and agencies, if such regulation affects a "traditional government function."

Concurrence: (Blackmun, J.) In order to properly determine whether or not to allow federal regulation of state and local governments and agencies, a balancing test must be applied. Where a federal interest outweighs a state interest, a federal statute should be upheld.

Dissent: (Brennan, J.) The Tenth Amendment only reserves to the states those powers not delegated to the federal government. Otherwise, there is nothing in the Constitution that grants sovereignty to the states. Moreover, the resulting displacement of state policies by a challenged federal statute is no greater than when the federal government chooses to ouster state laws (which is clearly within federal authority). The *Gibbons* doctrine, which looks to the political (not judicial) process for restraints on commerce power, should not be disregarded.

Dissent: (Stevens, J.) The challenged amendments are no different from other federally imposed regulations on state activities that all would agree are permissible.

McCray v. United States (S. Ct. 1904)

Facts: Congress enacted legislation to tax butter-colored margarine at a rate of ten cents per pound, while uncolored margarine was taxed at one-fourth of a cent per pound.

Issue: May the Judiciary curtail Congress' lawful taxing power because of a tax's burdensome effects?

Rule: (White, J.) Congress has constitutional authority to select the subjects of an excise tax. It is the people's role, not the Judiciary's, to check Congress' lawful exercise of its taxing power.

Mulford v. Smith (S. Ct. 1939)

Facts: The Agricultural Adjustment Act of 1938 provided marketing quotas for flue-cured tobacco. The quota was to be apportioned among tobacco-growing farms when the supply of tobacco surpassed the "reserve supply level." Tobacco auction warehouse-men were required to pay a penalty on the excess tobacco marketed through their warehouses. The warehousemen were allowed to deduct the penalty from the purchase price paid to producers who supplied the excess tobacco.

Issue: May Congress establish marketing quotas and impose penalties in areas of commerce that are traditionally regulated by the state?

Rule: (Roberts, J.) Congress may regulate local marketing of goods destined for interstate commerce.

Kleppe v. New Mexico (S. Ct. 1976)

Facts: The Wild Free-Roaming Horses and Burros Act of 1971 was enacted to protect "unbranded and unclaimed horses and burros on public lands of the United States." To appease a New Mexico cattle rancher, the New Mexico Livestock Board rounded up and removed 19 burros from federal land in New Mexico in violation of the Act.

Issue: Does the Property Clause, which empowers Congress to make all "needful Rules and Regulations" respecting federal territories, extend to regulating wildlife living on federal lands?

Rule: (Marshall, J.) Congress has complete proprietary and legislative power over federal lands and may regulate the lands and everything thereon through powers granted by the Property Clause.

City of Rome v. United States (S. Ct. 1980)

Facts: Section 5 of the Voting Rights Act of 1965 required a covered jurisdiction to obtain pre-approval from the U.S. Attorney General or the U.S. District Court for the District of Columbia to enact any "standard, practice, or procedure" with respect to voting.

Issue: May Congress, through the exercise of its remedial powers to enforce the voting rights guarantees of the Fifteenth Amendment, prohibit a local government from instituting structural changes in its electoral system if those changes would have unintended, discriminatory effects?

Rule: (Marshall, J.) Congress may use its broad legislative authority to enforce voting rights under §2 of the Fifteenth Amendment to invalidate voting procedures that it deems discriminatory in effect.

Dissent: (Powell, J.) Preclearance is intrusive on local autonomy in the structuring of democratic procedures. To deny the municipality the "bail out" option renders the Act unconstitutional as applied to it.

Dissent: (Rehnquist, J.) The Court's decision is inconsistent with the *City of Mobile v. Bolden* decision, which held that city was under no constitutional obligation to structure its electoral system to maximize a minority group's ability to elect a candidate of its choice. Denial of pre-clearance is a great intrusion on state autonomy.

Mississippi University for Women v. Hogan (S. Ct. 1982)

Facts: The oldest all-female university in the nation denied a male admission to its nursing program. P was permitted to audit classes but was required to attend one of the state's coeducational nursing schools to obtain credits toward a degree.

Issue: May Congress, pursuant to §5 of the Fourteenth Amendment, authorize states to maintain practices otherwise violative of the Amendment?

Rule 1: (O'Connor, J.) Though Congress has broad powers to enforce the equal protection guarantees of the Fourteenth Amendment, its powers are limited to adopting measures to secure those guarantees. Congress has no powers to restrict, abrogate, or dilute the guarantees.

Rule 2: (O'Connor, J.) The party seeking to uphold a statute on gender-based classification bears the burden of showing an "exceedingly persuasive justification" for the classification. Further, this burden is met only by showing at least that the classification serves important governmental objectives and that the discriminatory means are closely related to the achievement of those objectives.

Dissent: (Powell, J.) As the Equal Protection Clause was never intended to apply to this kind of case, the heightened level of scrutiny analysis employed by the Court is inappropriate. Further, the Court's decision curtails valuable diversity in the type of higher education a state can offer to women.

City of Boerne v. Flores (S. Ct. 1997)

Facts: P, a Catholic archdiocese, sued D city alleging that the city's failure to allow it to expand a church in a historic district violated the federal Religious Freedom Restoration Act, which required that states imposing restrictions that affected religious practice show that the restriction was narrowly tailored in order to serve a compelling government interest.

Rule: (Kennedy, J.) Congress' power to enforce the Fourteenth Amendment does not give it the power to reinterpret the Fourteenth Amendment, and there was an insufficient factual showing to convince the Court that the statute was "congruent and proportional" to the Fourteenth Amendment rights the statute sought to protect.

Note: This case introduced the "congruence and proportionality" test as the test for legislation enforcing the Fourteenth Amendment.

Kimel v. Bd of Regents (S. Ct. 2000)

Facts: P sued state university under the Age Discrimination in Employment Act (ADEA).

Issue: Did the ADEA validly abrogate state sovereign immunity?

Rule: (O'Connor, J.) For statutes to validly abrogate state sovereign immunity as measures enforcing the Fourteenth Amendment, there must be congruence and proportionality, which is not shown when both the amount of unconstitutional conduct restricted by the statute is relatively small, and when the statute's scope and remedies are broad.

Dissent: (Stevens, J.) Congress should have the authority to abrogate state sovereign immunity under its Article I authority; thus in this case it is unnecessary to reach the question of Congress' powers under the Fourteenth Amendment.

Board of Trustees v. Garrett (S. Ct. 2001)

Facts: P sued state university under the Americans With Disabilities Act provision banning employment discrimination against disabled people.
Issue: Did this provision validly abrogate state sovereign immunity?
Rule: (Rehnquist, C.J.) In order to satisfy the congruence and proportionality standard, there must be a record of state action that would be unconstitutional if considered in a lawsuit, on the precise type of conduct regulated by the statute.
Concurrence: (Kennedy, J.) The requirement of a precise record of unconstitutional conduct by states reflects the seriousness of an abrogation of states' immunity from lawsuits.
Dissent: (Breyer, J.) Congress is better suited than courts to determine when disparate treatment rises to the level of invidious discrimination that violates the Equal Protection Clause and triggers Congress' remedial power.

Nevada Dep't of Human Resources v. Hibbs (2003)

Facts: P sued D state for violating the federal Family and Medical Leave Act (FMLA).
Issue: Is the FMLA a valid abrogation of state sovereign immunity?
Rule: (Rehnquist, C.J.) Because the FMLA targets gender discrimination, which receives higher scrutiny than most other classifications, it is easier for Congress to demonstrate a pattern of unconstitutional conduct that triggers Congress' remedial powers.
Dissent: (Kennedy, J.) The FMLA is inappropriate legislation to enforce the Fourteenth Amendment because there's been no showing of significant unconstitutional conduct by the states.
Dissent: (Scalia, J.) If the question was the validity of the FMLA as applied to Nevada, it would have been necessary to show that Nevada itself had been engaging in unconstitutional conduct.

Tennessee v. Lane (S. Ct. 2004)

Facts: P sued D state under the provision of the Americans With Disabilities Act (ADA) requiring nondiscrimination in the provision of public services when he was assigned a nondisabled accessible courtroom for a case he was litigating.
Issue: Does that provision of the ADA validly abrogate state sovereign immunity with regard to access to judicial proceedings?

Rule: (Stevens, J.) Because the right at issue in this case is a fundamental right, and because the scope and depth of the ADA's provisions mirror the constitutional rule for access to courts, the statute validly abrogates states' sovereign immunity.

Dissent: (Rehnquist, C.J.) There is insufficient evidence that states are unconstitutionally denying people access to courts; thus, Congress overstepped in imposing these restrictions.

Dissent: (Scalia, J.) The congruence and proportionality standard is too difficult to apply in a principled way; thus, for congressional action enforcing racial equality the appropriate test is simply rational basis, while other congressional enforcement action is limited to providing remedies for court-adjudicated violations.

South Carolina v. Katzenbach (S. Ct. 1966)

Facts: The Voting Rights Act authorized the Attorney General to suspend state voting statutes that were found to appear discriminatory. Only limited judicial review was allowed.

Issue: May Congress pass a law pursuant to the Fifteenth Amendment that enables it to strike state voting statutes it deems to be discriminatory, whether intentional or not, with limited or no judicial review?

Rule: (Warren, C.J.) As long as Congress adopts a rational means of enforcing the Fifteenth Amendment guarantee of the right to vote regardless of race, it is constitutional. Since the state has none of the constitutional protections that individuals have, the established procedures formulated by the Voting Rights Act are considered to be rational under the circumstances and therefore within Congress' power under the Fifteenth Amendment.

Concurrence/Dissent: (Black, J.) While most of the provisions of the Voting Rights Act are constitutional, the provisions limiting a state's ability to amend its own constitution and not allowing the state to obtain a hearing in the Court are unconstitutional.

Katzenbach v. Morgan (S. Ct. 1966)

Facts: The Voting Rights Act of 1965 provided that, subject to certain restrictions, no person shall be denied the right to vote because of an inability to read or write English. New York required an ability to read or write English in order to vote.

Issue: May Congress constitutionally legislate based on its own interpretation of the reach of the Equal Protection Clause of the Fourteenth Amendment and defeat a state voting requirement?

Rule: (Brennan, J.) Congress may legislate based on its own judgment of the reach of the Equal Protection Clause of the Fourteenth Amendment. The Voting Rights Act of 1965 was enacted to enforce the Equal Protection

Clause of the Fourteenth Amendment, and the states have no power to withhold voting rights on conditions that are forbidden by the Fourteenth Amendment.

Dissent: (Harlan, J.) In cases where there is room to differ on whether equal protection or due process has been violated, it is up to the Judiciary, not the legislature, to resolve the conflict. The Act here allows the Fourteenth Amendment to swallow the state's constitutional authority in this field.

CHAPTER 4

State Regulation and the National Economy

I. THE DORMANT COMMERCE CLAUSE

A. The Constitution imposes certain limitations on state power.
These limitations may be express or implied. The most fertile ground for litigation in this field is the dormant Commerce Clause. This chapter is primarily concerned with the issue of whether, when faced with federal inaction, a state may enact legislation that affects interstate commerce.

The Constitution grants Congress the power to regulate interstate commerce. Congressional silence in certain areas may not be construed as congressional approval of state actions. Nonetheless, the Court has recognized the legitimacy of certain state action taken pursuant to a state's police power to protect its citizens and its environment. A state regulation that affects interstate commerce must meet each of the following requirements:

1. The regulation must pursue a legitimate end;
2. The regulation must be rationally related to that legitimate end; and
3. The state interest must outweigh the burden and discrimination imposed by the regulation on interstate commerce.

B. State Regulation of Transportation
States generally regulate transportation in interstate commerce in furtherance of public safety. Because the existence of a legitimate state interest is usually not in doubt, the Court has focused on the rational relationship between the state objective and regulation. The Court applies a balancing test, weighing the burden of the regulation on interstate commerce and the putative state benefit. In this area, the Court usually shows deference to legislative findings.

C. Discrimination and Protectionism

However, a state may generally not enact laws that, on their face or by effect, discriminate against interstate commerce. State laws discriminate against interstate commerce when they provide an economic advantage to intrastate commerce while burdening interstate commerce. State laws enacted pursuant to a state's police powers that impose equal burdens on interstate and intrastate commerce are usually upheld as nondiscriminatory. However, the Court will not allow a state to isolate itself economically from the commercial interplay among the states.

1. Incoming Commerce

   a. Protection of Economy

   A state may not bar the importation of certain goods into its borders in order to protect its in-state industries from out-of-state competition. Protectionist regulations are *per se* invalid.

   b. Health, Safety and Environmental Regulations

   If the state is pursuing legitimate aims to protect the health and safety of its citizens and its environment, the Court will generally balance the putative benefits to the state against the burdens to interstate commerce and determine if the state aims could be achieved through other, less burdensome means.

2. Outgoing Commerce: Protection of Natural Resources

   A state regulation that restricts the use of its natural resources to its residents or that bars their movement in interstate commerce warrants strict review by the Court. The Court usually upholds such discriminatory regulations only if a compelling state interest exists and less discriminatory measures are unavailable.

3. Market Participant Exception

   a. Market Participant: When a state acts as a market participant and not a regulator, dormant Commerce Clause analysis is usually not applied. The state, as market participant, may discriminate against interstate commerce in favor of its residents. However, a state as market participant in one market may not exert its influence to affect the operation of another market in which it is not a participant.

   b. The Privileges and Immunities Clause of Article IV, §2, cl. 1 provides that the "Citizens of each State shall be entitled to all the Privileges and Immunities in the several States." Hence, a state acting as a market participant that discriminates against out-of-state individuals or corporations might be vulnerable to a challenge based on this Clause even though the state's action does not violate the dormant Commerce Clause.

II. CONGRESSIONAL REGULATION OF FEDERAL-STATE RELATIONS

A. Preemption of State Authority

Article VI of the Constitution (the Supremacy Clause) grants federal law the status of the "supreme law of the land." If federal and state law regulate the same subject matter, the state law is preempted if:

1. Joint compliance is impossible;
2. The objectives of the two laws conflict;
3. Congress preempts the entire field; or
4. There is substantial national need for uniformity in regulation.

Absent the above, the test for preemption of state regulation in the subject area centers around the finding of:

1. An unmistakable congressional intent to preempt;
2. The pervasiveness of federal regulation; or
3. A state's historic power to regulate within the subject matter area.

B. Congressional Consent to State Law

The restrictions that the dormant Commerce Clause imposes on state power are not explicitly stated in the Constitution but are inferred from the exclusive grant to Congress of the power to regulate interstate commerce. Therefore, the limitations that the Court imposes on state authority to regulate commerce may be reversed by Congress. Congress may enact laws empowering the states to interfere with interstate commerce in any given manner. Congress may also prohibit states from regulating in a way previously upheld by the Court.

III. OTHER ELEMENTS OF FEDERALISM

A. State Taxation and Free Trade

Although it is widely recognized that "interstate business must pay its way by bearing its share of local tax burdens," states may not impose discriminatory or unduly burdensome taxes on businesses engaged in interstate commerce. Such state taxation violates the Commerce Clause. The decisions in this area are not always clear and consistent, but the Court has nevertheless tried to distinguish between permissible and impermissible state tax. The most commonly litigated taxes have been property taxes, sales and use taxes, net and gross receipts taxes, and license and franchise taxes. The typical subjects of state taxation have been interstate transportation and interstate sales.

1. Commerce Clause Restriction

The general principles the Court applies under Commerce Clause analysis to test the validity of a tax upon a multi-state company doing business in the taxing state are:

a. Whether the company's business activity is sufficiently connected to the taxing state;

b. Whether the tax imposes a heavier financial burden on interstate companies; and

c. Whether the tax is fairly apportioned.

2. Fourteenth Amendment Restriction

A state tax must also withstand the challenge of the Due Process Clause of the Fourteenth Amendment. An out-of-state company may not be taxed unless it has "minimum contacts" with the taxing state.

B. Intergovernmental Relationships

1. Tax Immunities

a. Federal Immunity from State Taxation

The general theory supporting federal immunity from state taxation is that a government may not tax those it does not represent. *McCulloch v. Maryland*. Therefore, when a state taxes the federal government or a constituent part thereof, it would in effect be taxing the whole nation, which it does not represent.

b. State Immunity from Federal Taxation

The federal government may not tax a state in a way that "unduly interfere[s] with the state's performance of its sovereign functions of government." The Constitution does not explicitly forbid the federal government from taxing a state. This prohibition is inferred from the Tenth Amendment, which reserves certain powers to the state.

2. Regulatory Immunities

The general theory supporting federal immunity from state regulation is that a government may not regulate those whom it does not represent. *McCulloch v. Maryland*.

Therefore, a state may not regulate the federal government or a constituent part thereof. The immunity a state enjoys from federal regulation is inferred from the Tenth Amendment, which reserves certain powers to the state.

3. Interstate Relations

a. Article IV, §2, cl. 1 of the Constitution (Privileges and Immunities Clause) provides: "The Citizens of each State shall be entitled to all Privileges and Immunities of Citizens in the several States." The purpose of this Clause is to prevent states from discriminating against out-of-staters. For purposes of this Clause, citizens and residents are interchangeable terms and only rights that bear on the vitality of the nation as a single entity are protected.

b. Article I, §10, cl. 1 of the Constitution provides that no state "shall, without the consent of the Congress [enter into] any agreement or compact with another State." Interstate compacts have been used by Congress to remedy many interstate and regional problems such as boundary disputes, natural resources regulations, etc.

c. Article IV, §2, cl. 2 provides for interstate extradition, and Congress has supplemented the force of the duty among the states by enactment of legislation.

d. Article IV, §1 (the Full Faith and Credit requirement) is the most litigated provision of Article IV. This provision requires states to give "Full Faith and Credit to the public Acts, Records, and Judicial Proceedings of every other State."

CASE CLIPS

Gibbons v. Ogden (S. Ct. 1824)

Facts: P, the holder of a New York monopoly right to operate steamboats between New York and New Jersey, challenged a federal law of 1793 that gave D the right to operate steamboats along the same route.
Issue: Does Congress' authority automatically preempt state authority when the subject to be regulated falls within both federal and state powers?
Rule: (Marshall, C.J.) When a state enacts laws which collide with acts of Congress and the laws operate to deprive a citizen of a congressionally conferred right, the state law must yield to the federal law.

Willson v. Black Bird Creek Marsh Co. (S. Ct. 1829)

Facts: A dam built by P upon authorization from the State of Delaware blocked navigable waters affecting interstate commerce. D, owner of a sloop licensed under federal navigation laws, broke the dam in order to pass through.
Issue: Absent direct congressional prohibition, may a state enact a statute to protect the health and property of its citizens when the statute adversely interferes with interstate commerce?
Rule: (Marshall, C.J.) Congress continues to regulate interstate commerce via the dormant Commerce Clause. A state may not enact laws which contravene the dormant Commerce Clause.

Cooley v. Board of Wardens of the Port of Philadelphia (S. Ct. 1851)

Facts: A Pennsylvania law required ships entering or leaving the Port of Pennsylvania to engage a local pilot to guide them through the harbor. A congressional statute provided that "all pilots in the bays, inlets, rivers, harbors, and ports in the United States shall continue to be regulated in conformity with the existing laws of the states ... and such laws as the states may respectively hereafter enact for the purpose."
Issue: Does the grant of the commerce power to Congress deprive the states of all regulatory powers in the area of commerce?
Rule: (Curtis, J.) The grant of the commerce power to Congress is not exclusive, and states may regulate certain subjects of interstate commerce that do not require a uniform system of regulation.

Southern Pacific Co. v. Arizona (S. Ct. 1945)

Facts: An Arizona statute prohibited the operation of railroad trains of more than 14 passengers or 70 freight cars within the state.

Issue: May a state, pursuant to its general police powers, impose health and safety transportation regulations that adversely affect interstate commerce?

Rule: (Stone, C.J.) A state may not enact transportation regulations that substantially burden interstate commerce and deprive interstate commerce of uniformity when Congress has deemed uniformity to be of importance.

Dissent: (Black, J.) The balancing of state safety interests against national concern for uniformity and the smooth flow of interstate commerce is not a matter for judicial determination but for legislative consideration.

Dissent: (Douglas, J.) When the propriety of local regulation has been recognized in an area, the grounds for judicial intervention should be more than the burdensome effects on interstate commerce. Further, when the question arises under the Commerce Clause, the state legislation is entitled to a presumption of validity.

Kassel v. Consolidated Freightways Corp. (S. Ct. 1981)

Facts: Iowa exercised its police powers to enact a safety statute that prohibited the use of certain large trucks within its borders.

Issue: May a state, pursuant to its police powers, enact legislation precluding the use of certain vehicles on its highways in an effort to promote its parochial interests?

Rule: (Powell, J.) When a state statute that promotes local interests yields only marginal gains and the interference with interstate commerce is substantial, the state statute is invalid under the Commerce Clause.

Dissent: (Rehnquist, J.) It is not the Judiciary's task to balance state benefits against the burden to interstate commerce. Because Congress can preempt the rational policy determination of a state legislature, a state statute carries a strong presumption of validity.

Philadelphia v. New Jersey (S. Ct. 1978)

Facts: A New Jersey law prohibited the importation of most "solid or liquid waste which originated or was collected outside the territorial limits of this State."

Issue: May a state enact legislation to combat local health and environmental problems when the legislation discriminates against articles of commerce coming into the state?

Rule: (Stewart, J.) A state statute which effects a ban on items of commerce entering the state is invalid because a state may not isolate itself from interstate commerce.

Dissent: (Rehnquist, J.) The fact that a state must dispose of its own waste does not mean that it must serve as a depository for those of other states. The state should be free under the Court's past precedents to ban the importation of items for health and safety reasons.

Dean Milk Co. v. Madison (S. Ct. 1951)

Facts: A local ordinance barred the sale of milk that was not processed and bottled at an approved pasteurization plant within a five-mile radius of the city.

Issue: May a city, pursuant to its powers to protect the health and safety of its citizens, enact laws to regulate the processing and sale of consumer items even though the laws adversely affect interstate commerce?

Rule: (Clark, J.) A state may not enact legislation that burdens interstate commerce when other adequate alternatives are available by which the state could achieve its regulatory goals.

Dissent: (Black, J.) The fact that the ordinance, like all health regulations, imposes some burden on trade is not dispositive of its discriminatory effect on interstate commerce.

Hunt v. Washington Apple Advertising Comm'n (S. Ct. 1977)

Facts: North Carolina enacted a statute that required all closed containers of apples to display either the applicable USDA grade or a notice indicating no classification. State grades were also prohibited.

Issue: May a state, pursuant to its police powers to protect its citizens, enact laws that are nondiscriminatory on their face but that burden interstate commerce?

Rule: (Burger, C.J.) When a state regulation has the practical effect of burdening interstate sales, it conflicts with the "common market" doctrine of the Commerce Clause and must be struck down.

H.P. Hood & Sons v. Du Mond (S. Ct. 1949)

Facts: A Boston milk distributor who obtained milk from New York producers and maintained three receiving depots in New York was denied a license to establish a fourth depot. A New York State law prohibited additional licensing unless the Commissioner was satisfied that the issuance of the license would not adversely affect the milk market.

Issue: May a state deny an out-of-state business access to its local market when such denial of access would protect and advance local economic interests?

Rule: (Jackson, J.) States are not separate economic units, and a state may not exclude out-of-state business in order to protect and advance local economic interests.

Dissent: (Black, J.) As the language of the statute is not discriminatory, the Court should not attribute an invidious purpose to the Commissioner's actions.

Dissent: (Frankfurter, J.) The case should be remanded because unanswered questions persist, without which the Court is unable to apply the proper test to balance national concerns of interstate commerce against local interests.

CTS v. Dynamics Co. of America (S. Ct. 1987)

Facts: Indiana enacted a statute that regulated the acquisition of "control shares" in an issuing public corporation. Under the statute, an entity acquired "control shares" whenever it acquired shares that, but for the operation of the Act, would have brought its voting power in the corporation to or above 20%, 33 ⅓%, and 50%. A majority vote of all disinterested shareholders holding each class of stock was required to pass a resolution that converted the control shares into voting rights. The practical effect of this requirement was to condition acquisition of control of a corporation on approval of a majority of the pre-existing disinterested shareholders.

Issue 1: May a state statute regulate subject matter already regulated by federal law?

Rule 1: (Powell, J.) When regulatory conditions imposed by state statutes are consistent with the text and purpose of a federal law, the federal law does not preempt the state law.

Issue 2: May a state law regulate the acquisition and control of a corporation if it does not openly contravene a federal law but interferes with interstate commerce?

Rule 2: (Powell, J.) A state law which regulates interstate commerce and local business evenhandedly, but which more frequently affects out-of-state businesses, is not discriminatory and is a valid exercise of a state's regulatory authority under the Commerce Clause.

Dissent: (White, J.) A state law which undermines the policies of a federal law is necessarily preempted by the federal law. Further, a state law regulating the transaction of stocks of corporations incorporated within its state will be used to block interstate transactions. Such a state law violates the Commerce Clause.

Reeves, Inc. v. Stake (S. Ct. 1980)

Facts: Reacting to a serious cement shortage, D instituted a preference policy by which all in-state cement orders and contract commitments were given preference over out-of-state orders at a state-owned and operated cement factory.

Issue: May a state, in a time of shortage, confine the sale of an item it produces solely to its residents without violating the Commerce Clause?

Rule: (Blackmun, J.) A state, acting as a market participant and not a market regulator, may discriminate against interstate commerce and sell its products on a preferential basis to its state residents.

Dissent: (Powell, J.) When a state becomes a participant in the private market to engage in nontraditional governmental functions, the Constitution forbids actions that would impede the flow of interstate commerce.

United Bldg. & Constr. Trades v. Camden (S. Ct. 1984)

Facts: A municipal ordinance required that at least 40% of the employees of contractors and subcontractors working on city construction projects be city residents.

Issue: May a municipality of a state enact laws that discriminate in the area of employment against non-municipality residents without violating the Privileges and Immunities Clause guaranteeing to U.S. citizens all privileges and immunities afforded to citizens in the several states?

Rule: (Rehnquist, J.) Absent a substantial reason for the difference in treatment, a municipality may not institute policies which discriminate against residents of other states. Such policies violate the Privileges and Immunities Clause, which guarantees U.S. citizens all privileges and immunities afforded to citizens in the several states.

Dissent: (Blackmun, J.) Because the Privileges and Immunities Clause does not afford state residents any protection against their own state's laws, intrastate discrimination based on municipal residency should not implicate the concerns of the Clause.

Pacific Gas & Elec. Co. v. State Energy Comm'n (S. Ct. 1983)

Facts: A California law imposed a moratorium on the certification of nuclear energy plants pending the federal government's acceptance of a long-term solution for the disposal of nuclear wastes.

Issue: May a state attempt to legislate in an area that Congress has earmarked for national regulation?

Rule: (White, J.) When federal and state law intersect in an area traditionally reserved for state regulation, a state retains its historic police powers unless the state action is contrary to Congress' manifest purpose.

Exxon Corp. v. Governor of Maryland (S. Ct. 1978)

Facts: In response to complaints of inequitable distribution of gasoline among retail stations during a period of short supply, Maryland enacted a statute forbidding producers or refiners of petroleum products to operate retail service stations within the state.

Issue: Is a state law, enacted pursuant to a state's regulatory powers, discriminatory and violative of the Commerce Clause if it imposes operating burdens on some, but not all, interstate firms?

Rule: (Stevens, J.) The Commerce Clause protects the interstate market, not particular interstate firms, from prohibitive or burdensome regulations. Therefore, a state law which regulates the particular structure or methods of operation in a retail market is constitutional.

South-Central Timber Development v. Wunnicke (S. Ct. 1984)

Facts: The State of Alaska proposed to sell 49 million board feet of timber but stipulated that the purchaser must process the timber before it was shipped out of the state. The local processing requirement was designed to protect the local processing and related industries.

Issue: In an effort to promote its local industries, may a state, acting as a market participant in one market, use its influence to exert a regulatory effect in another market in which it is not a participant?

Rule: (White, J.) The market-participant exception is inapplicable when a state attempts to regulate in a market in which it is not a participant. Such action blocks the flow of interstate commerce at the state's borders and therefore violates the dormant Commerce Clause.

South Carolina State Highway Dep't v. Barnwell Brothers, Inc. (S. Ct. 1938)

Facts: A 1933 South Carolina statute prohibited the use of certain trucks on its state highways.

Issue: May a state, pursuant to its police powers, enact a statute to effect safety and efficiency goals while restricting the movement of items in interstate commerce?

Rule: (Stone, J.) In the absence of federal legislation, a state may impose nondiscriminatory restrictions on interstate commerce in order to promote local goals.

Baldwin v. G.A.F. Seelig, Inc. (S. Ct. 1935)

Facts: New York enacted the Milk Control Act, which established a system of minimum prices to be paid by milk dealers to milk producers. The Act also prohibited the in-state sale of milk bought outside the state unless the price paid to the producers was one that would be lawful under a similar transaction within the state.

Issue: May a state, pursuant to its police power, enact legislation to ensure the health and economic welfare of its citizens by taxing products entering the state from other states?

Rule: (Cardozo, J.) A state may not use its police or taxing powers to establish an economic barrier against competition with products originating in another state. Further, a state may not dictate the prices at which other states may sell their products and establish economic barriers against the entry of the products as punishment for nonconformity.

Henneford v. Silas Mason Co., Inc. (S. Ct. 1937)

Facts: D enacted a statute that imposed a 2% use tax on tangible personal property in the State of Washington.
Issue: May a state impose a nondiscriminatory use tax on personal property that was in interstate commerce but has since reached its final destination?
Rule: (Cardozo, J.) A use tax on an item after it has reached its final destination is not a tax upon the operation of interstate commerce but a tax upon the privilege of using the item. Such taxes are within a state's taxing power.

Hughes v. Oklahoma (S. Ct. 1979)

Facts: An Oklahoma statute provided that "No person may transport or ship minnows for sale outside the state which were seined or procured within the waters of th[e] state."
Issue: May a state enact legislation prohibiting the exportation of wildlife found within its boundaries in an effort to preserve the ecological balance of its environment?
Rule: (Brennan, J.) When wildlife becomes an article of commerce, a state cannot limit its use to citizens within its boundaries at the exclusion of citizens of other states.

Hicklin v. Orbeck (S. Ct. 1978)

Facts: Alaska passed a statute that required that qualified Alaskan residents be given preference over nonresidents for jobs involving "all oil and gas leases, easements or right-of-way permits for oil or gas pipeline purposes, unitization agreements or any renegotiation of any of the preceding to which the state is a party."
Issue: Does a state's enactment of employment legislation aimed at alleviating local unemployment problems but resulting in discrimination against nonresidents violate the Privileges and Immunities Clause?
Rule: (Brennan, J.) A state's proprietary right in its natural resources is insufficient justification for the enactment of discriminatory legislation in employment. Such actions violate both the Privileges and Immunities Clause and the Commerce Clause.

Silkwood v. Kerr-McGee Corp. (S. Ct. 1984)

Facts: P's daughter was contaminated by plutonium from D's plant, which was subject to licensing and regulation by the Nuclear Regulatory Commission, a federal agency. After her death in an unrelated auto accident, P initiated a tort action seeking, among other remedies, punitive damages.

Issue: Does the federal government's exclusive authority to regulate an area necessarily preempt all remedies under state law?

Rule: (White, J.) When a remedy under state law does not conflict or frustrate Congress' objective for the subject earmarked for federal regulation, the state remedy is not preempted by the federal regulation.

Dissent: (Blackmun, J.) When the remedy sought under the state law is within the area regulated by federal regulation, such state remedy would be incompatible with federal regulations and is therefore preempted.

Complete Auto Transit, Inc. v. Brady (S. Ct. 1977)

Facts: Mississippi imposed a business tax "for the privilege of doing business within its state."

Issue: Does the imposition of a state tax for the privilege of doing business within a state violate the Commerce Clause when a company's only business within the state arises through interstate commerce?

Rule: (Blackmun, J.) The imposition of a tax on interstate activity for the privilege of doing business within a state is valid if the tax is fairly apportioned and the activity is sufficiently connected to the state.

Boston Stock Exchange v. State Tax Comm'n (S. Ct. 1977)

Facts: New York State imposed a "transfer tax" on the sale, transfer, or delivery of shares or certificates of stock in any corporation. In order to reduce competition with other state exchanges, New York amended its transfer tax law to extend financial advantage to sales and transfers on the New York exchanges at the expense of the regional exchanges.

Issue: May a state enact legislation to tax in a manner that discriminates against interstate transactions in order to favor local commercial interests over out-of-state business?

Rule: (White, J.) The fundamental purpose of the Commerce Clause is to assure that there is free trade among the several states. Therefore, no state may impose a tax which discriminates against interstate commerce by providing a direct commercial advantage to local business.

Mayor of the City of New York v. Miln (S. Ct. 1837)

Facts: An 1824 New York State law required the master of a vessel arriving in New York from a foreign country or another state to provide a detailed report on each passenger transported into New York or transferred to another vessel with the intention of proceeding to New York. The law also required that the master post security for the maintenance of immigrants and their children who became wards of the City and to remove any non-citizen whom the mayor deemed likely to become a dependent of the City.

Issue: May a state, pursuant to its powers to provide for the protection and welfare of its citizens, impose conditions upon the entry of immigrants into its state from foreign countries and other states?

Rule: (Barbour, J.) A state retains certain internal police powers, and it acts within those powers when it dictates terms upon which it will accept immigrants into its state who might adversely affect the safety, happiness and prosperity of its present citizens.

Prigg v. Pennsylvania (S. Ct. 1842)

Facts: The Fugitive Slave Act of 1793, enacted pursuant to the Article IV, required an owner of a fugitive slave to establish satisfactory proof of ownership and a judge or magistrate to issue a certificate thereto, prior to the extradition of the slave. P, the agent of a Maryland slave owner, applied for such a certificate and upon being refused, illegally removed the slave. P's action violated a Pennsylvania statute explicitly enacted to prevent such forms of self-help in the removal of fugitive slaves.

Issue: May a state law, pursuant to its police powers to regulate state matters, enact laws prohibiting owners from seizing and removing fugitive slaves from the state's borders?

Rule: (Story, J.) The Constitution secures an owner's right to the return of fugitive slaves and Congress is empowered to enforce that right through appropriate legislation. When Congress has exercised its constitutional power and enacts laws to safeguard rights guaranteed by the Constitution, state legislatures may not interfere with the protection of those rights.

Concurrence: (Taney, C.J.) States are not prohibited from interfering for the purpose of protecting the right of the owner over his property, but it is enjoined upon them as a duty, to protect and support the owner when he is endeavoring to regain possession of his property found in other states.

Dissent: (McLean, J.) In my judgment, there is not the least foundation in the Fugitive Slave Act for the right to take a fugitive slave by force and remove him out of the state. Such a proceeding can receive no sanction under the Act, for it is in express violation of the procedures of the Act. If a state magistrate refuses to act even though duty bound to do so, a recourse to a United States judge is the appropriate response.

Dred Scott v. Sandford (S. Ct. 1857)

Facts: In 1834, Dred Scott, a slave, was taken by his master from Missouri to Illinois. After two years they moved to Minnesota, then to part of the Louisiana Territory. They eventually returned to Missouri where Scott was sold to Sandford. Slavery was prohibited in Illinois by the state constitution and in the Louisiana Territory by federal statute. Scott argued that the various provisions abolishing slavery in the areas he had traveled made him a free man.

Issue 1: Is the slave class a part of the citizenry and able to invoke the court's jurisdiction premised on diversity of citizenship?

Rule 1: (Taney, J.) The Constitution's use of the word "citizens" does not include and was never intended to include the slave class. Therefore, slaves are not entitled to the rights and privileges which the Constitution bestows on its citizens, including the invocation of diversity of citizenship jurisdiction.

Issue 2: Is Congress authorized to pass a law prohibiting the ownership of slaves in certain territories?

Rule 2: (Taney, J.) Slaves are property and Congress may not deprive citizens of their property without due process of law.

Charles River Bridge v. Warren Bridge (S. Ct. 1837)

Facts: P, a company incorporated pursuant to an act of the Massachusetts legislature, built the Charles River Bridge (a toll bridge) to replace the ferry service operated by Harvard College. P paid Harvard College a yearly fee to compensate for the lost income from the cessation of the ferry service. In 1828 the Massachusetts legislature chartered another corporation to build the Warren Bridge adjacent to the Charles River Bridge. Upon the surrender of the Warren Bridge to the State as its charter provided, the State abolished the toll, thereby destroying the commercial value of the Charles River Bridge.

Issue: Does the grant of a charter to establish a bridge over a public waterway give the grantee exclusive contractual rights over such waterway for the duration of the charter?

Rule: (Taney, C.J.) In granting a public charter to a corporation, no rights vest to the corporation beyond those expressly granted. Rights cannot be granted by implication. Therefore, absent express language in the charter, vesting exclusive contractual rights, a state may, pursuant to its power of improvement and public accommodation, continue to administrate in that area.

Dissent: (Story, J.) It should be kept in mind that in construing this charter, we are not construing a statute involving political powers and sovereignty. We are construing a grant of the legislature, which though in the form of a statute, is still a solemn contract. I maintain that upon the principles of common reason and legal interpretation, the present grant carries with it a necessary implication, that the legislature shall do no act to destroy or essentially impair the franchise.

Baldwin v. Montana Fish and Game Comm'n (S. Ct. 1978)

Facts: Montana instituted a hunting license system under which non-residents were forced to pay fees 7 to 25 times higher than those paid by Montana residents.

Issue: Does a state recreational policy discriminating against nonresidents violate either the Privileges and Immunities Clause or the equal protection guarantees of the Fourteenth Amendment?

Rule 1: (Blackmun, J.) A state must treat all citizens equally with respect to those privileges and immunities bearing upon the vitality of the nation as a single entity. As recreational policies are not vital to the unity of the nation, distinctions based upon residency do not violate the Privileges and Immunities Clause, which guarantees equal treatment for all citizens throughout the country.

Rule 2: (Blackmun, J.) A state policy that merely imposes a heavier economic burden on nonresidents to use a state's recreational facilities does not violate the equal protection guarantees of the Fourteenth Amendment. Such regulations are reasonable means to effect the state's substantial interest in preserving its natural resources.

Supreme Court of New Hampshire v. Piper (S. Ct. 1985)

Facts: Piper, a resident of Vermont, applied to take the New Hampshire bar examination. After passing the examination, the New Hampshire Board of Bar Examiners informed her that she would have to establish a residence in that state before admission. She sued in federal court, claiming a violation of the Privileges and Immunities Clause.

Issue: May a state exclude nonresidents from its bar?

Rule: (Powell, J.) The opportunity to practice law is a "fundamental right" and thus protected by the Privileges and Immunities Clause. While that Clause permits discrimination against nonresidents where there is a substantial reason for the difference in treatment and the discrimination bears a substantial relationship to the state's objective, New Hampshire's exclusion of nonresident lawyers satisfies neither of these tests.

Dissent: (Rehnquist, J.) A state may legitimately wish to maximize the number of resident lawyers, so as to increase the quality of the pool from which its lawmakers can be drawn.

McCulloch v. Maryland (S. Ct. 1819)

Facts: Congress enacted a law that granted a charter to the Second National Bank to issue bank notes. P, pursuant to a state law imposing a tax on banks operating in Maryland but not chartered by the state legislature, proceeded to tax the Maryland branch of the National Bank.
Issue: Is a federally created entity immune from state taxation?
Rule: (Marshall, C.J.) A federal entity created pursuant to Congress' constitutional powers represents the interest of the whole nation, and a state may not tax those whom it does not represent. Therefore, a state may not tax an entity created by the federal government.

Cooper v. Aaron (S. Ct. 1958)

Facts: The growing public hostility from Little Rock residents, fueled in part by the passage of laws by the Arkansas legislature to frustrate the desegregation efforts of the Little Rock School Board, caused William Cooper and other members of the Board to petition for a two-and-one-half-year postponement of their program for school desegregation. The postponement entailed that John Aaron and other African-American students who had been enrolled in Little Rock's Central High School for the coming term be transferred to segregated schools.
Issue 1: Are state governmental officials duty bound to obey federal court orders based on the court's interpretation of the federal Constitution?
Rule 1: (Warren, C.J.) The federal Judiciary is supreme in the exposition of the law of the Constitution. Consequently, the interpretation of the Fourteenth Amendment enunciated by the Judiciary in the *Brown* case is the supreme law of the land and state officials are bound thereby.
Issue 2: May the Court allow a local school board, in good faith, to postpone its desegregation program due to violent resistance by state governmental officials and local citizens?
Rule 2: (Warren, C.J.) Children have a constitutional right not to be racially discriminated against in public school admission. This right cannot be sacrificed or yielded to violence and disorder perpetrated to frustrate the implementation of programs to ensure those rights.

Garcia v. San Antonio Metropolitan Transit Authority (S. Ct. 1985)

Facts: An amendment to the Federal Labor Standards Act of 1938 brought all state and local government employees under the Act's provisions regulating overtime. After the decision in *National League of Cities*, which held that the overtime provisions could not be applied to "traditional governmental functions," D, a public mass-transit system in San Antonio, withdrew itself from the Act's overtime provisions.

Issue: May Congress, pursuant to its powers under the Commerce Clause, regulate state governmental functions without violating state sovereignty as guaranteed under the Tenth Amendment?

Rule: (White, J.) Congress may regulate a state activity if the activity falls within Congress' commerce power.

Dissent: (Powell, J.) Federal overreaching sanctioned under the Commerce Clause undermines the constitutionally mandated balance of power between the states and the federal government.

Steward Machine Co. v. Davis (S. Ct. 1937)

Facts: Congress, through the Social Security Act, required employers with eight or more employees to pay a payroll tax to the U.S. Treasury. Employers who made contributions to state unemployment funds received a credit against their federal tax.

Issue: Does Congress' adoption of measures conditioning the receipt of benefits upon participation in a state program violate the Tenth Amendment, which reserves undelegated national powers to the states?

Rule: (Cardozo, J.) Congress may adopt measures to alleviate a national unemployment crisis as long as those measures do not infringe on a state's quasi-sovereign powers.

Pennsylvania v. Nelson (S. Ct. 1956)

Facts: D appealed from a decision that held that the Smith Act superseded the Pennsylvania Sedition Act and therefore P could not be properly convicted thereunder.

Issue: Is a state law regulating seditious activity preempted by a federal statute regulating the same activity?

Rule: (Warren, C.J.) Preemption of state law by federal law occurs when (1) the scheme of federal regulation is so pervasive as to make reasonable an inference that Congress left no room for supplementary state regulation; (2) the federal interest is so dominant that the federal system must be assumed to preclude enforcement of state laws on the same subject; (3) enforcement of state laws presents a serious danger of conflict with the administration of the federal program. Should the states be permitted to exercise concurrent jurisdiction in this area, federal enforcement would encounter not only the difficulties of incompatible or conflicting adjudications but the added conflict engendered by different criteria of substantive offenses.

Dissent: (Reed, J.) Congress has not, in any of its statutes relating to sedition, specifically barred the exercise of state power to punish the same acts under state law. The Smith Act appears in 18 U.S.C., which codifies the federal criminal laws. Section 3231 of that Title provides: "Nothing in this title shall be held to take away or impair the jurisdiction of the courts of the several States under the laws thereof." This Court has interpreted the section to mean that states may provide concurrent legislation in the absence of explicit congressional intent to the contrary. The majority's position in this case cannot be reconciled with that clear authorization of Congress.

City of Burbank v. Lockheed Air Terminal (S. Ct. 1973)

Facts: An ordinance adopted by Burbank made it unlawful for a pure jet aircraft to take off from the Hollywood-Burbank Airport between 11 p.m. and 7 a.m.

Issue: May a local government, pursuant to its police powers to protect the health and welfare of its citizens, enact safety laws that regulate the use of its navigable airspace after Congress has delegated that authority to a federal agency?

Rule: (Douglas, J.) A state may not regulate the use of its navigable airspace once Congress, to achieve uniform regulation in air traffic control, has earmarked that area for federal regulation.

Dissent: Unless Congress' preemptive intent with respect to state law is abundantly clear, the Court should hesitate to invalidate state and local legislation.

Missouri v. Holland (S. Ct. 1920)

Facts: In 1916, the United States and Great Britain entered into the Migratory Bird Treaty to protect species of birds that annually migrated to certain areas of the United States and Canada.

Issue: May Congress, pursuant to its treaty power, enact federal statutes to regulate a subject area otherwise regulated by the states?

Rule: (Holmes, J.) Federal statutes enacted within the scope of the Treaty Power are "necessary and proper means" of executing an enumerated power of the national government. Therefore, such action does not violate the Tenth Amendment.

United States v. Belmont (S. Ct. 1937)

Facts: The United States, pursuant to an agreement with the Soviet Union in 1933, acquired ownership of funds of a Soviet company that had been deposited with a private banker in New York City. The Soviet Union had acquired the funds by nationalizing the company and appropriating its assets. Because acquisition of property by confiscation was contrary to

New York's expressed public policy, the estate of the New York City banker refused to acknowledge the United States' claim to the funds.

Issue: May a state refuse to honor an agreement made between the federal government and a foreign power because the application of the agreement violates the state's public policy?

Rule: (Sutherland, J.) Governmental power over external affairs is not distributed, but is vested exclusively in the national government. States exercise no preemptive power in the area of foreign relations and constitutional agreements and treaties made between the federal government and a foreign power are binding on states.

New Energy Co. of Indiana v. Limbach (S. Ct. 1988)

Facts: An Ohio state statute provided a tax credit for each gallon of ethanol sold by fuel dealers if the ethanol was produced in Ohio or in a state that granted similar tax advantages to ethanol produced in Ohio.

Issue: May a state enact regulatory measures that deprive out-of-state producers of a tax benefit that is available to in-state producers?

Rule: (Scalia, J.) The Commerce Clause prohibits a state's adoption of regulatory measures that discriminate against interstate commerce unless the state advances a substantial local concern that cannot be addressed by nondiscriminatory alternatives.

D. H. Holmes Co., Ltd. v. McNamara (S. Ct. 1988)

Facts: D, a Louisiana corporation, contracted with several New York companies for the design and printing of merchandise catalogs. The catalogs were designed in New York but printed in other states, and 82% were mailed to Louisiana customers. D did not pay any sales tax to New York or to the states in which the catalogs were printed. P determined after audit that D was liable for use taxes on the value of the catalogs.

Issue: Does a state statute violate the Commerce Clause by imposing a use tax on personal tangible property that is purchased out of state but used within the state?

Rule: (Rehnquist, C.J.) A state's use tax is valid under the Commerce Clause if (1) the activity being taxed bears a substantial relationship to the state; (2) the tax is fairly apportioned; (3) the tax does not discriminate against interstate commerce; and (4) the tax is fairly related to the benefits provided by the state.

Minnesota v. Clover Leaf Creamery Co. (S. Ct. 1981)

Facts: A Minnesota law banned the retail sale of milk in plastic, nonreturnable, nonrefillable containers, but permitted paperboard milk cartons.

Issue: May a state, in pursuit of local environmental goals, enact statutes that impose incidental burdens on interstate commerce?

Rule: (Brennan, J.) A nondiscriminatory state regulation serving substantial state interests does not violate the Commerce Clause, even though it imposes minor incidental burdens on interstate commerce.

Quill Corp. v. North Dakota (S. Ct. 1992)

Facts: North Dakota taxed property purchased for storage, use or consumption within the state. Retailers maintaining a place of business in North Dakota were required to collect the tax from consumers. Firms that placed three or more advertisements in North Dakota within a 12-month period were considered to be maintaining a place of business in the State. Quill was a Delaware corporation that successfully solicited business in North Dakota through catalogs, fliers, and national advertisements, but had no property or employees in North Dakota. Quill challenged the tax under the Commerce Clause, which prohibits discrimination and undue burdens on interstate commerce.

Issue: May a state require an out-of-state mail-order house that has neither outlets nor sales representatives in the state to collect and pay a use tax on goods purchased for use within the state?

Rule: (Stevens, J.) States may not impose sales and use taxes on vendors whose only connection with customers in the taxing state is by common-carrier or U.S. mail, because such vendors lack a *substantial nexus* with the state.

Dissent: (White, J.) In today's economy, it is no longer rational to require physical presence as part of the Commerce Clause analysis. It is unfair to give a tax advantage to vendors who can take advantage of a State's infrastructure, banking institutions, courts, etc. from outside the state.

Maine v. Taylor (S. Ct. 1986)

Facts: A federal statute made it a crime to "import, export, transport, sell, receive, acquire, or purchase in interstate or foreign commerce . . . any fish or wildlife taken, possessed, transported, or sold in violation of any law or regulation of any State or in violation of any foreign law."

Issue: May a state, in an effort to protect the ecological purity of its natural resources, enact laws that discriminate against interstate commerce?

Rule: (Blackmun, J.) A state statute that discriminates against interstate commerce is valid if the statute serves a legitimate and substantial local purpose that cannot be served by other nondiscriminatory alternatives.

Dissent: (Stevens, J.) When a state discriminates against interstate commerce, it carries the substantial burden of proving that its local goal cannot be achieved through other nondiscriminatory alternatives. This burden must be met with great specificity, which Maine fails to do in this instance.

White v. Massachusetts Council of Construction Employers, Inc. (S. Ct. 1983)

Facts: The Mayor of Boston issued an executive order that required that half the workforce on all construction projects funded by public monies consist of bona fide residents of Boston. A portion of those funds came from federal grants that permitted parochial favoritism.

Issue: May a city order preferential hiring of city residents on construction projects funded by the city?

Rule 1: (Rehnquist, J.) A local government acting as a market participant may discriminately expend its funds without violating the Commerce Clause.

Rule 2: (Rehnquist, J.) When a state or local government action is specifically authorized by Congress, the action is not subject to Commerce Clause restrictions even if it interferes with interstate commerce.

Lewis v. BT Investment Managers, Inc. (S. Ct. 1980)

Facts: Two Florida statutes prohibited an out-of-state bank holding company from owning or controlling a business that sells investment advisory services.

Issue: May a state enact legislation that regulates local banking and related activities, but that precludes certain out-of-state enterprises from competing in the state's local financial market?

Rule: (Blackmun, J.) When a state statute on its face and in actual effect displays a local favoritism or protectionism unnecessitated by substantial local concerns, such state action unreasonably burdens interstate commerce and must be held as violative of the Commerce Clause.

Bendix Autolite Corp. v. Midwesco Enterprises, Inc. (S. Ct. 1988)

Facts: Ohio's statute of limitations was tolled while a party was out of the state.

Issue: May a state withdraw legal defenses to out-of-state corporations that are engaged in commerce in the state, but that are not subject to the jurisdiction of the state court?

Rule: (Kennedy, J.) A state's denial of a legal defense to an out-of-state corporation cannot be conditioned upon a waiver or relinquishment of rights that the corporation would have otherwise retained, because this practice significantly burdens interstate commerce and is violative of the Commerce Clause.

Dissent: (Rehnquist, C.J.) If a state may require the licensure of foreign corporations engaged in intrastate commerce, it is consistent for the state to treat them like any other entity that has done intrastate business, incurred liability, and thereafter withdrawn from the state.

Supreme Court of Virginia v. Friedman (S. Ct. 1988)

Facts: The State of Virginia conditioned "on motion" admission to its bar on the showing, among other matters, that the applicant was a permanent resident of Virginia.

Issue: Does the imposition of a state residency requirement for "on motion" admission to the state bar violate the Privileges and Immunities Clause, which guarantees to all citizens the privileges and immunities that citizens of the several states enjoy?

Rule: (Kennedy, J.) Regulations discriminating against nonresidents seeking admission to the state bar violate the Privileges and Immunities Clause guaranteeing to all citizens the privileges and immunities enjoyed by citizens of the several states.

Bacchus Imports, Ltd. v. Dias (S. Ct. 1984)

Facts: A Hawaii liquor tax imposed a 20% excise tax on sales of wholesale liquor. Certain locally produced alcoholic beverages were exempted from the tax.

Issue: Does the Twenty-First Amendment, which repealed the prohibition on the manufacture, sale, or transportation of intoxicating liquors in the United States, empower a state to impose an excise tax that provides a commercial advantage to local business and discriminates against interstate commerce?

Rule: (White, J.) The Twenty-First Amendment's repeal of the prohibition on intoxicating liquor does not empower local legislatures to erect barriers against interstate commerce in favor of the local liquor industry.

Dissent: (Stevens, J.) A state legislature has the power to create a local monopoly by prohibiting the sale of non-local alcoholic beverages. Thus, it may engage in a less extreme form of discrimination that provides a specific benefit in the form of a subsidy or tax exemption for locally produced alcoholic beverages.

Capital Cities Cable, Inc. v. Crisp (S. Ct. 1984)

Facts: An Oklahoma state law required cable television operators to delete all advertisements for alcoholic beverages contained in the out-of-state signals that they transmitted to their subscribers within the state.

Issue: Does the Twenty-First Amendment, which reserves to the states certain powers to regulate the traffic of liquor, empower a state to countermand federal policies adopted under the commerce power to promote the widespread development of cable communications?

Rule: (Brennan, J.) When a state regulation squarely conflicts with the objective of a federal law, and the state's central power to regulate the traffic of liquor under the Twenty-First Amendment is not directly implicated, the balance between state and federal power tips decisively in favor of federal law, and the state law is preempted.

Gade v. National Solid Waste Mgmt. Ass'n (S. Ct. 1992)

Facts: Illinois enacted hazardous waste statutes to "promote job safety" and "protect life, limb, and property." The federal Occupational Safety and Health Act (OSA Act) and the Occupational Safety and Health Administration (OSHA) also regulated hazardous waste management to protect the safety of the workplace. National Solid Waste Management claimed that the Illinois act was preempted by the federal regulations. From the OSA Act language, the Court found that Congress intended to subject employers and employees to only one set of regulations.

Issue 1: Where Congress acts to establish a scheme of uniform standards, may States enact additional regulations that do not conflict with the federal regulations?

Rule 1: (O'Connor, J.) Where there is a federal scheme establishing uniform standards, state law is preempted and states may not supplement federal regulations with ostensibly nonconflicting standards.

Issue 2: May states enact laws that interfere with areas of federal regulation if the law is enacted for an objective not subject to federal regulation?

Rule 2: Whether a state law occupies a field preempted by the federal government is determined with reference to both the purpose and actual effect of that law. Therefore, a state law that has a direct and substantial impact on worker safety is preempted by the OSA Act, even if the state can demonstrate some additional impact outside the workplace.

Concurrence: (Kennedy, J.) The result in this case is correct because the terms of the OSA Act expressly provide for preemption. However, in the absence of express provisions, state laws should be preempted only if they impose prohibitions or obligations that directly contradict Congress' primary objectives.

Dissent: (Souter, J.) Federal law only preempts state law if there is a clear congressional purpose to supplant states' traditional police powers. The text of the OSA Act does not support such a conclusion.

Ray v. Atlantic Richfield Co. (S. Ct. 1978)

Facts: The State of Washington adopted a statute to regulate the size and movement of oil tankers in Puget Sound, a body of inland water lying along the northwest coast of Washington.

Issue: May a state, in order to protect the lives and property of its citizens and preserve its marine environment, promulgate safety requirements for vessels using its navigable waters when federal law already regulates those vessels?

Rule: (White, J.) When state regulations impose different and higher requirements than a federal law attempting to achieve the same objective, or when a state law frustrates the evident intention of Congress to establish a uniform standard, the state law is preempted by the federal law.

Dissent: (Marshall, J.) When there is no direct conflict between federal and state laws, the state law should be preempted only to the extent necessary to protect the achievement of the aims of federal law. Whenever possible, the Court should reconcile the operation of both statutory schemes, rather than holding the state law invalid.

United States v. New Mexico (S. Ct. 1982)

Facts: The federal government contracted with three private companies to manage and maintain its facilities in Albuquerque and Los Alamos, New Mexico. New Mexico imposed a gross receipts tax and a compensating use tax on those doing business within its state.

Issue: May a state tax a privately owned corporation contracted to work for the federal government?

Rule: (Blackmun, J.) Cost-plus contractors that are not designated agents are not constituent parts of the federal government. A state may therefore properly impose taxes upon them.

South Carolina v. Baker (S. Ct. 1988)

Facts: Congress passed the Tax Equity and Fiscal Responsibility Act of 1982 which, among other things, removed the federal income tax exemption for interest earned on unregistered, publicly offered long-term bonds issued by states and local governments.

Issue: May the federal government tax the interest earned by a state bond without violating the state's tax immunity?

Rule: (Brennan, J.) The federal government may constitutionally tax the income earned from a state bond because the tax is imposed and collected from bondholders, not the state, and because any increased administrative costs incurred by the states are not "taxes" within the meaning of the tax immunity doctrine.

Dissent: (O'Connor, J.) To federally tax income earned from state bearer bonds is an attempt by Congress to regulate the states by threatening to deprive them of this tax immunity. This type of congressional act should be invalidated because Congress should not be able to erode state sovereignty.

Leslie Miller, Inc. v. Arkansas (S. Ct. 1956)

Facts: An Arkansas statute required all contractors to obtain a license from the State's Contractors Licensing Board before bidding, executing a contract, and commencing work as a contractor in the State.

Issue: May contractors working for the federal government be subject to a state's general licensing regulations that ensure the reliability of contractors working within the state?

Rule: (per curiam) The federal government has its own standards to determine the reliability and competence of its contractors. Therefore, federal contractors are immune from state licensing regulations.

Federal Energy Regulatory Commission v. Mississippi (S. Ct. 1982)

Facts: A statute enacted to combat the nationwide energy crisis authorized the exemption of cogeneration and small power production facilities from financially burdensome state regulation that discouraged their development.

Issue: Does Congress violate state sovereignty, as guaranteed under the Tenth Amendment, by inducing a state to participate in a federal program and to use its regulatory machinery to advance the program's goals?

Rule: (Blackmun, J.) When Congress, in a preemptible area, conditions state participation in a federal regulatory scheme on adoption of the federal proposal and on the use of its regulatory machinery to achieve the regulation's goals, Congress is merely inducing the state to participate in the federal program. Such inducement is a proper exercise of congressional power and does not threaten a state's separate and independent existence guaranteed under the Tenth Amendment.

Dissent: (O'Connor, J.) The Court's decision is antithetical to the values of federalism and inconsistent with our constitutional history.

The structure of the act drains inventive energy from state governmental bodies, making them less able to pursue local conservation proposals.

South Dakota v. Dole (S. Ct. 1987)

Facts: A federal statute withheld a percentage of otherwise allocable federal highway funds from states "in which the purchase or public possession of any alcoholic beverage by a person who is less than twenty-one years of age is lawful."

Issue: May Congress, consistent with its powers under the Spending Clause, legitimately attach conditions to a state's receipt of federal funds?

Rule: (Rehnquist, C.J.) Congress may, pursuant to its broad spending power, encourage state action by attaching conditions to the receipt of federal funds. Congress' conditional grant under its spending power must be (1) exercised for the general welfare; (2) clearly and unambiguously stated; and (3) related to the federal interest in particular national programs and projects.

Dissent: (Brennan, J.) The Twenty-First Amendment strikes the proper balance between federal and state authority in the area of liquor regulation and reserves those powers to the states. Therefore, Congress may not condition a federal grant in a manner to abridge those powers.

Dissent: (O'Connor, J.) The conditional grant of federal funds does not meet the Court's three-prong test. Establishment of a minimum drinking age is not sufficiently related to interstate highway construction, as the Court asserts. The breadth of the spending power should not be limited to Congress' notion of the general welfare, because Congress could misuse this power to invade state sovereignty.

Lorillard Tobacco Co. v. Reilly (S. Ct. 2001)

Facts: Manufacturers and sellers of tobacco products challenged Massachusetts regulations restricting the sale, promotion, and labeling of tobacco products.

Issue: Did federal tobacco marketing and warning label information preempt state law on these topics?

Rule: (O'Connor, J.) Federal law on these issues was sufficiently detailed such that the federal law's statements of preemptive effects govern.

Healey v. West Lynn Creamery (S. Ct. 1995)

Facts: Massachusetts collected a tax on all wholesale milk whether domestic or imported but then put that money into a fund out of which domestic milk producers were subsidized.

Issue: Are a neutral tax and a domestic subsidy, both of which are independently constitutional, unconstitutional when combined?
Rule: (Blackmun, J.) Such a combination violates the dormant Commerce Clause because it amounts to a tax on imported milk, and because there is no internal political constituency that would oppose the scheme except for consumers, who might not be interested given the small impact it had on retail prices.
Dissent: (Rehnquist, C.J.) Political process analysis has no place in dormant commerce jurisprudence, and the state should be free if it wishes to subsidize local producers in whatever manner it wishes.

C & A Carbone Inc. v. Clarkstown (S. Ct. 1994)

Facts: City required that certain waste products be deposited with a particular facility rather than shipped out of the city for disposal.
Issue: Does the city ordinance restrict interstate commerce and violate the dormant Commerce Clause?
Rule: (Kennedy, J.) The ordinance restricts the interstate market in waste processing by directing that local waste be processed at the local facility. For the same reason it discriminates against interstate commerce and thus is unconstitutional.
Dissent: (Souter, J.) The Court's result expands the scope of the dormant Commerce Clause by striking down a law that regulates evenhandedly both local and interstate commerce in waste processing.

Granholm v. Heald (S. Ct. 2005)

Facts: New York and Michigan enact laws restricting direct sales of wine from out-of-state wineries to local consumers, but continue allowing local wineries to engage in such sales.
Issue: Do these state laws fall within states' powers to regulate liquor under the Twenty-First Amendment or do they violate the dormant Commerce Clause?
Rule: (Kennedy, J.) The Twenty-First Amendment does not give states the power to discriminate with regard to liquor sales, and the laws do not satisfy the test for laws that discriminate against interstate commerce; thus, they are unconstitutional.
Dissent: (Stevens, J.) We should rely on contemporaneous understandings of the Twenty-First Amendment, which stressed the uniqueness of liquor and the authority states have to restrict importation of liquor.
Dissent: (Thomas, J.) This type of discrimination is authorized by federal law and also by the Twenty-First Amendment, which is a limitation on the normal requirements of the dormant Commerce Clause.

United Haulers Ass'n v. Oneida-Herkimer (S. Ct. 2007)

Facts: Local ordinance requires private trash haulers to deliver trash to a public handling facility. The haulers sue, alleging that the ordinance discriminates against interstate commerce by preventing them from sending the waste to an out-of-state facility.

Issue: Does this type of "flow control" ordinance violate the dormant Commerce Clause?

Rule: (Roberts, C.J.) There is no violation when such an ordinance directs commerce to a publicly owned facility. The rule in *C.A. Carbone v. Clarkstown*, 511 U.S. 383 (1994), striking down a similar flow control ordinance is distinguishable because in that case the ordinance directed traffic to a private waste handling facility. There is a difference between private businesses and government facilities, with the result that there is no discrimination against interstate commerce when the ordinance discriminates in favor of a government-owned facility.

(Plurality) Applying the balancing test from *Pike v. Bruce Church*, 397 U.S. 170 (1970), the ordinance survives dormant Commerce Clause scrutiny.

Concurrence: (Scalia, J.) I do not join the part of the opinion doing *Pike* balancing, as I find that to be inappropriate policy judgment that is conferred to Congress.

Concurrence: (Thomas, J.) The power to regulate interstate commerce is given to Congress and not the Court: thus, we have no business striking down statutes such as this one.

Dissent: (Alito, J.) There is no difference between this statute and the one struck down in *Carbone*; therefore the ordinance should be struck down.

Department of Revenue of Kentucky v. Davis (S. Ct. 2008)

Facts: Kentucky resident purchased bonds issued by another state. Kentucky does not exempt income from other states' bonds from its own income tax, though it does exempt income from bonds issued by Kentucky governmental units.

Issue: Does this differential tax treatment violate the dormant Commerce Clause?

Rule: (Souter, J.) No. Financing local government activity with tax-exempt bonds is the type of traditional government activity that is exempt from dormant Commerce Clause analysis. Local government bonds constitute a distinctive market, given that they are generally ignored by out-of-state buyers; this suggests that it's not economic protectionism that's motivating the states. There is no need to do the benefit-burden balancing called for by *Pike v. Bruce Church*, especially given that in this particular case the Court is incapable of drawing the balance accurately.

Concurrence: (Stevens, J.) Actions that motivate state citizens to lend money to their state does not burden interstate commerce in the way condemned by the dormant Commerce Clause.

Concurrence: (Roberts, C.J.) There is no need to consider the market for local bonds; the first part of the Court's analysis is sufficient to answer the question.

Concurrence: (Scalia, J.) The first part of the Court's analysis is sufficient to answer the question; thus, I would not consider the market for local bonds. Moreover, I would abandon *Pike* balancing altogether, and not just in this case.

Concurrence: (Thomas, J.) I would abandon the dormant Commerce Clause doctrine, which has no basis in the Constitution's text.

Dissent: (Kennedy, J.) The majority misapplies precedent and reaches a result that will distort the interstate market, in opposition to the principle underlying the Commerce Clause.

Dissent: (Alito, J.) I agree with Justice Kennedy's dissent.

Altria Corp. v. Good (S. Ct. 2008)

Facts: P Smokers brought state-law misrepresentation claims against D cigarette makers. Ds argued that federal law regulating tobacco advertising preempted the state law claim.

Issue: Does federal tobacco advertising law preempt state law claims alleging that cigarette makers misrepresented the health consequences of smoking?

Rule: (Stevens, J.) There is no preemption. The federal law attempts to protect smokers' health while guarding against the harm to commerce from non-uniform advertising rules. Here the state law claim is not preempted by the federal law's explicit preemption of state law "requirements or prohibitions based on smoking and health." The duty to disclose information has nothing to do with "smoking and health" *per se*.

Dissent: (Thomas, J.) The Court should hold the lawsuit preempted since it imposes an obligation because of the effect of smoking on health.

CHAPTER 5

Separation of Powers

I. INTRODUCTION

Each branch of the federal government derives its authority from enumerated powers conferred by the Constitution and from additional powers implicit in those the Constitution expressly grants.

To prevent centralization of authority in any one government branch, no arm of the federal government may assume the powers of another. This is referred to as the "separation of powers" principle. For example, under this doctrine, Congress may not assign its legislative powers to the President; nor may it enact laws that reserve to it exclusive control over the official who executes that law. The precepts that follow, articulated through the Supreme Court, illustrate the attempt to achieve and maintain a balance among the three branches' fields of power.

II. LEGISLATIVE PROCESS AND ENFORCEMENT: CONGRESS AND THE PRESIDENT

A. Bicameralism and Presentment

Separation of powers goes hand in hand with the "checks and balances" system of government. To prevent tyranny by either the legislative or executive branch, legislation must pass through procedures of both bicameralism and presentment.

1. Bicameralism refers to the two-house approval system by which bills are passed through Congress. To be valid, all legislation must be approved by a majority of each congressional house.

2. Presentment requires that all congressionally ratified bills be presented to the President, who may either sign them into law or veto them. Congress can override the President's veto if two-thirds of each house approves the vetoed bill.

B. Operating Parameters

1. The President may not usurp official functions properly belonging to Congress. Because only Congress may devise and enact

laws (with presidential approval), a President's order must be based on an act of Congress or derive from the executive powers granted in the Constitution. Otherwise, the President's lawmaking role is limited to recommending, approving, and vetoing legislation.

2. Congress may not infringe on presidential powers. Thus, Congress may not pass an act outside the bicameral/presentment system and reserve veto power over a party Congress delegates to execute and administer the law.

3. Congress may also not delegate to an official the power to execute a law and then reserve exclusive power over that official's removal. Such executive discretion is an infringement of presidential authority. Congress may, however, delegate a non-legislative party to enforce a law, provided Congress establishes behavioral principles to which the delegate can adhere. Similarly, an act that authorizes a non-executive government branch to select and remove an "inferior" officer does not violate the separation of powers doctrine.

III. "NECESSARY AND PROPER" EXERCISE OF AUTHORITY

Article I, §8 authorizes Congress to "make all laws which shall be necessary and proper" for executing Congress' express or implied powers. This includes the authority to pass laws enforcing constitutional amendments.

Laws pursuant to amendments are valid if they are consistent with the letter and spirit of the Constitution. These statutes supersede state laws, particularly when they redress state law injustices that a constitutional amendment proscribes.

IV. FOREIGN AFFAIRS

A. As the sole national representative in the field of international affairs, the President's executive power in foreign relations is greater than that for domestic affairs. The exigencies of foreign affairs permit the President to wield executive authority even if it is not pursuant to a congressional act.

B. Treaty Power

The President has the power to make treaties, though two-thirds of the Senate must ratify them. As exercises of the national government's complete power over international affairs, treaties cannot be subject to any state interference. Valid treaties and the statutes that enforce them are part of the supreme law of the land and override state power.

1. When a treaty and statute conflict, the more recent supersedes the other.
2. International Agreements
   When Congress acquiesces to an international accord that the President enters in order to resolve a foreign relations problem, the President may have power to settle all U.S. citizens' pending claims against the foreign country.

C. War Power and Authority over Armed Forces
   1. Declaring War: Congress and the President
      Only Congress can declare a national or foreign war. It cannot declare war against a state. The President can never declare a war. However, as Commander-in-Chief of the armed forces, the President may call upon the military, without congressional approval, in such emergencies as when another country unilaterally declares war and/or invades the United States. Problems arise when the United States conducts "military actions" that are claimed to be different from true "wars."
   2. Harsher Measures Under the War Power
      The Supreme Court has determined that because a state of war does not end with termination of hostilities, the war power includes the authority to enact legislation redressing conditions directly and immediately caused by war. Such legislation might address housing shortages resulting from the diversion of wartime production from home building.

D. Immigration
   Congress has exclusive and absolute control over policies regarding admission of aliens. For example, the legislature may expel aliens and create a system for their registration and identification. Such broad power is an expression of national sovereignty and is a necessary part of Congress' role in managing foreign relations and national security.
   The scope of judicial review of immigration and alien residence policies is quite narrow. The Supreme Court defers to ostensibly legitimate exercises of congressional authority in this area.

V. FEDERAL CONTROL OF CITIZENSHIP STATUS

A. Citizenship Under the Fourteenth Amendment
   The Fourteenth Amendment confers citizenship on those born or naturalized in the United States. Congress does not have express or implied power to alter or remove citizenship granted under the Fourteenth Amendment unless the person consents. A citizen can voluntarily relinquish citizenship.

B. Citizenship Apart from the Fourteenth Amendment
Congress may validly pass a statute that imposes conditions on
citizenship created outside the Fourteenth Amendment. Such a
statute must neither violate constitutional restrictions nor be
unreasonable, arbitrary, or unlawful.

VI. EXERCISE OF GOVERNMENT POLICE POWER

A. Protection of Public Health and Safety
The liberties secured by the Constitution do not import an
absolute right to freedom from all state restraint. A state's statutory exercise of its police power does not abridge those liberties
when enacted to protect public health and safety. The Court may
only review laws enacted to ensure the general welfare when they
falsely purport to protect public health, morals, or safety and
invade constitutional rights.
B. Restraining Contract Obligations
Where vital public interests are at stake, a state may exercise
its protective police power through temporary and conditional
restraints to prevent the immediate enforcement of contract
obligations. Such state action is permitted where:
1. An emergency exists, calling for the state to protect the community's vital interests;
2. The restrictive legislation is designed to protect a basic societal
interest;
3. The relief is appropriate to and justified by the emergency;
4. The restrictions' conditions are reasonable; and
5. The legislation is temporary and limited to the exigency that
calls it forth.

VII. FEDERAL IMMUNITIES

A. The Speech or Debate Clause
1. The Speech or Debate Clause (Article I, §6) grants members
of Congress immunity from questioning and incriminating
evidence about their legislative activities. The Clause also
applies to congressional aides whose activity, if performed by
the member, would be a legislative function.
2. Protected legislative functions include speaking and debating
on the congressional floor, voting, participating in committee hearings, and assisting in preparing committee reports.
Congressional investigations that rely on compulsory disclosure of information also fall within legitimate protected
activity.

3. Congressional members' and aides' statements made outside the context of legislative functions or deliberations are not protected from inquiry by the Speech or Debate Clause. This includes public transmittal of congressional information. Similarly, members and aides are not shielded by either the Clause or by a so-called executive privilege from prosecution for violating criminal laws in preparing for or implementing legislative acts.

B. Executive Immunity

The President is absolutely immune from liability arising from his official acts. This immunity prevents the President from being distracted from his public duties by civil liability.

Alternative remedies and deterrents, however, ensure that complete immunity will not place the President above the law.

C. Executive Privilege

Executive privilege is a right occasionally claimed by Presidents to prevent disclosure of information they consider confidential. Scrutiny or disclosure of presidential records is permissible, despite executive privilege, where:

1. Public access is sufficiently restricted to preserve executive confidentiality;

2. The records' contents are of national and historic importance; and

3. Such scrutiny aids the legislative process and is within Congress' investigative power.

VIII. EXECUTIVE POWERS: APPOINTMENT, REMOVAL, AND PARDON

A. Removal Power

1. Removal Power Generally

The President has unfettered, exclusive power to remove his appointees without approval from the legislature. This includes both high-ranking officials who act as his "alter ego" and executive officers engaged in other normal duties. Such absolute removal power is a necessary outgrowth of Article II's grant to the President of general administrative control of those who execute the law.

2. Limitations

The President's absolute power of removal over government officials is restricted to those whose positions are units of, and subordinate to, the executive department. This removal power does not extend to officials in quasi-legislative or quasi-judicial agencies, such as administrative bodies created by

Congress to carry out a statute's legislative policies. Congress alone holds control over these agencies. This control includes the power to fix terms of office and conditions for removal.

B. The Power to Pardon

The President has unlimited pardoning power that may be exercised at any time before, during, or after legal proceedings. The power includes the authority to grant relief from criminal contempt penalties. A pardon is valid even if the one pardoned has not been indicted or convicted.

IX. POWER OF LEGISLATIVE INQUIRY

A. Congress may conduct investigations and compel private individuals to furnish information when necessary and proper to execute Congress' authority to legislate. When relevant to legislative ends, Congress may make inquiries into existent and proposed statutes, as well as make surveys of social, economic, or political defects. Where public interests outweigh private concerns, a congressional witness may not resist inquiry into pertinent subject matter of which the witness is apprised.

B. Limitations on Power of Inquiry

Because it is not a law enforcement or trial agency, Congress faces certain limitations on its authority to investigate. For example, Congress may not:

1. Expose individuals' private affairs for purposes outside the furtherance of legislative goals;

2. Inquire into matters exclusive to another governmental branch; or

3. Compel a group's disclosure of its membership where:

   a. Such disclosure would seriously inhibit or impair exercise of constitutional rights, and

   b. The legislature has not convincingly shown a substantial relation between the information sought and a subject of overriding and compelling governmental interest.

CASE CLIPS

Youngstown Sheet & Tube Co. v. Sawyer
[The Steel Seizure Case] (S. Ct. 1952)

Facts: Responding to a proposed work stoppage in the steel industry, President Truman issued an executive order directing the Secretary of Commerce to seize and operate most of the nation's steel mills.

Issue: Do presidential orders have the force of law when they are not based on either congressional statute or constitutional grants of executive power?

Rule: (Black, J.) Lawmaking power is entrusted solely to Congress. The President's power to issue and enforce an order must stem from either an act of Congress or from the Constitution itself. A presidential order to seize property is invalid if it is not founded on a legislative statute or in the constitutional provisions that grant and delimit executive powers. The Constitution limits the President's role in the lawmaking process to recommending and vetoing legislation.

Concurrence: (Frankfurter, J.) The President does not have power to issue such an order when Congress has already expressly negated such power through legislation.

Concurrence: (Jackson, J.) When the President takes measures incompatible with the expressed or implied will of Congress, he can rely only on his own constitutional powers, minus Congress' constitutional powers over the matter.

Dissent: (Vinson, C.J.) If the President has any power under the Constitution to meet a critical situation in the absence of express statutory authorization, there is no basis for criticizing the exercise of such power. History shows that Presidents have taken prompt action to enforce laws and protect the country whether or not Congress provided in advance for a method of execution.

Immigration and Naturalization Service v. Chadha
(S. Ct. 1983)

Facts: Chadha successfully sought a suspension of deportation from the INS and the Attorney General. Congress delegated the power to suspend a deportation order to the Attorney General, reserving the right of either the Senate or House of Representatives to veto a suspension ordered by the Attorney General. The House of Representatives vetoed the suspension. Because the Act's veto power clause permitted the vote of one congressional house to override the executive branch's deportation findings, P challenged the clause as an unconstitutional violation of the separation of powers doctrine.

Issue: Are statutory clauses that reserve to Congress legislative veto power violative of the separation of powers doctrine?

Rule: (Burger, C.J.) Congressional actions are legislative when they alter the legal rights, duties, and relations of persons or entities. To be valid, all legislation must pass through both houses of Congress and be signed by the President. By circumventing these requirements, the legislative veto denies the President his constitutional right to participate in the lawmaking process and thus violates the separation of powers doctrine.

Concurrence: (Powell, J.) Though Congress views its veto power as essential to controlling the delegation of authority to administrative agencies, it has assumed a judicial function in violation of the separation of powers principle.

Dissent: (White, J.) Without the legislative veto, Congress must either refrain from delegating necessary authority or, in the alternative, it must abdicate its lawmaking function to the executive branch and independent agencies. The former leaves major national problems unresolved; the latter risks unaccountable policymaking by those not elected to fill that role.

Dissent: (Rehnquist, J.) Legislative history shows that Congress has been unwilling to grant the executive branch permission to suspend deportations without Congress retaining a legislative veto. Thus, I disagree with the Court's decision to sever the legislative veto provision from the statute and retain the statute's delegation of suspension power to the executive.

Bowsher v. Synar (S. Ct. 1986)

Facts: The Balanced Budget and Emergency Deficit Control Act set an annual maximum deficit amount for federal spending and required spending cuts whenever the budget deficit exceeded the limit by a certain sum. It also provided to the U.S. Comptroller General the authority to facilitate enforcement of the Act.

Issue: Does Congress breach the separation of powers doctrine by conferring on an official the power to execute legislation while retaining sole right to remove that official?

Rule: (Burger, C.J.) Congress' role in lawmaking is limited to enacting legislation and passing new legislation to execute it. It is a violation of the separation of powers doctrine for Congress to delegate the power to execute a law to an official and for Congress to reserve to itself exclusive power over that official's removal. Doing so would involve an unconstitutional intrusion into the executive function.

Concurrence: (Stevens, J.) Congress may not exercise its fundamental power to formulate national policy by delegating that power to one of its two houses, to a legislative committee, or to an individual agent of the Congress.

Dissent: (White, J.) The Comptroller General's powers are not such that vesting them in an officer not subject to removal at will by the President would improperly interfere with presidential powers. This official's functions are not central either to the exercise of the President's enumerated powers or to his general duty to ensure execution of the laws.

Dissent: (Blackmun, J.) Rather than striking down this important statute in its entirety I would simply strike down Congress' authority to remove the Comptroller General.

Morrison v. Olson (S. Ct. 1988)

Facts: Congress enacted the Ethics in Government Act, which allowed the Attorney General to request and help appoint independent counsel to investigate and prosecute violations of federal criminal laws by government officials. Only the Attorney General could remove this counsel.

Issue: Is an act unconstitutional for authorizing a party other than the President to appoint and remove a government officer?

Rule: (Rehnquist, C.J.) An act authorizing a non-executive branch of the government to select and remove an officer does not violate Article II or the separation of powers doctrine if that officer's position is "inferior." The Attorney General's power to fire the counsel for "good cause" provides sufficient executive branch control over the enforcement of the laws.

Dissent: (Scalia, J.) The Court has avoided the inevitable conclusion that a statute is void for vesting purely executive power in one who is not the President. Because the independent counsel is not subordinate to another officer, he or she is not "inferior," and her appointment other than by the President with the Senate's consent is unconstitutional, as are the limits on the President's power to fire the counsel.

United States v. Curtiss-Wright Export Corp. (S. Ct. 1936)

Facts: A 1934 Congressional Joint Resolution permitted the President to forbid arms and munitions sales to select countries.

Issue: May Congress delegate legislative power to the President when delegation is required for the handling of foreign affairs?

Rule: (Sutherland, J.) Delegation of certain legislative powers to the President can be constitutional when necessary to govern foreign affairs. The parameters of the constitutionality of the President's legislative power differ when external, rather than internal, affairs are at stake. As the sole federal representative in the field of international affairs, the President does not require a congressional act to establish legislative authority in foreign relations. The President must be accorded a degree of discretion and freedom from statutory restriction, which would not be admissible were domestic affairs alone involved.

United States v. Nixon (S. Ct. 1974)

Facts: President Nixon filed a motion to quash a federal court subpoena directing him to produce tape recordings and documents of his conversations with aides and advisers. Nixon asserted absolute executive privilege against complying with the subpoena and claimed that the separation of powers doctrine precluded judicial review of the privilege claim.

Issue: Does judicial review of, and asserted preeminence over, claims of presidential privilege violate the separation of powers doctrine?

Rule: (Burger, C.J.) The Supreme Court's authority to interpret claims of powers allegedly derived from enumerated constitutional powers includes the authority to assess the validity of a claim of privilege. Neither the separation of powers doctrine nor a generalized need for presidential confidentiality can sustain an absolute presidential privilege of immunity when that privilege conflicts with courts' ability to administer justice.

Powell v. McCormack (S. Ct. 1969)

Facts: P was excluded from his seat in Congress due to allegations of misconduct, despite having met the standing requirements for congressional membership as stipulated in Article I, §2.

Issue: Does the Judiciary violate the separation of powers principle by interpreting Congress' constitutional power to control its own membership?

Rule: (Warren, C.J.) Federal courts may interpret the scope of the Constitution's grant of authority and responsibilities to coordinate branches of government. That includes the authority to hear cases involving explication of Congress' constitutional power to control its membership.

Buckley v. Valeo (S. Ct. 1976)

Facts: A federal statute authorized a Federal Election Commission composed of congressional appointees to make investigations and keep records regarding federal elections. The commission was also empowered to devise federal election rules and to penalize those who violated the act or commission regulations.

Issue: Does Congress violate the separation of powers doctrine by enacting a law that reserves to itself the power to appoint those who will execute and administer a statute?

Rule: (per curiam) Congress has been given explicit and plenary authority to statutorily regulate a field of activity. This does not give it the power to appoint those responsible for administering the statute. Congress may undoubtedly create "offices" in the generic sense and provide methods of appointment to those offices. But when these appointees are chosen by Congress, and not by the President in accordance with Article II, they do not qualify as "officers of the United States." Since only officers of the United States (i.e., appointed by the President) have power to execute law, congressional appointees may not administer or enforce the law that creates their positions.

Nixon v. Administrator of General Services (S. Ct. 1977)

Facts: Former President Nixon challenged the constitutionality of a federal act that directed the Administrator of General Services to take custody of presidential papers and tape recordings.

Issue: Does a federal act authorizing responsible, limited scrutiny of presidential records by appropriate parties violate the principles of separation of powers and executive privilege?

Rule: (Brennan, J.) Whether an act disrupts the balance between coordinate government branches depends on the extent to which the act prevents a branch from accomplishing its constitutionally assigned functions. A separation of powers violation is unlikely, however, where the activity complained of is under the complainant branch's exclusive, responsible control and where the activity's scope is limited by adequate safeguards.

Executive privilege does not bar an act permitting scrutiny or disclosure of presidential records where (a) public access is sufficiently restricted to preserve executive confidentiality; (b) the records' contents are of national and historic importance; and (c) such scrutiny aids the legislative process and is within Congress' investigative power.

Dames & Moore v. Regan (S. Ct. 1981)

Facts: As part of a settlement to free American hostages held in Iran, President Carter suspended all contractual suits against Iran that were pending in American courts.

Issue: May the President suspend and settle American citizens' pending court claims against non-Americans, when done with congressional acquiescence and in the interest of foreign relations?

Rule: (Rehnquist, J.) Congress has implicitly authorized the President to suspend the claims of American citizens against foreign powers by its long history of acquiescing to such presidential conduct.

Concurrence/Dissent: (Powell, J.) Nullification of attachments presents a separate question from whether the suspension and proposed settlement of claims may constitute a taking.

The Prize Cases (S. Ct. 1863)

Facts: President Lincoln proclaimed a blockade of Southern ports after several Southern states seceded.

Issue: May the President wield the power to use the military without congressional approval when the threat to the nation's security is from within the country?

Rule: (Grier, J.) The President may resist an internal threat by using the same powers available to fend off a foreign attack.

Dissent: (Nelson, J.) As Commander-in-Chief, the President has control over the military in times of invasion. However, only Congress may declare war; if Congress is in recess when an emergency arises, it can quickly be assembled to invoke the war power.

Missouri v. Holland (S. Ct. 1920)

Facts: A federal statute attempting to regulate the killing of migratory birds was invalidated as being outside any enumerated congressional authority. The United States and Great Britain enacted a treaty prohibiting the killing of certain migratory birds.

Issue: May a treaty concern a subject area that is not within Congress' powers?

Rule: (Holmes, J.) Congress may ratify a treaty concerning matter not within Congress' enumerated powers. Such a treaty falls within the Supremacy Clause and will therefore be binding on the states.

Whitney v. Robertson (S. Ct. 1888)

Facts: Ps imported goods from Santo Domingo that were subject to a duty imposed by law. Similar goods imported from Hawaii (then a separate country) were duty-free under a treaty with Hawaii and the congressional act that enforced it.

Issue: When a valid treaty and statute conflict, which controls?

Rule: (Field, J.) The Constitution deems both treaties and statutes to be the supreme law of the land and on equal footing. When the two address the same subject and do not conflict, the courts will try to give effect to both, without violating either. If the two are inconsistent, the one more recently passed supersedes the other.

Goldwater v. Carter (S. Ct. 1979)

Facts: Several members of Congress filed suit in federal court against President Carter for terminating a treaty with Taiwan.

Issue: Is the abrogation of a treaty a political question and therefore beyond the Judiciary's authority?

Rule: None. The Court granted the petition for certiorari.

Concurrence: (Rehnquist, J.) This case is "political" and therefore non-justiciable because it involves both the President's authority in foreign affairs and Congress' authority to negate presidential actions. The executive and legislative branches should resolve these issues; they should not rely on the Judiciary to settle a dispute between coequal governmental branches, each of which is competent to protect its interests.

Concurrence: (Powell, J.) A dispute between Congress and the President is not ripe for judicial review until each branch has acted to assert its constitutional authority. This case does not present a nonjusticiable political question because (1) no constitutional provision explicitly gives the President power to terminate treaties; (2) the Court need only apply normal principles of interpretation to the constitutional provisions at issue; and (3) adjudication would not produce an embarrassing diversity of pronouncements on the issue by various governmental departments.

Dissent: (Brennan, J.) The Court is competent to address the question of whether a governmental branch is constitutionally designated for political decision-making power. Here, the Constitution commits to the President alone the power to recognize, and withdraw recognition from, foreign regimes.

United States v. Pink (S. Ct. 1942)

Facts: The Soviet Union assigned to the United States its claims to the assets of a Russian insurance company's New York branch. The United States sued to recover those assets, asserting the priority of the government's claims over those of creditors earmarked for payment by New York State.

Issue: Are federal treaties and agreements, as instruments of national foreign policy, supreme over contravening state policies?

Rule: (Douglas, J.) All international compacts and agreements have the same dignity and legislative supremacy as treaties and therefore must be honored by the states.

Galvan v. Press (S. Ct. 1954)

Facts: P, a Mexican alien, was ordered deported for his membership in the Communist Party.

Issue: How broad is the scope of Congress' power over the presence of aliens?

Rule: (Frankfurter, J.) Congress has exclusive control to formulate policies pertaining to aliens' entry into and right to remain in the United States.

Dissent: (Black, J.) A resident alien should not be driven from this country for joining a political party that, at the time, was recognized as legal.

Fiallo v. Bell (S. Ct. 1977)

Facts: Alien fathers of U.S. citizens are granted special immigration preference. Unwed fathers of illegitimate offspring are denied the preference.
Issue: May the Judiciary question congressional immigration policy?
Rule: (Powell, J.) Congress' powers over immigration may not be regulated by the Judiciary.

Afroyim v. Rusk (S. Ct. 1967)

Facts: P, a naturalized American citizen, was denied renewal of his citizenship after voting in an Israeli political election.
Issue: May Congress constitutionally strip away the citizenship of one who has never voluntarily renounced or relinquished it?
Rule: (Black, J.) Congress does not have express or implied power to remove an American's citizenship without his or her consent. The Fourteenth Amendment (conferring citizenship on those born or naturalized in the United States) is best read as defining a citizenship that is retained until voluntarily relinquished.

Rogers v. Bellei (S. Ct. 1971)

Facts: A section of the Immigration and Nationality Act provided that a citizen from birth would lose his citizenship unless he or she stayed in the United States for five consecutive years between the ages of 14 and 28.
Issue: May Congress statutorily deprive the citizenship of one born outside the United States and a citizen because his parent was a citizen?
Rule: (Blackmun, J.) Congress may constitutionally enact a statute imposing conditions for citizenship upon those whose citizenship is created outside the parameters of the Fourteenth Amendment. The Supreme Court will deem such a statute valid if it fits within the restrictions of constitutional provisions other than the Fourteenth Amendment, and if the statute's conditions are not unreasonable, arbitrary, or unlawful.
Dissent: (Black, J.) The Constitution, and the Fourteenth Amendment in particular, cannot rise and fall with the Court's passing notions of what is "fair," "reasonable," or "arbitrary."

United States v. Helstoski (S. Ct. 1979)

Facts: A member of the House of Representatives was indicted for criminal acts. He claimed the Speech or Debate Clause protected him from having to produce a record of potentially incriminating statements made on the congressional floor.

Issue: Are members of Congress protected from production of incriminating evidence or questioning about legislative acts performed in Congress?

Rule: (Burger, C.J.) The Speech or Debate Clause (Article I, §6) does not protect members of Congress from questioning or the introduction of incriminating evidence concerning legislative functions outside Congress. Evidence referring only to acts to be performed in the future, however, may be admitted, since indications of future performance are not themselves legislative acts.

Concurrence/Dissent: (Stevens, J.) Precedent does not require rejection of evidence that merely refers to legislative acts when that evidence is not offered to prove the legislative act itself.

Dissent: (Brennan, J.) I would dismiss this indictment. A corrupt agreement to perform legislative acts, even if provable without reference to the acts themselves, may not be the subject of a general conspiracy prosecution.

Hutchinson v. Proxmire (S. Ct. 1979)

Facts: Hutchinson (P) sued Proxmire (D), a U.S. senator, for defamation arising out of D's criticism of allegedly wasteful federal funding of P's scientific research. D presented this criticism in a speech before Congress, in a press release, and in newsletters sent to the public; he also referred to the research on television.

Issue: Does the Speech or Debate Clause protect public transmittal of information?

Rule: (Burger, C.J.) The Speech or Debate Clause grants members of Congress immunity from liability solely for legislative activities. Protected activities include speeches and debates, and such integral, deliberative, and communicative endeavors as committee proceedings and in-house reports. Defamatory statements made outside are not protected.

Dissent: (Brennan, J.) Public criticism by legislators of unnecessary governmental expenditures is a legislative act shielded by the Speech or Debate Clause.

Nixon v. Fitzgerald (S. Ct. 1982)

Facts: Fitzgerald (P) sued President Nixon for civil damages, following a Civil Service Commission finding that P was wrongfully dismissed from his position with the Department of the Air Force.

Issue: Is the President immune from all civil damage liability?

Rule: (Powell, J.) The President of the United States is absolutely immune from damages liability predicated on his official acts. This immunity extends to actions within the outer perimeter of official responsibility.

Dissent: (White, J.) The Court's decision makes the President immune, regardless of the damage he inflicts, regardless of how violative of the statute and of the Constitution he knew his conduct to be, and regardless of his purpose. Absolute immunity places the President above the law. The separation of powers doctrine is not violated by subjecting the President and/or his actions to judicial scrutiny.

Mistretta v. United States (S. Ct. 1989)

Facts: The Sentencing Reform Act of 1984 created the Sentencing Commission as "an independent commission in the judicial branch." The Commission was empowered to establish sentencing guidelines that would be binding on the courts, but would preserve judicial discretion to depart from the guidelines in special cases. Of the seven commission members, at least three had to be federal judges.

Issue 1: Does Congress grant excessive legislative discretion, and thus violate the separation of powers doctrine, by delegating the power to promulgate sentencing guidelines for federal crimes to an independent body?

Rule 1: (Blackmun, J.) Although Congress generally cannot delegate its legislative power to another government branch, Congress may create an independent rulemaking commission to promulgate sentencing guidelines and locate that body in another government branch if (1) the integrity of the branch is not undermined; (2) the powers are appropriate for that governmental branch; and (3) Congress sets forth sufficiently specific and detailed standards for the exercise of that authority.

Issue 2: Does the separation of powers doctrine prohibit Article III judges from serving on independent commissions such as the sentencing commission?

Rule 2: Judges may serve on independent commissions so long as their participation does not threaten, in fact or in appearance, the impartiality of the judicial branch.

Dissent: (Scalia, J.) The decisions made by the Commission are not technical, but are heavily laden with value judgments and policy assessments. They also have the force and effect of laws prescribing the sentences criminal defendants are to receive. Creation of such a "junior-varsity Congress" is an unlawful and undemocratic delegation of pure legislative power.

McCulloch v. Maryland (S. Ct. 1819)

Facts: Congress chartered the Second Bank of the United States, which established an active branch in Baltimore, Maryland. Because the bank was not also chartered by the Maryland legislature, it was subject to a Maryland state tax that applied to all banks operating in Maryland without that state's authority.

Issue: Does Congress violate the Constitution by enacting laws that necessarily and properly execute powers not explicitly granted by the Constitution?

Rule: (Marshall, C.J.) The national government derives its power from the American people; its authority is not subordinate to the states. While some of those powers are explicitly stated in the Constitution, other powers, such as the power to charter a bank, are implied. In addition, Congress may enact all "necessary and proper" laws (Article I, §8) to execute both explicit and implied powers.

United States v. Kagama (S. Ct. 1886)

Facts: The Indian Appropriation Act outlawed the killing of one Indian by another on a reservation and subjected the offender to trial, judicial procedure, and sentencing in U.S. courts.

Issue: (Miller, J.) May Congress enact legislation to extend U.S. judicial jurisdiction over Native American peoples?

Rule: Congress may statutorily bring Native Americans under U.S. judicial jurisdiction. As wards of the nation, and as communities dependent on the United States, Native Americans are owed a federal duty of protection.

Fong Yue Ting v. United States (S. Ct. 1893)

Facts: A congressional statute enforced a policy of prohibiting Chinese people from entering the United States. Chinese people who were permitted to stay were required to obtain a certificate of residence.

Issue: Is legislation regulating the presence of foreigners a valid exercise of national power over U.S. foreign relations?

Rule: (Gray, J.) The national government's absolute authority over U.S. foreign relations includes complete power over foreigners' admission into and presence in this country. That power permits Congress to expel aliens and create a system for their registration and identification.

Dissent: (Brewer, J.) The legislation at issue deprives these foreigners of liberty and imposes punishment without due process of law. Aliens in the United States fall within the express protection of the Constitution. The asserted doctrine of powers inherent in sovereignty is both indefinite and dangerous. Its exercise in expelling a race is beyond the Constitution's protecting power.

South Carolina v. Katzenbach (S. Ct. 1966)

Facts: The Voting Rights Act of 1965 contained provisions attempting to prevent racial discrimination in the voting process by offering remedies against such unjust practices as requiring literacy or "good moral character" in order to vote.

Issue: May Congress pass laws to carry out the provisions of constitutional amendments or to exercise congressional powers?

Rule: (Warren, C.J.) Congress may constitutionally enact statutes that validly enforce a constitutional amendment or that are "necessary and proper" for carrying out enumerated or implied powers.

Concurrence/Dissent: (Black, J.) It is doubtful that this suit presents a justiciable case or controversy. In addition, at least one of the Act's provisions unjustly blurs the constitutional distinction between state and federal power by requiring federal approval of certain states' laws and constitutional amendments.

Katzenbach v. Morgan (S. Ct. 1966)

Facts: The Voting Rights Act of 1965 ensured the right to vote to those from Puerto Rico who met certain conditions, even if they couldn't read or write in English. New York election law, however, required English reading and writing ability as a prerequisite to voting.

Issue: When is a federal law a valid enforcement of the Equal Protection Clause, such that it overshadows conflicting state law?

Rule: (Brennan, J.) A federal statute pursuant to an amendment is an appropriate enforcement of the Equal Protection Clause if it is plainly adapted to such enforcement and it is consistent with the letter and spirit of the Constitution. Such a statute supersedes contravening state laws.

Dissent: (Harlan, J.) The disputed federal law is a legislative announcement that Congress believes a state law to entail an unconstitutional deprivation of equal protection. Our responsibility is to decide whether the state enactment violates federal constitutional rights. Federal law should not intrude on state law unless there has been a denial by the state of Fourteenth Amendment limitations.

Jacobson v. Massachusetts (S. Ct. 1905)

Facts: A municipal ordinance, enacted pursuant to a state law, required all city residents to receive a smallpox vaccine.

Issue: Is a state's exercise of its police power over public health, safety, and morals necessarily an infringement of constitutional liberties?

Rule: (Harlan, J.) The liberties secured by the Constitution do not import an absolute right to freedom from all state restraint. A state's statutory exercise of its police power does not abridge those liberties when enacted to protect public health and safety.

Hampton & Co. v. United States (S. Ct. 1928)

Facts: The Tariff Act of 1922 authorized the President to raise tariff duties on goods.

Issue: Is an act unconstitutional if Congress delegates a non-legislative party to enforce it and if the act's purposes go beyond that of raising revenue?

Rule: (Taft, C.J.) Each governmental branch may invoke the action of the other branches, provided it does not assume their constitutional field of action. For example, Congress may pass a law and authorize another party, including the President, to effectuate it, provided Congress has established general principles and rules of action to which that party must conform. Secondly, it is within Congress' power to pass revenue acts, the motives behind which include those unrelated to raising revenue.

McGrain v. Daugherty (S. Ct. 1927)

Facts: A Senate investigating committee ordered a warrant following Daugherty's failure to respond to successive subpoenas to appear before the committee for questioning.

Issue: May a house of Congress make inquiries of private individuals and compel their appearance to give information that will help Congress effectively shape informed legislation?

Rule: (Van Devanter, J.) The Constitution grants each house of Congress auxiliary powers to carry out those the Constitution expressly confers. The power to make inquiries and to compel private individuals to furnish information is valid when necessary and proper to execute Congress' primary and constitutionally granted authority to legislate.

Watkins v. United States (S. Ct. 1957)

Facts: In testifying before the House Committee on Un-American Activities about his and others' association with the Communist party, Watkins refused to give information about the former activities of those he believed were no longer connected with the party.

Issue: May Congress conduct inquiries (by compulsion or otherwise) into people's private affairs for reasons unconnected to its legislative functions?

Rule: (Warren, C.J.) Congress' power to conduct investigations is inherent and auxiliary to the authority to legislate. That power does not encompass the authority to expose individuals' private affairs for purposes outside the furtherance of legislative goals.

Barenblatt v. United States (S. Ct. 1959)

Facts: Barenblatt was convicted for contempt of Congress after refusing to answer certain questions before the Subcommittee of the House Committee on Un-American Activities. He objected to the Subcommittee's right to inquire into his political and religious beliefs or any "other personal and private affairs" or associations.

Issue: Does Congress deny First Amendment rights by compelling a witness to reveal information if the public importance outweighs private interests?

Rule: (Harlan, J.) Congress does not necessarily deny the rights guaranteed by the First Amendment by conducting inquiries that enable it to exercise a constitutionally granted legislative function. Of course, Congress may only investigate areas in which it may potentially legislate. Furthermore, it cannot inquire into matters exclusive to another governmental branch. But where public (particularly national) interests outweigh private concerns, the First Amendment does not permit a congressional witness to resist inquiry into pertinent subject matter of which the witness is apprised.

Dissent: (Black, J.) The Court affirms use of the contempt power to enforce questioning in the realm of speech and association. This questioning violates due process, abridges freedom of speech and association, and is not related to Congress' legislative function.

Gibson v. Florida Legislative Investigation Committee (S. Ct. 1963)

Facts: Gibson, president of the NAACP's Miami branch, was found in contempt for refusing to bring with him the NAACP's membership records to refer to for answering questions before the Investigation Committee.

Issue: Does a legislature's demand for disclosure of a group's membership violate the constitutional right of freedom of association?

Rule: (Goldberg, J.) The constitutionally protected freedom of association for the advancement of beliefs and ideas encompasses the right to protection of privacy of association. A legislature's demand for a group's disclosure of its membership is therefore impermissible where (a) such disclosure would seriously inhibit or impair exercise of constitutional rights and (b) the legislature has not convincingly shown a substantial relation between the information sought and a subject of overriding and compelling governmental interest.

Eastland v. United States Servicemen's Fund (S. Ct. 1975)

Facts: The U.S. Serviceman's Fund (P) sought an injunction when the Senate Subcommittee on Internal Security issued a subpoena for bank records of the Fund's financial transactions. The Fund claimed that the records were tantamount to a membership list and were therefore protected by the First Amendment as privileged information.

Issue: Is congressional investigation through compulsory disclosure of information a legitimate legislative activity protected by the Speech or Debate Clause?

Rule: (Burger, C.J.) The Speech or Debate Clause renders Congress immune from liability and judicial review when its actions fall within the scope of legitimate legislative activity.

Concurrence: (Marshall, J.) The Speech or Debate Clause protects the Senate's actions from judicial interference. However, the Clause cannot be used to avoid meaningful review of constitutional objections to a subpoena simply because the subpoena is served on a third party.

Dissent: (Douglas, J.) Congressional power may not be used to deprive people of their First Amendment or other constitutional rights. No regime of law may make those who wield such power immune from actions brought by people who have been wronged by official action.

Gravel v. United States (S. Ct. 1972)

Facts: Gravel and his congressional aide released government documents to a publisher.

Issue: Does the Speech or Debate Clause protect both congressional aides and commercial publication of congressional material?

Rule: (White, J.) The Speech or Debate Clause protects congressional members against lawsuits and investigations relating to legislative acts. The Clause also applies to congressional aides whose activity, if performed by the member, would be a legislative function.

Dissent: (Douglas, J.) The Speech or Debate Clause should insulate a congressional member and his aide from inquiry into private publication of legislative matter. Such publication is a way of informing the public of the executive branch's activities.

Dissent: (Brennan, J.) By not considering private publication of congressional matter within the scope of the Speech or Debate Clause, the Court excludes from the sphere of protected legislative activity a function lying at the heart of democratic government — informing the public about matters affecting the administration of government.

Dissent: (Stewart, J.) The Court's ruling permits a vindictive executive to subpoena a member of Congress to testify about informants who have not committed crimes and who have no knowledge of crime. It is not clear that the executive's interest in justice must *always* override public interest in having an informed Congress.

Myers v. United States (S. Ct. 1926)

Facts: A congressional act authorized the President, with the Senate's consent, to appoint and remove postmasters.

Issue: Does the President have exclusive power of removing executive officers of the United States whom he has appointed with the Senate's advice and consent?

Rule: (Taft, C.J.) The President has unfettered, exclusive power to remove his appointees without approval from the legislature. This includes both high-ranking officials who act as his "alter ego" and executive officers engaged in other normal duties.

Dissent: (Brandeis, J.) To imply a grant to the President of the uncontrollable power of removal from statutory inferior executive offices involves an unnecessary and indefensible limitation upon the constitutional power of Congress to fix tenure of such offices. It has been Congress' practice to control the exercise of executive removal power.

Dissent: (Holmes, J.) The President's duty to see that the laws be executed is one not exceeding the laws or requiring him to achieve more than Congress sees fit to leave within his power.

Humphrey's Executor v. United States (S. Ct. 1935)

Facts: President Roosevelt removed Humphrey, a Hoover appointee, from the Federal Trade Commission.

Issue: Does the President's unlimited power to remove executive officers extend to those in quasi-legislative or quasi-judicial agencies?

Rule: (Sutherland, J.) The President's absolute power of removal over government officials is restricted to those whose positions are units of, and subordinate to, the executive department. This removal power does not extend to officials in quasi-legislative or quasi-judicial agencies, such as administrative bodies created by Congress to carry out a statute's legislative policies.

United States v. Woodley (1985)

Facts: President Carter nominated Judge Heen to sit on a California federal court. He then granted Heen a recess commission to preside, pending Senate confirmation. Though President Reagan revoked Heen's nomination, Heen continued on the bench for several months. During that period, Heen convicted Woodley (D) of violating federal drug laws. An appeals panel overturned Woodley's conviction, claiming that recess appointments of federal judges contravened Article II of the Constitution.

Issue: May the President constitutionally confer temporary federal judicial commissions during a Senate recess?

Rule: (Beezer, Circuit Judge) Article II specifically empowers the President to appoint Supreme Court judges and to fill all office vacancies during a Senate recess. The Article's express language, as well as legislative history and historical practice, suggests that this authority extends to the appointment of federal judges.

Dissent: (Norris, J.) The Recess Appointments Clause, authorizing presidential appointments during congressional recess, should not apply to federal judges. Judges appointed under the Recess Clause lack the political independence and impartiality that only a confirmed federal judge, equipped with life tenure and guaranteed compensation, can afford to exercise.

Ex Parte Grossman (S. Ct. 1925)

Facts: A federal judge sentenced Grossman to one year in prison and fined him $1,000 for ignoring a restraining order. Although President Coolidge later limited Grossman's penalty to just the fine, the judge reinstated the prison sentence.

Issue: Does the President's power to pardon encompass criminal contempt penalties in addition to offenses against the federal government?

Rule: (Taft, C.J.) The federal government's "checks and balances" system confers on the President the power to afford relief, through pardon, from undue harshness or evident mistake in the operation or enforcement of criminal law. The President's power to pardon therefore includes the authority to grant relief from criminal contempt penalties.

Murphy v. Ford (1975)

Facts: President Ford granted former President Nixon a pardon for alleged misconduct while in office, despite that fact that legal proceedings had not commenced.

Issue: May a President grant a pardon in the interest of domestic tranquility, even though the recipient has not been subjected to legal proceedings?

Rule: The President has unlimited pardoning power that may be exercised at any time before, during, or after legal proceedings. A pardon is appropriately granted when offered to rebellious parties to restore national tranquility. A pardon is valid even if the one pardoned has not been indicted or convicted.

Ex Parte Milligan (S. Ct. 1866)

Facts: Sentenced to death by a military commission, D, a civilian, sought a circuit court order to release him from military custody so that he might have access to civil law procedures or be discharged.

Issue: May a civilian be denied the right to jury trial and, instead, be subjected to military justice?

Rule: (Davis, J.) A civilian's access to the civil judiciary, including trial by jury, is a fundamental right that cannot be abridged even by national emergency conditions. While the military may try its members in military tribunals, it may not try civilian citizens of states where the courts are open and where martial law is not established.

Home Building & Loan Ass'n v. Blaisdell (S. Ct. 1934)

Facts: The Minnesota Moratorium Law, enacted during the Depression, permitted homeowners to postpone mortgage payments until they re-established financial security.

Issue: Under what circumstances may a state legislate to enjoin enforcement of private contract obligations?

Rule: (Hughes, C.J.) Where vital public interests are at stake, a state may exercise its protective police power through temporary and conditional restraints to prevent the immediate enforcement of contract obligations. Such state action is permitted where (1) an emergency exists, calling for the state to protect the community's vital interests; (2) the restrictive legislation is designed to protect a basic societal interest; (3) the relief is appropriate to and justified by the emergency; (4) the restrictions' conditions are reasonable; and (5) the legislation is temporary and limited to the exigency that calls it forth.

Dissent: (Sutherland, J.) The statute at issue directly contravenes the Article I, §10 prohibition against laws impairing contract obligations. The Court's opinion sets precedent for future, gradual, but ever-advancing encroachments upon the sanctity of private and public contracts.

Woods v. Cloyd W. Miller Co. (S. Ct. 1948)

Facts: The 1947 Housing and Rent Act, enacted under Congress' war power during a housing shortage following World War II, set a ceiling on the rent charged in certain housing areas.

Issue: Does Congress' war power encompass laws addressing conditions directly caused by war after the cessation of hostilities?

Rule: (Douglas, J.) Because a state of war does not end with the termination of hostilities, Congress' war power includes the authority to enact legislation redressing conditions directly and immediately caused by war.

Concurrence: (Jackson, J.) Careful constitutional scrutiny is required when the war power is invoked to affect people's liberties, property, or economy. The war powers may not be indefinitely prolonged merely by keeping legally alive a state of war that had in fact ended.

Korematsu v. United States (S. Ct. 1944)

Facts: Korematsu, an American citizen of Japanese descent, was convicted for violating Exclusion Order No. 34, issued during World War II, which barred all persons of Japanese descent from a designated "military area" where Korematsu happened to live.

Issue: May the government constitutionally exclude or set apart sectors of the population to directly address a specific wartime threat?

Rule: (Black, J.) The Supreme Court cannot say that exclusion or segregation of a particular segment of the population during wartime is never commensurate with and appropriate to a perceived danger. Compulsory exclusion of large groups of citizens from their homes, except under circumstances of direst emergency and peril, is inconsistent with our basic governmental institutions. But when under conditions of modern warfare our shores are threatened by hostile forces, the power to protect must be equal to the danger posed.

Concurrence: (Frankfurter, J.) The validity of action under the war power must be judged wholly in the context of war. That action is not to be stigmatized as lawless because like action in times of peace would be lawless.

Dissent: (Roberts, J.) This is a case of convicting a citizen as a punishment for not submitting to imprisonment in a concentration camp, based on his ancestry, without evidence or inquiry concerning his loyalty and good disposition toward the United States.

Dissent: (Murphy, J.) There is no reasonable relation between this deprivation of constitutional rights and an immediate, imminent, and impending public danger to support this racial restriction. Such restraint is one of the most sweeping and complete deprivations of constitutional rights in this nation's history in the absence of martial law.

Dissent: (Jackson, J.) This case represents an attempt to make an otherwise innocent act a crime merely because this prisoner is the son of parents as to whom he had no choice, and belongs to a race from which there is no way to resign. A civil court cannot be made to enforce an order that violates constitutional limitations even if it is a reasonable exercise of military authority.

Mora v. McNamara (S. Ct. 1967)

Facts: After being drafted for military service in Vietnam, Ps sought a declaratory judgment that the U.S. activity in Vietnam was illegal. (The Court denied certiorari. Dissenting opinions were filed.)

Issue: What questions arise when U.S. military action and the military powers exercised by the President and Congress do not fit neatly into the Constitution's delegation of military authority?

Dissent: (Stewart, J.) The Court should have granted certiorari and squarely faced the problematic questions this case presents. These include (1) whether the U.S. military activity in Vietnam is a "war" according to Article I; (2) whether the President may constitutionally order Ps' participation in that military activity, when Congress has not declared war; and (3) what relevance such forced military service has to U.S. treaty obligations and to the Tonkin Gulf Resolution.

Dissent: (Douglas, J.) This case invokes historically conflicting views regarding the definition of "war" and the scope and distribution of the executive and legislative branches' military powers.

Clinton v. Jones (S. Ct. 1997)

Facts: P, former state employee while Bill Clinton was governor of Arkansas, brought suit again the President for sexual harassment.

Issue: Did it violate the separation of powers for a court to proceed with the lawsuit against the President while he was still in office, given the potential lawsuits have to distract the President from his Article II duties?

Rule: (Stevens, J.) There is no constitutional immunity for lawsuits growing out of non-official conduct that occurred before the President took office. There is no history of such suits so monopolizing the President's time as to make it impossible for him to carry out his constitutional duties.

Concurrence: (Breyer, J.) Congress if it wishes can legislate an immunity in these circumstances.

Whitman v. American Trucking Ass'n (S. Ct. 2001)

Facts: The Environmental Protection Agency (EPA) interpreted the Clean Air Act in a way so as to make it unclear how clean air had to be in order to comply, and the lower court rejected that interpretation on the ground that that interpretation would have violated the non-delegation doctrine.

Issue: Can an agency cure an otherwise overbroad delegation of power to it by means of a limiting interpretation?

Rule: (Scalia, J.) The non-delegation doctrine examines how broad congressional delegation is; thus an agency cannot cure an otherwise unconstitutionally overbroad delegation. In this case, however, the statute provides enough of an "intelligible principle" to satisfy non-delegation requirements.

Concurrence: (Stevens, J.) It is clear that the agency is exercising legislative power, and courts should recognize that reality when considering non-delegation challenges.

CHAPTER 6

The Bill of Rights and the States: Procedural Due Process

I. THE BILL OF RIGHTS AND THE STATES

A. Bill of Rights — Generally
The Bill of Rights (i.e., the first ten amendments to the Constitution), like most of the provisions of the Constitution, is only applicable to governmental entities.

B. Applicability to the States
1. Prior to the Civil War, the Bill of Rights was not applicable to the states. *Barron v. The Mayor and City Council of Baltimore.*
2. After the passage of the Fourteenth Amendment, *infra*, much of the Bill of Rights was made applicable to the states through its Due Process Clause.

II. FOURTEENTH AMENDMENT

The Fourteenth Amendment provides that "No state shall make or enforce any law which shall abridge the privileges or immunities of citizens of the United States; nor shall any State deprive any person of life, liberty, or property, without due process of law; nor deny to any person within its jurisdiction the equal protection of the laws."

A. Privileges and Immunities Clause
The Privileges and Immunities Clause of the Fourteenth Amendment only refers to uniquely federal rights and does not protect those rights that relate only to state citizenship, nor does it incorporate any of the Bill of Rights. *Slaughterhouse Cases.*
1. Federal Rights
Federal rights include the right to interstate travel or commerce, the right to petition Congress, the right to enter federal lands,

117

the rights of a citizen while in the custody of a federal officer, and the right to vote in federal elections.

2. State Rights

State rights include "fundamental" rights not explicitly stated in the Constitution, but generally given by the common law of any free nation. One such right is the right to practice one's trade. *Id.*

B. The Due Process Clause of the Fourteenth Amendment and Its Incorporation of the Bill of Rights

1. The Cardozo/Black/Frankfurter Debate

a. Cardozo in *Palko v. Connecticut* and Frankfurter in *Adamson v. California* held that the "selective incorporation" view (see *infra*) was historically the more correct way of interpreting the Due Process Clause of the Fourteenth Amendment. The historical evidence indicates that the drafters of the amendment did not intend to incorporate the Bill of Rights into the Due Process Clause. The Court therefore ought to define and interpret the Due Process Clause according to the plain meaning of the words and the ordinary concepts of what is *naturally* meant by "life, liberty, and property" and "due process of law." They further argued that if there was any intention of incorporating the Bill of Rights into the Due Process Clause, the drafters of the Amendment could have used language to that effect. Most of the pre-1937 cases adopted this approach. *Powell v. Alabama.*

b. Black's Dissent in *Adamson*

Black claimed that the history of the Fourteenth Amendment indicated that all portions of the Bill of Rights were to be made directly applicable to the states. He further argued that a selective incorporation policy would permit the Court to adopt a subjective, natural law approach to constitutional issues and hence empower it to overturn acts of the other branches of the government, merely because the Justices disagreed with the policy behind those acts. This was beyond the scope of the Supreme Court's authority.

c. The selective incorporation position has become the prevailing view.

2. Selective Incorporation

a. The Early Cases

The *Palko* and *Adamson* cases espoused that if an amendment was implicit in the concept of ordered liberty, it was to be applied to the states. The Court said that it would enforce rights so rooted in the traditions and conscience of our people as to be fundamental.

   b. The Current Model: *Duncan v. Louisiana*
   In 1968, the Court in *Duncan v. Louisiana* set a broader guide-
   line for expanding the scope of the Due Process Clause. The
   court held that those provisions that are considered
   fundamental to the American system of law are applied to
   the states through the Due Process Clause of the Fourteenth
   Amendment, even though they may not necessarily be
   fundamental for any system of democratic government.
   c. "Bag and Baggage"
   When a provision of the Bill of Rights is made applicable to
   the states, it applies to state and local acts in the same manner
   as it does to federal actions. *Id.* See also *Malloy v. Hogan;
   Williams v. Florida; Apodaca v. Oregon.*
   d. Modern Due Process
   Today, virtually all of the applicable amendments in the Bill of
   Rights have been incorporated into the Fourteenth Amendment, with the notable exception, among others, of the right
   to indictment by a grand jury when held to answer for a crime,
   guaranteed by the Fifth Amendment. *Hurtado v. California.*

III. PROCEDURAL DUE PROCESS

A. Defined
   The Fifth and Fourteenth Amendments prevent both the federal
   and state governments from depriving any person of "life, liberty,
   or property without due process of law."
   1. Application
      This does not mean that the Clause bars the government from
      any procedural irregularities. It only applies when life, liberty, or
      property are taken. *Board of Regents v. Roth.*
   2. Effect
      The Clause essentially means that the government may not act
      arbitrarily or unfairly.
B. Substantive Due Process Distinguished
   1. Substantive — Validity of Laws
      Substantive due process tests the validity of laws to see if there is
      a fundamental interest at stake and whether a legitimate state
      objective justifies impinging on that interest.
   2. Procedural — Validity of Process
      Procedural due process tests the process by which the law is
      administered. It guarantees the right to be heard, etc. Procedural
      due process guarantees that there is a full and fair decision-
      making process before the government takes some action directly
      impairing a person's life, liberty or property.

C. Liberty and Property
The Court has generally construed "liberty" and "property" broadly.
1. Liberty
Liberty includes, but is not limited to:
a. Freedom from bodily restraint
b. Right to contract
c. Right to engage in lawful occupations
d. Right to marry
e. Freedom of religion
f. Right against self-incrimination
2. Property
Property is generally construed liberally, but a person must have already acquired the benefit in question or have a legitimate claim of entitlement to the benefit, based on some legal source.
a. Welfare recipients have a property claim. *Goldberg v. Kelly.*
b. Public employees have some claim, but only if a legitimate claim of entitlement (a justifiable expectation) is proved. *Board of Regents v. Roth; Perry v. Sindermann.*
c. Students have a property interest in attending school.
3. Factors considered in deciding whether an interest is protected:
a. The breadth of the injury;
b. The state's prior characterization (by statute) of the interest as an interest in liberty or property.
D. What Process Is Due?
1. Right to Be Heard
Due process generally requires the "right to be heard," which can mean anything from the right to submit written statements in one's favor to the right to a full evidentiary hearing with witnesses, counsel, and judicial review. The procedure that is due is determined by the amount of information needed to ensure that erroneous deprivations will not be made.
2. Balancing Test — *Mathews v. Eldridge*
The cost of requiring a particular set of procedures is weighed against the benefits from those procedures. The principal reason for procedural safeguards is to prevent inaccurate decisions.
a. Benefit
On one side of the equation is the strength of the private interest in jeopardy. It is multiplied by the risk of an erroneous deprivation of the interest. The grievousness of the potential loss to the recipient must also be considered. *Goldberg v. Kelly.*

b. Cost

On the other side is the government's interest, which is the fiscal and administrative expense of the procedural requirement.

3. State Procedures

Where a state sets procedures for giving and terminating benefits, the procedures for termination will not automatically be upheld as constitutional. *Cleveland Board of Educ. v. Loudermill.*

E. Proceedings Other than Adversarial Proceedings

Due process requirements are also applicable to nonadversarial proceedings such as juvenile delinquency cases, *In re Gault,* and cases involving the involuntary commitment of the mentally ill.

F. Exceptions to the Due Process Requirements

1. Waiver

A person may waive his or her constitutional due process rights. However, before an individual may waive any rights, the person must be informed of his or her rights (e.g., Fifth Amendment rights against self-incrimination; *Miranda v. Arizona*).

2. Exclusionary Proceedings

The due process requirements do not apply where the government has refused to admit into the country persons from other nations who have arrived at U.S. borders. *Shaughnessy v. United States ex rel. Mezei.*

CASE CLIPS

Barron v. The Mayor and City Council of Baltimore (S. Ct. 1833)

Facts: Baltimore made Barron's wharf inaccessible by diverting streams during construction.

Issue: Does the Fifth Amendment guarantee that private property shall not be "taken for public use without just compensation" apply to local and state governments?

Rule: (Marsh, C.J.) The Bill of Rights is a specific check on the power of the national government, which itself was created by the Constitution, not a proclamation of rights to be protected by all governments. If the Bill of Rights had applied to the states, then the Constitution would have expressly stated so, as it has in other areas of the Constitution.

Slaughter-House Cases (S. Ct. 1873)

Facts: Plaintiffs claimed that the State of Louisiana deprived them of their right to exercise their trade in violation of the Fourteenth Amendment, which states that "[n]o state shall make or enforce any law which shall abridge the privileges or immunities of citizens of the United States."

Issue: Does the Privileges and Immunities Clause of the Fourteenth Amendment, which protects U.S. citizens against unconstitutional exercise of state power, extend to fundamental rights such as the right to exercise in one's trade?

Rule: (Miller, J.) The only guarantee that the Constitution gives with respect to fundamental rights is that the federal government will not infringe upon the rights. There is no constitutional guarantee that the federal government will protect fundamental rights from the exercise of state power.

Dissent: (Field, J.) The limits on states' powers to infringe on federally guaranteed rights existed before the Fourteenth Amendment was passed. The purpose of the Privileges and Immunities Clause is to guarantee to the citizens of the United States the most basic and fundamental rights.

Dissent: (Bradley, J.) The deprivation of a citizen's right to exercise his trade is a deprivation of property without due process of law, as well as a denial of the citizen's right to equal protection of the laws.

Duncan v. Louisiana (S. Ct. 1968)

Facts: Defendant was convicted of simple battery after a trial without a jury, pursuant to the Louisiana State Constitution.

Issue: Does the Due Process Clause of the Fourteenth Amendment require states to grant criminal defendants the Sixth Amendment right to trial by jury?

Rule: (White, J.) The right to a jury trial is fundamental to the American scheme of justice and is therefore binding on the states as a due process requirement.

Concurrence: (Black, J.) The entire Fourteenth Amendment should incorporate the Bill of Rights, making them applicable to the states.

Concurrence: (Fortas, J.) Although a jury trial is a fundamental right and should be made applicable to the states, the specific details of the jury rules should be determined by the states.

Dissent: (Harlan, J.) The Due Process Clause of the Fourteenth Amendment only requires that state procedures be fundamentally fair; it does not impose nationwide uniformity for its own sake by incorporating the Bill of Rights and defining the Bill of Rights as the *only* way to achieve individual libertarian goals.

Cleveland Board of Educ. v. Loudermill (S. Ct. 1985)

Facts: An Ohio statute provided that classified civil service employees could be terminated only for cause, and could obtain administrative review if discharged.

Issue: When a state legislature creates a new property interest by establishing certain procedures enabling the interest holder to preserve his interest, must the established procedures meet the criteria prescribed by the Due Process Clause?

Rule: (White, J.) While the legislature may elect not to confer a property interest in public employment, once such an interest is conferred, the state may not constitutionally authorize its deprivation without appropriate procedural safeguards.

Dissent: (Rehnquist, J.) A classified civil service employee is entitled to exactly what the state legislature grants, and no more. The same authority that confers a property right should also have the power to define the limits of the property right.

Mathews v. Eldridge (S. Ct. 1976)

Facts: Eldridge's disability benefits were terminated after he was offered an opportunity to submit a written statement opposing termination, but before he was given an opportunity for an evidentiary hearing.

Issue: What factors must be considered when deciding whether a particular set of procedures implemented in a decision to deprive a citizen of property satisfies due process requirements?

Rule: (Powell, J.) The essence of due process is the requirement that a person in jeopardy of serious loss be given notice of the case against him and an opportunity to meet it. Factors to consider include the private interest that will be affected by the official action; the risk of an erroneous deprivation of such interest through the procedures used, and the probable value, if any, of additional or substitute procedural safeguards; and the government's interest, including the function involved and the fiscal and administrative burdens that the additional or substitute procedural requirement would entail.

Dissent: (Brennan, J.) Based on an evaluation of the above enumerated factors, a pretermination evidentiary hearing should be implemented as part of a disability benefits recipient's due process rights.

Board of Regents v. Roth (S. Ct. 1972)

Facts: Roth, an untenured teacher in Wisconsin, was dismissed without cause after his one-year term had expired.

Issue: Is continued government employment a liberty or property interest protected by the Fourteenth Amendment?

Rule: (Stewart, J.) One does not have a property interest in his job when dismissal will not damage his reputation or bar him from a broader class of employment.

Dissent: (Marshall, J.) Every citizen who applies for a government job is entitled to it unless the government can establish some reason for denying the employment. This is a property right and is protected against arbitrary government action.

Perry v. Sindermann (S. Ct. 1972)

Facts: Sindermann had been employed for ten years under a series of one-year contracts at Odessa Junior College. The college had a *de facto* tenure program whereby Sindermann "understood" that he had tenure.

Issue: Does an implied, but not express, guarantee of government employment constitute a property interest so that a denial of a contract renewal without stated reasons or an opportunity to challenge the decision constitutes a due process violation?

Rule: (Stewart, J.) A person's interest in a benefit is a property interest for due process purposes if there are such rules or mutually explicit understandings that support his claim of entitlement to the benefit.

Goldberg v. Kelly (S. Ct. 1970)

Facts: New York State welfare payments were discontinued without prior notice or hearing.

Issue: What are the general procedural due process requirements with respect to the termination of welfare payments?

Rule: (Brennan, J.) Welfare benefits are property that may not be taken without procedural protection similar to that guaranteed in other judicial matters.

Dissent: (Black, J.) The government interest in taking unqualified people off the welfare rolls outweighs the private interests of individuals. Welfare payments are not property but charitable installments promised by the government. Furthermore, placing such a burden on the government will only result in a much stricter eligibility process at the outset, thus causing a situation the majority hopes to avoid.

Schneiderman v. United States (S. Ct. 1943)

Facts: Schneiderman became a naturalized citizen of the United States in 1927 while a high official of the American Communist Party. To attain citizenship, he had to behave as a person "attached to the principles of the Constitution." In 1939 the Department of Justice sought to revoke his citizenship, arguing that as a member of the Communist Party Schneiderman could not satisfy this requirement.

Issue 1: What is the government's burden of proof in a denaturalization proceeding?

Rule 1: (Murphy, J.) To prevail at a denaturalization proceeding, the government must prove by clear and convincing evidence that when citizenship was originally conferred, it was not done in accordance with strict legal requirements.

Issue 2: Is Communist Party membership inconsistent with the principles of the Constitution?

Rule 2: The Constitution did not forge a political strait jacket for the generations to come. Advocation of the nationalization of the means of production is not inconsistent with the general political philosophy of the Constitution, as many in our history have supported such measures in varying degrees. Nor can the Party's commitment to violent overthrow be attributed to an individual member without evidence to that effect.

Dissent: (Stone, C.J.) The question for decision here is merely whether Schneiderman, in securing his citizenship by naturalization, has fulfilled a condition for that citizenship created by Congress. Our task is not to answer the question ourselves, but to determine whether the record warranted such a finding by the district court. In this case there is ample such evidence.

Hurtado v. California (S. Ct. 1884)

Facts: The California Constitution provided that prosecution of crimes could be initiated on the basis of a formal accusation drawn up by a prosecutor after a review by a magistrate.

Issue: Does the Due Process Clause of the Fourteenth Amendment require that states must indict an accused by a grand jury?

Rule: (Matthews, J.) The only principles which should guide a procedural due process inquiry are the principles of liberty and justice. Indictment by a grand jury, though traditional in its usage, is not the only way in which the accused can be tried fairly and with due process of law.

Dissent: (Harlan, J.) The Fourteenth Amendment uses the same language limiting the states' powers as the Fifth Amendment uses to limit the power of the federal government. Therefore, since the prosecution of federal crimes requires indictment by a grand jury, so should the prosecution of crimes committed against the state.

Palko v. Connecticut (S. Ct. 1937)

Facts: A Connecticut statute provided that the state could appeal in criminal cases where the accused was convicted of a lesser crime than originally charged, and effectively try defendants twice for the same crime.

Issue: Does the Due Process Clause of the Fourteenth Amendment incorporate all provisions of the Bill of Rights and impose the rights on state governments?

Rule: (Cardozo, J.) The Due Process Clause of the Fourteenth Amendment incorporates those provisions of the Bill of Rights which are found to be implicit in the "concept of ordered liberty." A statute that allows the state to appeal a case where the accused was convicted on a lesser charge does not violate those fundamental principles of liberty and justice which lie at the base of all our civil and political institutions.

Adamson v. California (S. Ct. 1947)

Facts: A provision of the California Constitution allowed the refusal of an accused to testify to be admitted as evidence of guilt.

Issue: May a state statute allow a prosecutor to comment on a defendant's refusal to testify against himself?

Rule: (Reed, J.) The Fifth Amendment only prohibits the coercion of self-incriminating testimony. However, a law that merely allows inferences to be made in light of facts already determined is not violative of due process.

Concurrence: (Frankfurter, J.) In federal criminal cases, the prosecution may not comment on a defendant's refusal to testify against himself, but this prohibition is statutory. The Due Process Clause does not prohibit such a practice. When the states ratified the Fourteenth Amendment, they did not contemplate that the Amendment would preempt all of the states' own rules in conducting trials.

Dissent: (Murphy, J.) Not only should the Bill of Rights be carried over into the Fourteenth Amendment's Due Process Clause, but the latter should be read more broadly as to also prohibit fundamental due process violations aside from those enumerated in the Bill of Rights.

Dissent: (Black, J.) Legislative history shows that instead of the Court applying its own notions of what is the concept of fundamental justice, the Due Process Clause should incorporate the complete protection of the Bill of Rights.

Rochin v. California (S. Ct. 1952)

Facts: Defendant's stomach contents were forcibly removed to recover evidence of narcotics trafficking.

Issue: What are the judicial limits of due process interpretation?

Rule: (Frankfurter, J.) The Due Process Clause places upon the Court the duty of exercising a judgment, within the narrow confines of judicial power in reviewing state convictions, upon interests of society pushing in opposite directions. However, when situations shock the conscience, the constitutional violations are obvious.

Concurrence: (Black, J.) The invasion of a person's body should be equivalent to a Fifth Amendment violation against self-incrimination. The Fifth Amendment, as well as the rest of the Bill of Rights, should be incorporated into the Fourteenth Amendment Due Process Clause.

Williams v. Florida (S. Ct. 1970)

Facts: A Florida statute provided that criminal cases not involving capital offenses should be tried before a six-person jury.

Issue: Is a jury of six sufficient to satisfy procedural due process requirements?

Rule: (White, J.) The concept of a twelve-person jury is merely a historical accident and is only incidental to the Sixth Amendment guarantee of a jury trial. The number twelve has no significance except to mystics.

Concurrence: (Black, J.) Although we normally should apply the Bill of Rights in its entirety to the states and not distinguish between state and federal due process requirements, in this case since the number twelve has no real significance, a six-person jury will remain consistent with the Sixth Amendment right to a jury trial.

Dissent: (Marshall, J.) The requirement of a twelve-person jury that was read into the Sixth Amendment for federal cases should also be made a requirement for state criminal cases.

Concurrence: (Harlan, J.) This is an example of why the incorporation doctrine (i.e., the notion that the Due Process Clause of the Fourteenth Amendment incorporates the Bill of Rights in its entirety) does not work. There are some instances where the right alleged is not implicit in the concept of ordered liberty, and therefore the federal government should not stifle the states' flexibility in making its own rules. Procedural due process requirements as they apply to states should be decided on a case-by-case basis.

Concurrence: (Stewart, J.) This case represents some of the basic errors in the incorporation approach to the Fourteenth Amendment.

Apodaca v. Oregon (S. Ct. 1972)

Facts: Defendants were convicted by split jury votes.

Issue: Do the Sixth and Fourteenth Amendments require a unanimous vote in a jury trial?

Rule: (White, J.) The essential feature of a jury obviously lies in the interposition between the accused and his accuser of the common sense judgment of a group of laymen. Therefore, a requirement of unanimity does not materially contribute to the exercise of this common sense judgment, and is not required by the Sixth or Fourteenth Amendments.

Dissent: (Stewart, J.) If we are to apply the Sixth Amendment right to a jury trial to state criminal cases, then we must apply the same rules to state trials as we do to federal trials. Because the Sixth Amendment guarantees that a verdict must be unanimous to convict in a federal case, the same rule should apply in state cases.

Concurrence: (Blackmun, J.) Although the split vote rule is not unconstitutional, it's wrong.

Concurrence: (Powell, J.) Not all the elements required in a federal jury trial are required in a state trial.

Dissent: (Douglas, J.) Because both the federal and the state guarantees of jury trials stem from the same Sixth Amendment, they should have the same rules. The Due Process Clause should incorporate the Bill of Rights in its entirety and not allow the Supreme Court to act as a legislative body and determine what is and isn't included in the Fourteenth Amendment.

Dissent: (Brennan, J.) To allow a split vote conviction to be upheld is tantamount to denying the defendant the right to a jury trial.

Dissent: (Marshall, J.) To allow a split vote verdict would be to strip away the essential features of the jury, leaving it to be a jury in name only.

Powell v. Alabama (S. Ct. 1932)

Facts: Ds were convicted of rape without the benefit of counsel.

Issue: Does the denial of the right to counsel infringe on the Due Process Clause?

Rule: (Sutherland, J.) In capital cases, where the defendant is unable to employ his own counsel and is incapable of adequately making his own defense, it is the duty of the Court to assign counsel for him as a necessary requisite of due process of law.

Gideon v. Wainwright (S. Ct. 1963)

Facts: Defendant was charged with breaking and entering with intent to commit a crime, not a capital offense. He was denied the right to counsel and was subsequently convicted and sentenced to five years.

Issue: Does the Due Process Clause of the Fourteenth Amendment require state governments to guarantee an accused the right to counsel in all criminal cases?

Rule: (Black, J.) Those provisions of the Bill of Rights that are fundamental and essential to a fair trial are made obligatory on the states by the Fourteenth Amendment. The right to aid of counsel is of this fundamental character.

Concurrence: (Clark, J.) There should be no difference in the guarantee of the right to counsel whether the defendant is being accused of a non-capital offense where a person's liberty might be deprived, or whether he's being accused of a capital offense where a person's life might be deprived.

Concurrence: (Harlan, J.) Although the right to counsel should be recognized as a fundamental right embraced in the Fourteenth Amendment, we shouldn't automatically carry over an entire body of federal law and apply it in full sweep to the states.

Escobedo v. Illinois (S. Ct. 1964)

Facts: Defendant was denied the assistance of counsel during a pre-indictment interrogation.

Issue: Does the constitutional right to counsel include the right to the assistance of counsel during a police interrogation before indictment?

Rule: (Goldberg, J.) The fact that many confessions are obtained during pre-indictment interrogation points out its critical nature as a stage when legal aid and advice are surely needed. If the right to legal counsel were denied during this period, then the trial would be over before it started.

Dissent: (Harlan, J.) I think the rule announced today is most ill-conceived and that it seriously and unjustifiably fetters perfectly legitimate methods of criminal law enforcement.

Dissent: (Stewart, J.) The constitutional right to counsel begins when the criminal investigation ends and the adversary proceeding begins. This is at the time of the indictment and not beforehand.

Dissent: (White, J.) The Constitution does not provide for a right to counsel during a criminal investigation, but there is a right to avoid self-incrimination. However, this does not mean that no one may confess to crime voluntarily; it just means that a person has a right against *compelled* incrimination.

Miranda v. Arizona (S. Ct. 1966)

Facts: Defendant had confessed while in custody without being informed of his constitutional rights.

Issue: Is a confession obtained during a police interrogation when the defendant has not yet been apprised of his rights a violation of Fifth Amendment privileges?

Rule: (Warren, C.J.) When an individual is taken into custody or otherwise deprived of his freedom by the authorities in any significant way, and is subjected to questioning, the privilege against self-incrimination is jeopardized.

Dissent: (Harlan, J.) The role of the Constitution is only to sift out *undue* pressure, not to assure spontaneous confessions. The social costs of crime under the new rules promulgated by this decision will be staggering.

Malloy v. Hogan (S. Ct. 1964)

Facts: Petitioner was ordered to testify as a witness in a gambling inquiry, not as a defendant in a criminal prosecution.

Issue: Does the right against self-incrimination extend to someone's refusal to testify in an inquiry not directly involving the person?

Rule: (Brennan, J.) The Fifth Amendment's exemption from compulsory self-incrimination is also protected against abridgment by the states under the Fourteenth Amendment. This includes the right to avoid compulsory testimony as a witness in a statutory inquiry, and is not limited to testimony as a defendant in a criminal prosecution.

Dissent: (Harlan, J.) The notion of incorporating a whole body of law which surrounds a specific prohibition, and binding it on the states, represents an encroachment on the concept of federalism and results in compelled uniformity.

Dissent: (White, J.) In witness testimony, the judge rather than the witness should determine when an answer sought is incriminating.

Schmerber v. California (S. Ct. 1966)

Facts: Defendant sustained injuries from a drunken driving accident. While in the hospital, the police instructed the attending physician to withdraw blood from the defendant in a medically acceptable manner, over the defendant's objections. The blood sample was used as evidence of the defendant's intoxication.

Issue 1: Does withdrawing a blood sample over a defendant's objections constitute a violation of the defendant's due process rights?

Rule 1: (Brennan, J.) The withdrawal of blood by a physician in a simple, medically acceptable manner in a hospital environment for the purpose of proving intoxication does not offend notions of justice so as to violate the Due Process Clause.

Issue 2: Does the forcible withdrawal of blood from a defendant for evidentiary purposes in a state case constitute a violation of the Fifth and Fourteenth Amendment privilege against self-incrimination?

Rule 2: (Brennan, J.) The Fifth and Fourteenth Amendment privilege against self-incrimination in a state case protects an accused only from being compelled to testify against himself or otherwise provide the state with evidence of a testimonial or communicative nature. The withdrawal of blood for evidentiary purposes does not involve compulsion to these ends.

Issue 3: Is removal of blood for evidentiary purposes from a defendant accused of drunken driving considered reasonable in light of the Fourth and Fourteenth Amendment's restraint on unlawful searches and seizures?

Rule 3: (Brennan, J.) The Fourth Amendment provides a right against unreasonable searches and seizures. This is binding on the states through the Fourteenth Amendment. The taking of blood from a defendant does not violate this right when there is a reasonable belief that the extraction will lead to incriminating evidence and when the procedure is done by a physician in a hospital environment according to accepted medical practices.

Concurrence: (Harlan, J.) While agreeing with the Court that the taking of this blood test involved no testimonial compulsion, I would go further and hold that apart from this consideration the case in no way implicates the Fifth Amendment.

Dissent: (Black, J.) Blood test evidence is, in all respects, the actual equivalent of testimony taken from the defendant and therefore within the scope of the Fifth Amendment.

New York v. Quarles (S. Ct. 1984)

Facts: In the midst of apprehending D, it became apparent to the police that he had discarded a gun during the pursuit. D was frisked and a gun was not found, but he was wearing a holster. Before reading him his *Miranda* rights, one of the officers asked D where the gun was, and he obliged.

Issue: When a detained suspect is asked questions regarding the public safety, must the apprehending officer first advise him of his rights, even if the circumstances and the impending danger of the situation would lead one to reasonably believe that there is no time to adhere to a police manual?

Rule: (Rehnquist, J.) There is a public safety exception to the requirement that *Miranda* warnings be given before a suspect's answers may be admitted into evidence, and the availability of that exception does not depend on the motivation of the officers involved. The original *Miranda* rule was an attempt to curtail the practices of coercing testimony out of a suspect to use as evidence against him, but it was not meant to inhibit the officers from making split second judgments in ensuring the public safety.

Concurrence/Dissent: (O'Connor, J.) While *Miranda* has never been read to prohibit the police from asking questions to secure the public safety, the cost of securing public safety when such questions are asked and answered must be borne by the state, not by the defendant. However, the *Miranda* rule only applies to testimonial evidence and not real or physical evidence.

Dissent: (Marshall, J.) The policies underlying the Fifth Amendment's privilege against self-incrimination are not diminished simply because testimony is compelled to protect the public's safety. Custodial interrogations are inherently coercive. The Fifth Amendment does not prohibit the interrogation only to the extent that the defendant may not be incriminated by his own testimony, absent a waiver of his constitutional rights. If the cost of soliciting statements from the defendant to ensure the public safety is inadmissible into evidence, then that is the price we have to pay to protect the Fifth Amendment.

Dunaway v. New York (S. Ct. 1979)

Facts: Dunaway was questioned after being read his *Miranda* rights while in custody but no warrant was issued for his arrest.

Issue 1: When may one be detained for questioning without being formally arrested?

Rule 1: (Brennan, J.) Although an individual has not been formally arrested, the standard for intrusion into someone's privacy such as detention for questioning or some other investigatory purpose should be no different than for an arrest, i.e., probable cause. Both are, in effect, a seizure and should be subject to Fourth Amendment standards which prohibit unreasonable search and seizure without probable cause.

Issue 2: What is the status of evidence obtained while an individual has been unlawfully detained?

Rule 2: (Brennan, J.) In order to effectuate the Fourth Amendment, evidence obtained as a result of an unlawful detention or arrest is inadmissible.

Dissent: (Rehnquist, J.) Only when an officer, by means of physical force or show of authority, has in some way restrained the liberty of a citizen may we conclude that a seizure has occurred in violation of the Fourth

Amendment if probable cause cannot be shown. Therefore any evidence obtained from a person while in custody but not while involuntarily detained is admissible.

Shaughnessy v. United States ex rel. Mezei (S. Ct. 1953)

Facts: Mezei, a resident alien for 25 years, left the country. When he returned, he was detained on Ellis Island and not allowed reentry. When a writ of *habeas corpus* was granted, the government refused to disclose any affirmative evidence of the risk in admitting him.
Issue: What are the constitutional ramifications of the government not allowing disclosure of reasons for denial of reentry into the country by a resident alien?
Rule: (Clark, J.) The power to expel or exclude aliens is a fundamental sovereign attribute exercised by the government's political departments and is largely immune from judicial control.
Dissent: (Jackson, J.) A resident alien must be given a fair hearing to test an official claim that he is one of a deportable class.

Robinson v. California (S. Ct. 1962)

Facts: A California law made it a misdemeanor, punishable by 90 days in jail, to be addicted to narcotics.
Issue: Is a law making the status of narcotics addiction a criminal offense punishable by imprisonment a violation of the Eighth Amendment prohibition against cruel and unusual punishment?
Rule: (Stewart, J.) While imprisonment in the abstract is not cruel and unusual, the punishment must fit the crime. Narcotics addiction has been medically categorized as an illness and therefore should not be made punishable.
Dissent: (Clark, J.) The state constitutionally may attempt to deter and prevent acts through punishment which are not harmful to society in themselves, because of the grave threat of future harmful conduct which they pose. Narcotics addiction is no different.
Dissent: (White, J.) The crime of narcotics addiction is not a punishment for having an illness but rather a crime of the regular, repeated or habitual use of narcotics immediately prior to the arrest.

Furman v. Georgia (S. Ct. 1972)

Facts: A Georgia statute imposed the death penalty for rape or murder.
Issue: Is the death penalty cruel and unusual punishment?
Rule: (per curiam) The death penalty constitutes cruel and unusual punishment in violation of the Eighth and Fourteenth Amendments.

Concurrence: (Douglas, J.) The discriminatory application of the death penalty, in addition to being violative of the Equal Protection Clause, is also "unusual" punishment in the sense that the punishment discriminates on the basis of race, religion, wealth, social position, or class.

Concurrence: (Brennan, J.) Whether or not a punishment is considered cruel and unusual depends upon whether or not the punishment comports with human dignity. There are four principles: the punishment must not be unusually severe or degrading; it may not be inflicted arbitrarily; it may not be rejected by contemporary society; it must serve some type of penal purpose.

Concurrence: (Stewart, J.) The death penalty is unique in its total irrevocability. It is unique in its rejection of rehabilitation of the convict as a basic purpose of criminal justice. And it is unique in its absolute renunciation of all that is embodied in our concept of humanity. For these reasons the death penalty is constitutionally impermissible under the Eighth and Fourteenth Amendments.

Concurrence: (White, J.) The death penalty *per se* is not unconstitutional. However, the policy of leaving the imposition of the death penalty to the discretion of the jury is a violation of the Eighth Amendment.

Concurrence: (Marshall, J.) The death penalty is immoral and unconstitutional in that it serves none of the useful social functions of punishment other than retribution. In our society, retribution as the sole justification for certain modes of punishment shocks the conscience. Furthermore, the death penalty is applied discriminatorily.

Dissent: (Burger, C.J.) When the Constitution prohibits cruel and unusual punishment it means only to exclude punishments of extreme and barbarous cruelty. The death penalty has not been considered by the majority to be *per se* violative of the Eighth Amendment. The death penalty was considered cruel and unusual only because it was applied infrequently, but history shows that this is a wrong interpretation of cruel and unusual.

Dissent: (Blackmun, J.) It is beyond the Court's power to decide that the death penalty is unconstitutional based on policy reasons if it cannot be found that the death penalty is in and of itself cruel and unusual punishment, which it is not.

Dissent: (Powell, J.) The majority's action constitutes an infringement on the legislative powers of federal and state lawmakers and policy setters.

Dissent: (Rehnquist, J.) As is the case here, judicial overreaching results in the sacrifice of the important right of the people to govern themselves.

In re Gault (S. Ct. 1967)

Facts: Defendant was tried in juvenile court without numerous procedural guarantees normally required in adult criminal trials by the Fourteenth Amendment.

Issue: Is a juvenile court system that does not have procedural rules to ensure fairness and the preservation of fundamental rights of juveniles constitutional?

Rule: (Fortas, J.) The juvenile court process has, in effect, evolved into a criminal court system for youngsters under the age of 18 and therefore should be treated with the same accord and procedural notions of ordered liberty as does an adult court.

Concurrence/Dissent: (Harlan, J.) There is no constitutional basis for employing a system that denies anyone certain constitutional guarantees. A juvenile court system must have timely notice of a juvenile proceeding, the right to counsel, and the right for appellate review.

Dissent: (Stewart, J.) Juvenile proceedings are neither criminal nor civil trials. They are not adversarial proceedings. Accordingly, Fourteenth Amendment requirements have no applicability to juvenile proceedings.

O'Connor v. Donaldson (S. Ct. 1975)

Facts: Donaldson was confined against his will to a mental institution where he was not being treated for his illness and did not pose a threat either to himself or to others if set free.

Issue: Is a statute authorizing a hospital to confine a nondangerous, untreated mental patient against his will just to "improve his standard of living" constitutional?

Rule: (Stewart, J.) "A state cannot constitutionally confine a nondangerous individual who is capable of surviving safely in freedom by himself or with the help of willing and responsible family members or friends."

Concurrence: (Burger, C.J.) A state may not lawfully confine an individual thought to need treatment without due process of law and justify that deprivation of liberty solely by providing some treatment.

Mapp v. Ohio (S. Ct. 1961)

Facts: P challenged her conviction for the possession of obscene materials because the evidence used against her was obtained unlawfully.

Issue: May a state court admit evidence that was unreasonably or unlawfully acquired in violation of the Fourth Amendment's guarantee to the right to privacy?

Rule: (Clark, J.) The Fourth Amendment's right to privacy is enforceable against the states through the Due Process Clause of the Fourteenth Amendment, and therefore all evidence obtained by unconstitutional searches and seizures violates the Fourth Amendment and is inadmissible in state courts.

Dissent: (Harlan, J.) The issue in this case is not as the majority asserts, but rather whether the Ohio law outlawing the mere knowing possession or control of obscene materials is consistent with First Amendment rights assured against state action by the Fourteenth Amendment.

United States v. Leon (S. Ct. 1984)

Facts: P searched several private residences of D, an alleged drug trafficker, pursuant to a facially valid search warrant obtained on the strength of an affidavit summarizing the police officers' observations during their surveillance of D.

Issue: Does the Fourth Amendment's prohibition against unlawful searches and seizures bar the admission of evidence obtained by police officers acting in reasonable and good faith reliance on a search warrant that is ultimately found to be unsupported by probable cause?

Rule: (White, J.) The Fourth Amendment does not explicitly preclude the use of evidence obtained in violation of its prohibition against unlawful searches and seizures. The exclusionary rule is a judicially created remedy to safeguard the rights of the Amendments generally through its deterrent effect, rather than a personal constitutional right of the person aggrieved. The marginal or nonexistent benefits produced by suppressing evidence obtained in objectively reasonable reliance on a subsequently invalidated warrant cannot justify the substantial cost of exclusion of the evidence.

Dissent: (Brennan, J.) The Court's decision represents the *piece de resistance* of the Court's past efforts to strangulate the exclusionary rule. The Court seeks to justify its decision on the ground that the "costs" of adhering to the exclusionary rule in cases like these exceed the "benefits." The language of deterrence and cost benefit analysis creates an illusion of technical precision. However, we have not been subjected to an honest assessment of the merits of the exclusionary rule, but have instead been draw into a curious world where the "costs" of excluding illegally obtained evidence loom to exaggerated heights and where the "benefits" of such exclusion are made to disappear with a mere wave of the hand.

Cupp v. Murphy (S. Ct. 1973)

Facts: D voluntarily appeared at a police station for questioning upon hearing of the murder of his wife. The police, upon observing a dark spot on D's finger, despite D's refusal and without a warrant, obtained a sample of scrapings from D's fingernails. At the time, D was not under arrest.

Issue: May the police, absent an official arrest and a warrant, search the body of a person for evidence under circumstances where probable cause for an arrest exists?

Rule: (Stewart, J.) Police searches and seizures in which probable cause exists, the intrusion is limited, and the evidence is readily destructible do not violate the Fourth and Fourteenth Amendments.

Dissent: (Brennan, J.) Before we take the serious step of legitimating even limited searches merely upon probable cause, without a warrant or as incident to an arrest, we ought first to be certain that such probable cause existed. Whether or not probable cause existed is difficult to determine from the record. Because the Court of Appeals did not address this question, the proper course would be to remand to that court so that it might decide in the first instance whether there was probable cause to arrest and search.

Schneckloth v. Bustamonte (S. Ct. 1973)

Facts: D was a passenger in a car that was stopped by police during a routine patrol. The driver of the automobile verbally assented to a police search, even though no one had been arrested or threatened with arrest. The search turned up checks previously stolen from a carwash.

Issue: Is voluntary, uncoerced consent to a search a valid waiver of a subject's right against unlawful searches and seizures even though the subject did not understand that the consent could be freely and effectively withheld?

Rule: (Stewart, J.) When the subject of a search is not in custody and voluntarily consents to the search, the Fourth and Fourteenth Amendments require that the state demonstrate that the consent was in fact given voluntarily and not the result of duress or coercion, express or implied. Although the subject's knowledge of a right to refuse is a factor to be taken in account, the state is not required to demonstrate such knowledge as a prerequisite to establishing a voluntary consent.

Dissent: (Douglas, J.) "Verbal assent" to a search is insufficient; the fact that consent was given to the search does not imply that the suspect knew that the alternative of refusal existed.

Chimel v. California (S. Ct. 1969)

Facts: D's wife admitted police officers to her home where they waited for and arrested D, pursuant to an arrest warrant issued in connection with a coin burglary. The officers, absent a search warrant, also searched D's home where they uncovered certain coins that were later admitted into evidence against D's objections.

Issue: May the police obtain evidence through a warrantless search of an arrestee's home but incident to a lawful arrest without violating the Fourth Amendment's prohibition against unlawful searches and seizures?

Rule: (Stewart, J.) There is no constitutional justification, absent a search warrant, to extend a search pursuant to a lawful arrest beyond the person and the immediate area from where the arrestee might obtain a weapon or destroy evidence.

Dissent: (White, J.) The scope of the search in this case was "reasonable" under the Fourth and Fourteenth Amendments.

Coolidge v. New Hampshire (S. Ct. 1971)

Facts: Based upon information gathered during the murder investigation and clothing and weapons D's wife voluntarily delivered to the police, the state attorney general, acting in his capacity as a justice of the peace, issued an arrest warrant and four search warrants. An inspection of D's car, obtained pursuant to one of the search warrants, yielded further evidence that was used at D's trial to convict him of the brutal murder of a teenager.
Issue: Is a search warrant issued by a state prosecutor who is also a justice of the peace a valid warrant through which admissible evidence may be obtained?
Rule: (Stewart, J.) The Fourth Amendment's prohibition against unlawful searches and seizures demands that a search warrant be issued by a neutral and detached magistrate. The search and seizure of premises cannot constitutionally rest upon a warrant issued by the state official who is the chief investigator and prosecutor in the case.
Dissent: (Black, J.) The Fourth Amendment contains no constitutional rule barring the admission of illegally seized evidence. The Amendment does not require that every search be made pursuant to an arrest. It prohibits only "unreasonable searches and seizures." The relevant test is not the reasonableness of the opportunity to procure a warrant, but the reasonableness of the seizure under all the circumstances.

Warden v. Hayden (S. Ct. 1967)

Facts: Acting on information that gave the precise location and description of an armed robber who fled the scene of the robbery, the police arrived and were given permission to search the house in which the suspect was seen to have fled. A thorough search yielded the suspect and several items, including weapons and clothing.
Issue 1: May the police enter a building without a warrant and conduct a warrantless search for a robbery suspect without violating the Fourth Amendment's prohibition against unreasonable searches and seizures?
Rule 1: (Brennan, J.) The Fourth Amendment does not require police officers to delay an investigation if to do so would gravely endanger their lives or the lives of others. In instances where speed is of the essence and a thorough search of the premises for persons and weapons is the only way to ensure the apprehension of the correct suspect and the confiscation of all weapons, the Fourth Amendment is not violated.
Issue 2: Does the Fourth Amendment's prohibition against the unreasonable searches and seizures preclude the seizure and introduction into

evidence of certain "evidentiary" items obtained pursuant to a lawful search?

Rule 2: (Brennan, J.) The Fourth Amendment allows intrusion upon privacy under certain circumstances, and there is no viable reason to distinguish intrusions to secure "mere evidence" from intrusions to secure fruits, instrumentalities, or contraband.

Concurrence: (Fortas, J.) The Fourth Amendment should not be held to require exclusion from evidence of certain items found by the police during a search. However, there is no need to repudiate the so-called mere evidence rule.

Dissent: (Douglas, J.) The right to privacy sustained in *Griswold v. Connecticut* is kin to the right of privacy created by the Fourth Amendment. That there is a zone of privacy that no police can enter, whether in "hot pursuit" or armed with a meticulously proper warrant, has been emphasized by prior cases. I would adhere to them and leave to the individual the choice of opening his private effects (apart from contraband and the like) to the police or keeping their contents a secret and their integrity inviolate.

Camara v. Municipal Court (S. Ct. 1967)

Facts: A provision of the San Francisco Housing Code provided that city department employees could enter buildings without a warrant to perform duties imposed by the Municipal Code.

Issue: Do local administrative inspection programs allowing local city officials to enter and inspect private premises without a search warrant violate Fourth Amendment's prohibition against unreasonable searches?

Rule: (White, J.) Administrative inspection programs which include warrantless searches are significant intrusions upon the interests protected by the Fourth Amendment. Warrantless searches lack the traditional safeguards which the Fourth Amendment guarantees to the individual.

Dissent: (Clark, J.) To permit the issuance of warrants, in area inspection programs, with probable cause resting on inspection standards as outlined in municipal codes, degrades the Fourth Amendment.

Michigan v. Tyler (S. Ct. 1978)

Facts: A police detective, summoned by the fire chief who suspected arson as the cause of a fire, entered a building while the fire was being put out and took pictures of two plastic containers and the gutted building. Upon the complete extinguishing of the fire, the police detective and the fire chief confiscated the containers. Police officials returned to the site on several different occasions to inspect the premises and removed additional evidence.

Issue: Does a warrantless entry and search of a burning building by fire-fighters and police for evidence of a crime violate the Fourth Amendment's prohibition against unreasonable searches and seizures?

Rule: (Stewart, J.) Except in certain carefully defined classes of cases, entry and search of private property without proper consent is "unreasonable" unless it has been authorized by a valid search warrant. A burning building clearly presents an exigency of sufficient proportion to render a warrantless entry by firefighters "reasonable." Once in the building, officials may remain there for a reasonable time to investigate the cause of the fire.

Concurrence: (Stevens, J.) When there is no probable cause to believe a crime has been committed and when there is no special enforcement need to justify an unannounced entry, the Fourth Amendment neither requires nor sanctions an abrupt and peremptory confrontation between state officials and a citizen.

Dissent: (White, J.) To hold that some subsequent re-entries are "continuations" of earlier ones is confusing for it will be difficult to predict in advance how a court might view a re-entry. Those investigating fires and their causes deserve a clear demarcation of the constitutional limits of their authority.

Dissent: (Rehnquist, J.) Warrant Clause analysis has no application to routine, regulatory inspections of commercial premises. Because the searches in this case fall within that category, the only remaining question is whether the searches were reasonable. The subsequent searches of the premises were reasonable for purposes of the Fourth Amendment as notice of the search of an apparently abandoned, burnt-out building would have served no purpose.

Terry v. Ohio (S. Ct. 1968)

Facts: Ds, convicted for carrying concealed weapons, had been stopped and searched after a police detective observed their "suspicious" behavior in front of a store.

Issue: When does the police procedure to "stop and frisk" suspicious persons become unreasonable in violation of the Fourth Amendment's prohibition against unreasonable searches and seizures?

Rule: (Warren, C.J.) When a police officer is lawfully confronting a possibly hostile person in the line of duty he has a right, springing only from the necessity of the situation and not from any broader right to disarm, to frisk for his own and others' protection. Weapons discovered pursuant thereto are properly admissible in evidence.

Concurrence: (Harlan, J.) The Court's holding offers the only satisfactory basis for admitting evidence obtained through police's "stop and frisk" procedure. An officer's right to interrupt a citizen's freedom of movement and invade his privacy arises only because circumstances warrant a forced encounter in an effort to prevent or investigate a crime. Once that forced encounter is justified, however, the officer's right to take suitable measures for his and others' safety follows automatically.

Dissent: (Douglas, J.) The defendants in this case were seized and the frisking of them was a search within the meaning of the Fourth Amendment. It is mysterious how the search and seizure can be constitutional under the Fourth Amendment unless there was probable cause to believe that a crime had been committed, was in the process of being committed, or was about to be committed. If loitering were in issue and that was the offense charged, there would be "probable cause" shown. But the crime was the carrying of concealed weapons; and there is no basis for concluding that the officer had "probable cause" for believing that crime was being committed.

Sibron v. New York; Peters v. New York (S. Ct. 1968)

Facts: A New York statute provided that police could "stop and frisk" citizens upon suspicion.

Issue: What are the parameters within which police "stop and frisk" procedures must be conducted?

Rule: (Warren, C.J.) A warrantless "stop and frisk" procedure comports with the Fourth Amendment's prohibition against unreasonable searches and seizures only if the search is reasonable in scope and the police are able to demonstrate (a) probable cause for an arrest in order to intrude upon an individual's personal security or (b) reasonable grounds to believe that the individual might be armed and dangerous. Evidence gathered pursuant to an unreasonable search and seizure is inadmissible.

Delaware v. Prouse (S. Ct. 1979)

Facts: D sought to suppress evidence of marijuana obtained by the patrolman who stopped his car during a routine spot check for drivers' licenses and registration. The patrolman had not observed any traffic or equipment violation.

Issue: Is it a violation of the Fourth Amendment's prohibition against unreasonable searches and seizures for a patrolman, absent probable cause or reasonable suspicion of any illegal activity, to routinely stop vehicles being driven on a public highway?

Rule: (White, J.) The permissibility of a particular law-enforcement practice is judged by balancing its intrusion on the individual's Fourth Amendment interests against its promotion of legitimate governmental interests. Even when there is no probable cause to believe that a driver is committing a traffic or equipment violation, random license and registration checks of vehicles and detaining the driver are unreasonable under the Fourth Amendment.

Dissent: (Rehnquist, J.) No one questions that a state may require the licensing of those who drive on its highways and the registration of vehicles which are driven on those highways. If a state insists on these requirements, it obviously may take steps necessary to enforce compliance.

Olmstead v. United States (S. Ct. 1928)

Facts: Ds sought to suppress incriminating evidence obtained through wiretapped telephone lines at points between their homes and offices.

Issue: Does the Fourth Amendment's prohibition against unreasonable searches and seizures preclude governmental officials from wiretapping telephone lines to obtain evidence of illegal activity?

Rule: (Taft, C.J.) The Fourth Amendment's prohibition against unreasonable searches and seizures is to prevent the use of governmental force to search someone's house, their person, papers and effects, and to prevent their seizure against the person's will. This prohibition cannot be extended and expanded to include telephone wires.

Dissent: (Brandeis, J.) In giving effect to the principle underlying the Fourth Amendment, the Court should refuse to place an unduly literal construction upon it. The Framers of the Constitution conferred, as against the government, the right to be let alone — the most comprehensive of rights and the right most valued by civilized men. To protect that right, every unjustifiable intrusion by the government upon the privacy of the individual, whatever the means employed, must be deemed a violation of the Fourth Amendment. The use of facts ascertained by such intrusion as evidence in a criminal proceeding is a violation of the Fifth Amendment.

Dissent: (Butler, J.) The contracts between telephone companies and users contemplate the private use of the facilities employed in the service. The communications belong to the parties between whom they pass. During the transmission the exclusive use of the wires belongs to the persons served by it. Tapping the wires and listening in by the officers literally constituted a search for evidence.

Berger v. New York (S. Ct. 1967)

Facts: A New York state statute provided that New York judges could authorize wiretaps and bugging "upon oath or affirmation" that there is reasonable ground to believe that evidence of crime might be procured by such means.

Issue: May a court official, pursuant to a state statute and absent a showing of probable cause, authorize the wiretapping of an individual's telephone lines when there is reasonable ground to believe that evidence of crime may be obtained by such means?

Rule: (Clark, J.) The Fourth Amendment commands that a warrant issues not only upon probable cause supported by oath or affirmation, but also "particularly describing the place to be searched, and the persons or things to be seized." A state statute not particular in these details and overbroad in connection with the duration of the wiretapping violates the guarantees of the Fourth Amendment.

Concurrence: (Douglas, J.) The Court's decision is correct because at long last it overrules *sub silentio Olmstead v. United States* and brings wiretapping and other electronic eavesdropping fully with the purview of the Fourth Amendment. My overriding objection to electronic surveillance is that it is a search for "mere evidence," which as I have maintained on other occasions is a violation of the Fourth and Fifth Amendments.

Dissent: (Black, J.) The literal language of the Fourth Amendment imports tangible things, persons, houses, papers and effects, and it would require an expansion of the language used by the Framers in the interest of privacy or some equally vague judge-made goal to hold that it applies to the spoken word.

Dissent: (Harlan, J.) Time-honored distinctions between the constitutional protections afforded against federal authority by the Bill of Rights and those provided against state action by the Fourteenth Amendment have been obliterated, thus increasingly subjecting state criminal enforcement policies to oversight by this Court. Newly contrived constitutional rights have been established without any apparent concern for the empirical process that goes with legislative reform.

Katz v. United States (S. Ct. 1967)

Facts: D was convicted for the interstate telephonic transmission of gambling information in violation of a federal statute.

Issue: May the government electronically listen to and record an individual's telephone conversation made through a public telephone booth without violating the Fourth Amendment's prohibition against unreasonable searches and seizures?

Rule: (Stewart, J.) A government act in electronically listening to and recording an individual's conversation made through a public telephone booth violates the privacy upon which the individual justifiably relies while using the booth. Such government action constitutes a "search and seizure" within the meaning of the Fourth Amendment.

Concurrence: (Harlan, J.) The rule emerging from prior decisions is that there is a two-fold requirement, first that a person have exhibited an actual (subjective) expectation of privacy and, second, that the expectation be one that society is prepared to recognize as "reasonable." Conversations in the open would not be protected against being overheard, for the expectation of privacy under the circumstances would be unreasonable.

Dissent: (Black, J.) The Fourth Amendment cannot be construed to apply to eavesdropping. The words of the Amendment should not be distorted to "keep the Constitution up to date" or "to bring it into harmony with the times."

United States v. United States District Court for Eastern District of Michigan (S. Ct. 1972)

Facts: The government sought to direct the district court to vacate its disclosure order in connection with the sealed wiretap logs the government submitted as evidence against three defendants charged with the destruction of government property. The government refused to permit disclosure on the ground that secrecy was vital to national security.

Issue: May the President, acting through the Attorney General, authorize electronic surveillance in internal security matters without prior judicial approval?

Rule: (Powell, J.) The Fourth Amendment freedoms cannot be properly guaranteed if domestic security surveillance may be conducted solely within the discretion of the executive branch. The Amendment does not contemplate the executive officers of government as neutral and disinterested magistrates. The powers emanating from the President's domestic security role must be exercised in a manner compatible with the Fourth Amendment and this requires an appropriate warrant procedure.

Hoffa v. United States (S. Ct. 1966)

Facts: D, convicted of attempting to bribe jurors in his previous trial, which ended in a hung jury, challenged the admissibility of the testimony of the prosecution's chief witness on the ground that when he made incriminating statements to the witness, D did not know that the witness was a government informer.

Issue: Does the Fourth Amendment's prohibition against unreasonable searches and seizures preclude the admission of evidence of wrongdoing that has been mistakenly but voluntarily communicated to a government informer?

Rule: (Stewart, J.) The Fourth Amendment's prohibition against unreasonable searches and seizures protects the security one relies upon when one places oneself within a constitutionally protected area. It does not protect a wrongdoer's misplaced belief that a person to whom one voluntarily confides one's wrongdoing will not reveal it.

Dissent: (Warren, C.J.) Although the defendant erects his main arguments on constitutional grounds, it should not even be necessary for the Court to reach those questions. For the affront to the quality and fairness of federal law enforcement which this case presents is sufficient to require an exercise of our supervisory powers. The use of an informer of questionable character and with a great incentive to act as such evidences a serious potential for undermining the integrity of the truth-finding process in the federal courts.

Bishop v. Wood (S. Ct. 1976)

Facts: D, the City Manager of Marion, North Carolina, terminated the employment of P, a policeman, without affording him a hearing. Because a city ordinance classified P as a "permanent employee," P claimed a constitutional right to a pretermination hearing.

Issue: Does a permanent, public employee have a property interest in continued employment that is protected under the Due Process Clause of the Fourteenth Amendment?

Rule: (Stevens, J.) Only a state law or a contract can vest in an employee a property right in continued employment. Therefore, a permanent public employee, absent a contract or a governing state law, is an at-will employee who may be discharged at any time without cause.

Dissent: (Brennan, J.) Before a state law is construed as not securing a "property" interest, the Court should determine the reasonableness of the employee's belief that the law did confer such an interest.

Dissent: (White, J.) Contrary to the Court's ruling, the ordinance in question did confer a property right to continued employment unless there is cause for dismissal. Thus, having granted the right, it is the federal Constitution, not state law, which determines the process to be applied in connection with any state decision to deprive an individual of that right.

Vitek v. Jones (S. Ct. 1980)

Facts: A Nebraska statute provided that when a designated physician or psychologist found that a state prisoner "suffer[ed] from a mental disease or defect" and could not be treated in the facility in which the prisoner was incarcerated, the Director of Correctional Services could transfer the prisoner for examination and treatment to another institution within or without the Department of Corrections.

Issue: Does the involuntary transfer of a state prisoner to a mental hospital violate a liberty interest that is procedurally protected under the Due Process Clause of the Fourteenth Amendment?

Rule: (White, J.) An objective expectation, firmly fixed in state law and official Penal Complex practice, that a prisoner would not be transferred unless he suffered from a mental disease or defect that could not be adequately treated in the prison, creates a liberty interest. The protection of this liberty interest demands that the minimum requirements of procedural process appropriate under the circumstances be observed in determining whether the condition warranting the transfer to the mental hospital has occurred.

Michael H. v. Gerald D. (S. Ct. 1989)

Facts: Under California law a child born within a marriage was deemed a child of the marriage. Only the husband or wife, under very limited circumstances, could rebut the presumption of legitimacy.

Issue: Does a state law presuming paternity of a child born within a marriage violate the due process rights of a man who is the natural father of a child born to the wife of another man?

Rule: (Scalia, J.) A state law may declare that it is generally irrelevant for paternity purposes whether a child conceived during and born into an existing marriage was begotten by someone other than the husband. The Court defers to the state legislature's determination that as a matter of overriding social policy, the husband is to be held responsible for the child.

Concurrence: (Stevens, J.) A natural father can have a constitutionally protected interest in his relationship with a child whose mother was married and cohabitating with another man at the time of conception. The California statute, at least as applied in this case, protects that interest.

Dissent: (Brennan, J.) A parent-child relationship is a liberty interest that is protected by the Due Process Clause. The California statute cuts off this relation without affording the least bit of process.

Dissent: (White, J.) A father has a liberty interest entitled to due process protection if he has come forward to participate in the rearing of the child (i.e., held the child out as his own and provided financial support). The California statute does not protect this interest.

Kentucky Dep't of Corrections v. Thompson (S. Ct. 1989)

Facts: The Kentucky State Reformatory adopted regulations governing general prison visitations. The Reformatory reserved the right to deny visitation to anyone whose presence constituted a "clear and probable danger to the safety and security of the institution or would interfere with the orderly operation of the institution."

Issue: Does a state law establishing visitation criteria grant prison inmates a liberty interest protected by the Due Process Clause of the Constitution?

Rule: (Blackmun, J.) A state law creates a liberty interest by explicitly using mandatory language in connection with the establishment of specific substantive predicates to govern official decision making. A regulation lacking the requisite mandatory language requiring that a particular result is to be reached upon a finding that the substantive predicates are met does not create a liberty interest properly protectible under the Due Process Clause. **Dissent:** (Marshall, J.) The exercise of such unbridled governmental power over the basic human need to see family members and friends strikes at the heart of the liberty protected by the Due Process Clause. Recognizing a liberty interest in this case would not create a right to "unfettered visitation," but would merely afford prisoners rudimentary procedural safeguards against retaliatory or arbitrary denials of visits. Further, I fail to see why mandatory language is always an essential element of a state-created liberty interest. Absent concrete evidence that state officials routinely ignore substantive criteria set forth in statutes or regulations, it is only proper to assume that the criteria are regularly employed in practice, thereby creating legitimate expectations worthy of protection by the Due Process Clause.

Daniels v. Williams (S. Ct. 1986)

Facts: P sought to recover damages for back and ankle injuries allegedly sustained when he fell on the stairway of the prison stairway in which he was incarcerated. The state provided itself with tort immunity.
Issue: Does a negligent act by state officials resulting in injury and/or loss of property amount to a deprivation under the Due Process Clause of the Fourteenth Amendment?
Rule: (Rehnquist, J.) The Due Process Clause was intended to secure the individual from the arbitrary exercise of the powers of government and has historically been applied to deliberate decisions of government officials to deprive a person of life, liberty, or property. The negligent actions of prison custodians do not implicate the concerns of the Due Process Clause.

Vlandis v. Kline (S. Ct. 1973)

Facts: Connecticut, pursuant to a statute, required that the nonresidency status of out-of-state students entering its state university system remain in force throughout their period of attendance.
Issue: In allocating tuition rates at its state universities, does an irrebuttable presumption of nonresidency, resulting in higher tuition fees to nonresidents, violate the Due Process Clause of the Fifth and Fourteenth Amendments?
Rule: (Stewart, J.) A state, concerned with residency in allocating the rates for tuition and fees at its university system, may not deny an individual the resident rates on the basis of a permanent and irrebuttable presumption of nonresidence, when that presumption is not necessarily or universally true in fact, and when the state has reasonable alternative means of making the crucial determination.

Dissent: (Rehnquist, J.) The opinion accomplishes the invalidation of a state law by a highly theoretical analysis that relies heavily on notions of substantive due process that have been authoritatively repudiated by subsequent decisions of the Court.

Cleveland Board of Educ. v. LaFleur (S. Ct. 1974)

Facts: Several school board rules required that pregnant teachers take maternity leave without pay at least five months prior to the expected birth of a child.

Issue: Does a rule forcing a pregnant public school teacher to take maternity leave without pay several months prior to her due date violate rights protected by the Constitution?

Rule: (Stewart, J.) Childbearing is a constitutionally protected right and regulations impinging that right must be rationally related to a valid state interest. Arbitrary cut-off dates embodied in mandatory maternity leave rules are not rationally related to the state interest in preserving continuity of instruction.

Dissent: (Rehnquist, J.) The Court rests its invalidation of the school regulations on the Due Process Clause rather than on any claim of sexual discrimination under the Equal Protection Clause of that Amendment. The opinion presents another example of the Court's unending war on irrebuttable presumptions.

Weinberger v. Salfi (S. Ct. 1975)

Facts: A provision of the Social Security Act imposed duration-of-relationship requirements denying survivorship benefits to surviving wives and stepchildren who had not had their respective relationships with the deceased wage earner for more than nine months prior to his death.

Issue: Does the imposition of a statutory eligibility requirement for the receipt of survivorship benefits under a government benefit program violate equal protection guarantees under the Fourteenth Amendment?

Rule: (Rehnquist, J.) The receipt of benefits under a government benefit program is a noncontractual claim, and therefore not constitutionally protected. A classification with respect to a noncontractual claim need only be rationally related to the congressional objective. The duration-of-relationship requirement is rationally related to the congressional objective of guarding against abuse of the system.

Dissent: (Brennan, J.) When certain factors are present, as in this case, the government's interests in efficiency must be surrendered to the individual's interest in proving that the facts presumed are not true as to her.

Hamdi v. Rumsfeld (S. Ct. 2004)

Facts: An American citizen was captured during military operations in Afghanistan and held as an enemy combatant. His father sued, demanding a right to a hearing to prove his innocence.

Issue: Does an American citizen have a right to a hearing to claim innocence when captured abroad as part of military operations when the President deems him an enemy combatant?

Rule: (O'Connor, J.) (plurality) Due process demands that on these narrow facts, an American citizen has a due process right to a hearing at which he can contest his innocence.

Concurrence: (Souter, J.) Congress did not authorize detentions without hearings in these circumstances; on these facts due process requires that the detainee be given a hearing.

Dissent: (Scalia, J.) Unless Congress suspends the writ of habeas corpus, or criminal charges are promptly brought against the detainee, he must be released.

Sandin v. Connor (S. Ct. 1995)

Facts: Prisoner P brought a claim seeking a hearing where he could call witnesses before being disciplined for misconduct.

Issue: Did due process require a hearing when a prison regulation requires that discipline be imposed after a finding, based on substantial evidence, of misconduct?

Rule: (Rehnquist, C.J.) While in most cases liberty interests can be created by the existence of regulations that cabin officials' decision-making discretion, the unique characteristics of prisons require that before an interest rises to the level of being protected by due process, it had to be an atypical, significant deprivation.

Wilkinson v. Austin (S. Ct. 2005)

Facts: Ohio transferred P, a prisoner, into a Supermax (highest security) facility.

Issue: Does the transfer into a Supermax facility deprive a prisoner of a liberty interest, and if so, do the state's procedures for deciding these transfers violate the Due Process Clause?

Rule: (Kennedy, J.) A transfer like this does deprive a prisoner of a liberty interest, given the conditions at Supermax facilities and the impact it has on parole eligibility. However, the state's procedures comport with due process under the test from *Matthews v. Eldridge*, 424 U.S. 319 (1976): the individual's interest, while significant is still limited by the basic fact of his incarceration, the state's informal review procedures are adequate to reach accurate transfer decisions, and the state has a high interest in quick transfers of prisoners who are potentially dangerous to guards and other prisoners. If the state in practice does not follow these procedures the prisoner can return to court.

Tennessee Secondary School Athletic Ass'n v. Brentwood Academy (S. Ct. 2007)

Facts: A scholastic athletic conference sanctioned member school for violating the conference rules about recruiting middle-school students, after providing a hearing to the school.

Issue: Does the sanction violate the school's First Amendment associational rights or its procedural due process rights?

Rule: (Stevens, J.) There are no violations. The school joined the conference voluntarily, and whatever restrictions on its associational rights flowing from the recruiting restrictions are justified by the conference's need to ensure the integrity of its academic competition and prevent pressure on students. The hearing the conference gave the school was adequate, even though the process included an *ex parte* hearing.

Concurrence: (Kennedy, J.) I agree with the result but not with some of the case citations the Court makes in its First Amendment analysis.

Concurrence: (Thomas, J.) I do not believe the conference is a state actor and subject to the Constitution.

CHAPTER 7

Fourteenth Amendment Substantive Rights, Constitutional Economic Rights, Bills of Attainder, and Ex Post Facto Laws

I. INTRODUCTION

A. Fourteenth Amendment

The Fourteenth Amendment of the Constitution guarantees that "No State shall make or enforce any law which shall abridge the privileges and immunities of citizens of the United States; nor shall any State deprive any person of life, liberty, or property, without due process of law."

B. Privileges and Immunities Clause

The Privileges and Immunities Clause forbids state infringement of the rights of national citizenship, but not the rights of state citizenship. Consequently, the Clause protects uniquely federal rights such as the right to petition the federal government and the right to interstate travel.

In 1999 the Court decided *Saenz v. Roe*, which for the first time in 50 years and only the second time since Reconstruction relied on the Fourteenth Amendment Privileges and Immunities Clause to strike down a state law.

C. Due Process Clause

The Due Process Clause protects life, liberty, and property. The doctrine of substantive due process is derived from the Due Process Clause and is invoked to protect "fundamental rights" emanating from life, liberty, and property.

Initially, the Court used the substantive due process doctrine to protect fundamental economic and property rights. However, more recently, substantive due process has been used to protect fundamental rights to privacy and personal freedom.

The basic issue raised in substantive due process litigation is whether the Court may extend protection to rights not explicitly protected in the Constitution by including them within the "fundamental rights" of citizens. The Court tests for substantive due process violation by evaluating the governmental act in terms of its reasonableness as a means of effectuating a legitimate state objective.

II. SUBSTANTIVE DUE PROCESS — ECONOMIC REGULATION

A. Judicial Intervention — *Lochner* Era

During the *Lochner* era, which lasted from approximately 1890-1937, the Court subjected state economic legislation to strict judicial scrutiny. Invoking substantive due process doctrine, the Court invalidated state laws deemed violative of economic and property rights. In the face of such invalidation, the Court recognized state police powers to safeguard the welfare of its citizens, and expressed no wish to substitute its judgment for those of the state legislature. Nonetheless, the Court reserved unto itself the right to determine whether the enactment of a regulation was properly within the police power of the state. State regulation of prices, labor relations, and participation in business were particularly susceptible to attack.

The Court established the following criteria by which a state regulation would be judged.

Mnemonic: **MEE**

1. **M**eans

The means employed must bear a substantial relation to the objective of the legislation.

2. **E**nds

The ends or objectives of the legislation must be legitimate and substantial.

3. **E**ffect

If the effect of the legislation is to substantially infringe upon liberty or property interests, then the law may violate due process.

B. The Decline of Judicial Scrutiny — Post-*Lochner* Era
The post-*Lochner* era was marked by decisions in which the Court moved away from strict scrutiny of state regulations and deferred more to the judgment of state legislatures as to the reasonableness of state regulations.

III. OTHER CONSTITUTIONAL PROTECTION OF ECONOMIC RIGHTS

A. Taking Clause
Incorporated into the Fourteenth Amendment's due process guarantee is the Fifth Amendment's proscription against the taking of private property for "public use, without just compensation." This proscription limits the exercise of Congress' implied eminent domain power. However, governments may, pursuant to their police and other regulatory powers, impose land-use restrictions that substantially reduce property value. The issue is when a regulatory restriction becomes a taking for which the owner must be compensated.

1. Interference with the Use of Land
When a government substantially interferes with the use or enjoyment by an individual of his property, the government may be held to have "taken" the property although physical possession has not occurred. Note, however, that not every injury to an individual's property amounts to a taking.

2. Zoning and Environmental Protection
A state's zoning and environmental regulations are usually upheld as valid exercise of a state's police power if the regulations:
a. Do not destroy all beneficial use of the land; and
b. Do not bar other types of development on the land.

3. Landmark Protection
Landmark protection regulations must be nondiscriminatory and be part of a comprehensive plan for achieving a significant public purpose.

B. Contracts Clause
Article I, §10 of the Constitution provides that "no state shall pass any law impairing the obligations of contract."

1. Federal Regulation
Although there is no similar constitutional prohibition that can be applied against the federal government, the Due Process Clause of the Fifth Amendment has been held broad enough to extend the prohibition to the federal government. The prohibition applies to both public and private contracts.

2. State Regulation
The Court has recognized that the constitutional prohibition against the impairment of contract is not absolute. States may, pursuant to their police power, restructure contractual obligations when vital state interests are involved.
To survive a Contracts Clause attack, a state legislation must:
a. Be applicable to a widespread economic or social problem;
b. Regulate an area already subject to state regulation;
c. Modify only temporarily the contractual obligations; and
d. Apply to a broad class of persons.

IV. PROTECTION OF NON-ECONOMIC RIGHTS

A. Right to Privacy
The right to privacy is not explicitly mentioned in the Constitution. However, the Court has recognized that a right of personal privacy, or a guarantee of certain areas or zones of privacy, does exist under the Constitution, emanating from the First, Fourth, Fifth, and Ninth Amendments, in the penumbras of the Bill of Rights, and in the concept of liberty guaranteed by the Fourteenth Amendment.
Only personal rights that can be deemed "fundamental" rights or rights "implicit in the concept of ordered liberty" are included in this guarantee of personal privacy. The rights to marry, raise children, and acquire knowledge are among some of the essential "liberties" protected under the Due Process Clause of the Fourteenth Amendment.

B. Personal Freedom
Not all aspects of personal freedom and autonomy are protected as fundamental rights. Thus far, the Court has refused to protect certain unconventional lifestyles, such as adulterous relations, as fundamental rights. However, in 2003 the Court took a major step by striking down a Texas same-sex sodomy law as violating the rights of gay men and lesbians to sexual intimacy. Also, the Court has recognized state power to regulate the living arrangements of non-family members and the personal appearance of city workers. In these instances, the Court has ruled that a state showing of a rational connection between the regulation and the promotion of safety to persons and property is sufficient to withstand a right to privacy attack.

C. Family Relations
Because the right to marry and raise children are fundamental rights protected under the Fourteenth Amendment, any state regulation of familial rights can only be justified by a compelling

state interest. Also, the regulation must be narrowly constructed so as to protect only the legitimate state interest involved. Extended familial rights are protected as fundamental rights of privacy.

D. Abortion

The Court has struggled with the constitutional status of the right to abortion. In 1973 in *Roe v. Wade* the Court held that abortion was a fundamental right that a state could infringe on only in very limited circumstances. That decision created an enormous amount of controversy, both in courts and across the nation. Throughout the 1980s *Roe* came under more and more pressure, and many commentators predicted its overruling. But in the 1992 case *Casey v. Planned Parenthood of S.E. Pennsylvania*, the Court reaffirmed what it called the "core holding" of *Roe*. The modern rule is that abortion restrictions must not impose an "undue burden" on the woman's right to an abortion.

V. SCOPE OF LIBERTY AND PROPERTY

A. Property

The Due Process Clause of the Fourteenth Amendment protects "life, liberty and property." The term "property" as used in the Clause incorporates more than ownership of real estate, chattels, or money. It includes "interests already acquired in specific benefits." However, to have a property interest in a benefit, there must be more than an abstract need or desire for it. There must be a legitimate claim of entitlement to such property interest under state or federal law.

B. Liberty

Liberty under the Due Process Clause of the Fourteenth Amendment is expansive and extends beyond the freedom from physical restraints. The Court has ruled that the phrase "life, liberty and property" is a "unitary concept embracing all interests valued by sensible men." In the area of substantive due process litigation, usually the issue presented is the constitutionality of a state infringement on a liberty. The Court then focuses on the degree of justification a state must show to defend that infringement successfully.

VI. OTHER RESTRICTIONS

A. Bills of Attainder

In Article I, §10, cl. 1 and in Article I, §9, cl. 3, the Constitution prohibits a state or the federal government respectively from legislatively enacting Bills of Attainder. The Clauses proscribe any legislative act "no matter what its form, that applies either to named individuals or to easily ascertainable members of a group in such a way as to inflict punishment on them with a judicial trial."

However, the fact that a legislative act imposes burdens on an individual or an easily identifiable group of persons does not mean the act is a Bill of Attainder.

To classify an act as a Bill of Attainder, the Court must first determine whether:

1. The punishment imposed by the act is "traditionally judged to be prohibited by the Bill of Attainder Clause";
2. The act furthers non-punitive goals, given the type and severity of the burden imposed;
3. The legislative motive evidences a congressional intent to punish; and
4. Less burdensome alternatives are available.

B. Ex Post Facto Laws

An ex post facto law imposes criminal liability on past transactions. Article I, §10, cl. 1 and Article I, §9, cl. 3 prohibit the state and the federal government respectively from enacting penal laws that have a retroactive effect. Laws violate the ex post facto prohibition when they:

1. Impose a penalty for past conduct that was lawful when performed;
2. Impose a harsher penalty for unlawful conduct than existed before the passage of the law; or
3. Alter penal provisions.

CASE CLIPS

Lochner v. New York (S. Ct. 1905)

Facts: A New York law prohibited the employment of bakery employees for more than 10 hours a day or 60 hours a week.

Issue: May a state enact a law prescribing working hours for certain privately contracted employees without violating the Due Process Clause of the Fourteenth Amendment?

Rule: (Peckham, J.) A state law interfering with contract freedom between employers and employees is invalid. Such a law can be justified only if it has a direct relation to a legitimate state objective.

Dissent 1: (Harlan, J.) It is not the province of the Court to determine the wisdom of a state law, but to assess the law on the basis of its consistency with the Constitution. If a state law does not contravene the Constitution, the Court should defer to the fact-findings of the state legislature.

Dissent 2: (Holmes, J.) The majority of a state has the right to embody their opinions in law. The dominant opinion should not be invalidated unless it infringes upon the fundamental principles of our tradition.

Nebbia v. New York (S. Ct. 1934)

Facts: New York established the Milk Control Board to fix the minimum retail prices at which store owners could sell certain items consumed off their premises.

Issue: May a state, in order to correct economic ills, establish retail prices at which store owners must sell certain items without violating the Due Process Clause of the Fourteenth Amendment?

Rule: (Roberts, J.) A state may, in pursuit of a reasonable economic policy and consistent with the Due Process Clause of the Fourteenth Amendment, establish retail prices of consumer items to promote public welfare.

Williamson v. Lee Optical Co. (S. Ct. 1955)

Facts: Oklahoma law prohibited any person not a licensed optometrist or ophthalmologist to fit, duplicate, or replace lenses or other optical appliances, except upon the written prescriptive authority of an Oklahoma licensed ophthalmologist or optometrist.

Issue: Does a state health and safety regulation prescribing the manner in which certain health care practitioners may supply services to the public violate the Due Process Clause of the Fourteenth Amendment?

Rule: (Douglas, J.) When pursuing a legitimate state objective, a state may, consistent with the Due Process Clause of the Fourteenth Amendment, define practice areas for practitioners within an industry.

Pennsylvania Coal Co. v. Mahon (S. Ct. 1922)

Facts: A Pennsylvania Act prohibited the mining of anthracite coal in such a way as to cause the subsidence of any structure used as human habitation. P contracted with D to remove the coal under P's property. P assumed all the risks and waived all claims for damages that might have arisen from the mining of coal.

Issue: Does a law that removes private citizens' property and contract rights of private parties violate the Due Process Clause of the Fourteenth Amendment?

Rule: (Holmes, J.) A state may not enact laws destroying previously reserved contract rights. Such state action constitutes a taking without compensation and violates the Due Process Clause of the Fourteenth Amendment.

Dissent: (Brandeis, J.) A state public health law which prevents a property owner from using property in a publicly harmful way, but which confers incidental benefits on other individuals, is within the police powers of the state.

First English Evangelical Lutheran Church of Glendale v. County of Los Angeles (S. Ct. 1987)

Facts: D adopted an Interim Ordinance forbidding replacement or construction of any structures within an interim flood protection area. The Ordinance affected D's campground where buildings had been destroyed by flood rains.

Issue: May a landowner, whose property had been temporarily "taken" pursuant to a land-use regulation, recover damages for the period prior to final determination that the regulation constituted a taking of his property?

Rule: (Rehnquist, C.J.) Where government regulation has temporarily "taken" all use of property from its owner, the Fifth Amendment prohibiting the taking of property without compensation demands that the government compensate the owner for the whole period over which the taking had occurred.

Dissent: (Stevens, J.) Precedent demonstrates that the type of regulatory taking at issue here is not a constitutional taking. Whether a temporary taking has occurred should not be answered by simply looking at the reason a temporary interference with an owner's use of his property is terminated.

Home Building & Loan Ass'n v. Blaisdell (S. Ct. 1934)

Facts: Minnesota's Mortgage Moratorium Law authorized relief against mortgage foreclosures and execution sales of real property. Local courts were allowed to extend the period of redemption from foreclosure sales, and no action for a deficiency judgment could be brought during this period.

Issue: May a state, in an economic emergency, enact legislation temporarily restructuring contractual obligations of private parties without violating the Contract Clause of the Constitution, which prohibits any state from passing laws impairing contractual obligations?

Rule: (Hughes, C.J.) The Contract Clause prohibition on a state's impairment of contractual obligations is not an absolute restriction of a state's protective power. Therefore a state may, pursuant to its police power to protect the public interest, adopt reasonable means to safeguard the economic interest of the whole state.

Dissent: (Sutherland, J.) A state has no constitutional power to alter contractual rights of parties to a contract. A statute which delays enforcement of a mortgagee's contractual right is an alteration of the terms of a contract in violation of the Contract Clause prohibiting state impairment of contract obligations.

Griswold v. Connecticut (S. Ct. 1965)

Facts: A Connecticut law prohibited the use of any drug or medicinal article or instrument to prevent conception. Another Connecticut law punished anyone who abetted, assisted, counseled, caused, hired or commanded another to commit any offense.

Issue: May a state enact legislation preventing married couples from associating with their physician?

Rule: (Douglas, J.) The right of association is a freedom within the zone of privacy protected by constitutional guarantees. Therefore, a state may not, to promote a local objective, impose unnecessarily broad regulations which invade the zone of privacy.

Dissent: (Black, J.) Only those rights specifically protected by the Bill of Rights or other constitutional provisions are protected under the Fourteenth Amendment. The right of privacy does not emanate from these constitutional provisions and the Court should not invalidate a state law merely because it offends a personal taste.

Dissent: (Stewart, J.) The Court's role is not to determine the wisdom of a state law but to test its constitutionality. The right to privacy as a guaranteed right is not found in the Constitution. Therefore, the Court should validate the state law.

Roe v. Wade (S. Ct. 1973)

Facts: Texas law made it a crime for a woman to procure an abortion except "by medical advice for the purpose of saving the life of the mother."
Issue: May a state impose regulation restricting a woman's right to terminate her pregnancy?
Rule: (Blackmun, J.) A woman's right to terminate her pregnancy, in consultation with her physician, is an area of privacy protected by constitutional provisions, and state regulations limiting those rights are justified only by showing a "compelling state interest." Further, a state's limitation of those rights of privacy must be narrowly drawn to express only the legitimate state interest at stake.
Dissent: (White, J.) Since this is an issue upon which reasonable men may disagree and to which there is no constitutional bar, the Court should leave such decisions to the people and the political processes of each state.

Board of Regents v. Roth (S. Ct. 1972)

Facts: P was hired by D to teach for one year. D advised P, without explanation, that he would not be rehired for the following year. P lacked tenure rights and under state law, "the decision whether to rehire a nontenured teacher was left to the unfettered discretion of university officials." P claimed that the failure to give him a reason for nonretention or an opportunity for a hearing violated his procedural due process rights.
Issue: Does the dismissal by a state university of an untenured teacher without a statement of reasons or a hearing violate the Due Process Clause of the Fourteenth Amendment?
Rule: (Stewart, J.) An untenured individual has no legitimate claims to property or liberty interests and may not activate the Due Process Clause of the Fourteenth Amendment to prevent nonretention by employers.
Dissent: (Marshall, J.) In order that citizens may feel secure and protected against arbitrary government action, federal and state governments should establish reasons for the denial of employment.

Bishop v. Wood (S. Ct. 1976)

Facts: D terminated P's employment as a policeman without affording him a hearing. Since a city ordinance classified P as a "permanent employee," P claimed a constitutional right to a predetermination hearing.
Issue 1: Does a permanent, public employee have a property interest in continued employment that is protected under the Due Process Clause of the Fourteenth Amendment?
Rule 1: (Stevens, J.) Only state law or a contract can vest in an employee a property right in continued employment. Therefore, a permanent public

employee, absent a contract or a governing state law, is an at-will employee who may be discharged at any time without cause.

Issue 2: Does wrongful dismissal from employment violate an interest in liberty?

Rule 2: There is no constitutional right to a correct personnel decision. Therefore, a wrongful discharge does not violate an individual's interest in liberty.

Dissent 1: (Brennan, J.) Before a state law is construed as not securing a "property" interest, the Court should determine the reasonableness of the employee's belief that the law did confer such an interest.

Dissent 2: (White, J.) The ordinance in question did confer a property right to continued employment unless there is cause for dismissal. Thus, having granted the right, it is the federal Constitution, not state law, which determines the process to be applied in connection with any state decision to deprive an individual of that right.

Penn Central Transportation Co. v. City of New York (S. Ct. 1978)

Facts: The New York Landmarks Preservation Commission denied two applications of UGP to construct a multi-story office building above P's Grand Central Terminal property, a designated landmark. P asserted that the Landmarks Preservation Law had "taken" its property without just compensation.

Issue: May a city, as part of a comprehensive program to preserve historic landmarks and historic districts, restrict the development of individual historic landmarks without effecting a "taking" requiring the payment of "just compensation"?

Rule: (Brennan, J.) When a city, in pursuit of a program to preserve certain historic sites, restricts from use a portion of a designated property, while permitting the remainder of the property to be used in a gainful manner, such action does not constitute a "taking" requiring the payment of "just compensation."

Slaughter-House Cases (S. Ct. 1872)

Facts: A Louisiana statute made it illegal to slaughter animals in New Orleans. However, D was allowed to "establish themselves at any point or place." Butchers wishing to slaughter animals had to use D's facilities and pay a reasonable compensation for the use.

Issue: Does a state violate the Privileges and Immunities Clause of the Fourteenth Amendment when it regulates its citizens' participation in a local industry thereby infringing on their rights to engage in free trade?

Rule: (Miller, J.) The Privileges and Immunities Clause of the Fourteenth Amendment guarantees the privileges of national citizenship. The right to engage in industry is not a privilege of national citizenship and a state may regulate its citizens' participation therein.

Allied Structural Steel Co. v. Spannaus (S. Ct. 1978)

Facts: Minnesota's Private Pension Benefits Protection Act subjected a private employer to a "pension funding charge" if it either terminated its plan or closed its Minnesota office. The charge was assessed if the pension funds were not sufficient to cover full pensions for all employees who had worked at least ten years for the employer.

Issue: May a state enact legislation to alter the mutually agreed-upon contractual responsibility of an employer to its employees without violating the Contract Clause prohibiting the state from impairing contract obligations?

Rule: (Stewart, J.) A state law which severely and permanently alters the prior contractual obligations of an employer and is not necessitated by an important social objective violates the Contract Clause prohibiting a state from impairing contract obligations.

Dissent: (Brennan, J.) The Act, rather than diluting pre-existing contractual obligations, creates new, additional obligations on a particular class of persons. Therefore, it is the Due Process Clause of the Fourteenth Amendment and not the Contract Clause which is implicated under these conditions.

United States v. Causby (S. Ct. 1946)

Facts: P owned land near an airport used by various aircraft owned by the United States. The aircraft that flew over P's property produced startling noise, preventing P's household from sleeping properly and forcing P to abandon his commercial chicken farm.

Issue: Do the frequent and regular flights of aircraft in airspace immediately above another's property constitute a taking in violation of the Fifth Amendment?

Rule: (Douglas, J.) Flights over private property constitute a taking if the flights are so low and so frequent as to be a direct and immediate interference with the enjoyment and use of the land.

Dissent: (Black, J.) The Court in this instance has given the concept of taking property a sweeping meaning not heretofore known. The adjustment of rights and remedies of property-owners made necessary by the flight of planes at safe altitude is a job for Congress.

Village of Belle Terre v. Boraas (S. Ct. 1974)

Facts: D restricted land use to one-family dwellings. "Family" meant "one or more persons related by blood, adoption, or marriage, living and cooking together as a single housekeeping unit, exclusive of household servants."
Issue: May a city impose land-use regulations discriminating against unrelated individuals on the basis of choice and number of household companions?
Rule: (Douglas, J.) It is within the power of a city or state to impose land-use regulations that are reasonable, are not arbitrary, and bear a rational relationship to a permissible state objective.
Dissent: (Marshall, J.) The ordinance unnecessarily burdens unrelated individuals' First Amendment freedom of association and their constitutionally guaranteed right to privacy.

Moore v. City of East Cleveland, Ohio (S. Ct. 1977)

Facts: An East Cleveland housing ordinance limited occupancy of a dwelling unit to members of a single family. The ordinance's definition of family recognized only a few categories of related individuals as a family. D lived with her son and two grandsons who were first cousins. This combination of related individuals failed to qualify as a family under the ordinance.
Issue: May a city impose restrictions on the living arrangements of family members without violating the Due Process Clause of the Fourteenth Amendment?
Rule: (Powell, J.) Freedom of personal choice in family matters is one of the liberties protected under the Due Process Clause of the Fourteenth Amendment. A city may not issue regulations to abridge that liberty without showing important governmental interests substantially served by the regulation.
Dissent: (Stewart, J.) The claim for associational freedom and for privacy in family matters is not of a level which invokes constitutional protection. This extends the contours of the Due Process Clause beyond recognition.

Bailey v. Alabama (S. Ct. 1911)

Facts: An Alabama statute criminalized breach of written labor contracts if the money for such services had been paid in advance and the employee was unable to refund that money. The statute required proof of the breaching employee's intent to injure or defraud, but such intent could be presumed through the employee's failure to repay the advance.
Issue: Does the Thirteenth Amendment prohibit the use of criminal penalties to enforce employment contracts?

Rule: (Hughes, J.) The Thirteenth Amendment was intended to prohibit all forms of involuntary servitude, not just slavery. A state may impose involuntary servitude as punishment for crime, but State may not compel one to labor for another in payment of a debt by punishing him as a criminal if he does not perform the service.

Dissent: (Holmes, J.) Any legal liability for breach of a contract is a disagreeable consequence which tends to make the contractor do as he said he would. Criminal penalties merely make such consequences more disagreeable, intensifying the legal motive for performing the contract.

Trustees of Dartmouth College v. Woodward (The Dartmouth College Case) (S. Ct. 1819)

Facts: The New Hampshire Legislature in 1816 amended the Dartmouth College corporate charter received from the British Crown in 1716. The amended charter, among other things, increased the number of trustees and created a board of overseers with the power to review important decisions of trustees. The amendments effectively rendered the trustees powerless. The trustees refused to recognize the legislation as binding upon them.

Issue: Does a state act, legislatively altering the terms of a corporate charter under which a college functions, constitute an impairment of contract in violation of the Contract Clause?

Rule: (Marshall, C.J.) The grant of a corporate charter to incorporate an institution for perpetuating the beneficence of the donors toward a specific object is a contract. Legislative alteration is impermissible under the Contract Clause of the Constitution which precludes states from impairing contractual obligations.

Stone v. Mississippi (S. Ct. 1880)

Facts: In 1869 the Mississippi legislature adopted a new constitution, which prohibited the authorization of the sale of lottery tickets. In 1870 the legislature enacted a statute making it unlawful to conduct a lottery in the state. Two years previously, the legislature had granted Ds a 25-year franchise to sell tickets for their lottery.

Issue: Does a state legislature's rescission of a franchise that a prior legislature had granted violate the Contract Clause of the Constitution precluding a state from impairing contracts?

Rule: (Waite, C.J.) The Constitution's Contract Clause protects contracts relating to property rights, not governmental rights. A lottery franchise is a permit, good against existing laws but subject to future legislative constitutional control or withdrawal. Therefore, the grant of such a charter is subject to governmental withdrawal at will.

City of El Paso v. Simmons (S. Ct. 1965)

Facts: P purchased land in Texas but was forced to relinquish title to the state in 1947. Texas law, under which P purchased the land, guaranteed that purchaser could regain title to forfeited property if a third party had not obtained title to the property. However, P's application to regain title was denied because under the 1941 amendment to the Texas law, the right to reinstate a claim could not be exercised beyond five years from the forfeiture date. P challenged the amendments as an abrogation of contractual obligation in violation of the Constitution.

Issue: Does a state law violate the Contract Clause's prohibition against the impairment of contract by amending its land-sale laws to have a retrospective effect on previous contracts?

Rule: (White, J.) Not every modification to a contractual promise violates the Contracts Clause. Laws restricting a party to those gains reasonably to be expected from the contract are not subject to attack under the Contract Clause, notwithstanding that they technically alter an obligation of a contract. A technical alteration of a public contract is justified because of the strong public interest in restoring confidence in the stability of land titles.

Dissent: (Black, J.) The Contracts Clause plainly guarantees that no state shall pass any law impairing the obligation of contracts. The Court should not allow Texas to now alter its contractual obligations with purchasers simply because those contracts have proven more costly to the state.

Munn v. Illinois (S. Ct. 1877)

Facts: The State of Illinois enacted a statute establishing maximum rates that warehouses and elevators had to charge for the storage of grain and also required these businesses to procure operating licenses. D, a grain elevator operator, claimed that the state statute violated the Due Process Clause of the Fourteenth Amendment.

Issue: Does a state law setting maximum prices and operating standards for certain businesses deprive owners of their property without due process in violation of the Due Process Clause of the Fourteenth Amendment?

Rule: (Waite, C.J.) When property is devoted to use in which the public has an interest, the property is subject to the public control and regulation, pursuant to a state's police power, for the common good.

Dissent: (Field, J.) The principle upon which the opinion proceeds is subversive of the rights of private property, heretofore believed to be protected by constitutional guarantees against legislative interference.

Wolff Packing Co. v. Court of Industrial Relations (S. Ct. 1923)

Facts: P, an industrial relations board created pursuant to state law to settle labor-management disputes from certain vital industries when the disputes threatened the public peace and health, initiated action against D when D refused to comply with P's order setting wages higher than what D had been willing to pay.

Issue: May a governmental agency, created to settle labor disputes between management and its employees, establish wages for private employees with which employers must comply without violating Due Process Clause of the Fourteenth Amendment?

Rule: (Taft, C.J.) The freedom to contract and of labor is a liberty protected under the Due Process Clause of the Fourteenth Amendment. A state's regulation of that liberty is justified only if the business is clothed with a public interest.

West Coast Hotel Co. v. Parrish (S. Ct. 1937)

Facts: The Industrial Welfare Committee of the State of Washington, pursuant to state law, established minimum wages for women and minors. The state law was passed to protect the health and welfare of women and minors by ensuring them a minimum wage from their employers. P sued to recover the difference between her wages and the minimum wage established by the Committee.

Issue: May a state, pursuant to its police powers to protect the health and welfare of its citizens, enact minimum wage law governing the employment of women and minors, without violating the Due Process Clause of the Fourteenth Amendment?

Rule: (Hughes, C.J.) The freedom of contract protected under the Due Process Clause is not absolute, and a state may regulate contracting between employers and employees in order to protect the public interest. A state may direct its lawmaking powers to correct the exploitation of a class of workers that, because of unequal bargaining power, is unable to effect a decent wage from its employers.

Dissent: (Van Devanter, J.) The meaning of the Constitution does not change with the ebb and flow of economic events, and the Court should not reconsider its previous holding, because of, among other reasons, "the economic conditions which have supervened."

Lincoln Federal Labor Union v. Northwestern Iron & Metal Co. (S. Ct. 1949)

Facts: In 1946 Nebraska amended its constitution by including "right to work" laws, which provided, among other things, that no "individual or corporation or association of any kind shall enter into any contract, written or oral, to exclude persons from employment because of membership in or nonmembership in a labor organization." Several labor unions challenged the amendment, asserting that, among other things, it impaired contractual obligations of existing labor-management contracts and denied unions and employers due process of law.

Issue: Does the Due Process Clause of the Fourteenth Amendment forbid a state from passing laws designed to safeguard the opportunities of non-union workers to obtain and keep employment free from discrimination against them because of their non-union status?

Rule: (Black, J.) States have the power to legislate against injurious practices in their internal commercial and business affairs, so long as their laws do not run afoul of some specific federal constitutional prohibition or of some valid federal law. If the federal Constitution affords protection for union members against discriminatory employment practices, the Constitution likewise protects non-union workers from similar practices.

Matter of Quinlan (1976)

Facts: P, father of a comatose patient, sought to have his daughter declared incompetent and to be appointed guardian of her person and property. P asked that the guardianship should empower him to discontinue the life support systems that sustained his daughter's life.

Issue: May the state deny a guardian of a dying incompetent patient the right to stop the use of life-sustaining systems?

Rule: The constitutionally protected right to privacy encompasses a patient's right to refuse medical treatment. A state may not destroy an incompetent's right to privacy by preventing a properly appointed guardian from exercising that right on behalf of the incompetent.

United States v. Carolene Products Co. (S. Ct. 1938)

Facts: Congress' Filled Milk Act prohibited the shipment in interstate commerce of skimmed milk filled with any fat or oil other than milk fat.

Issue: May Congress, in order to protect the public health and to guard against fraudulent substitutions, enact regulatory legislation prohibiting the shipment in interstate commerce of certain manufactured food products without violating the Due Process Clause of the Fifth Amendment?

Rule: (Stone, J.) When acting to protect the public health, congressional regulatory legislation affecting ordinary commerce should be presumed constitutional.

Ferguson v. Skrupa (S. Ct. 1963)

Facts: Kansas enacted a statute that prohibited the practice of debt adjusting except as an incident to "the lawful practice of law in the state."

Issue: May a state enact a statute outlawing certain business activities it deems contrary to the public welfare without violating the Due Process Clause of the Fourteenth Amendment?

Rule: (Black, J.) A state is free to exercise its legislative judgment to enact laws to protect its citizens. It is not the judiciary's role to sit as a super-legislature to weigh the wisdom of legislation and to substitute its social and economic beliefs for those of a state legislature.

United States Trust Co. of New York v. New Jersey (S. Ct. 1977)

Facts: New Jersey and New York repealed a 1962 Statutory Covenant that guaranteed that revenues and reserves pledged to pay bondholders of the New York and New Jersey Port Authority would not be used to finance deficits of other future mass transit facilities.

Issue: May a state enact legislation repealing its contractual obligations with bondholders without violating the Contract Clause?

Rule: (Blackmun, J.) The Contract Clause of the Constitution, which prohibits a state from impairing contractual obligations, bars a state, who is a contract party, from imposing drastic impairment on its contractual obligations when there is an evident and more moderate alternative to achieve the state objective.

Dissent: (Brennan, J.) The Court has moved away from the established principle that lawful exercises of a state's police powers stand paramount to private rights held under contract. The decision substantially distorts modern constitutional jurisprudence governing regulation of private economic interests.

Keystone Bituminous Coal Ass'n v. DeBenedictis (S. Ct. 1987)

Facts: The Pennsylvania Bituminous Mine Subsidence Act prohibited mining that caused subsidence damage to public buildings, dwellings, and cemeteries. The Department of Environmental Resources required 50% of the coal beneath a protected structure to be kept in place as a means of providing surface support.

Issue: May a state impose restrictions on the use of private property without effecting a taking requiring the payment of compensation?

Rule: (Stevens, J.) A land-use regulation that is enacted to advance substantial legitimate state interests and does not deny an owner economically viable use of the land is not a taking in violation of the Fifth and Fourteenth Amendments.

Dissent: (Rehnquist, C.J.) A regulation taking away property interests and rooted more in economic concerns than in public safety should not be insulated from Fifth Amendment attack.

Lucas v. South Carolina Coastal Council (S. Ct. 1992)

Facts: Lucas paid $975,000 for two residential lots in South Carolina for the purpose of building single-family homes. For the purpose of preventing beach erosion, the South Carolina Legislature passed an act that prohibited development of the property, rendering it valueless.

Issue: Does a use restriction that dramatically reduces the value of private property constitute a taking under the Fifth and Fourteenth Amendments that requires payment of just compensation?

Rule: (Scalia, J.) When a regulation precludes *all* economically productive or useful uses of land, compensation must be paid, unless the state can identify common law principles (nuisance, property law, etc.) that would have prohibited the intended use under the circumstances.

Dissent: (Blackmun, J.) The majority decision is incorrect because the state has the power to prevent any use of property it finds to be harmful to its citizens, and a state statute is entitled to a presumption of constitutionality.

Dissent: (Stevens, J.) The chance that property might be rendered valueless is a risk inherent in investment. If this is the result of a generally applicable act motivated by a compelling purpose, such an act does not constitute a taking.

Nollan v. California Coastal Comm'n (S. Ct. 1987)

Facts: Ps, owners of beachfront property, received permission from D to rebuild their home on condition that the public gain an easement across their beach property between the seawall and the oceanside boundary.

Issue: May a state, as part of a continuous program to provide access to public areas, condition the issuance of a land-use permit upon the uncompensated conveyance of property for public access without effecting a taking under the Fifth and Fourteenth Amendments?

Rule: (Scalia, J.) A state's imposition of a permit condition on the use of private land must serve the same governmental purpose as an outright ban on development of the land. The lack of connection between the condition and the original purpose of the building restriction converts the permit condition into a taking requiring compensation.

Dissent: (Brennan, J.) The Court's demand for an exact match between the permit condition and the original governmental purpose of the building restriction is inconsistent with our standard for reviewing the rationality of a state's exercise of its police power for the welfare of its citizens.

Zablocki v. Redhail (S. Ct. 1978)

Facts: A Wisconsin statute provided that members of a certain class of Wisconsin residents could not marry, within the state or elsewhere, without first obtaining a court order granting permission to marry. Marriages contracted in violation of the statute were both void and punishable as criminal offenses.
Issue: May a state, in pursuit of state interests, impose classifications on its residents significantly interfering with the exercise of a fundamental right?
Rule: A statutory classification significantly interfering with a fundamental right is invalid unless it is supported by sufficiently important state interests and is closely tailored to effectuate only those interests.
Dissent: (Rehnquist, J.) Traditional presumption of validity should be extended to this statute. Under the Equal Protection Clause the statute need only pass the "rational basis test" and under the Due Process Clause it need only be shown that it bears a rational relation to a constitutionally permissible objective.

Thornburgh v. American College of Obstetricians and Gynecologists (S. Ct. 1986)

Facts: The Pennsylvania Abortion Act imposed disclosure and reporting requirements on physicians and counselors of women seeking abortions.
Issue: May a state, to further legitimate compelling state interests, regulate the transmission of information between a woman and her professional medical advisor on issues involving childbearing?
Rule: Childbearing is a private sphere of individual liberty constitutionally protected from the reach of government. A state may not require the transmission of information within this private setting that would be an impediment to a woman's decision to have an abortion.

DeShaney v. Winnebago Dep't of Social Serv. (S. Ct. 1989)

Facts: DeShaney was beaten and permanently injured by his father, with whom he lived. Although social workers and other local officials received complaints regarding this abuse, they did not act to remove DeShaney from his father's custody. DeShaney asserted that this failure to act deprived him of his liberty in violation of the Due Process Clause.

Issue: Does the Due Process Clause protect against deprivations of liberty by private actors?

Rule: (Rehnquist, C.J.) The Due Process Clause is phrased as a limitation on the State's power to act, not as a guarantee of certain minimal levels of safety and security. It was intended to protect people from the state, not to ensure that the state protected them from each other. Thus, the Due Process Clause confers no affirmative right to governmental aid, even where such aid may be necessary to secure interests which the government itself may not deprive the individual.

Dissent: (Brennan, J.) While it is true that there is no general affirmative right to government assistance, if a state cuts off private sources of aid and then refuses aid itself, it cannot wash its hands of the harm that results from its inaction.

Dissent: (Blackmun, J.) The Fourteenth Amendment was designed to undue the formalistic legal reasoning that the Court engages in today. This case should be decided upon principles of fundamental justice, rather than rigid lines of action/inaction.

Saenz v. Roe (S. Ct. 1999)

Facts: California enacted a law restricting newcomers to the state to the level of welfare benefits they would have received from the recipient's former home state for a period of one year.

Issue: Does such a restriction impede a constitutionally protected right to travel?

Rule: (Stevens, J.) Such a restriction prevents newcomers into a state from being full and equal citizens of the new state upon establishing a bona fide residence in the new state, and thus violates the Fourteenth Amendment's Privileges and Immunities Clause. Both the majority and the dissents in the *Slaughter-House* cases recognized this aspect of the right to travel as a privilege or immunity of national citizenship.

Dissent: (Rehnquist, C.J.) The Court uses a provision that had previously lain dormant for over a century. Anyone affected by the California law has stopped traveling; thus the right to travel is not implicated. The Court's decision is inconsistent with decisions allowing states to charge higher college tuition rates for out-of-staters.

Lawrence v. Texas (S. Ct. 2003)

Facts: D was convicted of sodomy after police entered his home on a false tip and found him having sex with his same-sex partner.

Issue: Does the Due Process Clause protect non-commercial same-sex intimacy in a private home?

Rule: (Kennedy, J.) Case law, history and evolving understandings of privacy make it clear that same-sex intimacy is protected as a component of due process liberty.

Concurrence: (O'Connor, J.) The Texas law, by criminalizing same-sex but not opposite-sex sodomy, violates equal protection.

Dissent: (Scalia, J.) Laws restricting same-sex sex have a long history, and the precedential case of *Bowers v. Hardwick* was correct.

Note: This case overruled *Bowers v. Hardwick* (S. Ct. 1986), which upheld a sodomy prohibition against a due process challenge.

Washington v. Glucksberg (S. Ct. 1997)

Facts: P, a terminally ill patient, wished to have a doctor's assistance in committing suicide.

Issue: Does the Due Process Clause protect a terminally ill individual's right to commit suicide, or to seek the assistance of others in committing suicide?

Rule: (Rehnquist, C.J.) Such a right does not exist since there is no history of protecting this right in American society.

Concurrence: (Stevens, J.) While there is no open-ended constitutional right to commit suicide, there may be times when an individual's interest in hastening one's death is entitled to constitutional protection.

Stenberg v. Carhart (S. Ct. 2000)

Facts: P challenged Nebraska's law restricting "partial birth" abortions.

Issue: Do bans on certain types of abortion procedures, without exceptions for maternal health, constitute an "undue burden" on the right to an abortion?

Rule: (Breyer, J.) Restrictions on particular types of abortions, when those types may sometimes be the safest or most effective methods, constitute undue burdens when they lack an exception for the health of the mother.

Dissent: (Kennedy, J.) The undue burden test was not meant to impose such draconian limits on states' authority to restrict abortions.

Troxel v. Granville (S. Ct. 2000)

Facts: P challenged Washington law allowing a state court to allow child visitation any time such visitation was in the best interest of the child, even if the parent objected.

Issue: Does the lack of parental control over court-ordered visitation decisions violate parental rights under the Due Process Clause?

Rule: (O'Connor, J.) (plurality of four Justices) The statute's complete lack of deference to the parent's wishes, the lack of any determination that the parent is unfit, and the parent's willingness to accept some child visitations all combine to make the statute an unconstitutional abridgement of the parent's fundamental right to make decisions about her children.

Dissent: (Stevens, J.) Attention should be paid to the due process interests of the child in being able to continue to develop relationships with other family members such as the grandparents seeking visitation in this case.

Dissent: (Scalia, J.) There is not an unenumerated due process right of a parent to control the upbringing of her child.

Dolan v. Tigard (S. Ct. 1994)

Facts: P, a store owner, sued D city when, as a condition of approving her request to pave and expand her parking lot, D required her to devote some of her land to a bike path and some land as green space.

Issue: Are these requirements, which would constitute takings of private property if simply demanded of the owner, constitutional as conditions for the granting of a permit?

Rule: (Rehnquist, C.J.) There must be rough proportionality between the harm caused by the requested development and the conditions demanded for the permit; thus, for example, there must be at least some showing of the amount of extra traffic the larger parking lot would cause, in order to justify the requirement of a bike path.

Dissent: (Stevens, J.) Local governments need the flexibility to demand conditions for permits, in order to mitigate problems such development might cause, without having to prove exactly the magnitude of the harm caused.

Palazzolo v. Rhode Island (S. Ct. 2001)

Facts: P, owner of property, took title after enactment of a land-use regulation, which he then challenged as a taking.

Issue: Did the regulation constitute a background principle of property law under *Lucas v. South Carolina Coastal Comm'n*, to which the property was subject upon purchase, and thus not a taking, since it was in force when the owner purchased the property?

Rule: (Kennedy, J.) The date of the enactment's restriction is irrelevant to the takings question; a contrary rule would effectively put an expiration date on the Takings Clause.

BMW of North America v. Gore (S. Ct. 1996)

Facts: P, purchaser of a new BMW, sued BMW after he learned that his car had been repainted to repair damage from a hailstorm. P won a verdict and was awarded compensatory damages of $4,000 and punitive damages of $4 million, later reduced to $2 million. BMW appealed.

Issue: Does the Due Process Clause place limits on the imposition of punitive damages?

Rule: (Stevens, J.) The damage awards violate the Due Process Clause, given the massive disparity between it and the compensatory award, the lack of reprehensibility of BMW's conduct, and the lack of any domestic interest Alabama might have in punishing such conduct.

Dissent: (Scalia, J.) The Due Process Clause does not impose limits on punitive damage awards.

Roe v. Wade (S. Ct. 1973)

Facts: Ps, a pregnant single woman, a childless married couple, and a physician, challenged a Texas law that made it a crime for a woman to procure an abortion except "by medical advice for the purpose of saving the life of the mother."

Issue: May a state impose regulations restricting a woman's right to terminate a pregnancy?

Rule: (Blackmun, J.) A woman's right to terminate a pregnancy in consultation with her physician is an area of privacy constitutionally protected. State regulations limiting those rights are justified only by showing a "compelling state interest" narrowly drawn to effect only the legitimate state interest at stake.

Dissent: (White, J.) Since this is an issue upon which reasonable men may disagree and to which there is no explicit constitutional bar, the Court should leave such decisions to the people and the political processes of each state.

Harris v. McRae (S. Ct. 1980)

Facts: Congress prohibited the use of any federal funds to reimburse the cost of abortions under the Medicaid program, except under certain specified circumstances.

Issue: Does Congress' selective subsidization of certain medically necessary abortions contravene the liberty or equal protection guarantees of the Constitution?

Rule 1: (Stewart, J.) The liberty protected under the Due Process Clause affords protection against unwarranted government interference with freedom of choice in the context of certain personal decisions. It does not confer an entitlement to such funds as may be necessary to realize all the advantages of that liberty.

Rule 2: (Stewart, J.) Selective subsidization of certain medically necessary abortions does not violate any substantive liberties or create a constitutionally suspect classification. Selective subsidization creates incentives that make childbirth a more attractive alternative than abortion for persons eligible for federal medical assistance. Therefore, the measure is rationally and directly related to the congressional objective in protecting potential life.

Dissent: (Brennan, J.) The Court has established that a pregnant woman has a right to be free from state interference in her choice to have an abortion. The denial of public funds for medically necessary abortions plainly intrudes upon this constitutionally protected right, as by design and effect it serves to coerce indigent pregnant women to bear children that they would otherwise elect not to have.

Webster v. Reproductive Health Services (S. Ct. 1989)

Facts: Reproductive Health Services challenged the constitutionality of a Missouri statute regulating the performance of abortions. Of the act's 20 provisions, 5 were under consideration: (1) "findings" by the state legislature that "life begins at conception," and "unborn children have protectable interests in life, health, and well-being"; (2) a requirement that all state laws be interpreted to provide unborn children with the same rights enjoyed by other persons; (3) a provision requiring physicians, prior to performing an abortion on a woman whom they reasonably believe to be more than 20 weeks pregnant, perform medical tests to determine whether the fetus is viable; (4) a prohibition on the use of public employees and facilities to perform abortions not necessary to save the mother's life; and (5) a prohibition on the use of public funds, employees, or facilities to "encourage or counsel" a woman to have an abortion not necessary to save her life.

Issue 1: May a state express a value judgment that favors childbirth over abortion?

Rule 1: (Rehnquist, C.J.) *Roe v. Wade* does not limit the authority of a state to make a value judgment favoring childbirth over abortion, but merely prevents the state from using that value judgment to justify an otherwise invalid abortion regulation.

Issue 2: May a state prohibit the use of public facilities for the performance of abortions not necessary to save the mother's life?

Rule 2: The Due Process Clauses generally confer no affirmative right to government aid. The decision to withhold the use of public facilities for the performance of abortions leaves the woman with the same choices as if the state had decided not to operate any public hospitals at all.

Issue 3: May a state require the performance of viability tests after only 20 weeks of pregnancy before allowing a physician to perform an abortion?

Rule 3: (Rehnquist, C.J., writing for a plurality) The viability testing requirement permissibly furthers the state's legitimate interest in protecting potential human life. Although the performance of these tests occurs before the start of the third trimester, and thus would permit the state to regulate abortions during the second trimester for reasons other than the protection of the mother's health (in direct conflict with *Roe*), the doubt cast upon the constitutionality of this statute is a result of the unworkability of the rigid *Roe* trimester framework, and not a flaw in the statute itself.

Concurrence: (O'Connor, J.) The viability testing requirement does not conflict with any of the Court's past decisions concerning state regulation of abortion, including *Roe*. The tests merely further the state's legitimate interest in protecting potential life when viability is possible.

Concurrence: (Scalia, J.) *Roe v. Wade* should be overruled. To keep control of this political issue distorts the public perception of the role of this Court.

Dissent: (Blackmun, J.) There is no need to reconsider *Roe*. The viability testing provisions impose significant additional health risks on both the pregnant woman and the fetus, and bear no rational relation to the state's interest in protecting fetal life.

Partial Dissent: (Stevens, J.) The viability testing provisions are constitutional for the reasons stated by Justice O'Connor. However, the legislature's finding that life begins at conception, in the absence of a secular purpose, violates the Establishment Clause of the First Amendment.

Cruzan v. Director, Missouri Dep't of Health (S. Ct. 1990)

Facts: Nancy Cruzan was severely injured in a car accident. She was left in a "persistent vegetative state" and had virtually no chance of regaining her mental faculties. Her parents brought suit to have the hospital terminate the artificial nutrition and hydration procedures.

Issue 1: Does the Constitution grant individuals a "right to die"?

Rule 1: (Rehnquist, J.) A competent person has a constitutionally protected liberty interest in refusing unwanted medical treatment.

Issue 2: May a state require a surrogate decision maker acting in behalf of an incompetent patient to provide clear and convincing evidence of the incompetent's wishes as to the withdrawal of life-sustaining treatment?

Rule 2: As a state has a legitimate interest in protecting an individual's "right to die," a state may require an incompetent patient's surrogate decision maker to demonstrate clear and convincing evidence that the action of the surrogate conforms as best it may to the wishes expressed by the patient while competent.

Concurrence: (O'Connor, J.) Because our notions of liberty are inextricably entwined with our idea of physical freedom and self-determination, requiring a competent adult to endure life-sustaining procedures against her will burdens the patient's liberty, dignity, and freedom to determine the course of her own treatment. Furthermore, states may have a duty to give effect to the decisions of a surrogate decision maker in order to protect the patient's liberty interest in refusing medical treatment.

Dissent: (Brennan, J.) The clear and convincing standard imposed by the state in determining whether the decision of a surrogate decision maker comports with the wishes of an incompetent individual in terminating life-sustaining treatment is unrealistic and burdens the right of an individual to forgo life-sustaining treatment. Too few people execute living wills in anticipation of becoming vegetative, and the testimony of close friends and family members may be the best evidence available of what the patient's choice would be.

Dissent: (Stevens, J.) The meaning and completion of an incompetent patient's life should be controlled by persons who have her best interests at heart, not by a state legislature concerned only with the "preservation of human life."

Thornburgh v. American College of Obstetricians and Gynecologists (S. Ct. 1986)

Facts: Pennsylvania law imposed information, disclosure, and reporting requirements on physicians and counselors of pregnant women seeking abortions. P challenged the constitutionality of those provisions.

Issue: May a state regulate the transmission of information between a woman and her professional advisors on issues involving childbearing?

Rule: (Blackmun, J.) Childbearing is a private sphere of individual liberty constitutionally protected from the reach of government. A state may not require the transmission of information within this private setting which would be an impediment to a woman's decision to have an abortion.

Dissent: (O'Connor, J.) The state has imposed no undue burdens on the parties involved, so the state is justified in imposing such requirements.

Planned Parenthood of S.E. Pa. v. Casey (S. Ct. 1992)

Facts: Planned Parenthood challenged the Pennsylvania Abortion Control Act. It provided: (1) women seeking an abortion must give informed consent prior to the procedure and must be provided with certain information 24 hours in advance; (2) a minor must obtain informed consent of one of her parents or, if not feasible, a court; (3) a married woman must sign a statement indicating that she notified her husband; (4) compliance with these procedures is necessary if there is a medical emergency; and (5) reporting requirements were imposed on abortion facilities.

Issue: To what extent may states regulate abortion?

Rule: A state may enact laws that have the incidental effect of making it more difficult or expensive to procure an abortion, provided the law serves a valid purpose, is not designed to strike at the right itself, and does impose an *undue burden* (i.e., a substantial obstacle) on the woman's ability to make this decision. The various provisions of the Pennsylvania act are constitutional, except for the spousal notification requirement, which is a substantial obstacle to a woman's choice. Thus, this decision rejects the trimester framework established in *Roe v. Wade*. It reaffirms *Roe*'s essential holding by recognizing a woman's right to abortion before viability, confirming the state's power to restrict abortion after viability, and confirming the state's interest in protecting the health of the woman and the life of the fetus that may become a child.

Dissent: (Stevens, J.) A burden is undue if it is too severe or if it lacks a legitimate, rational justification. The 24-hour delay requirement and the provision of dissuasive information fail both parts of this test.

Dissent: (Blackmun, J.) The provisions requiring content-based counseling, a 24-hour delay, informed parental consent, and reporting of abortion-related information have been adjudicated before and should therefore be invalidated under principles of *stare decisis*.

Dissent: (Rehnquist, J.) The majority opinion claims to uphold *Roe* on the basis of *stare decisis* while in actuality it created a new undue-burden standard and never claimed that *Roe* was correct as an original matter. In fact, it should be reversed; abortion is not a fundamental right.

Dissent: (Scalia, J.) The states may permit abortion on demand but the Constitution does not require them to do so because (a) the Constitution says absolutely nothing about it, and (b) the traditions of American society have permitted abortion to be legally proscribed. The issue should be resolved by citizens trying to persuade one another and voting.

Bowers v. Hardwick (S. Ct. 1986)

Facts: A Georgia statute made it a criminal offense for anyone to engage in any form of sodomy.

Issue: May a state law criminalize certain private sexual activities between consenting adults without violating the federal Constitution?

Rule: (White, J.) The right of consenting adults to engage in particular sexual acts is not a fundamental right. Therefore, it is within the proper powers of a state to enact criminal sanctions to discourage sexual behavior it deems inappropriate.

Dissent: (Blackmun, J.) The issue in this case was not about "a fundamental right to engage in homosexual sodomy" as the Court asserts, but rather, about the broader issue of the "right to be left alone." That right should be analyzed in the light of the values underlying the constitutional right to privacy. Also, the Court erred in refusing to consider whether the

Georgia statute violates the Eighth or Ninth Amendments or the Equal Protection Clause of the Fourteenth Amendment.
Note: This case was overruled by *Lawrence v. Texas*.

Maher v. Roe (S. Ct. 1977)

Facts: Connecticut limited state Medicaid benefits for first-trimester abortions to those that are "medically necessary." To obtain the requisite authorization for the abortion, the woman had to submit a certificate from her attending physician stating that the abortion was medically necessary.
Issue: May a state limit the receipt of state medical benefits for first-trimester abortions only to abortions that are medically necessary without impinging upon a fundamental right protected by the Constitution?
Rule: (Powell, J.) The Constitution protects a woman from unduly burdensome interference with her freedom to decide whether to terminate her pregnancy. However, there is no constitutional limitation on the authority of a state to make a value judgment favoring childbirth over abortion and to implement that judgment by the allocation of public funds.
Dissent: (Brennan, J.) As a practical matter, many indigent women feel they have no choice but to carry their pregnancies to term because the state will pay for the associated medical services, even though they would have chosen to have abortions if the state had also provided funds for that procedure or if the state had provided funds for neither procedure. This disparity in funding clearly operates to coerce indigent pregnant women to bear children they would not otherwise choose to have. Also, the claim that the regulation impinges one's fundamental right to privacy is never addressed by the Court.

City of Akron v. Akron Center for Reproductive Health (S. Ct. 1983)

Facts: A 1978 Akron ordinance regulated abortion by requiring that all abortions performed after the first trimester be performed in a hospital; parental notification and consent for abortions to be performed on minors; physician statements regarding the viability of the fetus; a 24-hour waiting period before the abortion could be performed; and humane disposal of fetal remains.
Issue: When may a state regulate abortions to further its health interests?
Rule: (Powell, J.) A state's interest in health regulation becomes compelling at approximately the end of the first trimester. Even then, however, the state's regulation may only be upheld if it is reasonably designed to further that state interest. The Akron regulations at issue do not serve to inform a woman's decision in this area, but rather place constitutionally significant obstacles in her path.

Dissent: (O'Connor, J.) The *Roe* trimester framework is on a collision course with itself. As the medical risks of abortion decrease, the point at which the state may regulate for reasons of maternal health is moved further toward actual childbirth; as medical science advances, the point of viability is moved further back toward conception. At any stage of the pregnancy there is the potential for human life. Thus, a state may regulate abortion at any time so long as it does not unduly burden a woman's freedom to terminate her pregnancy.

Lingle v. Chevron USA (S. Ct. 2005)

Facts: A Hawaii statute limited the rents oil companies could charge to their retail dealers for leasing service stations. P, an oil company, alleged that the statute took its property without just compensation. The appellate court tested the statute by asking whether it "substantially advanced a legitimate government interest," a standard taken from *Agins v. Tiburon*, 447 U.S. 255 (1980).

Issue: Did the appellate court apply the right standard?

Rule: (O'Connor, J.) No. While a takings case, *Agins* imported the "substantially advances" standard from due process cases. Takings claims, unless they involve (1) a physical appropriation, (2) destruction of all economic value of the property, or (3) an exaction in exchange for a permit, are tested by the standard from *Penn Central v. New York*, 438 U.S. 104 (1978), which requires examination of the economic effect of the regulation, the extent to which it destroys investment-backed expectations, and the character of the regulation.

Concurrence: (Kennedy, J.) The holding today does not remove the possibility that a statute may so unfairly impose retroactive liability on a party as to violate substantive due process.

Kelo v. City of New London (S. Ct. 2005)

Facts: The City of New London began a redevelopment plan that involved condemning houses in a neighborhood, paying compensation to the owners, and transferring the land to other private parties who would use it to build various private facilities it was hoped would create jobs. P, a homeowner in the affected area, sued, alleging that the redevelopment project was not a public purpose and thus that the city did not have the authority to condemn her home under the Takings Clause.

Issue: Is a redevelopment plan involving transfer of private property from one private party to another a "public use" that authorizes government to take private property as long as it pays just compensation?

Rule: (Stevens, J.) When, as here, the redevelopment plan is not adopted simply to benefit a group of private individuals, the public use requirement does not stand in the way of a redevelopment plan that the government had concluded would produce jobs. The "public use" requirement is satisfied if there is a public purpose to the condemnation plan.

Concurrence: (Kennedy, J.) When confronted with a plausible allegation that government is using its eminent domain power to favor particular private parties a court should undertake a careful scrutiny of the record to make sure this is not the case. The lower court did that here and found no such favoritism.

Dissent: (O'Connor, J.) The majority's analysis would allow government to take property and transfer it to another owner anytime the second owner could put it to a higher use, thus making the "public use" clause useless as an assurance that private property can only be taken for reasons that benefit the public.

Dissent: (Thomas, J.) The Court's equation of "public use" with public purpose, dating from the late nineteenth century, is flawed. "Public use" should be understood to mean, literally, use by the public or the government.

Town of Castle Rock v. Gonzalez (S. Ct. 2005)

Facts: P was the beneficiary of a restraining order taken out against her ex-husband. When the ex-husband violated the order P notified the police and sought enforcement of the order. The police delayed and the ex-husband returned and killed P's children. P sued, alleging violation of her due process rights to prompt enforcement of the restraining order.

Issue: Did P have a property interest, protected by procedural due process, in prompt enforcement of the restraining order?

Rule: (Scalia, J.) There is no property interest where, as here, enforcement of the restraining order was subject to the police's discretion to make decisions about which laws to enforce. State law did not mandate arrest in response to violations of restraining orders, thus it did not create an entitlement amounting to a property interest protected by procedural due process.

Concurrence: (Souter, J.) P seeks a property interest in a procedure, rather than in a substantive entitlement. Such interests in procedure do not constitute property for due process purposes.

Dissent: (Stevens, J.) The trial court found that the state restraining order statute imposed a mandatory obligation on police departments, thus creating a property interest. We should defer to that court's understanding of the law of the state in which it sits.

Gonzalez v. Carhart (S. Ct. 2007)

Facts: After the Supreme Court struck down a state law banning "partial-birth" abortions because the law lacked an exception for the health of the mother, Congress enacted a similar law, including in it a fact-finding that this type of procedure was never necessary for the mother's health. Doctors who perform abortion sued.

Issue: Is the law unconstitutional under the requirement that abortion restrictions must always include an exception for the health of the mother?
Rule: (Kennedy, J.) The law is constitutional. It was not enacted for the purpose of creating an obstacle to a woman's right to choose an abortion; rather, it was enacted to protect innocent life from a brutal procedure and to protect the medical community's ethics and reputation. Moreover, there is scientific dispute about whether the procedure is ever necessary for a woman's health; thus, Congress has the latitude to make a finding on this contested issue. We reject here a facial challenge; if a particular woman alleges that the prohibition would harm her health she can sue to have the law struck down as applied to her.
Concurrence: (Thomas, J.) The majority correctly applies our abortion precedent. But I would overrule that precedent, including *Roe v. Wade*.
Dissent: (Ginsburg, J.) The Court's decision is contrary to our precedents, which require that abortion restrictions have exceptions for women's health. This procedure has been found necessary and proper in certain cases by the American College of Obstetricians and Gynecologists, the doctors most intimately involved with abortion decisions. If there is doubt about an issue like this then there is a risk that women's health will be harmed by this type of prohibition.

District of Columbia v. Heller (S. Ct. 2008)

Facts: D.C. law prohibits the keeping of a loaded gun in the home.
Issue: Does this law violate the Second Amendment's right to keep and bear arms?
Rule: (Scalia, J.) At the time of its enactment the Second Amendment was understood to protect an individual right to keep and bear arms. The prefatory statement about a "well regulated militia" only provided the reason for protecting the right, not the substance of the right itself. While certain gun restrictions remain constitutional, a ban on the home possession of a loaded gun for self-defense by someone not mentally ill or a felon is not constitutional.
Dissent: (Stevens, J.) The history from the drafting era shows that the Amendment was designed to protect the right of Americans to form effective militias. Even if the evidence were close respect for precedent favoring the militia interpretation would counsel rejecting the claim.
Dissent: (Breyer, J.) Even assuming that the right at issue is an individual right the D.C. law should be upheld as a reasonable restriction on the right, given the problem of gun violence and the only slight degree to which the law restricts individuals' rights to possess guns.
Note: The *Heller* decision did not face the question of whether the Second Amendment applies against the states, since the law was a federal one for the District of Columbia. As of 2009, this issue remains potentially unsettled.

CHAPTER 8

Equal Protection

I. OVERVIEW

A. The Equal Protection Clause

The Fourteenth Amendment provides that "no state shall make or enforce any law which shall deny to any person within its jurisdiction the equal protection of the laws." The Due Process Clause of the Fifth Amendment applies to the federal government. Both Clauses employ the same tests.

B. The Equal Protection Clause applies to:

1. State and federal actions, and

2. The making of classes. This does not include the determination of whether an individual falls within a specified class. Note, however, that the Court has allowed plaintiffs to state an equal protection claim even without alleging that they are members of a particular class that is suffering discrimination. *Village of Willowbrook v. Olech* (2000).

C. Standards

The Court employs three standards of review to determine constitutional violations under the Equal Protection Clause:

1. Mere Rationality Test;

2. Mid-Level or Heightened Scrutiny Test; and

3. Strict Judicial Scrutiny Test

II. STANDARDS OF REVIEW

A. Mere Rationality Test

1. Generally

Usually, a state's economic and social laws would be subjected to the mere rationality test. The statutory classification is upheld if it could conceivably bear a rational relationship to a permissible governmental objective.

2. Arbitrariness

In determining whether a law bears a rational relationship to a permissible governmental objective, the Court looks to see if the law is "purely arbitrary" in its classification. A state law will not be stricken merely because it is underinclusive, nor is it necessary to prove mathematically the means-end link.

3. Usually Stricken

If a state law is stricken under the mere rationality test, it is usually because the government objective involved is illegitimate. The invocation of the mere rationality test usually signals that the state law will withstand the equal protection challenge. At times, however, the Court performs a more stringent version of rational basis review.

B. Mid-Level Scrutiny Test

1. Generally

This test is usually applied to actions concerning neither a suspect class nor a fundamental right, but a quasi-suspect class.

2. Substantial Relation

To be valid under the Mid-Level Scrutiny test, a law must be substantially related to achieving an important governmental objective. Therefore, the means-end fit must be reasonably tight, but need not be the only way of achieving the objective.

3. Explicit Objective

The statutory objective itself must be explicitly stated by the legislature; the Court will not hypothesize (as it would in a Mere Rationality Test) about the aims of the legislature.

C. Strict Judicial Scrutiny Test

1. Generally

Strict Judicial Scrutiny is employed when the classification is "suspect" or when a fundamental right protected by the Constitution is involved.

2. When Upheld

Under Strict Judicial Scrutiny, a classification is upheld only if both of the following components are fulfilled:

a. Necessary

The classification must be necessary in that there is no alternative method of accomplishing the state objective.

b. Compelling

The state interest must be compelling rather than merely important or permissible.

3. Rarely Upheld

When strict judicial scrutiny is applied, the classification is rarely upheld. There are exceptions, however, e.g., *Grutter v. Bollinger* (2003).

III. SUSPECT CLASSIFICATIONS

A. Factors

In determining whether a classification is suspect, the Court looks at two factors:

1. Perennial Loser

Whether the classified group is frequently the object of discrimination such that the group is deemed a "perennial loser in the political struggle"; and

2. Intentional

Whether the discrimination in the challenged statute was intentional.

Intentional discrimination can be shown in three ways:

a. *De jure* discrimination, in that the statute is facially discriminatory;

b. Discriminatory administration exists;

c. *De facto* discrimination, in that a showing has been made by circumstantial evidence of a discriminatory purpose. This occurs when a statute is not facially discriminatory but has such an effect that purposeful discrimination can be inferred. Purposeful discrimination can be inferred from:

MNEMONIC: **CLAD**

   i. **C**ommunity's prior acts of discrimination;

   ii. **L**egislative history of statute;

   iii. **A**bsence of other reasons for passing the statute; and

   iv. **D**eparture from normal procedures in passing the statute.

   Note: A showing of disproportionate racial impact is not in itself sufficient to prove discriminatory purpose.

B. Suspect Classes

1. Race or National Origin

Under equal protection analysis, the only truly "suspect" classification is one based on race or national origin, as the Equal Protection Clause was designed to remedy invidious discrimination against blacks.

However, strict judicial scrutiny is not applied to racial classifications when they are used in affirmative action programs. Instead, a slightly more relaxed version of strict scrutiny is applied, in which the classification must be tightly connected (but not absolutely necessary) to an important governmental objective.

a. Employment and Admissions

In minority employment and admissions practices, the race or national origin of applicants may be considered as a factor, but strict quotas are unconstitutional.

b. Gender
Mid-level scrutiny is applied to affirmative action classifications based on gender.

2. Alienage
The Court has applied the strict scrutiny standard to alienage classification in the cases of state welfare benefits and civil service employment. However, exceptions to the application of the strict scrutiny standard are abundant.

C. Quasi-Suspect Classes
Since statutes are nearly always stricken when strict scrutiny is invoked and nearly always upheld under the mere rationality test, the Court has informally designated most classifications as semi-suspect, requiring mid-level or heightened review.

1. Gender Classifications
a. While the Court has fluctuated in its treatment of gender as a classification, it has settled upon mid-level scrutiny.
b. The Equal Protection Clause does not call for equal treatment when an actual difference between the classes exists. For example, the physical differences between men and women justify a criminal law making men and not women capable of committing statutory rape.

2. Alienage
a. Mid-level scrutiny is generally applied where the federal government is involved, since the federal government has exclusive responsibility for the supervision of aliens, even in the administration of welfare benefits.
b. Mid-level scrutiny is also applied where aliens might endanger representative government, for example, with a citizenship requirement in order to hold elective office.

3. Illegitimacy
a. The Court applies mid-level scrutiny to illegitimacy classifications, since discrimination against illegitimates has never been as severe as racial and gender discrimination. However, the Court applies greater than minimal scrutiny because the government has no legitimate interest in promoting "legitimate" family relationships.
b. Statutes requiring proof of acknowledged paternity, dependency, and support prior to deceased's death before the distribution of survivor benefits are generally upheld. However, statutes that create insurmountable barriers to an illegitimate inheriting from a deceased's estate are generally struck down.

D. Non-Suspect Class
Mental retardation or mental illness is not a quasi-suspect class, since the class is neither politically powerless nor the victim of

discrimination. However, the mere rationality test is applied with rigor when a statute makes a classification adversely affecting the mentally impaired.

IV. FUNDAMENTAL RIGHTS

A. Generally

An equal protection challenge involving a fundamental right triggers strict judicial scrutiny. Two kinds of rights are deemed "fundamental":

1. Those explicitly guaranteed by the Constitution, and
2. Those felt to be so important that they are considered implicitly granted by the Constitution, such as the right to vote.

B. Right to Privacy

1. The right to privacy was guaranteed in *Roe v. Wade*. If the equal protection challenge involves a privacy right, the strict scrutiny standard is applied.
2. This right does not extend very far with respect to providing monetary aid to indigent women seeking abortions. The Court declared that the poor are necessarily limited in many choices because of their lack of money, and while the choice to have an abortion is guaranteed, the state need not provide money for that choice. State statutes selectively subsidizing the cost of abortion are adjudged under the mid-level scrutiny test.

C. Access to Courts

Access to a court is a fundamental right if the right granted by the court is fundamental or if the court is the sole forum in which state-created relationships can be resolved. Fees are often waived in criminal cases and in divorce proceedings. However, if the court is not granting a fundamental right, then filing fees and other such restrictions may be upheld.

D. Right to Travel

1. The right to travel within the United States is guaranteed to all persons by the federal system of government.
2. States may not penalize newer residents (e.g., denying them welfare benefits) or reward older residents (e.g., preferential civil service policy or issuing greater rewards to older residents).
3. State universities can deny lower tuition rates to non-residents, since higher education is not a fundamental right.

E. Voting

1. The right to vote, even in state elections and other local elections, is fundamental, since it stems from the First Amendment.
2. States may not condition the exercise of a citizen's franchise upon the payment of a poll tax. However, states may require

that voters be of reasonable age and have resided in the state for a reasonable period of time. Other restrictions on voting, if they are necessary to achieve a compelling state interest, are upheld. For example, states may impose voter identification requirements as an anti-fraud measure if they do not impose a significant burden.

V. NON-FUNDAMENTAL PRINCIPLES

A. Necessities

Necessities such as welfare and education are not fundamental rights. While they are important, they are neither implicitly nor explicitly guaranteed by the Constitution. However, if a lack of wealth or education somehow deprives a person of the right to vote or the right to a day in court, deprivation of a fundamental right might be found.

CASE CLIPS

Railway Express Agency v. New York (S. Ct. 1949)

Facts: New York City prohibited advertising on business delivery vehicles unless the advertisement was for the owner's business. P sold space on its trucks for advertising that was unconnected with its own business.

Issue: Do practical road-safety regulations that discriminate against some motor vehicle operators violate the Equal Protection Clause?

Rule: (Douglas, J.) When a classification is rationally related to the accomplishment of a valid objective and is of a type not barred by the equal protection analysis, the regulation does not violate the Equal Protection Clause.

United States Railroad Retirement Board v. Fritz (S. Ct. 1980)

Facts: In 1974, the Railroad Retirement Act fundamentally restructured the railroad retirement system. Because the cost of paying of windfall benefits threatened the solvency of the system, the Act divided employees into groups, some of whom were denied the windfall benefits. The plaintiff class (which was denied windfall benefits) sought a declaratory judgment that the Act was unconstitutional under the Due Process Clause of the Fifth Amendment because it irrationally distinguished between classes of beneficiaries.

Issue: What is the standard of judicial review for determining whether social and economic legislation enacted by Congress violates the Fifth Amendment's Equal Protection Clause?

Rule: (Rehnquist, J.) Review of social and economic legislation that does not burden fundamental constitutional rights ends when Congress posits plausible reasons for the enactment of the legislation, thereby showing a rational relation to a permissible government objective.

Concurrence: (Stevens, J.) The classification is rationally related to the objective.

Dissent: (Brennan, J.) The classification is not rationally related to the objective.

Lyng v. International Union, United Auto Workers (S. Ct. 1988)

Facts: A 1981 amendment to the Food Stamp Act (OBRA §109) stated that no household shall become eligible to participate in the food stamp program during the time that any member of the household was on strike. In addition, a household allotment could not increase merely because, due to the strike, the striker's income decreased.

Issue: Does the 1981 Food Stamp Act amendment, which denies food stamps to households of striking workers, infringe upon associational or expressive rights under the First Amendment?

Rule: (White, J.) Denial of a government benefit to striking workers does not violate the First Amendment because it is rationally related to a legitimate governmental interest in maintaining neutrality in private labor disputes.

Dissent: (Marshall, J.) The amendment is unconstitutional because it excludes persons who may have no option of returning to work, and is not neutral in labor disputes.

Loving v. Virginia (S. Ct. 1967)

Facts: A Virginia statute prohibited interracial marriages. P, an African-American woman, married a white man out-of-state. Upon return to Virginia, they were convicted of violating the ban on interracial marriages.

Issue: Does a state statute prohibiting interracial marriages violate the Equal Protection Clause of the Fourteenth Amendment?

Rule: (Warren, C.J.) Restricting the freedom to marry solely because of racial classifications violates the central meaning of the Equal Protection Clause of the Fourteenth Amendment. The Equal Protection Clause demands that racial classifications be subjected to the most rigid scrutiny and can only be justified on the showing of their necessity to some permissible state objective.

Palmore v. Sidoti (S. Ct. 1984)

Facts: P, a white man, sued his ex-wife, a white woman, for custody of their infant because of D's remarriage to an African-American man.

Issue: May a state divest a natural mother of custody of her infant because of her remarriage to a man of a different race without violating the Equal Protection Clause of the Fourteenth Amendment?

Rule: (Burger, C.J.) A core purpose of the Fourteenth Amendment is to eradicate governmentally imposed discrimination based on race. A state's goal of granting custody based on the best interest of an infant does not justify a racial classification which denies a natural mother who is a fit parent her constitutional right to rear her infant.

Brown v. Board of Education [Brown I — Constitutional Ruling] (S. Ct. 1954)

Facts: Kansas, South Carolina, Virginia, and Delaware prohibited African-American children from attending public schools on a nonsegregated basis in their respective communities.

Issue: Does the racial segregation of children in public schools, even though the facilities and other tangible factors are "equal," deprive minority children of equal educational opportunities in violation of the Equal Protection Clause of the Fourteenth Amendment?

Rule: (Warren, C.J.) In the field of public education, the doctrine of "separate but equal" has no place. Separate educational facilities are inherently unequal and state-provided education must be available to all on equal terms. If not, such educational policies violate the Equal Protection Clause of the Fourteenth Amendment.

Brown v. Board of Education [Brown II—The Implementation Decision] (S. Ct. 1955)

Facts: *Brown I* held racial discrimination in public education unconstitutional. All federal, state, and local laws requiring or permitting such discrimination had to conform to this holding.

Issue: How is the nondiscriminatory policy in public education enunciated in *Brown I* to be implemented in local public schools?

Rule: (Warren, C.J.) As full implementation of the nondiscriminatory policy of *Brown I* requires the solution of varied local school problems, the cases are remanded to the courts where they were heard originally. The courts must judicially review the actions of local school authorities to ensure good faith implementation of the principle of *Brown I*. In fashioning and effectuating the decrees, the courts will be guided by equitable principles.

Craig v. Boren (S. Ct. 1976)

Facts: An Oklahoma statute prohibited the sale of "non-intoxicating" 3.2% beer to males under the age of 21 and to females under the age of 18.

Issue: May a state impose gender-based distinctions in regulating the purchase of intoxicating and "non-intoxicating" drinks?

Rule: (Brennan, J.) To withstand an equal protection challenge, a gender-based classification must serve an important governmental objective and be substantially related to the achievement of a state objective. If not, the gender-based classification violates equal protection.

Concurrence: (Powell, J.) There is no fair and substantial relation between the distinction and the object.

Concurrence: (Stevens, J.) The regulation does not cope with the objective of traffic safety.

Dissent: (Rehnquist, J.) The Court subjected the statute to a more stringent standard of judicial review than most other types of classification. The challenged law need only pass the "rational basis" equal protection analysis.

City of Cleburne v. Cleburne Living Center (S. Ct. 1985)

Facts: D, acting pursuant to a municipal zoning ordinance, denied a special-use permit to operate a group home for the mentally retarded.

Issue 1: What is the appropriate standard of review for a city ordinance classification dealing with mental retardation?

Rule 1: (White, J.) Mental retardation is not a suspect classification. Thus, the rationality test and not the heightened standard of review is applied to a city ordinance dealing with mental retardation.

Issue 2: May a city require a special permit for the operation of a group home for the mentally retarded when other care and multiple dwelling facilities are freely permitted?

Rule 2: (White, J.) A city ordinance discriminating against the mentally retarded is valid if it is rationally related to a governmental objective; otherwise, the city action violates equal protection.

Concurrence/Dissent: (Marshall, J.) The principle that mental retardation *per se* cannot be a proxy for depriving retarded people of their rights without regard to variation in individual ability is correct. However, the city ordinance should be invalidated under the heightened scrutiny test, as it sought to deny the retarded the right to establish a home, which is a fundamental right embraced by the Due Process Clause.

Washington v. Davis (S. Ct. 1976)

Facts: P, an African-American police officer, challenged the validity of a qualifying test administered to applicants for positions as police officers. Whites had a higher pass rate than African Americans.

Issue: Is a qualifying test for public employment, neutral on its face and serving legitimate governmental objectives, invalid under equal protection because it adversely impacts a disproportionate number of one race than another?

Rule: (White, J.) A qualifying test for public employment with a racially disproportionate impact is valid under the equal protection guarantees of the Fifth and Fourteenth Amendments, unless the test can be traced to a racially discriminatory purpose.

McClesky v. Kemp (S. Ct. 1987)

Facts: A Georgia state court convicted, and sentenced to death, McClesky, a black, of murdering a white. Citing "the Baldus Study," which alleged that blacks were 4.3 times as likely to receive a death sentence than whites, McClesky contended that the Georgia capital sentencing scheme was administered in a racially discriminatory manner in violation of the Equal Protection Clause.

Issue: Does a defendant who alleges an equal protection violation have the burden of proving purposeful discrimination in his situation?

Rule: (Powell, J.) A defendant who alleges an equal protection violation has the burden of proving the existence of purposeful discrimination. McClesky must prove, which he has failed to do, that the decision makers in his case acted with discriminatory purpose. The inferences drawn from general statistics are not dispositive here.

Dissent: (Brennan, J.) There is unconstitutionality in the different risks of death sentencing faced by black defendants in Georgia.

Rogers v. Lodge (S. Ct. 1982)

Facts: The Burke County Board of Commissioners consisted of five members elected at-large by all qualified voters in the county. The county was never divided into districts, and no African-American candidate had ever been elected to the Board. P filed this suit on behalf of all African-American citizens of Burke County.

Issue: Does an at-large electoral system, neutral on its face but effecting a dilution of a minority group's voting power, violate the equal protection guarantees of the Fourteenth Amendment?

Rule: (White, J.) Purposeful discrimination must be proven to invalidate an at-large voting system on equal protection grounds. Evidence of historical discrimination and enforced socioeconomic depression are relevant factors from which to infer purposeful discrimination.

Dissent: (Powell, J.) This sociological evidence was rejected in *Mobile v. Bolden* as inadequate to show purposeful discrimination. Primary emphasis should be placed instead on objective factors to determine purposeful discrimination.

Swann v. Charlotte-Mecklenburg Board of Education (S. Ct. 1971)

Facts: Dissatisfied with the school authorities' progress to implement the public school desegregation program, the District Court appointed an expert and accepted his plan, which involved some grouping of outlying white schools with inner-city black schools and some busing of elementary school students in both directions.

Issue: When a local authority charged with correcting a constitutional violation fails, may a district court intervene and formulate policies to enforce the constitutional guarantees?

Rule: (Burger, C.J.) A district court possesses broad equitable powers to remedy constitutional violations and may intervene when local officials fail to effect constitutional guarantees.

Wengler v. Druggists Mutual Insurance Co. (S. Ct. 1980)

Facts: Under Missouri law, a widower was not entitled to death benefits unless he was mentally or physically incapacitated from wage earning or proved actual dependence on his wife's earnings. By contrast, a widow was entitled to death benefits without having to prove actual dependence on her husband's earnings.

Issue: Is administrative convenience a sufficient objective to support a gender-based classification?

Rule: (White, J.) To withstand an equal protection challenge, gender-based discrimination must serve important governmental objectives and the discriminatory means must be substantially related to the objective. Administrative convenience is an insufficient governmental objective to justify a gender-discrimination law.

Regents of the University of California v. Bakke (S. Ct. 1978)

Facts: D's medical school at U.C. Davis operated a dual admissions program. The special admissions program did not apply the regular admissions program's 2.5 grade point average cut-off point. P was a white applicant whose application was rejected twice.

Issue 1: In furtherance of a goal to diversify the student body, may a state university establish admissions qualifications based on race and ethnic background?

Rule 1: (Powell, J.) Admissions qualifications based on race and ethnic backgrounds, even those enacted to further a benign purpose, must be held to the same exacting judicial scrutiny as other racially discriminatory policies. Those policies are justified only upon the showing of compelling state interest.

Issue 2: May a state university consider the race or ethnic background of its applicants as relevant to its admissions program?

Rule 2: (Powell, J.) The substantial state interest in a diversified student body may be served by a properly devised admissions program involving competitive consideration of race and ethnic background. Such consideration does not violate the Equal Protection Clause.

Concurrence: (Brennan, J.) The Court's opinion means that government may take race into consideration when it acts not to demean or insult any racial group, but to remedy disadvantages cast on minorities by past racial prejudice which are substantiated by appropriate findings.

Metro Broadcasting, Inc. v. FCC (S. Ct. 1990)

Facts: In an effort to increase minority participation in the broadcast media, the FCC adopted two policies. First, the Commission considered minority ownership as a "plus" in comparative hearings, to be weighed together with all other relevant factors. Second, the FCC permitted licensees under investigation to assign their licenses to FCC-approved minority enterprises, in contrast to the general rule prohibiting such transfers.

Issue: Do minority preference policies violate the Fifth Amendment's equal protection provision?

Rule: (Brennan, J.) Benign race-conscious measures mandated by Congress, even if those measures are not remedial, are constitutionally permissible to the extent that they serve important governmental objectives within the power of Congress and are substantially related to achievement of those objectives.

Dissent: (Kennedy, J.) The minority preference policies at issue here should be subjected to strict scrutiny analysis, just as all other race-conscious legislation. Policies favoring certain races, especially when not enacted for remedial purposes, pose all the problems associated with the racially discriminatory legislation condemned by this Court in the past.

Dissent: (O'Connor, J.) The racial classifications used here by the FCC are not authorized by Section 5 of the Fourteenth Amendment, which grants Congress such power in remedial situations only. The lessened equal protection standard adopted by the Court, therefore, cannot be supported by precedent or by the text of the Constitution.

Fullilove v. Klutznick (S. Ct. 1980)

Facts: The Public Works Employment Act required that a state or local grantee of federal funds must use at least 10% of the funds to procure services or supplies from statutorily identified minority business enterprises.

Issue: May Congress, pursuant to its spending power, require racial and ethnic participation as a condition to the receipt of federal funds?

Rule: (Burger, C.J.) Congress possesses broad remedial powers to correct past and present discrimination and effect equal protection guarantees. Therefore, Congress may, upon appropriate findings, induce voluntary action to assure compliance with existing federal statutory or constitutional antidiscrimination provisions or may authorize and induce state action to avoid unlawful conduct.

Concurrence: (Powell, J.) Such a classification is valid to remedy an actual statutory or constitutional violation.

Dissent: (Stewart, J.) Equal protection prohibits invidious discrimination by government. The challenged provision of the Act bars a class, solely on the basis of race and ethnic background, from having the opportunity to receive a government benefit and should be invalidated.

Dissent: (Stevens, J.) This remedy is too general and does not try to right specific, previous discriminatory practices.

Wygant v. Jackson Board of Educ. (S. Ct. 1986)

Facts: In order to ease racial tensions in the community, D protected employees of certain minority groups against layoffs. As a result, nonminority teachers were laid off, while minority teachers with less seniority were retained.

Issue: In order to remedy the effects of prior discrimination, may preferential protection against layoffs be extended to some state employees based on their race or national origin without violating the Equal Protection Clause?

Rule: (Powell, J.) Discrimination based on a race classification violates the Equal Protection Clause of the Fourteenth Amendment unless the discrimination serves a compelling state purpose and is specifically and narrowly tailored to accomplish only that purpose. Societal discrimination is an insufficient and overexpansive basis on which to justify a racially classified remedy.

Dissent: (Marshall, J.) Any *per se* prohibition against layoff protection must rest upon a premise that the tradition of basing layoff decisions on seniority is so fundamental that its modification can never be permitted. Protection from layoff should be an available tool for achieving legitimate societal goals.

City of Richmond v. J.A. Croson Co. (S. Ct. 1989)

Facts: D adopted the Minority Business Utilization Plan requiring prime contractors to whom it awarded construction contracts to subcontract at least 30% of the dollar amount of the contract to one or more statutorily defined Minority Business Enterprises. The 30% set-aside did not apply to city contracts awarded to minority-owned prime contractors.

Issue: May a state or local entity, in order to ameliorate the effects of past discrimination, establish racial qualifications for the distribution of advantageous contracts?

Rule: (O'Connor, J.) Racial classifications are suspect classifications requiring strict judicial scrutiny. Such racially discriminatory provisions must serve a compelling state purpose and be narrowly tailored. An overly inclusive provision enacted primarily for administrative convenience without defining the scope of the discrimination and the extent of the necessary remedy violates equal protection.

Dissent: (Marshall, J.) Strict judicial scrutiny is the incorrect standard by which the set-aside provision should be adjudged. Intermediate level scrutiny is a more appropriate standard to judge a race-conscious classification designed to further remedial goals. The use of strict scrutiny discourages the remedying of past discrimination.

San Antonio Independent School District v. Rodriguez (S. Ct. 1973)

Facts: D relied heavily on local property taxes for funding, which resulted in substantial interdistrict disparities in expenditures per student. P sued on behalf of children of poor families living in districts with a low property tax base.

Issue: What is the proper equal protection test to be applied to a state public education financing system that relates per-pupil expenditure to the property wealth of the district?

Rule: (Powell, J.) Public education is not a right granted to individuals by the Constitution, and state financing of public education is a local fiscal matter. Therefore, the traditional standard of review, under which a state only has to show that its system bears some rational relationship to legitimate state purposes applies.

Dissent: (White, J.) The means of property taxes are not rationally related to the goal of public education.

Plyler v. Doe (S. Ct. 1982)

Facts: A Texas law allowed the withholding of state funds to school districts for the education of children not "legally admitted" into the United States. It also authorized the denial of enrollment in public schools to these children.

Issue: May a state deny school-age children who are illegal aliens access to the free public education it provides to citizens and legal aliens of the same age?

Rule: (Brennan, J.) Resident aliens are not a suspect class and education is not a fundamental right. Thus, free public education may be denied a given class if it is rationally related to a substantial state purpose. However, denial of education to aliens is not rationally related to such a purpose.

Dissent: (Burger, C.J.) Once the Court concedes that illegal aliens are not a suspect class and that education is not a fundamental right, the inquiry should be limited to whether the classification bears a rational relationship to a legitimate state purpose. A state could conclude that it has less responsibility to provide benefits for illegal aliens than it does for citizens.

Harper v. Virginia Board of Elections (S. Ct. 1966)

Facts: Virginia required residents to pay a poll tax of $1.50 as a precondition to voting. Proceeds from the tax supported local governmental programs, including schools.

Issue: Is a poll tax that is required to vote constitutional?

Rule: (Douglas, J.) Because wealth is a suspect classification and voting is a fundamental right, poll taxes are strictly scrutinized. Since wealth is irrelevant to intelligent participation in the voting process, poll taxes are violative of equal protection guarantees.

Dissent: (Black, J.) A state's desire to collect revenue and a belief that voters who pay a poll tax will be interested in furthering the state's welfare are rational reasons for a poll tax.

Kramer v. Union Free School District No. 15 (S. Ct. 1969)

Facts: New York education law provided that residents could vote in school district elections only if they owned or leased taxable real property or were parents or custodians of children enrolled in the local public schools within the district.

Issue: May a state condition the exercise of a resident's franchise in school district elections to holders of taxable real property within the district and parents and custodians of children enrolled in the local public schools?

Rule: (Warren, C.J.) Equal protection demands that a law that selectively distributes the franchise be scrutinized. Thus, the law must be necessary to achieve the articulated state goal and be narrowly drawn to affect only the goal involved.

Dissent: (Stewart, J.) Only the rational relationship test need be applied when the right invoked is not fundamental and the classification is not racial.

Douglas v. California (S. Ct. 1963)

Facts: P, an indigent criminal, sought to be represented by counsel in his direct appeal as of right to the appellate court in California. The court denied P's request after reviewing the record and concluding that "no good whatever would be served by appointment of counsel."

Issue: Does a state court procedure resulting in the denial of counsel to an indigent defendant pursuing an appeal as of right violate equal protection under the Fourteenth Amendment?

Rule: (Douglas, J.) Denial of counsel based on economic circumstances is a type of invidious discrimination which violates the equality demanded by the Fourteenth Amendment.

Dissent: (Harlan, J.) This case should be judged under the Due Process Clause and not the Equal Protection Clause, and the California procedure does not offend due process. Equal protection does not impose on the states "an affirmative duty to lift the handicaps flowing from differences in economic circumstances."

Shapiro v. Thompson (S. Ct. 1969)

Facts: Various states provided that welfare assistance would be denied to those applicants who had not lived within their jurisdictions for at least one year.

Issue: May a state, to protect the integrity of a fiscal assistance program, deny assistance to otherwise qualified welfare recipients who have not resided within its jurisdiction for at least one year?

Rule: (Brennan, J.) A state assistance program imposing a durational residency requirement on some recipients of public aid penalizes those who exercise the fundamental right to travel. To withstand a constitutional challenge, the state must show that the program promotes a compelling state interest and not just show a rational relation.

Dissent: (Warren, C.J.) Congress has imposed residence requirements under the commerce power. States should be allowed to make similar requirements under the commerce power, too.

Zobel v. Williams (S. Ct. 1982)

Facts: Alaska enacted a dividend program to distribute proceeds of a mineral fund directly to citizens 18 years or older. Each adult citizen received one dividend unit for each year of residency subsequent to 1959, the first year of statehood.

Issue: Does a statutory scheme by which a state distributes income derived from its natural resources based on the length of each citizen's residence violate the equal protection rights of newer citizens?

Rule: (Burger, C.J.) A state statute creating distinctions based on length of residency is valid under equal protection analysis only if the statute serves a legitimate state interest that is rationally related to the distinction. There is no such relation involving length of residency.

Dissent: (Rehnquist, J.) This is an economic regulation that is presumptively valid. It is also rationally related to a legitimate state interest.

State v. Post (1845)

Facts: Proponents for the abolition of slavery argued that the institution of slavery violated the New Jersey Constitution, which declared that "all men are by nature free and independent, and have certain natural and unalienable rights, among which are those of enjoying and defending life and property, acquiring, possessing and protecting property, and of pursuing and obtaining safety and happiness."

Issue: Does the existence of slavery within a state violate a state constitution that upholds the freedom and independence of all men?

Rule: (Nevius, J.) Freedom and independence are not absolute terms, and rights emanating from these concepts must be understood within the context of their declaration. The state constitution recognized the existence of slavery, and absent clear and definite provision for its abolition, the institution of slavery continues to be compatible with those unalienable rights enunciated in the Constitution.

Dred Scott v. Sandford (S. Ct. 1857)

Facts: P, a slave, was taken by his master from Missouri to Illinois. After two years they moved to Minnesota, then to part of the Louisiana Territory. They eventually returned to Missouri where P was sold to D. Slavery was prohibited in Illinois by the state constitution and in the Louisiana Territory by federal statute. P argued that the various provisions abolishing slavery in the areas he had traveled made him a free man.

Issue 1: Is the slave class a part of the citizenry and able to invoke the court's jurisdiction premised on diversity of citizenship?

Rule 1: (Taney, C.J.) The Constitution's use of the word "citizens" does not include and was never intended to include the slave class. Therefore, slaves are not entitled to the rights and privileges which the Constitution bestows on its citizens, including the invocation of diversity of citizenship jurisdiction.

Issue 2: Is Congress authorized to pass a law prohibiting the ownership of slaves in certain territories?

Rule 2: (Taney, J.) Slaves are property and Congress may not deprive citizens of their property without due process of law.

Plessy v. Ferguson (S. Ct. 1896)

Facts: A Louisiana statute provided for separate railway carriages for whites and African Americans. P, a man of seven-eighth Caucasian and one-eighth African blood, violated the statute when he occupied a vacant seat in a coach reserved for white passengers.

Issue: May a state, pursuant to its police powers, promulgate laws requiring the separation of the black and white races in public conveyances without violating the equal protection guarantees of the Fourteenth Amendment?

Rule: (Brown, J.) A state may, pursuant to its police power, enact reasonable legislation requiring the separation of white and African-American citizens in places where they are liable to be brought into contact. Established usages, customs, and traditions; the promotion of comfort; and the preservation of public peace and good order may be considered in determining what is reasonable.

Dissent: (Harlan, J.) The fundamental objection is that the statute interferes with personal freedom. If a white man and an African-American man choose to occupy the same public conveyance on a public highway, it is their right to do so. No government, proceeding alone on the grounds of race, can prevent it without infringing the personal liberty of each.

Keyes v. School District No. 1 (S. Ct. 1973)

Facts: The Denver school system was racially segregated, but evidence of *de jure* segregation was only found with regard to one outlying community. The district court ordered district-wide desegregation.
Issue: Upon a finding of intentional school segregation in one part of the school system, who has the burden of proving intentional segregation in the remaining parts of the school system?
Rule: (Brennan, J.) A finding of intentional segregation in a meaningful portion of a school system creates a *prima facie* case of unlawful segregative design on the part of school authorities. The burden of proving that other segregated schools within the system are not also the result of intentionally segregative actions shifts to the school authorities.
Dissent: (Rehnquist, J.) A finding of racial segregation in one area of a school district is not enough to require that school boards affirmatively act to achieve racial mixing in schools where such mixing is not achieved through neutrally drawn boundaries.
Dissent: (Powell, J.) The Court should abandon the *de jure/de facto* distinction and hold that wherever segregated public schools exist, public authorities are presumed to be responsible and must meet a nationally applicable burden to demonstrate they are operating genuinely integrated schools.

New York City Transit Authority v. Beazer (S. Ct. 1979)

Facts: One of D's rules prohibited the employment of persons using narcotic drugs. This rule was applied to persons using methadone, which is widely used to fight heroin addiction.
Issue: Does a public entity's policy against employing narcotic drug users, including individuals using narcotic drugs for medical treatment, violate the Equal Protection Clause?
Rule: (Stevens, J.) Narcotic drug users are not a suspect class. A policy which excludes this class from employment need only be rationally related to the achievement of its objective. The prohibition against the employment of narcotic drug users is rationally related to the objective of safety and efficiency in the transportation business.
Dissent: (White, J.) Many persons now suffer from or may again suffer from some handicap related to employability. To single out narcotic drug

users is an arbitrary assignment of burdens among classes that are similarly situated with respect to the proffered objective, and that is the type of invidious choice forbidden by the Equal Protection Clause.

Strauder v. West Virginia (S. Ct. 1879)

Facts: A West Virginia statute precluded African Americans from serving on juries. P, an African-American man, challenged the constitutionality of his conviction for murder because African Americans were ineligible to serve on the grand or petit jury that convicted him.

Issue: In prescribing qualifications, may a state preclude citizens on the basis of race?

Rule: (Strong, J.) The Equal Protection Clause of the Fourteenth Amendment prohibits a state from withholding from any citizen the equal protection of the law. To deny otherwise qualified African Americans the right to participate in the administration of the law is a denial of equal protection of the law.

Korematsu v. United States (S. Ct. 1944)

Facts: P, an American citizen of Japanese descent, was convicted of violating Civilian Exclusion Order No. 34, which excluded all persons of Japanese ancestry from San Leandro, California, a Military Area.

Issue: During wartime, may Congress exclude some American citizens considered to be security risks from certain areas to prevent espionage and sabotage?

Rule: (Black, J.) Restrictions on the movement of citizens are constitutionally justified only under circumstances of direct emergency and peril. A threatened attack by hostile forces poses the gravest imminent danger, and Congress, pursuant to its power to protect, may take prompt and adequate security measures to ensure safety.

Dissent: (Murphy, J.) The exclusion of all persons of Japanese descent must rely for its reasonableness upon the assumption that all persons of such ancestry may have a dangerous tendency to commit sabotage and espionage. It is difficult to believe that reason, logic, or experience could be marshaled to support such an assumption.

Washington v. Seattle School District No. 1 (S. Ct. 1982)

Facts: The Seattle School Board voluntarily adopted a plan to racially integrate the schools. Opponents of the plan sponsored an initiative that prohibited school boards from requiring students to attend schools not nearest or next nearest to a student's home. Initiative 350 was adopted by an overwhelming statewide majority, including a majority of Seattle voters.

Issue: May a locally elected school board use the equal protection guarantees of the Fourteenth Amendment to defend its program of racial integration from attack by the state?

Rule: (Blackmun, J.) When a decision-making mechanism used to address racially conscious legislation is singled out by a state for peculiar and disadvantageous treatment, the state action plainly rests on racial distinctions in violation of the Equal Protection Clause of the Fourteenth Amendment.

Dissent: (Powell, J.) The error of the Court's decision cuts deeply into the heretofore unquestioned right of a state to structure the decision-making authority of its government. Undoubtedly, the school district could have canceled its integration program at any time without violating the Constitution. Yet, the Court now holds that neither the legislature nor the people of the state could alter what the school district had unilaterally decided.

Michael M. v. Sonoma County Superior Court (S. Ct. 1981)

Facts: The California "statutory rape" law defined unlawful sexual intercourse as "an act of sexual intercourse accomplished with a female not the wife of the perpetrator, where the female is under the age of 18."

Issue: Does a state's statutory rape law violate equal protection under the Fourteenth Amendment in punishing only the male participant?

Rule: (Rehnquist, J.) A gender-based criminal statute which furthers a state's legitimate interest in deterring behavior and which punishes only the participant who suffers few of the consequences of his conduct is constitutionally valid.

Dissent: (Brennan, J.) Sex-based classifications are unconstitutional. The Court reached the incorrect result by placing too much emphasis on the desirability of achieving the State's asserted goal: prevention of teenage pregnancy, and not enough emphasis on the fundamental question of whether sex-based discrimination is substantially related to the achievement of that goal.

Califano v. Goldfarb (S. Ct. 1977)

Facts: Under the Federal Old-Age, Survivors and Disability Insurance Benefits program widows received automatic payment of survivor benefits upon the death of their husbands. However, the program required a widower to prove dependency on his deceased wife for one-half of his support before receiving survivor benefits.

Issue: Does a statutory survivor benefit provision allowing women to receive survivor benefits automatically upon the death of a spouse but imposing a proof-of-dependency requirement on men violate the equal protection guarantees of the Fourteenth Amendment?

Rule: (Brennan, J.) A gender-based distinction created by a statute that would deprive deceased women of protection for their families which deceased men receive as a result of their employment is forbidden by the Constitution.

Dissent: (Rehnquist, J.) The distinction in no way perpetuates the economic discrimination which has been the basis for heightened scrutiny of gender-based classifications, and is, in fact, explainable as a measure to ameliorate the characteristically depressed condition of aged widows.

Sugarman v. Dougall (S. Ct. 1973)

Facts: A New York statute excluded aliens from all government civil service positions filled by competitive examination. This exclusion did not apply to other classes of civil service employment.

Issue: Does a state law prohibiting the employment of aliens from civil service positions in the competitive class violate equal protection?

Rule: (Blackmun, J.) Classifications based on alienage are inherently suspect and subject to strict judicial scrutiny. To withstand an equal protection challenge, a classification based on alienage must be narrowly drawn to accomplish a substantial purpose. The general exclusion of all aliens from a type of civil service employment is too broadly drawn to accomplish the state objective of having only employees with undivided loyalty.

Dissent: (Rehnquist, J.) The principal purpose of the Fourteenth Amendment is to prohibit states from invidiously discriminating by reason of race. However, there is no evidence suggesting that it was intended to render alienage a "suspect" classification.

Skinner v. Oklahoma ex rel. Williamson (S. Ct. 1942)

Facts: An Oklahoma statute allowed the state attorney general to institute a judicial proceeding to permit sterilization of imprisoned "habitual criminals."

Issue: May a state, pursuant to its police powers to protect the welfare of its citizens, enact legislation depriving habitual criminal offenders of their right to reproduce sexually?

Rule: (Douglas, J.) The right to sexually reproduce is a fundamental right protected under the liberties guaranteed by the Constitution. State law impairing that right by creating a classification demands strict judicial scrutiny, and the state law is valid only upon a showing of a narrowly drawn statute to effect a compelling state interest. Since there is no correlation between the criminal offense and genetic traits, the classification is not valid.

Reynolds v. Sims (S. Ct. 1964)

Facts: P challenged one existing and two proposed plans for the apportionment of seats in the two houses of the Alabama Legislature. The present scheme had no proportional relationship between population and number of senate seats for a county. The proposed plans would have reduced only some of the disparities.

Issue: Does a state scheme for non–population-based apportionment of legislative districts constitute an invidious discrimination violative of equal protection rights under the Fourteenth Amendment?

Rule: (Warren, C.J.) The Equal Protection Clause requires that the seats in both houses of a bicameral state be apportioned on a population basis. A non–population-based system unconstitutionally impairs an individual's right to vote for state legislators, as one's vote is weighted less in comparison to votes of citizens living in other parts of the state.

Mobile v. Bolden (S. Ct. 1980)

Facts: Mobile was governed by a city commission consisting of three members elected at large. Although Mobile had a substantial African-American population, no African-American person had ever been elected to the commission.

Issue: Does an electoral reapportionment into multimember districts that disadvantage a voting minority violate the Equal Protection Clause of the Fourteenth Amendment?

Rule: (Stewart, J.) The disproportionate impact on the voting strength of a group is insufficient to invalidate, on equal protection grounds, legislative reapportionment of districts into multimember districts. Purposeful discrimination for the reapportionment is a necessary component to achieve invalidation.

Dissent: (Marshall, J.) Although we have held that multimember districts are not unconstitutional *per se,* there is simply no basis for the plurality's conclusion that under our prior cases proof of discriminatory intent is a necessary condition for the invalidation of multimember districting.

Yick Wo v. Hopkins (S. Ct. 1886)

Facts: Ordinances gave the San Francisco Board of Supervisors the power to grant or withhold their consent to the use of wooden buildings as laundries. The board withheld consent from all Chinese applicants, and granted consent to most non-Chinese applicants. P was imprisoned for violating the ordinance.

Issue: May a city, pursuant to its police powers to protect the welfare of its citizens, vest its city officials with sole discretionary power to determine certain land-use policies?

Rule: (Matthews, J.) The vesting of sole discretionary powers in city offi-cials to determine land-use policies, which in practice turns out to be an arbitrary and oppressive exercise of power against a group of individuals, violates the equal protection guarantees of the Fourteenth Amendment.

Boiling v. Sharpe (S. Ct. 1954)

Facts: The District of Columbia denied African-American children admis-sion to the public schools that white children attended. The segregation policy was challenged as violative of the Due Process Clause of the Fifth Amendment.
Issue: Does the maintenance of racially segregated public schools by a territory of the federal government violate the Due Process Clause of the Fifth Amendment?
Rule: (Warren, C.J.) Racial classifications demand the highest level of judi-cial scrutiny because they are constitutionally suspect.

Segregation in public education is not reasonably related to any proper governmental objective and thus imposes on African-American children a burden that constitutes an arbitrary deprivation of liberty in violation of the Fifth Amendment.

Village of Arlington Heights v. Metropolitan Housing Development Corp. (S. Ct. 1977)

Facts: P applied to D for the rezoning of a parcel of land from single-family to multiple-family classification in order to build town-house units for low- and moderate-income tenants. P asserted that D's denial of their request was based on racial discrimination.
Issue: Does the denial of a rezoning request resulting in a racially discrim-inatory effect on the community violate the Equal Protection Clause?
Rule: (Powell, J.) When a local decision results only in a discriminatory effect and there is no proof that a discriminatory purpose is the motivating factor behind the decision, such a decision is accorded judicial deference.

Ambach v. Norwick (S. Ct. 1979)

Facts: A New York statute excluded from public school employment aliens who were eligible for naturalization but who refused to become citizens.
Issue: Does a state's imposition of a citizenship requirement in order to teach in public schools violate the Equal Protection Clause of the Fourteenth Amendment?
Rule: (Powell, J.) Governmental entities, when exercising the functions of government, may impose a citizenship requirement if it is rationally related to a state goal. Public school teachers fall within the "governmental

function" principle, and the citizenship requirement is rationally related to the governmental goal of promoting civic virtues.

Dissent: (Blackmun, J.) The citizenship requirement is not rationally related to the state goal because the statute is unconcerned with aliens teaching in private schools.

Mathews v. Diaz (S. Ct. 1976)

Facts: A congressional act granted medical insurance eligibility to resident citizens who were 65 years or older but denied eligibility to alien residents unless they had been admitted to permanent residence and had continuously resided within the United States for at least five years.

Issue: May Congress condition an alien's eligibility for participation in a federal medical insurance program on continuous residence and admission for permanent residence?

Rule: (Stevens, J.) Congress has exclusive control over the conditions of entry and residence of aliens and has no constitutional duty to provide all aliens with the welfare benefits provided to citizens. It is within Congress' power to condition an alien's receipt of welfare benefits upon the duration and the character of an alien's residence.

Lalli v. Lalli (S. Ct. 1978)

Facts: New York law required illegitimate children who would inherit from their fathers by intestate succession to provide a particular form of proof of paternity that was not required of legitimate children.

Issue: Does a succession law requiring proof of paternity from illegitimate children, but not legitimate children, violate the Equal Protection Clause of the Fourteenth Amendment?

Rule: (Powell, J.) Classifications based on illegitimacy are not subject to strict judicial scrutiny, but they must be substantially related to permissible state interests. A state's substantial interest in safeguarding the orderly disposition of property at death and devising an appropriate legal framework in furtherance thereof is sufficient to withstand an equal protection challenge.

Dissent: (Brennan, J.) The New York statute excludes forms of proof that do not compromise the state's substantial interest.

Therefore, the statute discriminates against illegitimates through means not substantially related to the legitimate interests that the statute purports to promote.

Frontiero v. Richardson (S. Ct. 1973)

Facts: Pursuant to federal statute, the military permitted a serviceman to claim his wife as a "dependent" without regard to whether she in fact was

dependent upon him for over one-half her support. Under the same program, a servicewoman could not claim her husband as a "dependent" unless he was in fact dependent upon her for over one-half of his support.
Issue: Does the uniformed services' program, which permits servicemen to automatically claim their wives as dependents while imposing a dependency determination requirement on the husbands of servicewomen, violate the Due Process Clause of the Fifth Amendment?
Rule: (Brennan, J.) Classification based on sex is inherently suspect and must be subjected to strict judicial scrutiny. It must serve an important governmental objective and the discriminatory means must be substantially related to the objective. Administrative convenience is not a sufficient governmental objective to justify a sex-discrimination law.

Personnel Administrator of Massachusetts v. Feeney (S. Ct. 1979)

Facts: Massachusetts law provided that all veterans who qualified for state civil service positions must be considered for appointment ahead of qualified nonveterans. The preference overwhelmingly advantaged males and applied to all positions in the state's classified civil service.
Issue: Do civil service hiring preferences for veterans violate the Equal Protection Clause of the Fourteenth Amendment as it operates overwhelmingly in favor of men?
Rule: (Stewart, J.) To determine the validity of a gender-neutral statute having a disproportionately adverse effect upon one gender, apply the two-prong test of (1) whether the statutory classification is actually non–gender-based and (2) whether the adverse effect reflects an invidious gender-based discriminatory purpose. Absent the finding of either actual discrimination and discriminatory purpose, a state statute is constitutionally valid.
Dissent: (Marshall, J.) The statute at issue is overinclusive to achieve the state objective of facilitating veterans' transition to civilian life and to encourage military service. Further, the state has at its disposal less discriminatory means to effect the objective of rewarding veterans.

Mississippi University for Women v. Hogan (S. Ct. 1982)

Facts: D denied P admission to its nursing program, but permitted him to audit classes.
Issue: May a state-funded university, pursuant to state law, maintain a single-sex admissions policy without violating the equal protection guarantees of the Fourteenth Amendment?
Rule: (O'Connor, J.) A gender-based classification is inherently suspect and must be subjected to strict judicial scrutiny. The "exceedingly

persuasive justification" demanded by strict scrutiny is met by showing that the discrimination serves important governmental objectives and that the discriminatory means are closely related to the achievement of those objectives. Since a state's single-sex admissions policy does not meet this test, it is violative of equal protection.

Dissent: (Powell, J.) As the Equal Protection Clause was never intended to apply to this kind of case, the heightened level of scrutiny analysis employed by the Court is inappropriate. Further, the Court's decision curtails valuable diversity in the type of higher education a state can offer.

Dandridge v. Williams (S. Ct. 1970)

Facts: Maryland participated in the federally created Aid to Families with Dependent Children Program but imposed a limit of $250 per month per family. Recipients with large families challenged the state version of the federal program as discriminatory because larger-sized families receive less aid per child than smaller-sized families.

Issue: May a state, in participating in a federally created welfare assistance program, impose its own limit on the amount a recipient may receive?

Rule: (Stewart, J.) Under equal protection analysis, state economic and social regulations with some rational basis are valid, though they might result in disparate treatment among individuals.

Dissent: (Marshall, J.) The classification process effected by the maximum grant regulation produces a basic denial of equal treatment, since persons similarly situated are not afforded equal treatment. Rather than on the definition of a "right," concentration should be placed upon the character of the classification, the relative importance of the lost benefit to the discriminated class, and the asserted state interest. Under this formulation of the analysis, the state regulation is invalid.

Griffin v. Illinois (S. Ct. 1956)

Facts: Under Illinois law, indigents could obtain a free transcript to obtain appellate review of constitutional questions but not of other alleged trial errors. P, convicted of armed robbery, alleged that there were nonconstitutional errors made in his trial and moved that a transcript be provided without payment as he was too poor to pay the necessary fees.

Issue: May a state, consistent with the Due Process and Equal Protection Clauses of the Fourteenth Amendment, provide free transcripts only to indigents appealing on constitutional error and not to indigents appealing on nonconstitutional grounds?

Rule: (Black, J.) In criminal proceedings, a state that grants appellate review may not discriminate on account of poverty. Indigent defendants must be afforded an adequate and effective appellate review process, regardless of whether the appeal is based on constitutional error. Where this includes the provision of a transcript, such must be provided.

Hill v. Stone (S. Ct. 1975)

Facts: In Texas' local bond elections, all persons owning taxable property rendered for taxation voted in one box, and all other registered voters voted in a separate box. A bond issue was passed only if it was approved by a majority vote both in the "rendered box" and in the aggregate of both boxes.

Issue: Does a state's restriction of the franchise in local elections by imposing a rendering requirement violate equal protection guarantees?

Rule: (Marshall, J.) A rendering requirement creates a classification which in effect disenfranchises those who have not rendered their property for taxation in the year of a bond election. Therefore, a state's restriction of the franchise in an election of general interest must meet the stringent test of compelling state interest, which it does not in this case.

Illinois State Board of Elections v. Socialist Workers Party (S. Ct. 1979)

Facts: The Illinois Election Code had two sets of signature requirements for parties and candidates to appear on a local or state ballot. More signatures were required for local elections than for state-wide elections.

Issue: Does a state's disparate signature procedure for entry onto electoral ballots violate the Equal Protection Clause of the Fourteenth Amendment?

Rule: (Marshall, J.) Restrictions on access to the ballot burden fundamental rights protected by the Constitution. To be valid, such restrictions must be necessary to serve a compelling state interest and be the least drastic means to achieve the state goal. A state's interest in avoiding overloaded ballots does not justify a more stringent signature requirement for some local elections.

Haig v. Agee (S. Ct. 1981)

Facts: D, Secretary of State, revoked P's passport. P was an American citizen and a former CIA employee residing in West Germany. D's action was predicated upon a determination that P's activities abroad threatened or were likely to threaten U.S. national security.

Issue: May the government revoke a passport on the ground that the holder's activity in foreign countries is causing or is likely to cause serious damage to national security or foreign policy?

Rule: (Burger, J.) When there is a substantial likelihood of serious damage to national security or foreign policy as a result of a passport holder's activities in foreign countries, the government may take action to ensure that the holder does not exploit the sponsorship of his travels afforded by the United States. The due process guarantees of the Constitution demand only a statement of reasons and an opportunity for a prompt postrevocation hearing.

Dissent: (Brennan, J.) The executive branch has attempted to use one of the only means at its disposal, revocation of a passport, to stop damaging speech. But just as the Constitution protects both popular and unpopular speech, it likewise protects both popular and unpopular travelers.

Griswold v. Connecticut (S. Ct. 1965)

Facts: Connecticut law prohibited the use of any contraceptive and punished principals, accomplices, and accessories equally. D, the Executive Director of Planned Parenthood League of Connecticut, advised married persons regarding the use of contraceptives.

Issue: Is there a right to privacy in a marital relationship that precludes a state from prohibiting any use of contraception?

Rule: (Douglas, J.) The various constitutional guarantees create penumbras of privacy. The privacy of the marital relationship is unconstitutionally invaded by unnecessarily broad regulation of marital affairs, such as total bans on any use of contraceptives.

Dissent: (Black, J.) Only those rights explicitly protected by the Bill of Rights or other specific constitutional provisions are protected under the Fourteenth Amendment. The right to privacy does not emanate from these constitutional provisions, and the Court should not invalidate a state law merely because it offends personal taste.

Roe v. Wade (S. Ct. 1973)

Facts: Ps, a pregnant single woman, a childless married couple, and a physician, challenged a Texas law that made it a crime for a woman to procure an abortion except "by medical advice for the purpose of saving the life of the mother."

Issue: May a state impose regulations restricting a woman's right to terminate a pregnancy?

Rule: (Blackmun, J.) A woman's right to terminate a pregnancy in consultation with her physician is an area of privacy constitutionally protected. State regulations limiting those rights are justified only by showing a "compelling state interest" narrowly drawn to effect only the legitimate state interest at stake.

Dissent: (White, J.) Since this is an issue upon which reasonable men may disagree and to which there is no explicit constitutional bar, the Court should leave such decisions to the people and the political processes of each state.

Rust v. Sullivan (S. Ct. 1991)

Facts: The Secretary of the Department of Health and Human Services promulgated new regulations in 1988 designed to prevent the use of federal grant money in the counseling of abortions. The regulations prohibited grant recipients from providing counseling or referral services for the use of abortion as a method of family planning. Further, the regulations prohibited grant recipients from engaging in activities that encouraged, promoted, or advocated abortion, and required grant-related activities to be physically and financially separate from prohibited abortion activities.

Issue 1: Do regulations that prohibit discussion of abortion in federally funded clinics violate the First Amendment?

Rule 1: (Rehnquist, C.J.) The Secretary's regulations are merely designed to ensure that the limits of the federal grant are observed. The government can, without violating the Constitution, selectively fund a program to encourage certain activities without funding alternate programs that deal with the problem in another way. Such selectivity is not viewpoint discrimination, but rather part of the normal decision-making process to expend limited funds.

Issue 2: Do restrictions on the subsidization of abortion-related speech impermissibly condition the receipt of a benefit on the relinquishment of a constitutional right?

Rule 2: The government in this instance is not denying a benefit to anyone, but is rather insisting that public funds be spent for the purposes for which they were authorized. Congress has not prevented grant recipients from engaging in abortion-related activities, but has simply declined to fund such activities from the public fisc.

Dissent: (Blackmun, J.) The counseling and referral provisions at issue are unconstitutional content-based regulations of speech. Although affected doctors and counselors could escape the prohibition by relinquishing their jobs, this has never been an acceptable justification for speech suppression. Furthermore, by suppressing medically pertinent information, the government places formidable obstacles in the path of a woman's freedom of choice in violation of her Fifth Amendment rights.

Harris v. McRae (S. Ct. 1980)

Facts: Congress prohibited the use of any federal funds to reimburse the cost of abortions under the Medicaid program, except under certain specified circumstances.

Issue: Does Congress' selective subsidization of certain medically necessary abortions contravene the liberty or equal protection guarantees of the Constitution?

Rule 1: (Stewart, J.) The liberty protected under the Due Process Clause affords protection against unwarranted government interference with freedom of choice in the context of certain personal decisions. It does not confer an entitlement to such funds as may be necessary to realize all the advantages of that liberty.

Rule 2: (Stewart, J.) Selective subsidization of certain medically necessary abortions does not violate any substantive liberties or create a constitutionally suspect classification. Selective subsidization creates incentives that make childbirth a more attractive alternative than abortion for persons eligible for federal medical assistance. Therefore, the measure is rationally and directly related to the congressional objective in protecting potential life.

Dissent: (Brennan, J.) The Court has established that a pregnant woman has a right to be free from state interference in her choice to have an abortion. The denial of public funds for medically necessary abortions plainly intrudes upon this constitutionally protected right, as by design and effect it serves to coerce indigent pregnant women to bear children that they would otherwise elect not to have.

Webster v. Reproductive Health Services (S. Ct. 1989)

Facts: Reproductive Health Services challenged the constitutionality of a Missouri statute regulating the performance of abortions. Of the act's 20 provisions, five were under consideration: (1) "findings" by the state legislature that "life begins at conception," and "unborn children have protectable interests in life, health, and well-being"; (2) a requirement that all state laws be interpreted to provide unborn children with the same rights enjoyed by other persons; (3) a provision requiring physicians, prior to performing an abortion on a woman whom they reasonably believe to be more than 20 weeks pregnant, perform medical tests to determine whether the fetus is viable; (4) a prohibition on the use of public employees and facilities to perform abortions not necessary to save the mother's life; and (5) a prohibition on the use of public funds, employees, or facilities to "encourage or counsel" a woman to have an abortion not necessary to save her life.

Issue 1: May a state express a value judgment that favors childbirth over abortion?

Rule 1: (Rehnquist, C.J.) *Roe v. Wade* does not limit the authority of a state to make a value judgment favoring childbirth over abortion, but merely prevents the state from using that value judgment to justify an otherwise invalid abortion regulation.

Issue 2: May a state prohibit the use of public facilities for the performance of abortions not necessary to save the mother's life?

Rule 2: The Due Process Clauses generally confer no affirmative right to government aid. The decision to withhold the use of public facilities for the performance of abortions leaves the woman with the same choices as if the state had decided not to operate any public hospitals at all.

Issue 3: May a state require the performance of viability tests after only 20 weeks of pregnancy before allowing a physician to perform an abortion?

Rule 3: (Rehnquist, C.J., writing for a plurality) The viability testing requirement permissibly furthers the state's legitimate interest in protecting potential human life. Although the performance of these tests occurs before the start of the third trimester, and thus would permit the state to regulate abortions during the second trimester for reasons other than the protection of the mother's health (in direct conflict with *Roe*), the doubt cast upon the constitutionality of this statute is a result of the unworkability of the rigid *Roe* trimester framework, and not a flaw in the statute itself.

Concurrence: (O'Connor, J.) The viability testing requirement does not conflict with any of the Court's past decisions concerning state regulation of abortion, including *Roe*. The tests merely further the state's legitimate interest in protecting potential life when viability is possible.

Concurrence: (Scalia, J.) *Roe v. Wade* should be overruled. To keep control of this political issue distorts the public perception of the role of this Court.

Dissent: (Blackmun, J.) There is no need to reconsider *Roe*. The viability testing provisions impose significant additional health risks on both the pregnant woman and the fetus, and bear no rational relation to the state's interest in protecting fetal life.

Partial Dissent: (Stevens, J.) The viability testing provisions are constitutional for the reasons stated by Justice O'Connor. However, the legislature's finding that life begins at conception, in the absence of a secular purpose, violates the Establishment Clause of the First Amendment.

Cruzan v. Director, Missouri Dep't of Health (S. Ct. 1990)

Facts: Nancy Cruzan was severely injured in a car accident. She was left in a "persistent vegetative state" and had virtually no chance of regaining her mental faculties. Her parents brought suit to have the hospital terminate the artificial nutrition and hydration procedures.

Issue 1: Does the Constitution grant individuals a "right to die"?

Rule 1: (Rehnquist, J.) A competent person has a constitutionally protected liberty interest in refusing unwanted medical treatment.

Issue 2: May a state require a surrogate decision maker acting in behalf of an incompetent patient to provide clear and convincing evidence of the incompetent's wishes as to the withdrawal of life-sustaining treatment?

Rule 2: As a state has a legitimate interest in protecting an individual's "right to die," a state may require an incompetent patient's surrogate decision maker to demonstrate clear and convincing evidence that the action of the surrogate conforms as best it may to the wishes expressed by the patient while competent.

Concurrence: (O'Connor, J.) Because our notions of liberty are inextricably entwined with our idea of physical freedom and self-determination, requiring a competent adult to endure life-sustaining procedures against her will burdens the patient's liberty, dignity, and freedom to determine the course of her own treatment. Furthermore, states may have a duty to give effect to the decisions of a surrogate decision maker in order to protect the patient's liberty interest in refusing medical treatment.

Dissent: (Brennan, J.) The clear and convincing standard imposed by the state in determining whether the decision of a surrogate decision maker comports with the wishes of an incompetent individual in terminating life-sustaining treatment is unrealistic and burdens the right of an individual to forgo life-sustaining treatment. Too few people execute living wills in anticipation of becoming vegetative, and the testimony of close friends and family members may be the best evidence available of what the patient's choice would be.

Dissent: (Stevens, J.) The meaning and completion of an incompetent patient's life should be controlled by persons who have her best interests at heart, not by a state legislature concerned only with the "preservation of human life."

Thornburgh v. American College of Obstetricians and Gynecologists (S. Ct. 1986)

Facts: Pennsylvania law imposed information, disclosure, and reporting requirements on physicians and counselors of pregnant women seeking abortions. P challenged the constitutionality of those provisions.

Issue: May a state regulate the transmission of information between a woman and her professional advisors on issues involving childbearing?

Rule: (Blackmun, J.) Childbearing is a private sphere of individual liberty constitutionally protected from the reach of government. A state may not require the transmission of information within this private setting which would be an impediment to a woman's decision to have an abortion.

Dissent: (O'Connor, J.) The state has imposed no undue burdens on the parties involved, so the state is justified in imposing such requirements.

Planned Parenthood of S.E. Pa. v. Casey (S. Ct. 1992)

Facts: Planned Parenthood challenged the Pennsylvania Abortion Control Act. It provided: (1) women seeking an abortion must give informed consent prior to the procedure and must be provided with certain information 24 hours in advance; (2) a minor must obtain informed consent of one of her parents or, if not feasible, a court; (3) a married woman must sign a statement indicating that she notified her husband; (4) compliance with these procedures is necessary if there is a medical emergency; and (5) reporting requirements were imposed on abortion facilities.

Issue: To what extent may states regulate abortion?

Rule: A state may enact laws that have the incidental effect of making it more difficult or expensive to procure an abortion, provided the law serves a valid purpose, is not designed to strike at the right itself, and does impose an *undue burden* (i.e., a substantial obstacle) on the woman's ability to make this decision. The various provisions of the Pennsylvania act are constitutional, except for the spousal notification requirement, which is a substantial obstacle to a woman's choice. Thus, this decision rejects the trimester framework established in *Roe v. Wade*. It reaffirms *Roe*'s essential holding by recognizing a woman's right to abortion before viability, confirming the state's power to restrict abortion after viability, and confirming the state's interest in protecting the health of the woman and the life of the fetus that may become a child.

Dissent: (Stevens, J.) A burden is undue if it is too severe or if it lacks a legitimate, rational justification. The 24-hour delay requirement and the provision of dissuasive information fail both parts of this test.

Dissent: (Blackmun, J.) The provisions requiring content-based counseling, a 24-hour delay, informed parental consent, and reporting of abortion-related information have been adjudicated before and should therefore be invalidated under principles of *stare decisis*.

Dissent: (Rehnquist, J.) The majority opinion claims to uphold *Roe* on the basis of *stare decisis* while in actuality, it created a new undue-burden standard and never claimed that *Roe* was correct as an original matter. In fact, it should be reversed; abortion is not a fundamental right.

Dissent: (Scalia, J.) The states may permit abortion on demand but the Constitution does not require them to do so because (a) the Constitution says absolutely nothing about it, and (b) the traditions of American society have permitted abortion to be legally proscribed. The issue should be resolved by citizens trying to persuade one another and voting.

Bowers v. Hardwick (S. Ct. 1986)

Facts: A Georgia statute made it a criminal offense for anyone to engage in any form of sodomy.

Issue: May a state law criminalize certain private sexual activities between consenting adults without violating the federal Constitution?

Rule: (White, J.) The right of consenting adults to engage in particular sexual acts is not a fundamental right. Therefore, it is within the proper powers of a state to enact criminal sanctions to discourage sexual behavior it deems inappropriate.

Dissent: (Blackmun, J.) The issue in this case was not about "a fundamental right to engage in homosexual sodomy" as the Court asserts, but rather, about the broader issue of the "right to be left alone." That right should be analyzed in the light of the values underlying the constitutional right to privacy. Also, the Court erred in refusing to consider whether the Georgia statute violates the Eighth or Ninth Amendments or the Equal Protection Clause of the Fourteenth Amendment.

Zablocki v. Redhail (S. Ct. 1978)

Facts: Wisconsin residents who had to support minor children not in their custody were required to receive permission from the state to marry. Marriages contracted in violation of the statute were both void and punishable as criminal offenses.

Issue: Does a state statute restricting an individual's right to marry violate the Constitution?

Rule: (Marshall, J.) The right to marry is a fundamental right guaranteed by the Constitution. A statutory classification significantly interfering with a fundamental right is invalid unless it is supported by sufficiently important state interests and is closely tailored to effectuate only those interests.

Dissent: (Rehnquist, J.) Traditional presumption of validity should be extended to this statute. Furthermore, there is a rational relation between this classification and the state objective.

New Orleans v. Dukes (S. Ct. 1976)

Facts: New Orleans prohibited pushcart food vending within the Vieux Carre district but exempted those vendors who had continually operated the same business for eight years prior to the amendment.

Issue: Does a city's enactment of economic regulations prohibiting newer businesses from operating within a specified section of the city violate the Equal Protection Clause of the Fourteenth Amendment?

Rule: (per curiam) When a local economic regulation is challenged on equal protection grounds and the regulation does not affect a fundamental right or establish suspect classifications, the Court defers to the local legislative determinations as to the desirability of imposing such discriminatory measures.

Columbus Board of Educ. v. Penick (S. Ct. 1979)

Facts: The Columbus public schools were highly segregated.

Issue: Upon a finding of a dual school system separated by race prior to 1954 and a school board's continued failure to eliminate the consequences of its past intentionally segregative policies, may a District Court order a system-wide desegregation plan?

Rule: (White, J.) A pre-1954 dual school system separated by race and a school board's continued failure to eliminate the consequences of past segregated policies evidence a discriminatory purpose and segregative impact sufficient to warrant the implementation of a system-wide desegregation plan.

Dissent: (Rehnquist, J.) Critically important questions were neither asked nor answered by the lower court. Thus, the record before the Court cannot inform as to whether so sweeping a remedy as a system-wide desegregation plan is justified.

Dayton Board of Educ. v. Brinkman [Dayton II] (S. Ct. 1979)

Facts: Dayton public schools were highly segregated. Although 43% of the students were African American, 51 of the 69 schools were virtually all-white or all-black.

Issue: Does a finding that purposeful racial segregation existed within a school system prior to 1954 warrant an inference that purposeful segregation currently exists in the school system?

Rule: (White, J.) A finding that purposeful segregation existed in a school system prior to 1954, absent sufficient countervailing evidence, warrants an inference that the school system remains deliberately segregated. This finding imposes an affirmative constitutional duty on school boards to eradicate the effect of discrimination within the school system.

Dissent: (Rehnquist, J.) A pre-1954 finding should not give rise to the presumption that current racial segregation in the school system is due to purposeful segregation.

Bernal v. Fainter (S. Ct. 1984)

Facts: P, an alien resident living in Texas, applied to become a notary public. Texas denied the application because P failed to satisfy the statutory requirement that a notary public be a U.S. citizen.

Issue: Does a statute imposing a federal citizenship requirement to be a notary public violate the Equal Protection Clause of the Fourteenth Amendment?

Rule: (Marshall, J.) State laws discriminating on the basis of alienage must be subjected to strict judicial scrutiny. The law must advance a compelling state interest by the least restrictive means practically available. A citizenship requirement governing eligibility to become a notary public does not serve a state's interest in ensuring that notaries public are familiar with its law.

Mathews v. Lucas (S. Ct. 1976)

Facts: The Social Security Act provided benefits to "dependent" children of a deceased parent. However, certain illegitimate children had to establish paternity and demonstrate dependency at the time of the parent's death in order to receive these benefits.

Issue: Does a statutory provision presuming dependency of legitimate offspring but requiring illegitimate offspring to demonstrate dependency to determine survivorship benefits violate the Due Process Clause of the Fifth Amendment?

Rule: (Blackmun, J.) Illegitimacy is not a suspect classification and a statutory provision using a nonsuspect classification need only be shown to have a rational basis. A classification distinguishing between legitimate and illegitimate offspring is rationally grounded in the congressional objective to aid the administration of survivorship benefits.

Dissent: (Stevens, J.) Legitimate children are no more likely to be "dependent" than are illegitimate children. Administrative convenience is insufficient grounds on which to justify a classification that is more probably the product of a tradition of thinking of illegitimates as less deserving persons than legitimates. That tradition should be rejected.

Califano v. Webster (S. Ct. 1977)

Facts: The method used to calculate benefits under the Social Security Act afforded female wage earners the chance of obtaining higher old-age benefits than similarly situated males.

Issue: Does a statutory program affording female wage earners higher old-age benefits than similarly situated males violate the equal protection guarantees of the Fourteenth Amendment?

Rule: (per curiam) To withstand scrutiny under equal protection, a classification based on gender must serve important governmental objectives and must be substantially related to achievement of those objectives. Remedying past economic discrimination against women is an important governmental objective served by the disparate treatment of the sexes under the Social Security Act.

Walton v. Arizona (S. Ct. 1990)

Facts: Walton was convicted of first-degree murder and sentenced by a judge in a separate proceeding. Arizona law required the sentencing judge to examine aggravating and mitigating circumstances of the crime, and required the imposition of the death penalty if one or more statutory aggravating circumstances were present and no mitigating circumstances were "sufficiently substantial to call for leniency." After finding two aggravating circumstances (the murder was for pecuniary gain and committed in an especially heinous, cruel, and deprived manner), the judge concluded that there was no mitigating factor sufficiently substantial to call for leniency and sentenced Walton to death.

Issue 1: Does the "especially heinous" aggravating circumstance vest too much discretion in the sentencer to impose the death penalty?

Rule 1: (White, J.) The "especially heinous" language used in the statute here is not too broad. Because the judge is the sentencer, he is presumed to know the law and the construction given the statutory language by the state supreme court. The language therefore provides meaningful guidance under *Furman v. Georgia*.

Issue 2: Does the statutory language noting that the sentencer "shall impose" the death penalty despite the presence of certain mitigating factors unduly restrict the sentencer's discretion to be merciful?

Rule 2: The state may, under *Woodson* and *Lockett*, impose on a defendant the burden of establishing the existence of sufficient mitigating circumstances so long as that procedure does not lessen the state's burden to prove the existence of the aggravating circumstances.

Concurrence: (Scalia, J.) The ultimate choice in capital sentencing is a unitary one — the choice between death and imprisonment. This Court's opinions *restricting* the exercise of discretion in the decision to impose the death penalty while *mandating* discretion in the decision to impose imprisonment are therefore irreconcilable. We cannot consistently hold that, under *Furman*, the state must specify in advance those aggravating factors that will be considered, while requiring, under *Woodson* and *Lockett*, that the state make individual assessments in each case regarding mitigating circumstances.

Dissent: (Brennan, J.) The *Lockett* and *Furman* principles speak to different concerns underlying our notion of civilized punishment; the *Lockett* rule flows primarily from the Eighth Amendment's core concern for human dignity, whereas the *Furman* principle reflects the understanding that the Amendment commands that punishment not be meted out in a wholly arbitrary and irrational manner.

Dissent: (Blackmun, J.) This statute impermissibly defines a wide range of mitigating evidence that may not be considered by the sentencer, while the words "especially heinous" do not serve to distinguish capital cases from other homicides where capital sentences are not imposed.

Dissent: (Stevens, J.) After narrowing the class of those eligible for the death penalty through narrow guidelines, it is entirely appropriate and consistent to then allow discretionary consideration of individual mitigating circumstances in the cases that remain.

Weinberger v. Salfi (S. Ct. 1975)

Facts: A provision of the Social Security Act imposed duration-of-relationship requirements denying survivorship benefits to wives and stepchildren who had not had their respective relationships with the deceased wage earner for more than nine months prior to his death.

Issue: Does the imposition of a statutory eligibility requirement for the receipt of survivorship benefits under a government benefit program violate equal protection guarantees under the Fourteenth Amendment?

Rule: (Rehnquist, J.) The receipt of benefits under a government benefit program is a noncontractual claim, and therefore not constitutionally protected. A classification with respect to a noncontractual claim need only be rationally related to the congressional objective. The duration-of-relationship requirement is rationally related to the congressional objective of guarding against abuse of the system.

Dissent: (Brennan, J.) When certain factors are present, as in this case, the government's interests in efficiency must be surrendered to the individual's interest in proving that the facts presumed are not necessarily that of a specific case.

New Jersey Welfare Rights Org. v. Cahill (S. Ct. 1973)

Facts: New Jersey's "Assistance to Families of the Working Poor" program limited benefits to families "which consisted of a household composed of two adults of the opposite sex ceremonially married to each other who have at least one minor child . . . of both, the natural child of one and adopted by the other, or a child adopted by both. . . ." The appellants claimed that the program effectively denied benefits to illegitimate children in violation of the Equal Protection Clause.

Issue: May a state deny rights to certain children based solely upon their illegitimate status?

Rule: (per curiam) The status of illegitimacy expresses society's condemnation of extramarital affairs. To visit this condemnation on the head of an infant, however, is unjust and contrary to the basic concept of our system that legal burdens should bear some relationship to individual responsibility.

Dissent: (Rehnquist, J.) The New Jersey statute distinguishes among types of families. Although the classification denies benefits to illegitimate children, this denial is imposed equally on the parents of these children.

The Civil Rights Cases (S. Ct. 1883)

Facts: Section 1 of the Civil Rights Act of 1875 provided that all people, regardless of race and color, were entitled to equal enjoyment of all public places of amusement.

Issue: Does Congress have the power to enact a law directly governing the behavior of citizens and prohibiting certain types of discriminatory practices, pursuant to the Thirteenth and Fourteenth Amendments?

Rule: (Bradley, J.) Congress only has the power granted by Section 2 of the Thirteenth Amendment and Section 5 of the Fourteenth Amendment to pass laws that will effectuate the goals and policies of their respective amendments. The Thirteenth Amendment prohibits slavery and involuntary servitude. To pass discrimination laws in no way effectuates the policies of this amendment. The Fourteenth Amendment prohibits the states from issuing legislation that denies equal protection of the laws, and any law which Congress passes to effectuate this policy must be directed specifically against a state that has a discriminatory law on its books. To pass a law directly governing the people of a state without deference to the just laws of that state represents a congressional usurpation of the states' lawmaking authority.

Dissent: (Harlan, J.) There are burdens and disabilities which constitute badges of slavery and servitude. The power to enforce the Thirteenth Amendment by appropriate legislation may be exerted for the eradication of these badges and incidents. Under its express power to enforce that amendment, Congress may enact legislation to protect people against deprivation of any civil rights granted to other freeman in the same state because of their race. The Act prohibits discrimination in access to public or quasi-public places. Racial discrimination practiced by entities in the exercise of their public or quasi-public functions is a badge of servitude which Congress may prevent under its power to enforce the Thirteenth Amendment. Congress also has the power to enact discrimination laws under the Fourteenth Amendment, which grants full citizenship rights to blacks. To effectuate this guarantee and to enforce this particular provision requires the ability to make a law directly affecting the status of federal and state citizens. Additionally, the Act is valid under Congress' power to enact laws pursuant to the Equal Protection Clause of the Fourteenth Amendment because the entities regulated by the Act, by virtue of the public services they render and resulting benefits, are instrumentalities of the state.

Hunter v. Erickson (S. Ct. 1969)

Facts: An Akron law provided that ordinances regulating the sale and lease of real property on the basis of "race, color, religion, national origin or ancestry" became effective only if approved by a majority voting at a general or special election. Most other ordinances became effective 30 days after passage, subject to repeal by referendum initiated by 10% of the voters.

Issue: May a city impose a more demanding approval procedure for ordinances regulating real estate transactions based on race, color, religion, national origin or ancestry without violating the equal protection guarantees of the Fourteenth Amendment?

Rule: (White, J.) Laws employing racial classifications are constitutionally suspect and subject to the most rigid judicial scrutiny. The imposition of a stricter approval system for certain types of legislation disadvantages the group on whose behalf the legislation is enacted, thus denying to that group equal protection of the law.

Palmer v. Thompson (S. Ct. 1971)

Facts: Jackson, Mississippi operated five public parks with swimming pools. Four of the pools were used by whites and one by African Americans. Rather than desegregate the pools, Jackson closed them.
Issue: Does the closing of public recreational facilities that were operated on a segregated basis constitute state action violating the equal protection guarantees of the Fourteenth Amendment?
Rule: (Black, J.) An official action closing public recreational facilities to all citizens does not constitute a denial of equal protection. The motivation behind an official act is irrelevant to the constitutionality of the act.
Dissent: (Brennan, J.) A state may not have an official stance against desegregating public facilities and implement it by closing those facilities in response to a desegregation order. The Equal Protection Clause is a hollow promise if it does not forbid such official denigration of the race which the Fourteenth Amendment was designed to protect.

Rostker v. Goldberg (S. Ct. 1981)

Facts: The Military Selective Service Act authorized registration of males, but not females, for military services.
Issue: Does Congress' exclusion of women from registration for the draft contravene the equal protection guarantees of the Constitution?
Rule: (Rehnquist, J.) Equal protection demands that similarly situated persons be treated similarly. Therefore, if a gender classification realistically reflects the fact that the sexes are not similarly situated, the classification is not invidious and does not violate equal protection. Women do not serve in combat, and the purpose of registration is to develop a pool of potential combat troops. Therefore, gender distinctions in this area are constitutionally permissible.
Dissent: (Marshall, J.) The gender-based military registration law violates the Constitution as it excludes women from a fundamental civic obligation.

Maher v. Roe (S. Ct. 1977)

Facts: Connecticut limited state Medicaid benefits for first-trimester abortions to those that are "medically necessary." To obtain the requisite authorization for the abortion, the woman had to submit a certificate from her attending physician stating that the abortion was medically necessary.

Issue: May a state limit the receipt of state medical benefits for first-trimester abortions only to abortions that are medically necessary without impinging upon a fundamental right protected by the Constitution?

Rule: (Powell, J.) The Constitution protects a woman from unduly burdensome interference with her freedom to decide whether to terminate her pregnancy. However, there is no constitutional limitation on the authority of a state to make a value judgment favoring childbirth over abortion and to implement that judgment by the allocation of public funds.

Dissent: (Brennan, J.) As a practical matter, many indigent women feel they have no choice but to carry their pregnancies to term because the state will pay for the associated medical services, even though they would have chosen to have abortions if the state had also provided funds for that procedure or if the state had provided funds for neither procedure. This disparity in funding clearly operates to coerce indigent pregnant women to bear children they would not otherwise choose to have. Also, the claim that the regulation impinges one's fundamental right to privacy is never addressed by the Court.

Boddie v. Connecticut (S. Ct. 1971)

Facts: Individuals in Connecticut seeking to dissolve their marriage had to pay a filing fee of $45 and an average of $15 for service of process. Ps sought a waiver of those costs due to indigence.

Issue: May a state deny access to its courts when one seeks a divorce but is unable to pay the necessary fees?

Rule: (Harlan, J.) When access to courts is the only effective means of resolving an issue for which state approval is required, denial of such access is equivalent to denial of an opportunity to be heard. Absent a sufficient countervailing justification, such denial violates due process.

City of Akron v. Akron Center for Reproductive Health (S. Ct. 1983)

Facts: A 1978 Akron ordinance regulated abortion by requiring that all abortions performed after the first trimester be performed in a hospital; parental notification and consent for abortions to be performed on minors; physician statements regarding the viability of the fetus; a 24-hour waiting period before the abortion could be performed; and humane disposal of fetal remains.

Issue: When may a state regulate abortions to further its health interests?

Rule: (Powell, J.) A state's interest in health regulation becomes compelling at approximately the end of the first trimester. Even then, however, the state's regulation may only be upheld if it is reasonably designed to further that state interest. The Akron regulations at issue do not serve to inform a woman's decision in this area, but rather place constitutionally significant obstacles in her path.

Dissent: (O'Connor, J.) The *Roe* trimester framework is on a collision course with itself. As the medical risks of abortion decrease, the point at which the state may regulate for reasons of maternal health is moved further toward actual childbirth; as medical science advances, the point of viability is moved further back toward conception. At any stage of the pregnancy there is the potential for human life. Thus, a state may regulate abortion at any time so long as it does not unduly burden a woman's freedom to terminate her pregnancy.

High Tech Gays v. Defense Indus. Sec. Clearance Office (9th Cir. 1990)

Facts: The Department of Defense subjected all homosexual applicants for Secret and Top Secret clearances to expanded investigations and mandatory adjudications.

Issue: What level of scrutiny must a court use to analyze an equal protection challenge to sexual-orientation based classifications?

Rule: Homosexual activity is not a fundamental right protected by substantive due process. Since homosexual conduct can be criminalized, homosexuals cannot constitute a suspect or quasi-suspect class entitled to greater than rational basis review for equal protection purposes.

Sweatt v. Painter (S. Ct. 1950)

Facts: The University of Texas Law School refused to admit P into its J.D. program because he was African American. Instead, the University founded a law school for African Americans, which P refused to attend.

Issue: Does the establishment of separate law school facilities for whites and African Americans violate the equal protection guarantees of the Fourteenth Amendment?

Rule: (Vinson, J.) The establishment of separate law school facilities for whites and African Americans does not offend the equal protection guarantees of the Fourteenth Amendment if the facilities afford equal educational opportunities to both races. To measure equality between the facilities, tangible and intangible factors contributing to the greatness of a law school must be included in the equation.

Stell v. Savannah-Chatham County Board of Educ. (1963)

Facts: P's public schools, as well as its teaching and administrative staffs, were racially segregated. The schools were equal in all respects except as to a slight advantage in favor of the black teaching staff in terms of graduate training and salaries. The county justified the segregation based on a showing that whites and African Americans had different educational aptitudes.

Issue: May a state classify the children in its public school system on the basis of their educational aptitudes if the purpose of the classification is the continued racial separation of the public school system?

Rule: A reasonable classification within the meaning of the Equal Protection Clause of the Fourteenth Amendment might be secured by a division of the schools on the basis of coherent groups having distinguishable educable capabilities. Educational aptitude is a reasonable classification.

Note: On appeal, this decision was reversed. The U.S. Court of Appeals for the Fifth Circuit determined that the District Court was bound by the decision in *Brown I* and may not refrain from acting as required by that decision, even if the court should conclude that the Supreme Court erred either as to its facts or as to the law.

Cooper v. Aaron (S. Ct. 1958)

Facts: Due to growing public hostility, D petitioned for a postponement of the program for school desegregation. The postponement entailed the transfer of African-American students to segregated schools.

Issue 1: Are state governmental officials duty bound to obey federal court orders based on the court's interpretation of the federal Constitution?

Rule 1: (Warren, C.J.) The federal Judiciary is supreme in the exposition of the law of the Constitution. Consequently, the interpretation of the Fourteenth Amendment enunciated by the Judiciary in the *Brown* case is the supreme law of the land and state officials are bound thereby.

Issue 2: May the Court allow a local school board, in good faith, to postpone its desegregation program due to violent resistance by state governmental officials and local citizens?

Rule 2: (Warren, C.J.) Children have a constitutional right not to be racially discriminated against in public school admission. This right cannot be sacrificed to violence and disorder perpetrated to frustrate the implementation of programs to ensure those rights.

Milliken v. Bradley (S. Ct. 1974)

Facts: P alleged past and present racial segregation in the operation of the Detroit public school system. The District Court upheld P's challenge and initiated a multidistrict remedial plan.

Issue: May a federal court impose a multidistrict, area-wide remedy to a single district's segregation problem, absent any finding that the other school districts have failed to desegregate the school systems within their districts?

Rule: (Burger, C.J.) When the schools of only one district are implicated in a deliberate segregation scheme, the federal court lacks constitutional power to institute a multidistrict, area-wide remedy.

Dissent: (Marshall, J.) The rippling effects on residential patterns caused by purposeful acts of segregation do not automatically subside at the school district border. By limiting the remedy to the single district implicated, a state can profit from its own wrong and perpetuate the separation of the races.

Smith v. Allwright (S. Ct. 1944)

Facts: A rule stating that only whites could vote in a primary election was established by a private, state, political party convention.

Issue: Is the administration of government elections by private parties a public function and therefore subject to constitutional limitations?

Rule: (Reed, J.) The administration of elections is a governmental function and therefore subject to constitutional limitations, even when the state has delegated its responsibility to a private party.

Gomillion v. Lightfoot (S. Ct. 1960)

Facts: Alabama redivided the boundaries of Tuskegee, which resulted in the exclusion of almost all African-American voters. No white voters were excluded.

Issue: May a state, pursuant to its police power, realign a political subdivision so as to exclude all African-American voters from political participation within the subdivision?

Rule: (Frankfurter, J.) The Fifteenth Amendment forbids a state from passing any law depriving citizens of their vote because of their race. A state's police power cannot be used as an instrument to circumvent a federally protected right.

South Carolina v. Katzenbach (S. Ct. 1966)

Facts: The Voting Rights Act authorized the Attorney General to suspend state voting statutes that were found to appear discriminatory. Only limited judicial review was allowed.

Issue: May Congress pass a law pursuant to the Fifteenth Amendment that enables it to strike state voting statutes it deems to be discriminatory, whether intentional or not, with limited or no judicial review?

Rule: (Warren, C.J.) As long as Congress adopts a rational means of enforcing the Fifteenth Amendment guarantee of the right to vote regardless of race, it is constitutional. Since the state has none of the constitutional protections that individuals have, the established procedures formulated by the Voting Rights Act are considered to be rational under the circumstances and therefore within Congress' power under the Fifteenth Amendment.

Concurrence/Dissent: (Black, J.) While most of the provisions of the Voting Rights Act are constitutional, the provisions limiting a state's ability to amend its own constitution and not allowing the state to obtain a hearing in the Court are unconstitutional.

Katzenbach v. Morgan (S. Ct. 1966)

Facts: The Voting Rights Act of 1965 provided that, subject to certain restrictions, no person shall be denied the right to vote because of an inability to read or write English. New York required an ability to read or write English in order to vote.

Issue: May Congress constitutionally legislate based on its own interpretation of the reach of the Equal Protection Clause of the Fourteenth Amendment and defeat a state voting requirement?

Rule: (Brennan, J.) Congress may legislate based on its own judgment of the reach of the Equal Protection Clause of the Fourteenth Amendment. The Voting Rights Act of 1965 was enacted to enforce the Equal Protection Clause of the Fourteenth Amendment, and the states have no power to withhold voting rights on conditions that are forbidden by the Fourteenth Amendment.

Dissent: (Harlan, J.) In cases where there is room to differ on whether equal protection or due process has been violated, it is up to the Judiciary, not the legislature, to resolve the conflict. The Act here allows the Fourteenth Amendment to swallow the state's constitutional authority in this field.

City of Richmond v. United States (S. Ct. 1975)

Facts: Richmond annexed adjacent territory in another county of Virginia. The result was a reduction in the percentage of African-American residents within the city limits.

Issue: Does a city's annexation of adjacent territory violate constitutional provisions if, as a result of the annexation, a racial group's voting percentage has decreased?

Rule 1: (White, J.) A city which has annexed new territory, thereby decreasing a racial group's voting strength, carries the burden of proving that the annexation had neither the purpose nor the effect of abridging any group's right to vote on account of race. The controlling factor in meeting this burden is a demonstration that there are objectively verifiable, legitimate reasons for the annexation.

Rule 2: (White, J.) An annexation reducing the relative political strength of the minority race in the enlarged city as compared with what it was before the annexation does not violate the provisions of the Voting Rights Act as long as the post-annexation electoral system fairly recognizes the minority's political potential.

Dissent: (Brennan, J.) To hold that an annexation agreement reached under purposeful discriminatory circumstances can be validated by objective economic justification offered many years after the fact, wholly negates the prophylactic purpose of Section 5 of the Voting Rights Act.

Baker v. Carr (S. Ct. 1962)

Facts: Tennessee apportioned its two Houses based on the number of qualified voters resident in each of its counties as reported in the 1901 census. The Assembly's failure to redistribute its legislative seats to reflect the large-scale migration into the urban areas caused P to charge that the devaluation of the urban citizens' votes denied them equal protection.

Issue: Does a constitutional challenge to a state's legislative apportionment scheme raise justiciability and jurisdiction questions that preclude a federal court from hearing such a case?

Rule: (Brennan, J.) A constitutional challenge to a state's legislative apportionment scheme implicates the equal protection guarantees of the Fourteenth Amendment. Dismissal for lack of jurisdiction is justified only if the claim is plainly without merit.

Dissent: (Frankfurter, J.) In order to hear a hypothetical claim resting on abstract assumptions, the Court has cast away an impressive body of rulings that reflect our political history regarding the relationship between population and legislative representation.

Lucas v. Forty-Fourth Gen. Assembly of Colo. (S. Ct. 1964)

Facts: An amendment to the Colorado state constitution provided for the apportionment of the lower house on the basis of population, but included additional factors in drawing state senate districts.

Issue: Does an apportionment scheme for one legislative house that is based on more factors than just population and that is approved by a majority of the electorate violate the Equal Protection Clause of the Fourteenth Amendment?

Rule: (Warren, C.J.) Both houses of a bicameral state legislature must be apportioned substantially on a population basis. Approval by a majority of electorate does not make an apportionment plan constitutional. It must still satisfy the basic requirements of the Equal Protection Clause.

Dissent: (Clark, J.) If one house is fairly apportioned by population, then the people should have some latitude in providing, on a rational basis, for representation in the other house.

Avery v. Midland County, Texas (S. Ct. 1968)

Facts: The Midland County Commissioners Court consisted of five members, of which one member was elected at large from the entire county and the other four members were chosen from districts with vast variances in population. The population variances resulted from placing virtually the entire City of Midland, in which 95% of the county's population resided, in a single district.

Issue: May a local government apportion its political system on a basis other than population without violating equal protection under the Fourteenth Amendment?

Rule: (White, J.) The actions of local governments are the actions of a state, and therefore, a state's political subdivisions must comply with the equal protection guarantees of the Fourteenth Amendment.

Dissent: (Harlan, J.) The administrative feasibility of judicial application of the "one man, one vote" rule to the apportionment even of state legislatures has not yet been demonstrated. Therefore, it seems unwise to extend the rule to the numerous units of local government whose variety is sure to multiply the problems which have already arisen and to cast further burdens on the federal courts.

Labine v. Vincent (S. Ct. 1971)

Facts: Ezra Vincent died intestate. Under Louisiana's law of intestate succession, collateral relations took the property of the intestate to the exclusion of acknowledged, but not legitimated, illegitimate children.

Issue: Does a statutory scheme for intestate succession precluding acknowledged but illegitimate children from automatically sharing in a father's estate violate the Due Process and Equal Protection Clauses of the Constitution?

Rule: (Black, J.) A statutory scheme prescribing the extent and the conditions under which illegitimate children may inherit from their father's estate, and which does not create insurmountable barriers to illegitimate children inheriting, does not violate the Equal Protection and Due Process Clauses of the Constitution.

Dissent: (Brennan, J.) A state's intestate succession laws, insofar as they treat illegitimate children whose fathers have publicly acknowledged them differently from legitimate children, plainly violate the Equal Protection Clause of the Fourteenth Amendment.

Massachusetts Board of Retirement v. Murgia (S. Ct. 1976)

Facts: The Massachusetts State Police Department required its officers to retire at age 50.

Issue: May a state impose a compulsory retirement age for certain government employees?

Rule: (per curiam) The right to government employment is not fundamental, and classifications based on age are not suspect. Therefore, such a classification need only be rationally related to the achievement of the state's objective. A mandatory retirement age of 50 for a state's uniformed police officers is rationally related to the state's objective of ensuring the physical preparedness of its uniformed police.

Dissent: (Marshall, J.) The Court is hesitant to expand the category of strict scrutiny rights and classifications. This is because legislation under strict scrutiny is usually struck down, while legislation generally passes the mere rationality test. However, the category of strict scrutiny is not complete and should be enlarged when the need arises.

Nordlinger v. Hahn (S. Ct. 1992)

Facts: In 1978, California voters passed Proposition 13, which limited property tax increases to 2% per annum. Actual property values had increased much more rapidly. Therefore, new owners bore a disproportionally large share of the tax burden because their property assessments were based on actual current value, rather than 1978 value plus artificially small annual increases.

Issue: Do preferential property tax rates for older owners violate the Equal Protection Clause?

Rule: (Blackmun, J.) Different treatment for newer and older property owners will satisfy the Equal Protection Clause if the classification rationally furthers a legitimate state interest. The state has a legitimate interest in local neighborhood preservation and in protecting owners' reliance interest in their expected tax liability. Because the tax scheme is rationally related to these interests, it does not violate the Equal Protection Clause.

Dissent: (Stevens, J.) Such disparate treatment of similarly situated taxpayers is arbitrary, unreasonable, and not rationally related to the stated interests.

United States v. Fordice (S. Ct. 1992)

Facts: Mississippi's state universities were founded as racially segregated institutions and remained so until 1962. As of the mid-1980s, 99% of

Mississippi's white students attended the schools that were formerly restricted to white students and 71% of the state's black students attended the schools that were formerly restricted to blacks.

Issue: What are the standards for determining whether a state university has met its obligation to dismantle prior *de jure* segregation?

Rule: (White, J.) To meet its obligation to dismantle prior *de jure* segregation, a state must show that any policies and practices traceable to the prior system that continue to have segregative effects — by influencing student enrollment decisions or by fostering segregation in other facets of the university system — have a sound educational justification and cannot be practicably eliminated. The court found that Mississippi did not meet its obligation because, *inter alia*: (1) it required higher ACT scores for admission to the historically white universities (at the time, the average score for white students was 18 and the average score for blacks was 7); and (2) most programs offered at the historically black schools were also offered at the historically white schools, and this practice was a primary component of the separate-but-equal system.

Dissent: (Scalia, J.) The burden created by the majority opinion has no application in the context of higher education, provides no genuine guidance to states and lower courts, and is as likely to subvert as to promote the interests of those citizens it seeks to protect. It confers virtually standardless discretion upon district judges while depriving them of the efficient remedy of mandatory student assignment.

Reed v. Reed (S. Ct. 1971)

Facts: An Idaho law provided that in the choice of persons to administer an intestate estate, preference should be given to males. Pursuant to that law, an Idaho probate court appointed the father rather than the mother to administer the intestate estate of a deceased child.

Issue: May a state, in the appointment of estate administrators, give preference to male applicants without violating the Equal Protection Clause?

Rule: (Burger, C.J.) A state may impose gender preferences if the difference in sex bears a rational relationship to a state objective. The objective of administrative convenience for the state probate courts is an insufficient ground on which to justify a gender classification to administer an intestate estate.

Kahn v. Shevin (S. Ct. 1974)

Facts: Florida law provided for a property tax exemption for widows, but offered no analogous benefit for widowers.

Issue: May a state grant a tax exemption based on the sex of a surviving spouse without violating the equal protection guarantees of the Fourteenth Amendment?

Rule: (Douglas, J.) When a state system of taxation imperils no specific federal right except equal protection, the Court defers to a state legislature's determinations of the proper classifications to produce a reasonable system of taxation.

Dissent: (Brennan, J.) Legislative classification that distinguishes potential beneficiaries solely by reference to their gender-based status must be subjected to strict scrutiny. Under this heightened scrutiny, the statute is invalid because the state's compelling interest can be served equally well by a more narrowly drafted statute.

Graham v. Richardson (S. Ct. 1971)

Facts: Arizona law precluded noncitizens residing within the United States for less than 15 years from receiving welfare benefits. Pennsylvania law excluded aliens from certain state-funded welfare benefits.

Issue: Does a state conditioning the receipt of welfare benefits upon federal citizenship or residency requirements violate the Equal Protection Clause of the Fourteenth Amendment?

Rule: (Blackmun, J.) Classifications based on alienage are inherently suspect and must be subjected to strict judicial scrutiny. A state's special public interest in preserving its limited welfare benefits for its own citizens and long-time resident aliens is inadequate justification for an alienage-based classification.

Karcher v. Daggett (S. Ct. 1983)

Facts: A New Jersey reapportionment plan contained population variances among the districts. Alternative plans had smaller population variances.

Issue: In reapportioning its congressional districts, by how far may a state deviate from achieving equal population among districts?

Rule: (Brennan, J.) Absolute population equality is the paramount objective of apportionment in the case of congressional districts. Minor deviations in population are permissible upon a showing of either that the population differences are genuinely unavoidable or that they are necessary to achieve a specific, legitimate state goal.

Dissent: (White, J.) The Court's insistence on attaining perfection in the equalizing of congressional districts is unreasonable. The population deviation before the Court is *de minimis,* and regardless of what other infirmities the plan may have, there is no violation of Article I, §2, the sole issue before the Court.

Davis v. Bandemer (S. Ct. 1986)

Facts: The Indiana Legislature started to reapportion the state's legislative districts. Several politicians challenged the reapportionment plan as constituting political gerrymandering intended to disadvantage Democrats.

Issue 1: Does a claim of political gerrymandering present a justiciable issue that can be properly decided by the courts?

Rule 1: (White, J.) A case of political gerrymandering presents the issue of fair representation for which judicially manageable standards exist to decide such cases.

Issue 2: May a state reapportion its legislative districts to favor a particular group of candidates without violating the equal protection guarantees of the Fourteenth Amendment?

Rule 2: (White, J.) Reapportionment necessarily favors one group over another. Therefore, in order for a reapportionment challenge to succeed, intentional discrimination against an identifiable political group and actual discriminatory effect on that group must be shown. A group's electoral power is not constitutionally diminished by a reapportionment scheme that makes winning elections more difficult, and a failure of proportional representation is insufficient to invalidate a reapportionment plan on equal protection grounds.

Dissent: (O'Connor, J.) Claims of partisan gerrymandering raise a nonjusticiable political question that the Judiciary should leave to the legislative branch. Racial gerrymandering should remain justiciable because the harms it engenders run counter to the central thrust of the Fourteenth Amendment.

Sosna v. Iowa (S. Ct. 1975)

Facts: P, after residing in Iowa for a month, filed a petition to dissolve her marriage. The court dismissed the petition because of P's failure to meet the durational residency requirement of one year for such an action.

Issue: Does a state's imposition of a durational residency requirement for the grant of a divorce violate constitutional guarantees?

Rule: (Rehnquist, J.) A state's interests in requiring divorce candidates to be genuinely attached to the state and its desire to insulate divorce decrees from the likelihood of collateral attack are sufficiently substantial to withstand equal protection and due process challenges.

Dissent: (Marshall, J.) It has been established that any classification that penalizes the exercise of the constitutional right to travel is invalid unless justified by a compelling governmental interest. The Court's failure to address this case in these terms suggests a new distaste for the mode of analysis we have applied to this area of equal protection law.

Attorney General of New York v. Soto-Lopez (S. Ct. 1986)

Facts: New York granted civil service employment preference to New York residents who were honorably discharged veterans of the armed forces, who served during a time of war, and who were residents of New York when they entered military service.

Issue: Does a preference in civil service employment opportunities offered by a state solely to resident veterans who lived in the state at the time they entered military service violate the constitutional rights of others?

Rule: (Brennan, J.) The right to interstate travel is a constitutionally protected right. A state law favoring "prior" residents and penalizing "newer" residents who have exercised this constitutional right must be subjected to heightened judicial review and is valid only if the state can demonstrate that its classification is necessary to accomplish a compelling state interest.

Dissent: (O'Connor, J.) Something more than a minimal effect on the right to travel must be required to trigger heightened scrutiny. Otherwise, the right to travel analysis will swallow up the traditional deference shown to state economic and social regulation.

Metropolitan Life Ins. Co. v. Ward (S. Ct. 1985)

Facts: Alabama showed preference to domestic insurance companies by imposing a substantially higher gross premium tax on out-of-state insurance companies.

Issue: Does a state's imposition of a more burdensome tax on foreign companies doing business within its state constitute a violation of equal protection?

Rule: (Powell, J.) A state's imposition of a more burdensome tax on foreign companies doing business within its borders violates equal protection unless the discrimination between foreign and domestic companies bears a rational relation to a legitimate state purpose. Promotion of domestic industry and encouragement of capital investment within the state are not legitimate state purposes to justify the imposition of the discriminatory tax at issue.

Dissent: (O'Connor, J.) Precedent imposes a heavy burden on those who would challenge local economic legislation solely on Equal Protection Clause grounds. Deference must be accorded to a legislature's judgment if the classification is rationally related to a legitimate state purpose.

Lyng v. Castillo (S. Ct. 1986)

Facts: The federal Food Stamp Program determined eligibility and benefit levels on a household basis rather than on an individual basis. A household was defined as parents, children, and siblings living together.

Issue: May Congress, in granting public assistance, distinguish between close relatives and other individuals living in the same household without violating equal protection guarantees?

Rule: (Stevens, J.) The class of "close relatives" is not a suspect classification triggering strict judicial scrutiny. The proper standard of review is whether the classification has a rational basis. Congress' determination that there is a distinction between close relatives and distant relatives sharing a home is a rational distinction upon which to base benefit levels.
Dissent: (Marshall, J.) When analyzing classifications affecting the receipt of governmental benefits, a court must consider the character of the classification in question, the relative importance of the benefits to individuals in the class discriminated against, and the asserted state interest. Under this formulation, equal protection analysis would preclude a distinction affecting a vital interest in family survival.

Kadrmas v. Dickinson Public Schools (S. Ct. 1988)

Facts: The North Dakota state legislature enacted legislation expressly indicating that nonreorganized school districts could charge a fee for transporting students to school.
Issue: Under the Equal Protection Clause, may a state allow some local school boards but not others to assess a fee for transporting pupils between their homes and the public schools?
Rule: (O'Connor, J.) Denial of free access to transportation to attend a public school does not interfere with a fundamental right or discriminate against a suspect class triggering strict judicial scrutiny. Under the rational relation test, a state's decision to allow local school boards the option of charging a user fee for bus service is rationally related to a state objective to encourage school boards to provide such service. Therefore, the state practice is constitutionally permissible.
Dissent: (Marshall, J.) The Court continues to retreat from the promise of equal educational opportunity by holding that a school district's refusal to allow an indigent child who lives far away from the nearest public school to use a school bus service without paying a fee does not violate the Equal Protection Clause. For the poor, education is often the only route by which to become full participants in our society. By allowing a state to burden the access of poor persons to an education, the Court denies equal opportunity and discourages hope.

Vieth v. Jubelier (S. Ct. 2004)

Facts: P, voters in a particular congressional district, challenged the drawing of the district's lines, claiming that the lines amounted to an unconstitutional political gerrymander.
Issue: Can congressional district lines that are drawn in order to concentrate voters of one party in one district ever deprive voters of the equal protection right to vote?

Rule: (Scalia, J.) (plurality) There is no judicially manageable standard for determining when such line-drawing, which is after all inherently political, crosses the line and so stacks the district with voters of one party that voters of the other party are unable to participate in the political process.

Concurrence: (Kennedy, J.) There may be standards that future courts will be able to discern; thus, it is inappropriate to label these claims non-justiciable political questions.

United States v. Virginia (S. Ct. 1996)

Facts: P challenged the male-only admissions policy of Virginia Military Institute (VMI), a state military school.

Issue: May a state-run military school maintain a male-only admissions policy because of asserted natural differences in the learning techniques and preferences of men and women, when it establishes a female-only military training program at a neighboring school and when the state defends the exclusionary policy on the desire to offer a diverse menu of educational options for men and women?

Rule: (Ginsberg, J.) Such asserted natural differences and desires to offer diverse educational options must be the real reasons for the policy, and not after-the-fact rationalizations. The female-only program is not equal to VMI's program, and thus does not cure the unconstitutional exclusion of women from VMI.

Dissent: (Scalia, J.) The state satisfied the intermediate scrutiny standard for gender classifications, and, at any rate, the Equal Protection Clause should not be thought of as having overthrown government policies that have existed since before the Clause was enacted.

Anh Nguyen v. INS (S. Ct. 2001)

Facts: A federal immigration rule treats foreign-born babies differently depending on which parent was an American citizen, with children of American mothers getting more favorable treatment than children of American fathers.

Issue: Does this differential treatment, depending on the gender of the American citizen-parent, violate the equality component of the Fifth Amendment's Due Process Clause?

Rule: (Kennedy, J.) It is reasonable for the government to recognize the inherent differences between men and women, in particular the differences between fathers and mothers with regard to the likelihood that they would form a close bond with a newborn.

Dissent: (O'Connor, J.) The careful scrutiny required of gender classifications requires that such justifications be reviewed skeptically, and must reflect real gender differences rather than stereotypes.

Grutter v. Bollinger (S. Ct. 2003)

Facts: P, a rejected applicant to the University of Michigan Law School, sued D school, alleging that its affirmative action program violated the Equal Protection Clause.

Issue: Under what circumstances can a school use race as part of its admissions criteria?

Rule: (O'Connor, J.) Universities have a compelling interest in the diversity of their classrooms, in order to ensure that students are exposed to a wide variety of experiences; this interest is protected as part of schools' First Amendment academic freedoms. As long as an admissions program is not a quota and as long as a person's race is treated as one factor among many in an individualized review of each application, the program passes muster. However, affirmative action programs should become unnecessary over the next 25 years.

Concurrence: (Ginsberg, J.) It is unnecessary to the decision of this case to determine whether strict scrutiny is the correct approach for affirmative action programs, since the Law School's program satisfies even that high level of scrutiny.

Dissent: (Rehnquist, C.J.) The Law School's use of race demonstrates a manipulation of applications in order to achieve the kind of racial balancing that the Court has determined to be unconstitutional.

Gratz v. Bollinger (S. Ct. 2003)

Facts: The University of Michigan undergraduate admissions department uses a numerical scale to determine admissions decisions, and that scale attaches 20 points to applications from members of certain historically underrepresented races, of the 100 points needed to guarantee admission. P, a rejected applicant, sued the school, claiming that the school's affirmative action program violated the Equal Protection Clause.

Issue: Under what circumstances can a school use race as part of its admissions criteria.

Rule: (Rehnquist, C.J.) The school's use of race is essentially a quota system, which does not include the individualized consideration of each application, and is thus unconstitutional.

Dissent: (Souter, J.) Effectively, the law school admissions system upheld in *Grutter* is no different than the system struck down in this case.

Adarand Constructors v. Pena (S. Ct. 1995)

Facts: P, a highway construction contractor, challenged the federal government's imposition of a minority-owned business set aside for highway construction funded with federal money, alleging that the set-aside violated the equality component of the Fifth Amendment's Due Process Clause.

Issue: Are federal affirmative action programs to be reviewed according to the same strict scrutiny accorded affirmative action plans established by states?

Rule: (Kennedy, J.) Federal affirmative action plans require the same strict scrutiny as analogous plans run by state governments.

Dissent: (Stevens, J.) There is good reason to accord more deference to federal affirmative action plans, given the national nature of Congress' constituency, the historical role of the federal government in ensuring equality, and the explicit grant to Congress to enforce the Equal Protection Clause of the Fourteenth Amendment.

Romer v. Evans (S. Ct. 1996)

Facts: Colorado voters enacted Amendment 2 to the Colorado Constitution, which prohibited any state agency or subdivision from recognizing any protected status to gays and lesbians.

Issue: Does Amendment 2 violate the equal protection rights of gays and lesbians?

Rule: (Kennedy, J.) Amendment 2 imposes such broad-based burdens on gays that it cannot be considered rationally related to any legitimate government interest, such as respect for the associational wishes of landlords who do not wish to rent to gays, or the state's desire to conserve scarce anti-discrimination enforcement resources. Amendment 2 also fails equal protection scrutiny by literally putting gays and lesbians outside of the law, by denying them protected status.

Dissent: (Scalia, J.) Amendment 2 merely prevents the granting of special privileges to gays. If a state can constitutionally prohibit sodomy, it can therefore take the lesser step of preventing gays from having protected class status.

Note: *Romer* was decided before *Lawrence v. Texas* (2003), which struck down prohibitions on sodomy.

Bush v. Gore (S. Ct. 2000)

Facts: Florida was recounting the vote in the 2000 presidential election, and different county election boards used different standards for deciding when a valid vote had been cast.

Issue: Does the existence of different counting standards used by different Florida election officials violate the Equal Protection Clause?

Rule: (per curiam) The use of different standards lacks a rational basis and therefore violates the rights of Florida voters to have their votes count equally. Because of the shortness of time before Florida's vote must be certified in order to escape a congressional challenge, the recount must be stopped.

Dissent: (Souter, J.) The use of different standards lacks a rational basis, but the proper remedy is to remand the case to state officials to let them determine how best to proceed.

Dissent: (Stevens, J.) There is no equal protection problem when there is a single "intent of the voter" standard to be applied. Any concerns about differing standards for determining voters' intent are mitigated by the presence of a single impartial magistrate to adjudicate all objections.

Shaw v. Reno (S. Ct. 1993)

Facts: In order to satisfy the federal Voting Rights Act, North Carolina created a congressional district that was heavily minority. White voters in the new district sued, alleging that the district had been drawn based on race.

Issue: What are the standards by which a court should determine whether a congressional district was created because of race, thus triggering strict scrutiny?

Rule: (O'Connor, J.) If the district is so bizarrely drawn as to be unexplainable on any other grounds but race, then it will be subject to strict scrutiny as a racial classification. The harms of race-based districting include concerns about stigmatizing minorities by suggesting they all think and vote alike, the message it sends to representatives from those districts that their duty is mainly to the minority voters in the district, and the overall racial balkanization it implies.

Dissent: (White, J.) The plaintiffs do not have standing to sue, as they have not shown that the districting decision caused them any injury, since they remain free to vote and participate in politics in the district.

Miller v. Johnson (S. Ct. 1995)

Facts: A congressional district was challenged as being drawn because of race, and thus subject to strict scrutiny.

Issue: Are there circumstances in which a district that is not bizarre, and thus doesn't come under the rule of *Shaw v. Reno*, nevertheless should be subject to strict scrutiny as a racial classification?

Rule: (Kennedy, J.) Race can play an appropriate role in the districting process, given the correlation between race and voting patterns. However, even a non-bizarre district will be subject to strict scrutiny if racial considerations predominated in its creation.

Dissent: (Stevens, J.) The plaintiffs here do not have standing, as they have not shown that they were injured in any way by the redistricting, since they can still participate fully in the district's politics.

Dissent: (Ginsberg, J.) There is a difference between considerations of race in the districting context that seek to exclude, and those, like this case, where the use of race seeks to ensure that historically excluded groups can participate effectively in politics.

Vacco v. Quill (S. Ct. 1997)

Facts: P, a terminal patient who wished to receive death-hastening medication, sued New York State, alleging that it violated equal protection for the state to allow patients to reject life-prolonging medication but to forbid patients to request and receive life-ending medication.

Issue: Can a state distinguish between allowing a person to refuse life-prolonging medication and forbidding a person from receiving death-hastening medication?

Rule: (Rehnquist, C.J.) As there is a long legal and medical tradition of distinguishing between assisted suicide and refusal of life-prolonging treatment, it cannot be said that the distinction in the New York law is unreasonable.

Concurrence: (Souter, J.) As all families can be expected to confront end-of-life issues in some context, there is no reason to think the political process will not be responsive to the need to draw appropriate lines governing decisions about prolonging life or hastening death.

Freeman v. Pitts (S. Ct. 1992)

Facts: After a number of years under federal court supervision, a school district was held to have achieved unitary status with regard to four of the six factors previous case law had identified as appropriate subjects for judicial supervision. The court relinquished control over those facets of the district's operations, and P appealed.

Issue: Does a district court have the discretion to relinquish control over some facets of school district operations before the district has completely reached unitary status?

Rule: (Kennedy, J.) Because of the inherent discretion a court has in fashioning equitable remedies, a district court has the discretion to relinquish control over facets of the district's operations that are no longer tainted by prior discrimination.

Board of Educ. v. Dowell (S. Ct. 1991)

Facts: After a finding that a school district had achieved unitary status, the district court closed the case against the school. Later when the district took action that would result in *de facto* re-segregation P sought to reopen the case. The district court refused but the appellate court reversed, holding that the injunction against the district was still in place. The district court then dissolved the injunction.

Issue: Under what circumstances can a district court dissolve an injunction against a school district that was held to have achieved unitary status?
Rule: (Rehnquist, C.J.) If the district court held that the district had achieved unitary status there was no further hurdle to that court dissolving the injunction; no further showing of grievous wrong to the district was necessary.
Dissent: (Marshall, J.) Injunctions should not be lifted so long as conditions likely to inflict the stigmatic injury condemned in *Brown v. Board of Educ.* persist and feasible methods remain to eliminate those conditions.

Missouri v. Jenkins (S. Ct. 1995)

Facts: The state appealed the district court's continued imposition of certain requirements on school districts found to have segregated, including teacher pay raises and continuation of magnet programs designed to make the district attractive to out-of-district white students.
Issue: What is the permissible scope of judicial supervision of school districts found to have segregated based on race?
Rule: (Rehnquist, C.J.) The ultimate inquiry in such cases is whether the district has complied in good faith with the injunction, and whether the vestiges of discrimination have been eliminated to the extent practicable. Federal court supervision is not designed to last forever. Remedies that seek to influence the conduct of innocent parties beyond the district's boundaries are not appropriate.

Parents Involved in Community Schools v. Seattle Sch. Dist. No. 1 (S. Ct. 2007)

Facts: A school district in Louisville that had recently been released from a federal court desegregation order, and a school distinct in Seattle that was never under such an order, adopted student assignment plans that include racial considerations. Parents sued.
Issue: Does a school district's use of race when not compelled by a federal court order violate the Equal Protection Clause?
Rule: (Roberts, C.J.) (plurality) Such uses of race are subject to the highest scrutiny. Here the districts cannot show that their use of race is narrowly tailored, given the minor effects the racial criterion has on student admission decisions and given their failure to demonstrate how less racially conscious measures were ineffective.
Concurrence: (Thomas, J.) Equal protection requires us to be extremely demanding before allowing school districts to use racial classifications in assigning students.
Concurrence: (Kennedy, J.) Districts must have more leeway than that suggested by the plurality to mitigate the past effects of racial segregation;

however, the districts' use of race fails equal protection scrutiny because the small number of students affected suggests that other more race-neutral means might have had the same effect of diversifying the racial mix in classrooms.

Dissent: (Stevens, J.) The Court's equation of this scheme of racial classification with the racial segregation in *Brown v. Board of Educ.* suggests the problems in the current strict three-tiered structure of equal protection scrutiny.

Dissent: (Breyer, J.) The position the districts were in when the school districts made modest use of race to assign students is analogous to the position of districts that are under federal court order; in both cases the districts are attempting to overcome the legacy of racial segregation.

Engquist v. Oregon Dep't of Agriculture (S. Ct. 2008)

Facts: P, an employee of D, was effectively fired. P sues, alleging that she was singled out for firing for reasons that were irrational and malicious.

Issue: Does the class-of-one theory of equal protection from *Village of Willowbrook v. Olech*, 528 U.S. 562 (2000), apply in the context of government employment?

Rule: (Roberts, C.J.) It does not. The workplace is different from the context in *Olech*, where government was acting as the sovereign regulator. The workplace, where government may necessarily have to single individuals out for reasons that are individualized and subjective, is simply not an appropriate context for a claim that government acts unconstitutionally when it treats similarly situated people differently.

Dissent: (Stevens, J.) Even if the class-of-one doctrine needs pruning, the Court's *per se* rule is too blunt of an instrument. The Court could simply have required that class-of-one plaintiffs prove that there was no conceivable rational basis for the government to single them out, and thereby preserved government flexibility to use its discretion to make subjective, individualized decisions.

League of United Latin American Citizens v. Perry (S. Ct. 2006)

Facts: In 2003 Republican legislators in Texas passed a reapportionment plan that redrew congressional districts in Texas, an unusual move given that it was not in response to the decennial census that is normally the trigger for redistricting. Minority groups sued, alleging that the legislature's action constituted a partisan gerrymander that violated their equal protection rights to equal participation in the political process. (They also raised statutory claims under the Voting Rights Act.)

Rule: (Kennedy, J.) (plurality) The plaintiffs have not established a partisan gerrymander, as they have offered no test that would provide a reliable standard for determining when redistricting constitutes an unconstitutional partisan gerrymander. The fact that the redistricting occurred in an unusual time frame does not by itself establish a violation.

Concurrence: (Roberts, C.J.) The question whether partisan gerrymandering claims are justiciable at all was not presented in this case; thus, in rejecting the plaintiffs' claims as presented I do not take a position on these claims' justiciability.

Concurrence: (Scalia, J.) Partisan gerrymander claims are not justiciable.

Concurrence: (Souter, J.) The procedure of any redistricting plan can theoretically provide the basis for a holding that the plan was an unconstitutional party gerrymander, in contrast to the plurality opinion.

Dissent: (Stevens, J.) The decision to redistrict in 2003 was made solely to advantage Republicans and disadvantage Democrats, and thus violated the Equal Protection Clause.

Dissent: (Breyer, J.) I agree with Justice Stevens' analysis of the partisan gerrymander issue.

Crawford v. Marion County Election Board (S. Ct. 2008)

Facts: Indiana law requires that voters produce a picture ID at the polling place, or otherwise execute a provisional ballot and sign an affidavit at the county clerk's office.

Issue: Does this law unconstitutionally restrict the right to vote so severely that it is facially invalid?

Rule: (Stevens, J.) (plurality) The few situations where the law may impose a severe burden on the right to vote do not justify a holding that the law is facially unconstitutional. However, persons denied the right to vote by this law may challenge the law as applied to their own particular circumstances.

Concurrence: (Scalia, J.) The law is constitutional because it imposes a reasonable, minimal and equal burden on the right to vote. The fact that some people are especially burdened by the law is irrelevant.

Dissent: (Souter, J.) The law imposes a serious burden on tens of thousands of Indiana voters, and the state has not pointed to specific facts about voter fraud or other interests that might justify this burden.

Dissent: (Breyer, J.) I would balance the burdens the law places on the right to vote with the state's interests. Based on this balancing, the law constitutes a disproportionate burden on the right to vote.

Village of Willowbrook v. Olech (S. Ct. 2000)

Facts: P homeowners requested D town to hook them up to the town's water system. D agreed, but only after demanding a larger easement than it normally requested for such hook-ups. Ps sued, alleging they were singled out for worse treatment due to D's bad faith growing out of a previous lawsuit.

Issue: Can an equal protection plaintiff state an equal protection claim without alleging that they were the victim of discrimination based on membership in a class, such as a racial group?

Rule: (per curiam) Yes. Equal protection protects every individual from irrational government singling-out, regardless of membership in a class.

Johnson v. California (S. Ct. 2005)

Facts: California segregates prisoners by race when they first enter a new facility, in order to minimize the possibility of violence from race-based gang warfare. P, a prisoner segregated by race when transferred to a new facility, sued, alleging the temporary segregation violated his Fourteenth Amendment rights.

Rule: (O'Connor, J.) All race-based classifications, including this one, must be tested according to strict scrutiny.

Concurrence: (Ginsburg, J.) Not all race-based classifications should be subject to the same level of scrutiny. Here, though, there is no pretense that the state's action is designed to correct previous racial inequalities, nor is it necessary to the safe operation of a prison. Therefore, strict scrutiny is appropriate.

Dissent: (Stevens, J.) The Court should simply declare this policy unconstitutional rather than sending the case back to the lower courts for application of strict scrutiny.

Dissent: (Thomas, J.) Prisoners lose many of their rights when they are incarcerated; the right to be free of racial segregation is one of them, when prison officials make a reasonable judgment that segregation is necessary to the efficient operation of a prison system.

CHAPTER 9

Post-Civil War Amendments and Civil Rights Legislation

I. INTRODUCTION

A. Bill of Rights

The first ten amendments to the Constitution are generally called the Bill of Rights. Originally, they were not directly binding upon state governments, as was held in *Barron v. The Mayor and City Council of Baltimore.*

B. Civil War Amendments

Upon enactment of the Civil War Amendments (the Thirteenth, Fourteenth, and Fifteenth Amendments), the individual was protected from the state as well as the federal government.

1. Thirteenth Amendment

The Thirteenth Amendment bars slavery.

2. Fourteenth Amendment

The Fourteenth Amendment provides that no state shall make or enforce any law that shall abridge the privileges or immunities of citizens of the United States, nor shall any state deprive any person of life, liberty, or property without due process of law, nor deny to any person the equal protection of the laws.

3. Fifteenth Amendment

The Fifteenth Amendment provides for the right to vote without racial discrimination.

C. Interpretation

When interpreting the Civil War Amendments and civil rights legislation, two considerations often arise:

1. State Action

   Only the state and federal governments are prohibited from interfering with civil rights (with the exception of the Thirteenth Amendment, which also governs private conduct). Private individuals' liberty is preserved. Thus, some "state action" must be shown before a court can grant relief.

2. Enforcement

   All of the Civil War Amendments provide that Congress shall have the power to enforce the Amendment by appropriate legislation. What legislation is "appropriate" is often questioned, since Congress is not authorized to regulate solely private conduct.

II. STATE ACTION

State action is apparent whenever the claim involves a statute, regulation, or direct action by the government or one of its subdivisions.

A. The Public Function Approach

   The actions of private individuals or corporations constitute state action when the state has entrusted the private actor with the performance of functions that are governmental in nature. The private actor is an agent of the state. There are several areas where the Court has found "public function":

   1. White Primary Cases

      Private political "organizations" may not hold primaries that are racially discriminatory. See *Terry v. Adams*.

   2. Company Towns

      Where a company town replaces the public streets such that nearly all forums of communication would be blocked if the private owner enforced his rights against trespassers, the operation of the land becomes a public function and the owner must yield to the free exercise of First Amendment rights. This approach had been held to include privately owned shopping centers, but these cases have been overruled.

   3. Parks and Recreational Facilities

      Operation of a park is generally considered a public function.

B. State Exclusivity

   The requirement of "state exclusivity" has narrowed the scope of the public function doctrine. It requires that the function be one that has traditionally been exclusively in the domain of the government.

   1. Utilities

      Operation of a privately owned utility, though licensed and regulated by the government, is not state action.

2. Nursing Homes and Private Schools
Operation of nursing homes and private schools, even if regulated and funded by the government and working under government contracts, is not state action.

C. The Nexus Theory
If the government has many "contacts" to the private action, the action may constitute state action.

1. Commandment
Even when applying facially neutral laws, a court's enforcement of a discriminatory agreement is state action violative of the Constitution. See *Shelley v. Kraemer.*

2. Encouragement
If the state somehow encourages the discrimination, the state has violated the Constitution. Such was the case in *Reitman v. Mulkey,* where California law prohibited the government from interfering with a private individual's right to discriminate in real estate transactions.

   a. Repeal
   However, mere repeal of a law prohibiting private discrimination is probably not "encouragement."

   b. Omission
   Also, mere failure to forbid private discrimination is not state action.

3. Symbiosis: When the action is mutually beneficial to the state and the private actor, state action might be found.

   a. But For
   In *Burton v. Wilmington Parking Authority,* the Court found that since the parking garage could not have existed but for the private discriminatory restaurant that leased space from the garage and helped defray its expenses, state action was present.

   b. Nursing Homes and Private Schools
   However, the Court has not found state action in the operation of nursing homes with Medicaid patients or private schools under government contract.

   c. State Licensing
   Also, the state has not found significant enough involvement in liquor licensing or public utilities licensing.

   d. Very Little Involvement
   In cases where state action is not found, it is usually because the state has not itself approved of the action or reviewed it, nor did it issue the regulations that caused the private action.

III. CONGRESSIONAL ENFORCEMENT

A. Introduction
  1. Power to Enforce
     With respect to Congress' power to enforce the Civil War Amendments, there are two main issues:
     a. To what extent can Congress enact legislation to regulate purely private conduct?
     b. What power does Congress have to interpret the Amendments differently from the Court, especially with respect to the remedies it can impose and the substantive content of the rights?
  2. Challenged Congressional Statutes
     Many statutes that grant civil rights have been challenged as beyond Congress' power. They include:
     a. 42 U.S.C. §1981, which is a general grant of civil rights that gives all persons the same rights "as is enjoyed by white citizens" to make and enforce contracts, use the courts, etc.;
     b. 42 U.S.C. §1982, which guarantees property rights regardless of race;
     c. 42 U.S.C. §1985, which prevents people from conspiring to deprive anyone of equal protection or equal privileges and immunities (this governs private conduct as well as state action);
     d. The Civil Rights Act of 1964, which guaranteed public accommodations, service, etc., enacted through Congress' power to regulate interstate commerce;
     e. The Voting Rights Act of 1965, which banned literacy tests; and
     f. The Fair Housing Act, Title VIII of the Civil Rights Act of 1968.
B. Power to Reach Private Conduct
   Congress is not empowered to reach private conduct under the Fourteenth and Fifteenth Amendments. Thus, Congress based its early statutes limiting private discriminatory conduct on the right to interstate travel, the right to vote, and other explicitly guaranteed federal rights.
  1. Enlarging the Scope
     Later, Congress' scope was enlarged to limit private conduct that interfered with another individual's access to state rights or a state official's attempts to furnish equal protection.
  2. Broadening of the Thirteenth Amendment
     Jones v. Alfred H. Mayer held that Congress had the power to determine what constituted a "badge of slavery." In *Jones,* a

private developer's refusal to sell land to black people constituted a badge of slavery.

C. Power to Interpret Constitutional Rights

1. Generally

Congress leaves to the federal courts the problem of defining the
substantive scope of constitutional rights. But in the area of civil
rights, Congress itself has had the view that it may define the
scope of the rights given by the Civil War Amendments. This
more aggressive view remains controversial.

2. Remedial Powers

Congress has very broad power to adopt remedial legislation, as
in the Voting Rights Act of 1965, which put strict limitations
upon the states where evidence of a history of discrimination
was found.

3. Voting Rights Act

Congress has also made substantive modifications in the Voting
Rights Act, in that it guaranteed the right to vote to all Puerto
Ricans that had finished the sixth grade, regardless of whether
they could speak English. It also granted the right to vote to
all people over the age of 18. In this sense, the right to vote,
a substantive right and not just a remedial correction, was
expanded.

4. Congruence and Proportionality

In general, congressional legislation enforcing the Civil War
Amendments must be congruent and proportional to the
underlying violations they address. Normally this requires
that there is some proportionate relationship between, on the
one hand, the scope of the remedial legislation and the severity
of the remedies it imposes and, on the other hand, the severity
or intractability of the constitutional violation the statute
attacks.

CASE CLIPS

The Civil Rights Cases (S. Ct. 1883)

Facts: The Civil Rights Act of 1875 provided that all people, regardless of race and color, were entitled to equal enjoyment of all public places of amusement.

Issue: Does Congress have the power to enact a law directly governing the behavior of citizens prohibiting certain types of discriminatory practices, pursuant to the Thirteenth and Fourteenth Amendments?

Rule: Congress only has the power granted by Section 2 of the Thirteenth Amendment and Section 5 of the Fourteenth Amendment to pass laws that effectuate the goals and policies of these Amendments. The Thirteenth Amendment prohibits slavery and involuntary servitude; discrimination laws in no way effectuate the policies of this Amendment. The Fourteenth Amendment prohibits the states from issuing legislation that denies equal protection of the laws; thus, any law that Congress passes to effectuate this policy must be directed specifically against a state that has a discriminatory law on its books.

Dissent: (Harlan, J.) Congress, under its express power to enforce the Thirteenth Amendment, may enact legislation of a direct and primary character to protect people against the deprivation, because of their race, of any civil rights granted to other freemen in the same state. Racial discrimination practiced by entities in the exercise of their public or quasi public functions is a badge of servitude the imposition of which Congress may prevent under its power to enforce the Thirteenth Amendment. Congress also has the power to enact discrimination laws of a direct character under the Fourteenth Amendment. To effectuate this guarantee of the rights of citizenship requires the ability to make a law directly affecting the status of federal and state citizens. Additionally, the Act should be held valid under Congress' power to enact laws pursuant to the Equal Protection Clause of the Fourteenth Amendment, because the entities regulated by the Act, by virtue of the public services which they render and the benefits that accrue to them as a result of such activity, are instrumentalities of the state.

Shelley v. Kraemer (S. Ct. 1948)

Facts: The Missouri and Michigan state courts enforced an agreement between a group of property owners restricting the occupancy of the properties to white people and excluding people of other races.

Issue: Is judicial enforcement by a state court considered state action with respect to the Fourteenth Amendment guarantee that no state shall deny its citizens equal protection of the laws?

Rule: The action of state courts and judicial officers in their official capacities is to be regarded as action of the state within the meaning of the Fourteenth Amendment. When the state has made available to private individuals its full coercive power to deny to citizens the equal enjoyment of property rights, the Fourteenth Amendment is violated.

Burton v. Wilmington Parking Authority (S. Ct. 1961)

Facts: D, a Delaware state agency, leased space to the Eagle Coffee Shoppe, Inc., a restaurant. The restaurant refused to serve blacks.

Issue: Does the state violate the Fourteenth Amendment when it engages in commercial dealings with private individuals who discriminate, and thereby become involved in the discriminatory practice?

Rule: Private conduct abridging individual rights does no violence to equal protection unless the state, in any of its manifestations, has been found to have become involved in it. Generally, when a state leases public property, the proscriptions of the Fourteenth Amendment must be complied with by the lessee as certainly as though they were binding covenants written into the agreement itself.

Concurrence: (Stewart, J.) Delaware Code provides that a restaurant keeper may refuse to serve persons whose reception or entertainment by him would be offensive to the major part of his customers. By classifying people as offensive on the basis of color, the state court violates the Fourteenth Amendment.

Dissent: (Harlan, J.) The majority is unclear in its determination of what standards are necessary to satisfy the requirements of state action.

Reitman v. Mulkey (S. Ct. 1967)

Facts: Article I, §26 of the California Constitution provided that private citizens had the right to sell or lease real property to whomever they wanted to and to refuse to sell to whomever they so chose.

Issue: Does a law, neutral on its face with respect to the rights of private citizens to engage in conduct as they wish, but that in effect sanctions racial discrimination, violate the Fourteenth Amendment?

Rule: A law that allows for the unregulated conduct of private individuals with respect to discrimination, especially when such a law effectively repeals previously enacted anti-discrimination laws, is an affirmative state action designed to make private discriminations legally possible. Such a law is considered to expressly authorize and constitutionalize the private right to discriminate in violation of the Fourteenth Amendment.

Dissent: (Harlan, J.) The enactment of a law repealing previously enacted laws has the same effect as if none of the laws had been passed in the first place. Therefore, there could be no Fourteenth Amendment violation. Additionally, a statute allowing for the freedom of the private individual is simply permissive in purpose and effect and inoffensive on its face. The state action required to bring the Fourteenth Amendment into operation must be affirmative and purposeful, actively fostering discrimination.

Jackson v. Metropolitan Edison Co. (S. Ct. 1974)

Facts: D, a public utility regulated by the state, did not provide for procedural due process standards in terminating electric service to a customer that did not pay his bill.

Issue: Are actions taken by entities strongly regulated by the state considered state actions for purposes of the Fourteenth Amendment?

Rule: The mere fact that a business is subject to state regulation does not by itself convert its action into that of the state for purposes of the Fourteenth Amendment. There must be a sufficiently close nexus between the state and the challenged action of the regulated entity so that the action of the latter may be fairly treated as that of the state itself. An entity's exercise of a choice allowed by state law, where the initiative comes from it and not from the state, does not make its action a "state action" for purposes of the Fourteenth Amendment.

Dissent: (Marshall, J.) State authorization and approval of "private" conduct should support a finding of state action. Furthermore, since the state action requirement is the same for all the elements of the Fourteenth Amendment, then according to the majority, there would not be sufficient state action to impose on a public utility an obligation to meet the constitutional mandate of nondiscrimination. Such a result would not make any sense.

DeShaney v. Winnebago Dep't of Social Serv. (S. Ct. 1989)

Facts: P was repeatedly beaten by his father. D was informed of the beatings but did not take the appropriate action to remove the child from his father's custody.

Issue: Is a governmental agency's failure to provide protection against the deprivation by a third party of one's personal liberty a violation of substantive due process?

Rule: There is nothing in the language of the Due Process Clause requiring a state to protect the life, liberty, and property of its citizens against the invasion of private actors. A state's failure to protect an individual against private violence does not constitute a violation of due process.

Dissent: (Brennan, J.) A state's actions, such as the monopolization of a particular path of relief, may impose upon the state certain positive duties. The Due Process Clause was intended to prevent government from abusing its power. Inaction can be every bit as abusive of power as action. **Dissent:** (Blackmun, J.) The Court's formalistic distinction between action and inaction has no place in the interpretation of the broad and stirring clauses of the Fourteenth Amendment.

United States v. Guest (S. Ct. 1966)

Facts: Ds were indicted under a federal statute criminalizing the restriction of blacks from access to public facilities and interstate roads and highways.

Issue: Does the federal government have the power to enact laws criminalizing private behavior with respect to the Fourteenth Amendment?

Rule: Purely private interference with a federally guaranteed right is constitutionally reachable by Congress since the right is fundamental to the concept of the federal union. However, the deprivation of rights that are only guaranteed under the Fourteenth Amendment may be criminalized by the federal government only if there is a sufficient nexus to state action.

Concurrence: (Clark, J.) All conspiracies interfering with Fourteenth Amendment rights, regardless of state action, should be subject to criminalization.

Concurrence/Dissent: (Harlan, J.) Congress only has the power to criminalize state interference with the freedom to engage in interstate travel.

Concurrence/Dissent: (Brennan, J.) Congress has the right to make a law involving private actions that inhibit another's rights if those rights emanate from the Constitution, even though not expressly guaranteed as against private citizens, and even though state action is not involved.

Jones v. Alfred H. Mayer Co. (S. Ct. 1968)

Facts: 42 U.S.C. §1982 states that all citizens shall have the same right as white citizens with respect to property.

Issue: Does Congress have the power to enact legislation regulating the practices of private individuals regarding racial discrimination?

Rule: Congress may legislate and regulate the conduct of private individuals regarding racial discrimination based on the Thirteenth Amendment's prohibition against slavery. The Thirteenth Amendment extends to all badges and incidents of slavery. Congress has the power to determine which practices constitute badges and incidents of slavery and has decided that the restraints upon an individual's liberty to live where he wants to live and to buy what he wants to buy violate the Thirteenth Amendment.

Dissent: (Harlan, J.) Section 1982 does not apply to purely private action.

Rome v. United States (S. Ct. 1980)

Facts: The Voting Rights Act of 1965 prohibited voting procedures that had a discriminatory effect on the voting power of blacks.

Issue 1: Does Congress have the power under the Fifteenth Amendment to ban practices if they are discriminatory in effect, but not in purpose?

Rule 1: Even though the Fifteenth Amendment bars only purposeful discrimination, any enforcement method that is appropriate can be used, and the prohibition of systems whose effect would be discriminatory is appropriate where there exists evidence of past discrimination.

Issue 2: Does Congress' regulation of state voting systems unconstitutionally interfere with a state government's integral operations?

Rule 2: Principles of federalism that might otherwise be an obstacle to congressional authority are necessarily overridden by the power to enforce the Civil War Amendments by appropriate legislation.

Dissent: (Powell, J.) A showing that one had not committed racial discrimination for a certain period of time should be sufficient for one to escape coverage of the Act. The Act's coverage should not last forever.

Dissent: (Rehnquist, J.) Congress was not empowered to determine that structural changes with a disparate impact on a minority group's ability to elect a candidate violate the Fourteenth and Fifteenth Amendments.

Katzenbach v. Morgan (S. Ct. 1966)

Facts: The Voting Rights Act of 1965 provided that, subject to certain restrictions, no person shall be denied the right to vote because of an inability to read or write English. New York had a requirement of an ability to read or write English in order to be able to vote.

Issue: May Congress constitutionally legislate based on its own interpretation of the reach of the Equal Protection Clause of the Fourteenth Amendment and defeat a state voting requirement?

Rule: Congress may legislate based on its own judgment of the reach of the Equal Protection Clause of the Fourteenth Amendment. The Voting Rights Act of 1965 was enacted to enforce the Equal Protection Clause of the Fourteenth Amendment, and the states have no power to withhold voting rights on conditions that are forbidden by the Fourteenth Amendment.

Dissent: (Harlan, J.) In cases where there is room to differ on whether equal protection or due process has been violated, it is up to the Judiciary, not the legislature, to resolve the conflict. The Act here allows the Fourteenth Amendment to swallow the state's constitutional authority in this field.

Oregon v. Mitchell (S. Ct. 1970)

Facts: The Voting Rights Act Amendments of 1970 guaranteed all citizens 18 years old or older the right to vote in all state and federal elections, even where the state's minimum age requirement was 21.

Issue: Does Congress have the power to determine whether or not a state law violates the Equal Protection Clause?

Rule: Congress does not have the power to decide matters of constitutional interpretation. This authority has been delegated to the Judiciary. Therefore, in passing a law requiring state elections to grant to 18-year-olds the right to vote, irrespective of state law, Congress has overstepped its authority by deciding on its own that the state law violates the Equal Protection Clause of the Fourteenth Amendment. However, Congress has full authority to regulate federal elections.

Dissent: (Brennan, J.) Congress may decide, if armed with sufficient evidence to that end, that a state's laws violate the Equal Protection Clause of the Fourteenth Amendment.

Concurrence/Dissent: (Stewart, J.) Congress may not decide on its own that a state law violates the Equal Protection Clause. It may make rules overriding state laws that either the Court has found to be violative of the Fourteenth Amendment or are so obviously discriminatory as to violate the Fourteenth Amendment.

Concurrence/Dissent: (Harlan, J.) Congress may neither define the extent nor interpret the Equal Protection Clause of the Fourteenth Amendment.

Flagg Bros. v. Brooks (S. Ct. 1978)

Facts: A state law allowed warehousemen to sell the property of their debtors.

Issue: Are functions traditionally performed by government, such as the replevin of goods in a debtor/creditor dispute, subject to the constitutional restraints of the Fourteenth Amendment even though the particular function has not been *exclusively* reserved to the state?

Rule: The only private activities that are within the constitutional constraints of the Fourteenth Amendment are those that are considered public functions. The fact that an activity is traditionally within the province of government does not make it a public function; such functions exist only when there is a history of exclusive governmental activity of the type at issue.

Dissent: (Stevens, J.) A formalized test as to what is considered a public function and what is not would not accomplish the objectives intended by the Fourteenth Amendment. Rather, we should look at the nature of the activity and the relevance of the constitutional value to the activity. State authorization of "strongman behavior" encourages procedures which are inherently unjust.

Blum v. Yaretsky (S. Ct. 1982)

Facts: A state regulation required that physicians evaluate whether a particular private nursing home patient's level of care was medically appropriate and imposed penalties for non-compliance with the regulation. These nursing homes were the beneficiaries of substantial government funding.

Issue 1: Does the imposition of penalties by the state on a private entity for not complying with a particular regulation establish compliance with the regulation as state action for purposes of constitutional constraints of the Fourteenth Amendment?

Rule 1: When the state does not specifically approve, enforce, or otherwise encourage a particular procedure practiced by a private entity, it is not necessarily considered a state action.

Issue 2: Does the fact that the state provides a private entity with public funding necessarily place that private entity within the constraints of the Fourteenth Amendment?

Rule 2: Granting state funds to a private agency does not necessarily render the private entity an arm of the state and hence subject to the Fourteenth Amendment.

Dissent: (Brennan, J.) Only by sifting facts and weighing circumstances can the non-obvious involvement of the state in private conduct be attributed its true significance. The policy implemented here is state policy, and where a private entity acts on behalf of the state to implement state policy, the action is state action.

Moose Lodge No. 107 v. Irvis (S. Ct. 1972)

Facts: The Pennsylvania Liquor Authority granted a liquor license to a fraternal organization that restricted its membership to whites.

Issue: Does the granting of a license to an organization by the state subject the organization to constitutional restraint?

Rule: When there is no official aid, encouragement, or involvement in an organization's decisions and policies on the part of the state, there is insufficient state action to subject the organization to constitutional restraints.

Dissent: (Douglas, J.) Although generally a private organization may discriminate and restrict its members to those of its own kind, in this case, since the amount of liquor licenses to be granted is limited by quota, the granting of a license to an organization that discriminates effectively restricts the ability of the discriminated group to obtain liquor. This restriction is essentially a result of state action.

Dissent: (Brennan, J.) Where the grant of a license imposes extensive regulations on an entity, it becomes intertwined with the state, and therefore a state action for Fourteenth Amendment purposes.

Marsh v. Alabama (S. Ct. 1946)

Facts: P was prohibited from distributing leaflets in a company-owned shopping center.

Issue: Does a company-owned shopping center constitute a public function for Fourteenth Amendment purposes?

Rule: When a private entity replaces all of the functions and activities that normally belong to the state or the municipality, constitutional restrictions apply.

Dissent: (Reed, J.) The rights of a private property owner outweigh any of the rights of a trespasser.

Hudgens v. National Labor Relations Board (S. Ct. 1976)

Facts: A group of strikers were prohibited from picketing in a privately owned shopping center.

Issue: Does a privately owned shopping center constitute a public function for Fourteenth Amendment purposes?

Rule: Unless there is sufficient state involvement in a private entity's operations, for example, a shopping center that is part of a company-owned town, and the property is used as a city, there is no state action and there is no assumption of a public function by a private person. So long as the state did not aid, command, or encourage the behavior in question, there is no state action for Fourteenth Amendment purposes. The rights of a private property owner outweigh any of the rights of a trespasser.

Dissent: (Marshall, J.) The shopping center has a monopoly on the places essential for communications about the shopping center, so it should assume governmental duties with respect to activities relating to the shopping center.

Terry v. Adams (S. Ct. 1953)

Facts: Clubs of white Democrats in Texas held their own private elections of nominees who then ran unopposed in the primaries.

Issue: Are private preprimary elections essentially providing the nominee for the Democratic Party in the general elections for state governmental offices, sufficiently considered state action for Fifteenth Amendment purposes?

Rule: Private preprimary elections are part of the electoral system, and therefore constitute a public function subject to the Fifteenth Amendment, even though there is a complete absence of formal state connection to any of the activities of any of the political clubs organizing the elections.

Concurrence: (Frankfurter, J.) By not taking any action to ensure a racially neutral election, the state has abdicated its responsibility and therefore should restrict the organizing private clubs to the Fifteenth Amendment.

Concurrence: (Clark, J.) If this system is allowed to continue, the black vote will be nullified.

Dissent: (Minton, J.) The situation here differs very little from situations where a candidate must obtain approval of a religious or ethnic group, which is permissible.

Evans v. Newton (S. Ct. 1966)

Facts: A tract of land was conveyed to the City of Macon, Georgia for use as a whites-only park. In 1955, the city resigned as trustee and had a private trustee appointed in order for the park to remain whites only and not to be subject to the Fourteenth Amendment restrictions. The city continued to provide maintenance services to the park.

Issue: Is a privately run park that was once in the trust of a municipality and currently enjoys some city services subject to the restrictions of the Fourteenth Amendment?

Rule: A park that was previously government run and then placed in the hands of a private trustee is imbued with state action because of the past and present aid given by the city to the running of the park and also because of the public and municipal nature of land used as a park within a city.

Concurrence: (White, J.) The original granting of the park was tainted by discriminatory state legislation validating the racial condition. Such a statute constitutes sufficient state action so as to subject the running of the park to the Fourteenth Amendment even while in the custody of private trustees.

Evans v. Abney (S. Ct. 1970)

Facts: The conveyance involved in *Evans v. Newton* stated that if for any reason the park could not continue as a whites-only park, the land would revert to the original grantor. The Court subsequently found that the current use of the park was unconstitutional, and therefore the land was to revert back to the original grantor.

Issue: Can a conveyance condition that requires that a parcel be put to unconstitutional use or revert be enforced?

Rule: Although minority and discriminated-against groups would be hurt by the reversion of property with an unconstitutional use condition, ordinary property law should prevail. The wishes of the original grantor must be honored.

Dissent: (Douglas, J.) Allowing for the reversion of the property to the original grantor would not further the cause of integration and civil rights.

Dissent: (Brennan, J.) This is a case of a state court's enforcement of a racial restriction to prevent willing parties from dealing with one another.

Let the beneficiaries to the trust and the claimants negotiate a deal that would benefit everybody rather than have the property revert so that no one should have anything.

Washington v. Seattle School District No. 1 (S. Ct. 1982)

Facts: A state statute allowed school busing by local school boards for any reason except to effect desegregation of public schools, but allowed for such determinations to be made on the state level.

Issue: Does a state statute, though facially neutral, but which uses the racial nature of an issue to determine the governmental decision-making structure, violate the Equal Protection Clause of the Fourteenth Amendment?

Rule: A state statute that uses the racial nature of an issue to determine the governmental decision-making structure violates the Equal Protection Clause of the Fourteenth Amendment because such a determination imposes a unique burden on racial minorities in their struggle for racial equality, a burden that other interest groups do not have.

Dissent: (Powell, J.) Since there is no requirement for the state to adopt on any level a mandatory racial integration policy, there should be no reason not to allow a state to determine when and how such a policy should be implemented.

Crawford v. Board of Education (S. Ct. 1982)

Facts: The California Constitution was amended to prevent state courts, but not federal courts, from ordering mandatory busing. This had the effect of preventing mandatory busing unless some constitutional provision had been violated.

Issue: Does a state have the right to amend its own constitution prohibiting state courts from ordering mandatory busing, but permitting federal courts to do so?

Rule: When a state chooses to do more in enforcing the right to racially balanced schools than is required by the federal constitution, it has the right to retreat to the federal standard whenever it wishes.

Concurrence: (Blackmun, J.) This case is distinguished from *Washington v. Seattle School District No. 1* because the amendment here did not distort the political process.

Dissent: (Marshall, J.) I fail to see how a redefinition of the decision-making structure with respect to the same racial issue can be unconstitutional when the state seeks to remove the authority from local school boards, yet constitutional when the state attempts to achieve the same result by limiting the power of its courts.

National Collegiate Athletic Ass'n v. Tarkanian (S. Ct. 1988)

Facts: The University of Nevada at Las Vegas (UNLV) suspended Coach Tarkanian after the NCAA reported that he had violated various association rules and required that disciplinary action be taken. Tarkanian successfully sued the NCAA on the grounds that he was deprived of his Fourteenth Amendment due process rights. NCAA appealed, claiming that its actions are not "state action" within the meaning of the Fourteenth Amendment because it is a private organization.

Issue: Where a state institution takes action to comply with the mandate of a private institution, do the private institution's acts constitute state action?

Rule: (Stevens, J.) Where a private party enjoys no governmental powers (such as the power to subpoena witnesses, impose contempt sanctions, etc.), the fact that it can impose its will on a state agency through monopoly power does not mean that it is acting under color of state law.

Dissent: (White, J.) There is state action where a private party is jointly engaged with state officials. Because UNLV "embraced" NCAA rules, agreed that NCAA would conduct the hearings, and accepted NCAA's findings of fact, the NCAA was jointly engaged with UNLV and its actions therefore constituted state action.

Edmonson v. Leesville Concrete Co. (S. Ct. 1991)

Facts: The defendant in a negligence action brought by an African American used peremptory challenges to strike prospective African-American jurors. The plaintiff, citing *Batson v. Kentucky,* claimed that the defendant must provide a race-neutral explanation for the peremptory strikes. The defendant prevailed on the issue at the district court, arguing that *Batson* applied only in criminal trials.

Issue: Does a private litigant's use of peremptory challenges involve state action?

Rule: (Kennedy, J.) Questions of state action focus first on whether the claimed constitutional deprivation resulted from the exercise of a right or privilege having its source in state authority and second, whether the private party charged with the deprivation could be described as a state actor. In this case, peremptory challenges exist only when the government allows parties, by statute or common law, to strike otherwise qualified jurors. Because a private party cannot exercise a peremptory challenge without the overt assistance of the court, that party must be considered a state actor.

Dissent: (O'Connor, J.) The state does not significantly participate in the peremptory challenge process, and the exercise of a peremptory challenge is not a traditional government function. A lawyer's actions in court do not become those of the state by virtue of their location.

Runyon v. McCrary (S. Ct. 1976)

Facts: Some private nonsectarian schools excluded blacks. 42 U.S.C.A. §1981 provided that all persons have the right to make contracts and to enforce them.

Issue: Does 42 U.S.C.A. §1981 prohibit private, commercially operated, nonsectarian schools from denying admission to prospective students because they are black, and, if so, is that federal law constitutional as applied?

Rule: Racial exclusion practiced by private nonsectarian schools violates the 42 U.S.C.A. §1981 provision guaranteeing the right of all persons to make and enforce contracts. Further, application of the statute to include the prohibition of private nonsectarian schools to engage in racially exclusionary practices does not violate constitutional rights to free association and privacy.

Concurrence: (Powell, J.) This case involves a public offer and therefore violates Section 1981. A personal contractual relationship would be protected by the right to freedom of association and would not violate Section 1981.

Concurrence: (Stevens, J.) Although Section 1981 was never intended to apply to private choices to engage in racially exclusionary practices, the line of authority indicates otherwise, and it must be followed.

Dissent: (White, J.) To contract means to have a meeting of the minds and for both parties to assent. The Section 1981 right to make and enforce contracts does not mean that a person must engage unwillingly in a contract; it merely states that when two parties willingly enter into a contract, the state must recognize the contract as binding and the courts must enforce it regardless of the parties' race.

South Carolina v. Katzenbach (S. Ct. 1966)

Facts: The Voting Rights Act of 1965 authorized the Attorney General to suspend certain state statutes based on administrative statistical findings that indicated a propensity for racial discrimination in voting in certain states or political subdivisions. The findings were generally subject, if at all, to limited judicial review.

Issue: May Congress pass a law pursuant to its powers under Section 2 of the Fifteenth Amendment that enables it to strike state voting statutes it deems to be discriminatory, whether intentional or not, with limited or no judicial review?

Rule: As long as Congress has adopted a rational means of enforcing the Fifteenth Amendment guarantee to all citizens of the right to vote regardless of race, the enforcement is constitutional. Since the state has none of the constitutional protections that individuals have, the established procedures formulated by the Voting Rights Act of 1965 are considered to be rational under the circumstances, and therefore within Congress' power under the Fifteenth Amendment.

Concurrence/Dissent: (Black, J.) While most of the provisions of the Voting Rights Act of 1965 are constitutional, the provisions limiting a state's ability to amend its own constitution and not allowing the state to obtain a hearing by the Court are unconstitutional.

Rendell-Baker v. Kohn (S. Ct. 1982)

Facts: A privately owned school for maladjusted students that received substantial government aid discharged some of its employees without an opportunity to be heard.

Issue: Does the granting of government aid to a private party subject that party's activities to constitutional review?

Rule: There is no imposition of constitutional limitations on the autonomy of private sector actors that receive government funding when there is no specific government encouragement of the activity challenged as violating an individual's constitutional rights.

Dissent: (Marshall, J.) When an entity's survival depends on the state and is subject to the state's complete control and supervision, the acts of the entity are generally approved by the state. Moreover, if the entity is engaged in an activity normally reserved to the state, then the acts done by the entity should be considered state action and therefore subject to constitutional review.

Pennsylvania v. Board of City Trusts (S. Ct. 1957)

Facts: A private trust established a school that was racially restrictive in its admission policy. Until 1869, the trustee was the city of Philadelphia. Since 1869 the school had been operated by the Board of Directors of City Trusts of the City of Philadelphia.

Issue: Does the conduct of a private trust in its administration of a school constitute state action with respect to the Fourteenth Amendment?

Rule: There is state involvement for a private trust to run a school on a racially restricted basis.

Brentwood Academy v. Tenn. Secondary School (S. Ct. 2001)

Facts: A private school sued an organization set up under Tennessee law to regulate interscholastic athletics.

Issue: Is an ostensibly private organization that is mainly comprised of state schools and whose employees participate in the state employee retirement system a state actor for Fourteenth Amendment purposes?

Rule: (Souter, J.) State action decisions are highly fact-intensive. Here, the function of the association, the fact that its employees are state employees for retirement purposes, and the fact that state officials sit ex officio on its board, render it a state actor.

City of Boerne v. Flores (S. Ct. 1997)

Facts: P, a Catholic archdiocese, sued D city alleging that the city's failure to allow it to expand a church in a historic district violated the federal Religious Freedom Restoration Act, which required that states imposing restrictions that affected religious practice show that the restriction was narrowly tailored in order to serve a compelling government interest.

Issue: Under what circumstances may Congress enforce the Fourteenth Amendment by prescribing a broader rule than that announced by the Court as the correct interpretation of the Fourteenth Amendment?

Rule: (Kennedy, J.) Congress' power to enforce the Fourteenth Amendment does not give it the power to reinterpret the Fourteenth Amendment, and there was an insufficient factual showing to convince the Court that the statute was "congruent and proportional" to the Fourteenth Amendment rights the statute sought to protect.

Note: This case introduced the "congruence and proportionality" test as the test for legislation enforcing the Fourteenth Amendment.

Kimel v. Board of Regents (S. Ct. 2000)

Facts: P sued state university under the Age Discrimination in Employment Act (ADEA).

Issue: Did the ADEA validly abrogate state sovereign immunity?

Rule: (O'Connor, J.) For statutes to validly abrogate state sovereign immunity as measures enforcing the Fourteenth Amendment, there must be congruence and proportionality, which is not shown when both the amount of unconstitutional conduct restricted by the statute is relatively small, and when the statute's scope and remedies are broad.

Dissent: (Stevens, J.) Congress should have the authority to abrogate state sovereign immunity under its Article I authority; thus in this case it is unnecessary to reach the question of Congress' powers under the Fourteenth Amendment.

Board of Trustees v. Garrett (S. Ct. 2001)

Facts: P sued state university under the Americans with Disabilities Act provision banning employment discrimination against disabled people.

Issue: Did this provision validly abrogate state sovereign immunity?

Rule: (Rehnquist, C.J.) In order to satisfy the congruence and proportionality standard, there must be a record of state action that would be unconstitutional if considered in a lawsuit, on the precise type of conduct regulated by the statute.

Concurrence: (Kennedy, J.) The requirement of a precise record of unconstitutional conduct by states reflects the seriousness of an abrogation of states' immunity from lawsuits.

Dissent: (Breyer, J.) Congress is better suited than courts to determine when disparate treatment rises to the level of invidious discrimination that violates the Equal Protection Clause and triggers Congress' remedial power.

Nevada Dep't of Human Resources v. Hibbs (S. Ct. 2003)

Facts: P sued D state for violating the federal Family and Medical Leave Act (FMLA).

Issue: Is the FMLA a valid abrogation of state sovereign immunity?

Rule: (Rehnquist, C.J.) Because the FMLA targets gender discrimination, which receives higher scrutiny than most other classifications, it is easier for Congress to demonstrate a pattern of unconstitutional conduct that triggers Congress' remedial powers.

Dissent: (Kennedy, J.) The FMLA is inappropriate legislation to enforce the Fourteenth Amendment because there's been no showing of significant unconstitutional conduct by the states.

Dissent: (Scalia, J.) If the question was the validity of the FMLA as applied to Nevada, it would have been necessary to show that Nevada itself had been engaging in unconstitutional conduct.

Tennessee v. Lane (S. Ct. 2004)

Facts: P sued D state under the provision of the Americans With Disabilities Act (ADA) requiring nondiscrimination in the provision of public services when he was assigned a non-disabled accessible courtroom for a case he was litigating.

Issue: Does that provision of the ADA validly abrogate state sovereign immunity with regard to access to judicial proceedings?

Rule: (Stevens, J.) Because the right at issue in this case is a fundamental right, and because the scope and depth of the ADA's provisions mirror the constitutional rule for access to courts, the statute validly abrogates states' sovereign immunity.

Dissent: (Rehnquist, C.J.) There is insufficient evidence that states are unconstitutionally denying people access to courts; thus, Congress overstepped in imposing these restrictions.

Dissent: (Scalia, J.) The congruence and proportionality standard is too difficult to apply in a principled way; thus, for congressional action enforcing racial equality the appropriate test is simply rational basis, while other congressional enforcement action is limited to providing remedies for court-adjudicated violations.

Katzenbach v. Morgan (S. Ct. 1966)

Facts: The Voting Rights Act of 1965 provided that, subject to certain restrictions, no person shall be denied the right to vote because of an inability to read or write English. New York required an ability to read or write English in order to vote.

Issue: May Congress constitutionally legislate based on its own interpretation of the reach of the Equal Protection Clause of the Fourteenth Amendment and defeat a state voting requirement?

Rule: (Brennan, J.) Congress may legislate based on its own judgment of the reach of the Equal Protection Clause of the Fourteenth Amendment. The Voting Rights Act of 1965 was enacted to enforce the Equal Protection Clause of the Fourteenth Amendment, and the states have no power to withhold voting rights on conditions that are forbidden by the Fourteenth Amendment.

Dissent: (Harlan, J.) In cases where there is room to differ on whether equal protection or due process has been violated, it is up to the Judiciary, not the legislature, to resolve the conflict. The Act here allows the Fourteenth Amendment to swallow the state's constitutional authority in this field.

CHAPTER 10

Freedom of Expression Regulation of Speech Because of Its Content

I. INTRODUCTION

The First Amendment states that "Congress shall make no law . . . abridging the freedom of speech, or of the press; or the right of the people peaceably to assemble."

Although the First Amendment explicitly guarantees freedom of speech and press, as well as the right to "assemble" for political and other purposes, Court decisions have inferred other rights extending from these. Such implicit rights include freedom of association and the freedom to engage in expressive behavior that does not fit neatly into the category of speech.

Federal and state governments may restrict expression, provided the restrictions are narrowly drawn to address the specific problems created by the expression. Laws regulating the time, place, and manner of expression must serve significant state interests and leave open alternative channels of communication.

II. RESTRICTING SPEECH BASED ON CONTENT: SUBVERSIVE ADVOCACY

A. General Policies
　　1. Whether or not the First Amendment protects certain speech often *depends* on its content. Government may use the content of expression as the basis for regulating it by considering it in a separate category from other expression.

2. The First Amendment does not absolutely bar regulation of speech based on content. For example, utterance of patently offensive words dealing with sex or other bodily functions may be regulated because of their content.

B. "Clear and Present Danger"

1. The First Amendment's Free Speech Clause does not protect speech that creates a clear and present danger of bringing about the substantive evils that Congress has a right to prevent. Under one view that danger need not be immediate or certain of success; the gravity of the danger must justify restraint of speech; other more recent cases have suggested that the danger must in fact be immediate.

2. Free speech may not apply to expression during wartime that presents a clear and present danger of compromising the U.S. war effort by advocating sympathy with the enemy or by criticizing U.S. military actions.

3. Mere criticism of law, as opposed to inciting violation of law, does not pose a clear and present danger and is therefore protected by the First Amendment. Such criticism, whether temperate or indecent, may not be suppressed because of its substance or lack of propriety.

C. Expression Inciting Illegal Conduct

1. The First Amendment does not protect speech or publication that incites, advocates, or teaches the violation of law or the overthrow of organized government by unlawful means.

2. Early precedent established that such advocacy may be outlawed even if it is cast in general terms, does not call for immediate action, and does not address particular people. Later cases held that advocacy of unlawful conduct may not be proscribed unless it is intended and likely to produce imminent disorder.

III. THE LIMITS OF FIRST AMENDMENT PROTECTION

A. "Fighting Words"

1. Free speech does not apply to "fighting words." These are words that by their very utterance inflict injury or tend to incite an immediate breach of the peace.

2. "Fighting words" fall outside First Amendment protection because they:

   a. Form no essential part of any exposition of ideas; and

   b. Are of such slight social value that society's interest in order and morality outweighs any benefit derived from them.

B. Defamation
   1. Public Officers
      First Amendment protection extends to defamation of a public officer's official conduct, since such conduct is a matter of public concern. It does not apply, however, to defamation made with actual malice, i.e., with knowledge of falsehood or with reckless disregard of whether or not a statement is false.
   2. Public Figures
      a. Erroneous statements about public figures receive First Amendment immunity, even if such statements intentionally inflict emotional distress. Immunity does not apply to defamation made with actual malice. Even without actual malice, however, publishers may be liable for defaming public figures when:
         i. The substance of the defamation risks substantial danger to reputation; and
         ii. The publisher engages in highly unreasonable conduct departing in the extreme from professional standards.
      b. The media are not protected by rights of free speech and press for obtaining news information through such misconduct as tortious or criminal activity. This is particularly true where the information is of minimal value to the public.
   3. Private Figures
      The First Amendment does not shield the media from liability for defamation of private figures.
      a. Private persons lack public figures' access to the media to counteract false statements. Private individuals' greater vulnerability to injury and states' interest in protecting such people justify media liability.
      b. People drawn into the public forum largely against their will are not public figures. Therefore, a publisher may be held liable, without proof of actual malice, for defaming a private person regarding a matter that is of purely private concern.
   4. Group Libel
      Libel is not within the area of speech protected by the First Amendment. Since libel aimed at individuals may be punished, government may proscribe libel directed at groups. Restrictions on libelous expression must not be willful, purposeless, or unrelated to maintaining peace and well-being.
C. Invasion of Privacy
   1. Public Record/Public Concern: Freedom of speech and press renders the media immune from liability for invasion of a non-public figure's privacy where the disseminated information is:
      a. Truthful;
      b. Of legitimate public concern; and

    c. Derived from publicly available records, such as official court documents.

    Government may constitutionally punish such dissemination only when the punishment is narrowly tailored to a state interest of the highest order.

D. Obscenity

  1. Definition

    Obscenity is that which, taken as a whole:

    a. Appeals to the prurient interest in sex;

    b. Portrays sexual conduct in a patently offensive way; and

    c. Has no serious literary, artistic, political, or scientific value.

  2. Determining Obscenity

    Determining whether expression is obscene depends, in part, on whether it is formulated or exploited entirely on the basis of its appeal to prurient interests. Contemporary community standards, not national standards, are to apply in determining whether expression is obscene.

  3. Obscenity and the First Amendment

    Obscenity is not protected by the First Amendment right of free speech and press. While ideas with even the slightest social value receive full constitutional protection, obscenity lacks redeeming social importance and may be restricted by law.

    a. Possession of Obscenity

      Criminalizing mere possession of obscene material violates the First Amendment right to receive information and ideas and is an unwarranted government invasion of privacy.

  4. Obscenity in Commerce

    Government may constitutionally restrict the use of obscene material in local commerce and in places of public accommodation. Legislation restricting obscenity is constitutional even if the social and moral evils the legislation seeks to cure are unquantifiable. However, pornography laws are unconstitutional if they are not narrowly tailored and if they result in suppression of expression based on content.

    a. Child Pornography

      States may statutorily prohibit child pornography, provided the restricted conduct is adequately defined. Child pornography laws do not require a showing that the restricted matter is obscene. Because the rationale for child pornography bans the protection of the child model, computer-generated "virtual" child pornography may not be prohibited.

E. Offensive or Indecent Speech

  1. Government may not statutorily restrict offensive speech based on content where the speech is merely indecent, but not obscene. Restrictions are valid only for those types of expression

that fall outside those protected by the First Amendment. Types of speech outside First Amendment protection include obscenity, expression violating privacy, and fighting words.

2. The government may regulate the content of indecent expression to promote a compelling interest if it chooses the least restrictive means to further that interest.

F. Commercial Speech

1. The First Amendment protects commercial speech (e.g., advertising) from unwarranted government regulation, provided such expression concerns lawful activity and is not misleading. Government restriction of commercial speech is constitutional if:

a. The restriction is not based solely on the speech's content;

b. The regulation reflects a substantial, asserted government interest;

c. The restriction directly advances that interest; and

d. The restriction is not more extensive than necessary to serve that interest.

THE PUBLIC FORUM PROBLEM

I. PERVASIVE THEMES

A. Introduction

In many cases, the Supreme Court has to decide whether a particular federal or state statute has violated the First Amendment guarantee to freedom of speech. Sometimes there is a valid government policy in restricting certain speech activity. In determining the validity of a statute with respect to First Amendment rights, the Court must balance speech interests against the governmental interests in the particular statute. The governmental interests must be unrelated to the suppression of free expression. *United States v. O'Brien*. Often, the Court analyzes the statute by determining whether or not the statute is *overly broad* or too *vague*. Though a narrowly drawn statute could validly restrict certain activity, the fatal flaw in that particular statute may be that it is drafted so that it may be read to restrict valid speech interests. Also, the Court will look at whether or not the regulation has the effect of restraining the activity prior to its occurrence. The Court will examine the regulation to see if it is content-based. Finally, the Court will examine whether or not the expressive conduct, if not verbal, falls under constitutionally protected conduct.

B. The Overbreadth Doctrine

An overbroad statute is one that is designed to burden or punish activities that are not constitutionally protected, but the statute includes within its scope activities that are protected by the First Amendment. Even where the conduct in a certain case is not constitutionally protected, but is restricted by an overbroad statute, the statute will be stricken and the conduct will be permitted. This is what is meant when a statute is stricken because it is overbroad *on its face*. This is only true in First Amendment cases. In other cases findings of unconstitutionality are generally made *as applied*.

C. Prior Restraint/Subsequent Punishment

1. Generally

   Prior restraint is considered a more drastic infringement on free speech than subsequent punishment. Prior restraint does not allow the speaker the choice of expressing his views and suffering the consequences for it. Subsequent punishment defines the illegality of certain conduct but does not prevent the speaker from actually engaging in such conduct. Therefore, while subsequent punishment may deter some speakers, at least the ideas or speech at issue can be placed before the public. Prior restraint limits public debate and knowledge more severely. Further, by using prior restraint the government may achieve its end by having a temporary restraining order issued and by the time the order is found to have been improperly granted, the subsequent allowance of the speech would have a negligible impact on the originally desired goal. *Walker v. City of Birmingham* (Douglas, J., dissenting).

2. Exceptions

   a. Obscenity

      Obscenity, particularly as it pertains to films, is an area of the law in which prior restraint has been upheld. *Freedman v. Maryland*. However, there are certain procedural safeguards that must be employed in the exercise of such prior restraint. A local censorship board:

      i. Has the burden of proving that the film in question is obscene;

      ii. Must defer to a judicial proceeding for the imposition of a valid final restraint on the film;

      iii. Must either permit the exhibition of the film or go to court for a restraining order, and;

      iv. Must assure a prompt final judicial decision.

   b. Court Orders/Statutes

      Courts usually treat violations of prior restraint orders as a more serious offense than refusals to abide by a statute. *Walker v. City of Birmingham*. While one is free to violate an unconstitutional statute restricting free speech, one is not free to violate the same words when written as a court injunction. There are two reasons for this phenomenon:

      i. Regardless of the constitutionality of a court order, disobedience constitutes a contempt of court, and;

ii. When a litigant objects to a trial court's ruling, he can always appeal, and does not have to violate a court order. On the other hand, often the only way to attack the constitutionality of a statute is to violate it.

D. Content-based Regulation

The state cannot ban speech based on its content. Such a ban would violate not only the First Amendment, but the Equal Protection Clause of the Fourteenth Amendment as well. *Carey v. Brown.*

E. Symbolic Expression

Symbolic speech is afforded the same First Amendment protection as verbal expression. The question that must be answered is what types of activities are considered "symbolic speech." Most of the time, however, application of standard First Amendment principles to any regulated conduct will resolve whether or not the particular activity is constitutionally protected. *United States v. O'Brien; Tinker v. Des Moines School District; Street v. New York; Spence v. Washington; Texas v. Johnson; Clark v. Community for Creative Non-Violence.*

II. GOVERNMENTAL INTERESTS AND THE PUBLIC FORUM

A. Introduction

As previously stated, in regulating speech activity, there must be some element of governmental interest in the regulation not related to the suppression of free expression. *United States v. O'Brien.*

B. The Public Forum

The level of substantiality needed to justify the governmental interest in the regulation of speech activity depends on the level of public forum where the activity occurs. The principles applied in the regulation of speech are different when the speech is taking place in a *true public forum* (e.g., parks, streets), a *semi-public forum* (e.g., schools, libraries), and public facilities that are considered non-public forums. *Perry Educational Ass'n v. Perry Local Educators' Ass'n.*

1. The Traditional Public Forum

The state may place reasonable time, place, or manner restrictions on speech that takes place in the traditional public forum, but these regulations must be implemented without regard to the content of the speech. The principles used in justifying speech restrictions are:

a. The government regulation is within the constitutional power of the government;

b. The regulation furthers an important or substantial governmental interest;

     c. The governmental interest is unrelated to the suppression of free expression;

     d. The incidental restriction on alleged First Amendment freedom is no greater than is essential to the furtherance of that interest. *United States v. O'Brien.*

     Alternatively, the regulation will be held valid if it is content neutral, is narrowly drawn to serve a substantial government interest, and leaves open ample alternative channels for communication. These tests are very similar.

Examples of the types of governmental interests that the Court has dealt with include keeping the peace (*Cantwell v. Connecticut*), cleanliness (*Schneider v. State*), protection of the public against fraud (*Schaumberg v. Citizens for a Better Environment; Secretary of State of Maryland v. Joseph H. Munson*), protection of privacy interests (which includes the interest in protecting the rights of the unwilling listener; *Cantwell v. Connecticut; Coates v. Cincinnati; Carey v. Brown*), the interest in preventing speech when there is a clear and present danger of substantive and immediate evil as a result of that speech (*Terminiello v. Chicago; Feiner v. New York; Cox v. Louisiana; Bridges v. California*), and the interest in allowing wider access to the various media (*Red Lion Broadcasting Co. v. FCC; City of Los Angeles v. Preferred Communications, Inc.; Columbia Broadcasting System, Inc. v. Democratic National Committee; Miami Herald Publishing Co. v. Tornillo*).

2. The Semi-Public Forum

     Public property that the state has opened for use by the public as a place for expressive activity is a semi-public forum. Although a state is not required to indefinitely retain the open character of the facility, as long as it does so it is bound by the same standards as apply in a traditional public forum. *Groyned v. City of Rockford; City Council v. Taxpayers for Vincent.*

3. The Non-Public Forum

     Public property that is not by tradition or designation a forum for public communication is governed by different standards. The state may reserve the forum for its intended purposes as long as the regulation on speech is reasonable and not an effort to suppress expression merely because public officials oppose the speaker's view. *Adderley v. Florida; Lehman v. Shaker Heights; Cornelius v. NAACP Legal Defense and Education Fund, Inc.; Perry Educational Ass'n v. Perry Local Educators' Ass'n.*

C. Private Property

    Private property owners do not have a duty to guarantee the First Amendment rights of the people on the owner's property. *Hudgens v. National Labor Relations Board.*

SPECIAL CONTEXTS

I. THE FIRST AMENDMENT AND THE POLITICAL CAMPAIGN PROCESS

A. As forms of communication, campaign expenditures and contributions qualify as "speech," not "conduct."

B. Campaign Expenditures vs. Contributions

1. Expenditures

Statutory limits on campaign expenditures unconstitutionally impede protected political expression. Expenditure restrictions reduce the quantity of expression by restricting the number of issues discussed, the depth of their exploration, and the size of the audience.

2. Contributions

It is constitutional to limit the amount a person or group may contribute to a campaign. Such restrictions involve little direct restraint on free political communication and do not infringe the contributor's freedom to discuss candidates and issues.

II. MORE SPECIAL CONTEXTS: EDUCATION AND LABOR

A. Education

1. School Boards

School board activities must comport with the First Amendment. Boards may not remove books from school libraries simply because board members dislike the ideas those books contain. Boards violate the First Amendment by removing books as a way of establishing an orthodoxy in politics, nationalism, religion, or other areas.

2. School Administration

a. Schools' basic educational mission includes inculcating societal values and preparing students to assume an active role in democratic government. When offensive speech delivered in school undermines that mission, the First Amendment rights of free speech and press do not prohibit schools from penalizing such speech.

b. First Amendment rights granted to adults do not extend equally to school students. Educators do not offend the First Amendment by exercising editorial control over the style and content of student speech in school-sponsored expressive activities, so long as their actions are reasonably related to legitimate educational purposes.

B. Labor

Qualifying as more than speech or communication, picketing involves patrol of a locality and may induce action. Therefore, a state, in enforcing some public policy, can constitutionally enjoin peaceful picketing aimed at preventing effectuation of that policy.

III. FREEDOM OF ASSOCIATION

A. Extension of Free Speech

The freedom of association logically extends from the right of free speech. The right to engage in activities protected by the First Amendment implies a corresponding right to choose associates with whom one can pursue group goals. Freedom to engage in association for the advancement of beliefs and ideas is an inseparable aspect of the liberties assured by the First and Fourteenth Amendments.

B. Compulsory Disclosure

Compelled disclosure of group membership places an impermissible restraint on freedom of association by exposing members to alienation and by discouraging future membership. Such consequences are only justified in light of a substantial government interest.

C. Statutory Restrictions

1. The Constitution protects freedom of association from statutory infringement. Restrictive statutes affecting this freedom must be narrowly construed. Vague, overly broad laws touching this freedom can impede its exercise. For example, it is unconstitutional to restrict or prohibit membership in an organization without regard to actual or prospective members' specific intent of furthering the organization's goals.

2. Where the association is widespread and public, rather than personal and private, laws prohibiting discrimination in association membership are constitutional.

IV. GOVERNMENT POWER AND THE FIRST AMENDMENT

A. The government may prohibit federal employees from engaging in political management and political campaigning. Such power is necessary to:

1. Prevent federal employees from practicing, or appearing to practice, political justice;

2. Prevent the government workforce from being used to build a powerful, perhaps corrupt, political machine; and

3. Ensure that such employees are not pressured to vote in a certain way or perform political chores rather than act out of their own beliefs.

B. A state cannot condition public employment on a basis that infringes employees' constitutionally protected freedom of expression. For example, the First Amendment protects public employees who speak out as citizens on matters of public concern. However, a public employee is not speaking as a citizen, and thus has no First Amendment rights, when his speech is made pursuant to his official duties.

C. Government Inquiry

1. Congress does not violate First Amendment rights by conducting inquiries enabling it to exercise a constitutionally granted legislative function. Congress may only investigate areas in which it may potentially legislate.

2. A legislature's demand for a group's disclosure of its membership is impermissible where:
    a. Such disclosure would seriously inhibit or impair exercise of constitutional rights; and
    b. The legislature has not shown a substantial relation between the information sought and an asserted, substantial government interest.

D. Government and the Press

1. Prior Restraint

    Absent compelling justification, the federal government may not exercise prior restraint on the press to prevent publication of sensitive government documents.

2. Revealing Information

    While the First Amendment protects news gathering, it does not violate First Amendment rights to require journalists to appear before a grand jury and answer questions relevant to a criminal investigation. The public interest in pursuing and prosecuting crimes reported to the press by informants outweighs the burden on news gathering that might result from people's reluctance to reveal information without assured anonymity.

3. Media in the Courtroom

    Photographic and broadcast coverage of certain types of judicial proceedings may not be constitutionally banned where adequate precautions exist to minimize the prejudicial effect such coverage may have on the jury or on the trial process.

4. Singling Out the Press

    While the First Amendment does not prohibit economic regulation of the press, regulation that singles out the press places a heavy burden of justification on the government. First Amendment rights are at risk when the government imposes differential taxation on the press alone.

CASE CLIPS

1. Regulation of Speech Because of Its Content

Schenck v. United States (S. Ct. 1919)

Facts: Ds mailed leaflets demanding that the public "Assert Your Rights" and peacefully express opposition to the draft during World War I.
Issue: May the First Amendment protection of expression and criticism be limited?
Rule: (Holmes, J.) The First Amendment does not protect the right to free speech when the nature or circumstances are such that the speech creates a clear and present danger of substantial harm to important national interests.

Masses Publishing Co. v. Patten (1917)

Facts: A publishing company sought an injunction against D, a postmaster, who refused to carry a magazine issue in the mail. D claimed the magazine violated the Espionage Act of 1917 in that its revolutionary material would encourage enemies of the United States and hamper conduct of war.
Issue: Does the Constitution protect criticism of law and government policies?
Rule: The First Amendment protects criticism of laws and government policies. Only direct incitement to violent resistance to the law is unprotected. First Amendment rights may not be limited based on the likelihood that speech may cause an indirect incitement against national interests.

Gitlow v. New York (S. Ct. 1925)

Facts: D, a member of the Socialist Party, was convicted of violating a statute that banned advocacy of the overthrow of the government for participating in the publication of political literature discussing the need for mass revolt to accomplish the "Communist Revolution."
Issue: Do the First and Fourteenth Amendments allow states to classify certain speech as involving danger of substantive evil, and to suppress any speech that falls into a classification regardless of the classification's generality?
Rule: (Sanford, J.) A state may prohibit any type of speech or publication which it has previously classified as dangerous to the foundations of law, organized government, or the public welfare, even if the speech is cast in general terms, does not call for immediate acts, and is not addressed to specific persons.

Dissent: (Holmes, J.) The Fourteenth Amendment makes freedom of speech applicable to the states. Therefore, a state may not prohibit speech unless it represents a clear and present danger of immediate and direct incitement.

Whitney v. California (S. Ct. 1927)

Facts: An active member of the Communist Labor Party, D was charged with knowingly becoming a member of an organization that advocated criminal syndicalism.

Issue: Is mere membership in an organization that is of a prohibited character sufficient to trigger the exception to the First Amendment protection of free speech?

Rule: (Sanford, J.) A state may make criminal any assembly or organization which advocates conduct that has been determined to endanger the public welfare, and may prosecute on the basis of membership rather than activity.

Concurrence: (Brandeis, J.) Fear of serious injury cannot alone justify the suppression of a fundamental constitutional right. To justify such suppression, there must be reasonable grounds for the belief that the free speech will result in substantial evil and that the danger of the evil is imminent. Each defendant must be given the opportunity to show that under the circumstances of a particular case, this was not so. The best way to combat injurious speech is not by repression but by rebuttal.

Dennis v. United States (S. Ct. 1951)

Facts: Ds were convicted of conspiracy for participating in the Communist Party, which was characterized as an advocate of the use of force and violence to overthrow the U.S. government.

Issue: Does a clear and present danger exist if the threat of harm is not immediately imminent?

Rule: (Vinson, C.J.) There need not be an immediately imminent threat, an actual attempt, or a high probability that an attempt will be successful for a clear and present danger to exist. Whether the gravity of the danger, discounted by its improbability, justifies restraint of speech to avoid the evil is a question for a *judge*, to determine in light of the evidence of each case.

Concurrence: (Frankfurter, J.) Congress should determine the relative weight of interests when balancing free speech and restrictions on expression.

Concurrence: (Jackson, J.) The "clear and present danger" standard should apply only to speech or writing which does not directly or explicitly advocate a crime, but which may incite criminal activity due to the circumstances under which it is expressed. However, direct incitement by speech should be made criminal regardless of its probability of success.

Dissent: (Black, J.) The First Amendment does not permit laws suppressing free speech on the basis of Congress' or judges' notions of reasonableness. This takes away the First Amendment's ability to protect radical or unorthodox views. Whether the speech presents a danger which is substantial enough to merit suppression should be a question for a jury.
Dissent: (Douglas, J.) Teaching the theory of overthrow of the government and hoping that it will come about does not amount to a substantial danger unless it is coupled with technical training for and intent to carry out the theory.

Brandenburg v. Ohio (S. Ct. 1969)

Facts: D, a Ku Klux Klan leader, was convicted under a state criminal syndicalism statute for advocating the use of unlawful means to accomplish his organization's political goals such as the possibility of revenge against the government's alleged suppression of whites.
Issue: May the government curtail free expression that does not advocate imminent, unlawful action?
Rule: (per curiam) The First Amendment does not permit a state to prohibit advocation of the use of force or unlawful conduct, except where such advocacy is directed to inciting imminent lawless action and is likely to produce such action.
Concurrence: (Douglas, J.) Speech should never be suppressed unless it is accompanied by or inseparable from an overt act. There is no constitutional line between advocacy of abstract ideas and advocacy of political action; the clear and present danger test is too easily manipulated to provide adequate protection.

New York Times v. Sullivan (S. Ct. 1964)

Facts: P, a police commissioner, sued *The New York Times* for libel. The *Times* ran an ad decrying recent violence against black demonstrators in the South. P claimed that, as commissioner, he was implicated in the ad's assertions of police abuses against Dr. Martin Luther King and other black demonstrators.
Issue: Does the First Amendment protect erroneous or defamatory criticism of a public officer's official conduct?
Rule: (Brennan, J.) Defamatory and factually erroneous statements are protected by the First Amendment when they relate to the official conduct of any public official, unless they are made with actual malice, i.e., with knowledge of falsehood or with reckless disregard of whether or not a statement is false.
Concurrence: (Black, J.) The First and Fourteenth Amendments should be interpreted to guarantee an absolute, unconditional right to criticize the conduct of public officials regardless of the presence of malice.

Roth v. United States; Alberts v. California (S. Ct. 1957)

Facts: Roth, a publisher, was convicted of violating a federal obscenity statute by mailing obscene advertising and a book. Alberts was convicted for selling and advertising obscene books in violation of state law.

Issue: Does obscenity fall within the scope of the First Amendment freedoms of speech and press?

Rule: (Brennan, J.) Obscenity is not protected by the First Amendment right of freedom of speech or press. Ideas which are not considered to have even the slightest social value may be statutorily restricted, regardless of whether or not they incite antisocial conduct.

Concurrence/Dissent: (Harlan, J.) Whether obscenity is protected by the First Amendment should be considered on a case-by-case basis. I concur in *Alberts*, because a state may have legitimate interests in controlling obscenity. I dissent in *Roth*, because the federal government does not have a direct substantive interest in the regulation of morality, and therefore does not have the power to do so.

Dissent: (Douglas, J.) A court should not judge the constitutionality of speech by weighing its social value or the purity of thought it instills in the reader's mind.

Miller v. California (S. Ct. 1973)

Facts: D was convicted of knowingly distributing by mail five unsolicited brochures containing sexually explicit material.

Issue: What factors apply in determining whether speech or printed matter is obscene and thus not protected by the First Amendment?

Rule: (Burger, C.J.) Obscene material need not be utterly without social value, but is that which by contemporary community standards, and taken as a whole, appeals to the lustful and lewd interest in sex; portrays sexual conduct in a patently offensive way; and has no serious literary, artistic, political, or scientific value.

Dissent: (Douglas, J.) Judges should not decide what is obscene absent clear and specific guidelines from the legislature which both the public and courts may follow.

Dissent: (Brennan, J.) The statute here is unconstitutionally overbroad, and therefore invalid on its face.

Paris Adult Theatre I v. Slaton (S. Ct. 1973)

Facts: P filed suit to enjoin the showing of obscene films at two "adult" theaters. No offensive depictions or words appeared on the marquee outside the theaters, and both posted an age requirement for admission and an advisory that those offended by nudity should not enter.

Issue: May government restrict obscenity that involves only consenting adults and takes place in a public place not in view of the general public?
Rule: (Burger, C.J.) A state may regulate the use of obscene material in a place which is open to the public, even if it is confined to consenting adults. A state's legitimate interests in doing so include the quality of life, the community environment, the tone of commerce and public safety.
Dissent: (Douglas, J.) In the absence of a captive audience, a merchant should not be held criminally liable for selling matter which is considered offensive by the majority.
Dissent: (Brennan, J.) In the absence of a very substantial state interest, sexually oriented materials should not be suppressed on the basis of their "obscene" contents. Obscenity cannot be clearly defined and separated from other sexually oriented but constitutionally protected speech. This vagueness denies adequate notice to persons engaged in the proscribed conduct, and creates a chilling effect on protected speech.

American Booksellers Ass'n, Inc. v. Hudnut (1985)

Facts: Indianapolis enacted an anti-pornography statute prohibiting "graphic sexually explicit subordination" of anyone by presenting them as sexual objects in situations of pain or physical abuse.
Issue: May the government classify and restrict expression on the basis of content?
Rule: (Easterbrook, J.) Laws that restrict expression on the basis of content violate the First Amendment. The First Amendment guarantees our absolute right to propagate opinions that the government and others find wrong or even hateful.

Hudnut v. American Booksellers Ass'n, Inc. (S. Ct. 1986)

Note: The judgment in *American Booksellers* was affirmed without opinion.

Cohen v. California (S. Ct. 1971)

Facts: D wore a jacket on which was written "Fuck the Draft" and was convicted under a state law that prohibited purposeful disturbance of peace or quiet by offensive conduct.
Issue: May government constitutionally regulate the manner in which ideas are conveyed when this manner involves only speech, and not conduct?
Rule: (Harlan, J.) A state may not restrict offensive speech unless it is obscene or directed at a specific person or group, with the intent and likelihood that it will provoke violent reaction. The fact that some may react violently or be unwilling receivers is not enough unless they are a captive audience.

Dissent: (Blackmun, J.) Speech that amounts to the willful use of profane language calculated to offend an unwilling audience should be considered provocative conduct.

Federal Communications Comm'n v. Pacifica Foundation (S. Ct. 1978)

Facts: D's radio station aired a George Carlin monologue that contained explicit, offensive language. After receiving a complaint, the FCC stated that such language could be regulated so as not to be aired at times when children would most likely be exposed to it.

Issue: Does the First Amendment proscribe the regulation of a non-obscene but indecent public broadcast due to its content?

Rule: (Stevens, J.) The public broadcast of non-obscene, but indecent language may be regulated on a case-by-case basis depending on its social value as determined by the context in which it is used and the likely audience.

Concurrence: (Powell, J.) Regulation of broadcasting may be justified due to its direct access into the home, and its accessibility to children. However, a court should not decide on the basis of its content, which speech is most valuable and hence deserving of the most First Amendment protection, and which is less so.

Dissent: (Brennan, J.) All speech which is not obscene deserves to be protected equally. The place for regulation of broadcasts is not in the marketplace at the hands of a censor, but in the home where the public can choose not to participate in such public discourse by not allowing a broadcast into the home.

Virginia Pharmacy Board v. Virginia Consumer Council (S. Ct. 1976)

Facts: P, a representative of prescription drug consumers, challenged a state law that forbade as "unprofessional" conduct the advertising of prescription drug prices on the grounds that the law had the effect of suppressing all prescription drug price information.

Issue: Is commercial speech, such as advertising, within the First Amendment's scope of protected expression?

Rule: (Blackmun, J.) Commercial speech, including paid advertising, is protected by the First Amendment, unless it is misleading or promotes an illegal product. Commercial speech may not be regulated, unless such restrictions (1) are not based on the speech's content; (2) serve a significant government interest; and (3) leave open alternative channels for communication of the information.

Dissent: (Rehnquist, J.) Commercial speech should be left within the state's right to regulate commerce, health, and welfare. First Amendment-protected public decision making should be restricted to social and political issues.

Central Hudson Gas v. Public Service Comm'n (S. Ct. 1980)

Facts: P, a gas company, challenged the constitutionality of the Public Service Commission's ban on promotional advertising by electrical utilities.
Issue: Under what circumstances may the government place restrictions on protected commercial speech?
Rule: (Powell, J.) First Amendment protection of commercial speech that is not misleading or concerning unlawful activity, may be limited if a state has a substantial interest which must be achieved by such restrictions. The restriction must directly advance the interest, and there must not be a less-restrictive alternative.
Concurrence: (Blackmun, J.) This test does not adequately protect truthful, non-misleading, noncoercive commercial speech. Absent a clear and present danger, government has no power to restrict expression because of the effect its message is likely to have on the public.
Concurrence: (Stevens, J.) Commercial speech does not encompass all promotional advertising. A blanket ban on all advertising by one particular industry should be declared unconstitutional if the perceived harm that may be caused by allowing the advertising is not serious enough to warrant direct regulation.
Dissent: (Rehnquist, J.) Commercial speech should not be accorded as much protection as non-commercial speech. A state should be entitled to broad discretion regarding the regulation and control of state-created monopolies.

Abrams v. United States (S. Ct. 1919)

Facts: Ds, Russian immigrants and socialist anarchists, distributed leaflets that urged a general worker strike in response to the U.S. shipment of Marines to Russia during World War I, which they perceived as an attempt to "crush the Russian Revolution."
Issue: May one be punished for the unintended consequences of one's speech?
Rule: (Clarke, J.) A person is judged to intend the consequences of his actions.
Dissent: (Holmes, J.) Speech should never be limited. The true test of the validity of government policies is whether they survive and are derived from the "marketplace of ideas" that is the uninhibited discussion of the

people. Speech may not be punished or suppressed under the First Amendment unless the speaker specifically intended to cause the criminal consequences and there is such a substantial threat to the important goals of the government that only immediate action may save them.

R.A.V. v. City of St. Paul (S. Ct. 1992)

Facts: After burning a cross on the lawn of a black family, R.A.V. was convicted of violating the St. Paul Bias Motivated Crime Ordinance, which provided, "Whoever places on public or private property a symbol . . . including, but not limited to, a burning cross or Nazi swastika, which one knows or has reasonable grounds to know arouses anger, alarm, or resentment in others on the basis of race, color, creed, religion, or gender commits disorderly conduct. . . ." The statute was construed by the state courts to apply only to "fighting words."

Issue: May "fighting words" be banned on the basis that they insult or provoke violence on the basis of race, color, creed, religion or gender?

Rule: (Scalia, J.) A statute that bans expression because it insults or provokes violence on the basis of race, color, creed, religion or gender is unconstitutional, even if limited to fighting words because it permits use of fighting words in connection with some ideas, but not others. The statute imposes special prohibitions only on speakers who express views on disfavored subjects and is thus an impermissible content and viewpoint regulation.

Concurrence: (White, J.) The statute should have been struck down because it is overbroad and does not pass equal protection review. Instead, the majority has created an "underbreadth" requirement, such that if the government wants to ban some fighting words, it must ban all fighting words.

Concurrence: (Stevens, J.) The statute should have been struck down because it is overbroad. By ruling that fighting words can be protected on the basis of subject matter, the majority affords such proscribable speech the same protection as core political speech (and greater protection than commercial speech).

United States v. Eichman (S. Ct. 1990)

Facts: Eichman was prosecuted for burning a U.S. flag in violation of the Flag Protection Act of 1989, which provided, "Whoever knowingly mutilates, defaces, physically defiles, burns, maintains on the floor or ground, or tramples upon any flag of the United States shall be fined . . . or imprisoned. . . ." The government asserted an interest in protecting the physical integrity of the flag under all circumstances without regard to the actor's motive, intended message, or the likely effects of the conduct on others.

Issue: May destruction or disfigurement of the flag be prohibited?

Rule: (Brennan, J.) Although a prohibition on destroying or disfiguring the flag is not an explicitly content-based limitation, the government's true interest is related to suppression of free expression; the statute focuses on disrespectful acts likely to damage the flag's status as a symbol of our nation and certain national ideals. Therefore, destruction or disfigurement of the flag may not be prohibited.

Dissent: (Stevens, J.) The government may and should protect the symbolic value of the flag without regard to the specific content of the flag-burner's speech.

Chaplinsky v. New Hampshire (S. Ct. 1942)

Facts: D called the city fire marshal a "damned fascist" and brawled with him on a public sidewalk.

Issue: Does the right of free speech apply to utterances that inflict injury or incite breach of the peace?

Rule: (Murphy, J.) The right of free speech is not absolute; it does not apply to "fighting words," i.e., words which by their very utterance tend to incite a violent reaction in the person to whom they are addressed.

Gooding v. Wilson (S. Ct. 1972)

Facts: D was convicted for using opprobrious, abusive language when police tried to move him and other antiwar demonstrators away from an army induction center.

Issue: Is a law unconstitutionally overbroad under the First Amendment if it may apply to speech that is outside the narrowly construed categories of unprotected expression?

Rule: (Brennan, J.) The constitutional guarantees of freedom of speech forbid states to punish the use of words or language not within narrowly limited classes of speech. Statutes must be carefully drawn or be authoritatively construed to punish only unprotected speech and not be susceptible of application to protected expression.

Dissent: (Burger, J.) The unconstitutionality for overbreadth of a statute should not be determined by whether the statute has been applied to protected conduct in past isolated incidents, but whether the language demonstrates the potential for broad harm to the protected right.

Dissent: (Blackmun, J.) The overbroad applications of this statute occurred in the distant and less-permissive past, and do not pertain to this issue.

Gertz v. Robert Welch, Inc. (S. Ct. 1974)

Facts: P, an attorney representing the family of a youth killed by a policeman, sued for libel when Robert Welch, Inc. (D) published an article claiming that P had "framed" the policeman, had a criminal record, and had Communist affiliations.

Issue: May the media claim a constitutional privilege against liability for publishing defamatory falsehood about those who are neither public officials nor public figures?

Rule: (Powell, J.) First Amendment protection does not apply to false statements about non-public figures because private individuals lack public personalities' power to counteract false statements. The burden of proof is on the victim to show negligence and falsehood.

Dissent: (Douglas, J.) There should be no "accommodation" of First Amendment freedoms.

Dissent: (Brennan, J.) The proper accommodation between avoidance of media self-censorship and protection of individual reputations lies in basing liability for defamation on knowledge or reckless disregard of a statement's falsity.

Dissent: (White, J.) The law has heretofore put the risk of falsehood on the publisher where the victim is a private citizen and no grounds of special privilege are invoked. The Court would now shift this risk to the victim, even though he has done nothing to invite the calumny, is wholly innocent of fault, and is helpless to avoid his injury.

Beauharnais v. Illinois (S. Ct. 1952)

Facts: D, president of an anti-African-American group, organized the distribution of literature that advocated political action against what he called an intrusion into white neighborhoods. D was then convicted of publication of material that portrayed any class of citizens as unwholesome or was likely to cause them to be subjected to contempt or derision.

Issue: Does the First Amendment prohibition against libel directed at specific groups extend to the states through the Fourteenth Amendment?

Rule: (Frankfurter, J.) Libel is not within the area of speech protected by the First Amendment. A state may criminally sanction libel aimed at defined groups, provided that the restrictions are neither willful and purposeless nor unrelated to the state's peace and well-being.

Dissent: (Black, J.) Every expansion of the law of criminal libel so as to punish discussions of matters of public concern means a corresponding invasion of the area dedicated to free expression by the First Amendment.

Dissent: (Douglas, J.) Substantial public interests should not be allowed to override First Amendment rights in the absence of a substantial and imminent danger.

Cox Broadcasting Corp. v. Cohn (S. Ct. 1975)

Facts: P, father of a rape victim, sued Cox Broadcasting (D) when one of its reporters revealed the daughter's name, which was in publicly available court documents, on television.
Issue: Is dissemination of truthful information derived from public records protected by the First and Fourteenth Amendments?
Rule: (White, J.) The First and Fourteenth Amendments protect from liability the publication or broadcasting of truthful information derived from publicly available records. This holds especially in areas of public concern. Privacy interests are secondary when the information already appears on the public records, since those records are inherently of interest to those concerned with government administration.

Young v. American Mini Theaters (S. Ct. 1976)

Facts: A city passed ordinances that prohibited "adult" theaters from being located within 1,000 feet of any two other "regulated uses" or within 500 feet of a residential area.
Issue: May the government use the content of expression as a criterion for its restriction?
Rule: (Stevens, J.) A government may use the content of expression as the basis for regulating expression, as long as it deals evenhandedly with all such expression, regardless of its political or philosophical message. This is especially so with regard to speech, such as sexually explicit speech, which is not as highly important to the proper functioning of society.
Concurrence: (Powell, J.) Expression may be regulated on the basis of content as long as the interests furthered by the law are important, substantial and wholly unrelated to any suppression of free expression, and the degree of incidental encroachment upon such expression was the minimum necessary to further the law's purpose.
Dissent: (Stewart, J.) Time, place, and manner restrictions of First Amendment rights should be content neutral except in the limited context of a captive or juvenile audience.

Hess v. Indiana (S. Ct. 1973)

Facts: D was convicted of violating a disorderly conduct statute for proclaiming to a crowd of antiwar demonstrators that they would continue to protest later.
Issue: May expression be restricted when it does not advocate unlawful or disorderly conduct and when it neither aims to nor is likely to create imminent disorder?
Rule: (per curiam) The government may not constitutionally restrict speech that neither advocates unlawful or disorderly action and that is not intended or likely to produce imminent disorder.

Dissent: (Rehnquist, J.) The defendant's speech clearly can be character-ized as an exhortation, particularly when uttered in a loud voice while facing a crowd.

Miami Herald Publishing Co. v. Tornillo (S. Ct. 1974)

Facts: A Florida statute required newspapers to give free reply space to political candidates whom they had attacked in their columns.

Issue: Is a statute that requires a newspaper to provide space for replies an unconstitutional abridgment of freedom of the press?

Rule: The right of newspaper editors to choose what they wish to print cannot be abridged to allow the public access to the newspaper media. This amounts to censorship.

Posadas de Puerto Rico Associates v. Tourism Company of Puerto Rico (S. Ct. 1986)

Facts: Puerto Rico enacted a law restricting advertising of casino gam-bling aimed at residents. P was fined by the Tourism Company (D) for violating the law.

Issue: Under what circumstances may commercial speech be restricted without abridging First Amendment rights?

Rule: The First Amendment provides limited protection to commercial speech that concerns a lawful activity and that is neither misleading nor fraudulent. Protected commercial speech may be restricted only if the government's interest in doing so is substantial, the restrictions directly advance the government's interest, and the restriction are not more exten-sive than necessary to serve that interest.

Dissent: (Brennan, J.) No differences between commercial and other kinds of speech justify protecting commercial speech less extensively where the government seeks to manipulate private behavior by depriving citizens of truthful information concerning lawful activities.

Dissent: (Stevens, J.) Blatant discrimination in punishment of speech depending on the publication, audience, and words employed should not be allowed. Such prohibitions establish a regime of prior restraint and articulate a standard that is hopelessly vague and unpredictable.

Dun & Bradstreet, Inc. v. Greenmoss Builders, Inc. (S. Ct. 1985)

Facts: Due to an error made by one of its employees, D, a credit reporting agency, published a false report that P had filed for bankruptcy. When D refused to furnish P with a list of the subscribers who received the report, P sued for defamation, alleging injury to its reputation.

Issue: Does First Amendment protection extend equally to speech and press on strictly private matters?

Rule: (Powell, J.) In cases of defamatory statements on strictly private matters, state interest in compensating injury to private individuals outweighs First Amendment interests in protecting such expression. Plaintiffs in such cases need not show negligence or "actual malice" to collect comprehensive damages, including presumed and punitive damages.

Concurrence: (White, J.) Public figures also should not be required to show actual malice to receive some damages.

Dissent: (Brennan, J.) The First Amendment requires significant protection from the chill of defamation law for a range of expression far broader than simply speech about pure political issues. The Court proposes an impoverished definition of "matters of public concern" that is irreconcilable with First Amendment principles. Offering no guidance as to what constitutes a "matter of public concern," the Court's distinction turns solely on the expression's subject matter.

Zacchini v. Scripps-Howard Broadcasting Co. (S. Ct. 1977)

Facts: A reporter for Scripps-Howard (D) filmed P's "human cannonball" act against P's wishes. When D aired the film during its late-night news program, P filed suit, claiming D's actions constituted an "unlawful appropriation of [his] professional property."

Issue: Do the First and Fourteenth Amendments protect the publication of another's artistic work without permission?

Rule: (White, J.) The First and Fourteenth Amendments protect a performer's entire act from publication without his consent. Such nonpermissive public exposure has qualities similar to copyright infringement and poses a substantial threat to that performance's economic value.

Dissent: (Powell, J.) When a film is used for a routine portion of a regular news program, I would hold that the First Amendment protects the station from suit, absent a strong showing by the plaintiff that the news broadcast was a subterfuge or cover for private or commercial exploitation.

New York v. Ferber (S. Ct. 1982)

Facts: D, owner of a store specializing in sexually oriented products, was convicted of knowingly promoting sexual performances by children under the age of 16 by distributing material depicting such performances.

Issue: Does the First Amendment protect child pornography from restriction?

Rule: (White, J.) The First Amendment does not prohibit statutory restrictions on child pornography, provided the conduct to be prohibited is adequately defined. A state's interest in protecting the physiological, emotional, and mental health of its children outweighs the risk of suppression of protected expression, especially when the value to society of such expression is minimal. Child pornography laws do not require a showing that the restricted matter is obscene.

Concurrence: (Acinar, J.) The compelling interests identified in today's opinion suggest that the Constitution might in fact permit a state to ban knowing distribution of works depicting minors engaged in explicit sexual conduct, regardless of the depictions' social value.

Concurrence: (Brennan, J.) Applications of child pornography statutes to depictions of children that in themselves do have serious literary, artistic, scientific or medical value would violate the First Amendment. In such cases, a state's regulatory interest would be far less compelling than in cases of true pornography.

Schad v. Borough of Mount Ephraim (S. Ct. 1981)

Facts: Ds, operators of an adult bookstore that showed live nude dancing, were found to have violated a local zoning ordinance forbidding live entertainment.

Issue: Do laws violate the First Amendment when they exclude a broad category of protected expression and do not serve significant state interests?

Rule: (White, J.) For the exclusion of a broad category of protected expression, the First Amendment requires that a statute restricting expression be narrowly drawn to respond to the distinctive problems arising from the restricted expression. Additionally, laws that regulate the time, place, and manner of such expression must serve significant state interests and leave open adequate alternative channels of communication.

Concurrence: (Blackmun, J.) Where protected First Amendment interests are at stake, zoning regulations have no immunity from constitutional challenge. Government cannot legislatively prevent access to forms of protected expression solely because these activities are sufficiently available elsewhere.

Concurrence: (Powell, J.) A residential community should be able to limit commercial establishments to essential neighborhood services permitted in a narrowly zoned area.

Concurrence: (Stevens, J.) The Borough bore the burden of demonstrating that the defendants' introduction of live entertainment had an identifiable adverse impact on the community.

Dissent: (Burger, C.J.) A community's willingness to tolerate certain commercial activities should not compel it also to tolerate every other commercial use, which may be incompatible with a residential atmosphere.

New York State Liquor Authority v. Bellanca (S. Ct. 1981)

Facts: D challenged the constitutionality of a state law that prohibited nude dancing in establishments licensed to sell liquor for on-site consumption.

Issue: Do a state's broad powers under the Twenty-First Amendment allow it to condition privileges granted under that Amendment on adherence to statutory restrictions on expression?

Rule: (per curiam) A state's power under the Twenty-First Amendment to ban entirely the sale of alcohol, or to regulate the time, place, and circumstances of such sale, includes the lesser power to prohibit the sale of liquor where statutorily proscribed expression is given vent. Whatever artistic or communicative value may be attached to prohibited expression is overcome by a state's exercise of its broad powers under the Twenty-First Amendment.

Dissent: (Stevens, J.) It is a mischievous suggestion that the Twenty-First Amendment gives states power to censor free expression in places where liquor is served. Neither the language nor the history of that Amendment provides support for this suggestion.

Florida Star v. B.J.F. (S. Ct. 1989)

Facts: A Florida statute made it unlawful to print, in any instrument of mass communication, the name of the victim of a sexual offense. The Florida Star was found civilly liable under this statute for publishing the name of a rape victim that it had obtained from a publicly released police report.

Issue: May a state punish the publication of true material obtained lawfully?

Rule: (Marshall, J.) If a newspaper lawfully obtains truthful information about a matter of public significance, state officials may not constitutionally punish publication of the information, absent a need to further a state interest of the highest order.

Concurrence: (Scalia, J.) A law cannot be regarded as protecting an interest of the highest order, and thus as justifying a restriction upon truthful speech, when it leaves appreciable damage to that supposedly vital interest unprohibited. In this case, the Florida statute does not prohibit the dissemination of such news through gossip and word of mouth, and is therefore invalid.

Dissent: (White, J.) There is no public interest in publishing the names, addresses, and phone numbers of persons who are the victims of crime — and no public interest in immunizing the press from liability in the rare cases where a state's efforts to protect a victim's privacy have failed.

United States v. Robel (S. Ct. 1967)

Facts: D, a Communist Party member, was indicted for violating a federal act that prohibited any member of a Communist-action organization from "engag[ing] in any employment in any defense facility."

Issue: Does a statute violate freedom of association by proscribing both protected and unprotected group membership?

Rule: (Warren, C.J.) An act that is overbroad in that it may touch on protected conduct in addition to regulating unprohibited conduct, is unconstitutional under the First Amendment.

Concurrence: (Brennan, J.) The constitutionality of overbroad acts should be determined on a case-by-case basis depending on their potential impact on fundamental rights, the importance of the end sought, and the necessity of the means adopted.

Dissent: (White, J.) The national interests behind the law in question are real and substantial. Given the Communist Party's characteristics, the exclusion of Communists from certain defense plants is well within Congress' powers.

Thomas v. Collins (S. Ct. 1945)

Facts: D, a high-ranking union officer, entered Texas to speak at a workers' meeting. The state attorney general obtained an order restraining D from speaking at the meeting because state law required union organizers to obtain a permit before engaging in union activity. D defied the order.

Issue: May a legislature pass laws that abridge free speech, absent a clear and present danger or other overriding government goals?

Rule: (Rutledge, J.) First Amendment rights cannot be abridged unless there is a clear and present danger that such abridgment seeks to curb, or unless public safety, health, morality, or the like, is at stake.

Ginzburg v. United States (S. Ct. 1966)

Facts: D was convicted of violating federal obscenity law for mailing allegedly obscene publications and advertisements for them.

Issue: Under the First Amendment, may materials that, standing alone, may not be considered obscene, be restricted because of the nature of their advertisement?

Rule: (Brennan, J.) Determining an expression's obscene nature may be based, in part, on whether the expression is marketed on the basis of its appeal to prurient interests.

Dissent: (Black, J.) The federal government is without any power under the Constitution to burden the expression of ideas of any kind.

The Court's obscenity guidelines are so vague and meaningless that they leave the defendant's fate to unbridled discretion.

Dissent: (Harlan, J.) Under the statute at issue, the government may only ban "hardcore pornography" from the mails. The Court's theory of obscenity is unrelated to the language, purposes, or history of the applicable statute.

Dissent: (Stewart, J.) The First Amendment stands for the principle that one cannot be imprisoned merely because his or her spoken or published expression offends a judge's aesthetic sensibilities.

Stanley v. Georgia (S. Ct. 1969)

Facts: While searching D's home under warrant to seize evidence of book-making activity, police found movie film and other items of an allegedly obscene nature. D was convicted of possession of obscene matter.

Issue: Do laws punishing private possession of obscene material violate of the First Amendment?

Rule: (Marshall, J.) Laws that criminalize mere possession of obscene material violate the First Amendment and constitute unwanted governmental intrusion into one's privacy.

Curtis Publishing Co. v. Butts; Associated Press v. Walker (S. Ct. 1967)

Facts: P, a college football coach, sued a publishing company for printing an article claiming that he rigged a game. In a case argued on the same day, P, a former Army general, sued the Associated Press for an article that claimed that he played a leading role in a campus riot against an African American's university enrollment.

Issue: Does the First Amendment freedom of speech and press protect media defamation of public figures?

Rule: (Harlan, J.) The First Amendment does not protect defamatory statements about public figures when the substance of the defamation risks substantial danger to reputation and where the publisher is engaged in highly unreasonable conduct departing in the extreme from the standards of responsible publishers.

Concurrence: (Warren, C.J.) Liability for defamation of both public officials and public figures should turn on a finding of "actual malice."

Concurrence/Dissent: (Black, J.) The "actual malice" rule concerning libel is wholly inadequate to save the press from being destroyed by libel judgments.

Concurrence/Dissent: (Brennan, J.) The "actual malice" standard should apply to public figures.

Time, Inc. v. Firestone (S. Ct. 1976)

Facts: P, wife to the heir of the Firestone tire fortune, sued Time, Inc. (D) for publishing a "false, malicious, and defamatory" article announcing her divorce.

Issue: Do First Amendment rights require a showing of "actual malice" for a publisher to be liable for defamation of a private person concerning a private matter?

Rule: (Rehnquist, J.) The First Amendment does not require a showing of "actual malice" for a publisher to be liable for defamation of a private person concerning a matter not of public concern. Those drawn into the public forum largely against their will are not public figures, regardless of their consequent social visibility.

Concurrence: (Powell, J.) A publisher should not be liable if he exercises the reasonably prudent care that a state may constitutionally demand of a publisher prior to a publication whose content reveals its defamatory potential.

Dissent: (Brennan, J.) The *New York Times* "actual malice" standard should apply here. Judicial proceedings are public events that cannot be reported without reference to those persons that are the subject matter of the controversy. Press coverage of court proceedings performs the indispensable role of subjecting the court system to public scrutiny.

Dissent: (White, J.) First Amendment values will not be furthered in any way by application of the fault standards imposed by *Gertz v. Robert Welch, Inc.*

Dissent: (Marshall, J.) The "actual malice" standard applied in public figure/public issue cases should apply here. Mrs. Firestone is a "public figure" within the meaning of prior decisions. She is a prominent high-society member who has easy access to the media, and she voluntarily acted in a manner that predictably attracted the attention of a sizable portion of the public.

Galella v. Onassis (1972)

Facts: P, a professional photographer, employed relentless, intrusive tactics to obtain candid shots of Jacqueline Onassis and her children. In light of Mrs. Onassis' efforts to evade the photography, P sued Mrs. Onassis and three Secret Service agents (Ds) for false arrest and malicious prosecution; he also sought an injunction to prohibit Ds from interfering with the practice of his trade.

Issue: Does the First Amendment protect all forms of conduct by the media in its coverage of public figures?

Rule: (Cooper, J.) The First Amendment does not immunize all conduct by the media, particularly tortious or criminal acts, in its efforts to gather information about a public figure, especially when the information sought is of minuscule societal importance.

Yates v. United States (S. Ct. 1957)

Facts: Ds, low-level members of the Communist Party, were convicted of violation of the Smith Act, which made it unlawful to "knowingly or willfully advocate or teach the duty of overthrowing or destroying any government in the United States by force or violence."

Issue: May a person be convicted under the Smith Act, which criminalizes the advocacy and teaching of the overthrow of government, for engaging in speech not designed to incite illegal action?

Rule: (Harlan, J.) One may not be convicted under the Smith Act for advocacy of forcible overthrow as an abstract doctrine. However, one may be convicted for advocacy of action for the actual overthrow of government.

Dissent: (Black, J.) The statutory provisions on which these prosecutions proceeded abridged freedom of speech, press, and assembly in violation of the First Amendment.

Scales v. United States (S. Ct. 1961)

Facts: D, a Communist Party chairman, was convicted of violating the Smith Act by becoming a member of an organization advocating the forcible or violent overthrow of the government, knowing the purposes of such organization.

Issue: Does an act that criminalizes membership in an organization based on what the organization advocates violate the First Amendment?

Rule: (Harlan, J.) Under the First Amendment, one may not be prosecuted for membership in an organization unless one is an active member who purposefully intends to act in the illegal aspects of the organization.

Dissent: (Black, J.) One should not be deprived of First Amendment freedoms based on a balancing test which weighs what a court considers to be a government interest which is significant enough to deprive one of freedom.

Jenkins v. Georgia (S. Ct. 1974)

Facts: D was convicted of distributing obscene material for showing the sexually oriented film "Carnal Knowledge" in a movie theater.

Issue: In determining obscenity under constitutional standards, does a jury's finding of patent offensiveness preclude further appellate review?

Rule: (Rehnquist, J.) Though questions of appeal to the "prurient interest" or of patent offensiveness are "essentially questions of fact," juries do not have unbridled discretion in determining what is "patently offensive." Appellate review courts may determine for themselves, after viewing the evidence, if the act is a public portrayal of hardcore sexual conduct for its own sake, and for ensuing commercial gain constituting "patent offensiveness."

City of Renton v. Playtime Theaters, Inc. (S. Ct. 1986)

Facts: P challenged a city ordinance prohibiting any "adult motion picture theater from locating in the vicinity of any residential zone, single or multiple-family dwelling, church, or park, and within one mile of any school."

Issue: Does a city ordinance prohibiting adult motion picture theaters from locating within one mile of certain types of buildings violate the freedom of speech guarantee of the First Amendment?

Rule: (Rehnquist, J.) A time, place and manner ordinance which is enacted primarily to combat the undesirable secondary effects of a type of business, and not to suppress free expression of unpopular views, is to be reviewed under the standard applicable to "content-neutral" time, place and manner regulations. If enacted to serve a substantial governmental interest, such ordinances are constitutionally valid.

Dissent: (Brennan, J.) The zoning ordinance should not selectively impose limitations on location based exclusively on content of expression.

Consolidated Edison Co. v. Public Service Comm'n (S. Ct. 1980)

Facts: P, a public utility, included inserts in billing envelopes to customers that stated its position on the use of nuclear power. Afterward, the Public Service Commission barred utility companies from including bill inserts that express viewpoints on controversial issues of public policy.

Issue: May government-regulated companies be prohibited from enclosing in billing envelopes materials setting out the company's views on issues of public policy?

Rule: (Powell, J.) Under the First Amendment, a government agency may not suppress the discussion of controversial issues by a government-funded utility unless suppression is necessary to advance a necessary policy goal.

Dissent: (Blackmun, J.) The Commission correctly concluded that use of the billing envelope to distribute management's pamphlets amounts to a forced subsidy of the utility's speech by the ratepayers. The state's attempt to protect the ratepayers from unwillingly financing the utility's speech and to preserve the billing envelope for the sole benefit of the customers who pay for it does not infringe upon the First Amendment rights of the utility.

Pittsburgh Press Co. v. Pittsburgh Comm'n on Human Relations (S. Ct. 1973)

Facts: The City of Pittsburgh enacted an ordinance that forbade newspapers from printing "help-wanted" advertisements in sex-designated columns except where the employer or advertiser was free to make hiring or employment referral decisions based on sex.

Issue: Does an ordinance forbidding hiring advertisement in sex-designated columns, except where the advertiser or employer is free to make hiring decisions based on sex, violate the freedoms of speech and of the press guaranteed by the First and Fourteenth Amendments?

Rule: (Powell, J.) Gender discrimination in employment is illegal and an ordinance narrowly drawn to prohibit placement in sex-designated columns of advertisements for nonexempt job opportunities does not infringe a newspaper's freedom of speech or press rights guaranteed under the First Amendment.

Dissent: (Stewart, J.) A government agency should not dictate the layout of a newspaper.

City of Erie v. Pap's AM (S. Ct. 2000)

Facts: The City of Erie banned nude dancing, and owners of dance clubs appealed.

Issue: Can a city ban nude dancing consistent with the First Amendment?

Rule: (O'Connor, J.) (plurality) The city had a right to seek to mitigate the secondary effects of nude dancing by requiring that the dancers put on clothing. The court should defer to the city's determination that this requirement would assist in mitigating those effects, and at any rate the city should not be penalized for requiring only minimal clothing rather than imposing more severe restrictions.

Concurrence: (Scalia, J.) The conduct here is without First Amendment protection, and if in pursuit of the public welfare the city wishes to banish it they can without any First Amendment scrutiny.

Dissent: (Stevens, J.) The majority for the first time allows a secondary effects justification to authorize the complete prohibition, rather than the zoning, of a type of protected expression.

City of Los Angeles v. Alameda Books (S. Ct. 2002)

Facts: The City of Los Angeles enacted an ordinance limiting the concentration of adult bookstores, in order to reduce the secondary effects of such businesses.

Issue: On what evidence may a city support a secondary effects regulation of protected speech?

Rule: (O'Connor, J.) (plurality) The city could rely on a study that did not establish that other means of combating the secondary effects would not have been as effective. The Court's prior cases do not set such a high bar for a city; instead, courts should defer to cities' judgment when a city determines that a particular approach will mitigate the problem.

Concurrence: (Kennedy, J.) Even though such regulations are effectively content-based speech restrictions, they should nevertheless receive only intermediate scrutiny given that they, as zoning restrictions, will not reduce the amount of speech that is made.

Wisconsin v. Mitchell (S. Ct. 1993)

Facts: D was convicted of assault and his sentence was increased under a statute that mandated higher sentences when crimes were based on the basis of race.

Issue: Does a sentence enhancement based on the perpetrator's racist intent violate his freedom of thought, in violation of the First Amendment?

Rule: (Rehnquist, C.J.) Because the statute penalizes conduct rather than thought there is very little chance of chilling protected thought. This distinguishes the statute from the one in *R.A.V.*, where the statute was aimed at expression. Bias-motivated crimes create distinct societal harm, and thus the state is justified in punishing them more harshly.

Reno v. ACLU (S. Ct. 1997)

Facts: P challenged the Communications Decency Act, which, among other things, made it a crime to use a computer to transmit or display a message available to someone under 18 that is patently offensive as measured by contemporary community standards.

Issue: Does the statute take in too much protected speech to be constitutional?

Rule: (Stevens, J.) The statute brings within its ambit too much protected speech, including, for example, emails from parents to their college student children about birth control and sexuality, and any website that has any offensive conduct on it unless it restricts access to adults, something most individual website creators will not have the expertise to do. Moreover, the Internet is not as invasive as radio, as users seldom encounter content by accident.

Concurrence/Dissent: (O'Connor, J.) It might be permissible to construe part of the statute as criminalizing offensive communications when specifically targeted at someone the sender knows is under 18. Thus construed, the statute would be constitutional, since it is permissible to restrict minors' access to certain content to which adults have a constitutional right.

44 Liquormart v. Rhode Island (S. Ct. 1996)

Facts: Rhode Island banned retailers from advertising the price of liquor, in order to prevent price-cutting wars that would increase alcohol consumption.

Issue: Does a prohibition on alcohol advertising violate the First Amendment?

Rule: (Stevens, J.) (plurality) The First Amendment requires courts to be skeptical of claims that speech restrictions on truthful, nonmisleading speech are necessary in order to protect the public from responding irrationally to the truth. At any rate, the restriction fails the existing *Central Hudson* test and thus should be struck down.

Concurrence: (O'Connor, J.) All that is necessary to decide this case is to apply *Central Hudson*, since under that case the state law must be struck down.

Thompson v. Western States Medical Center (S. Ct. 2002)

Facts: Federal regulations allow pharmacists to compound drugs for the unique needs of individual patients without having to submit such compounds to federal safety testing; however, the regulations prohibit the advertisement of such compounding services. Pharmacists challenged the restriction as a violation of the First Amendment.

Issue: Do such restrictions violate the First Amendment rights of pharmacists?

Rule: (O'Connor, J.) The restrictions fail the *Central Hudson* test, as there are other, less speech-restrictive means for the government to ensure that such particularized compounding not become generally available.

Dissent: (Breyer, J.) The restrictions are necessary to protect the public's health, and the Court's application of *Central Hudson* inappropriately limits government power to satisfy that goal.

Virginia v. Black (S. Ct. 2003)

Facts: D was convicted of violating a Virginia law that banned the burning of a cross with the intent to intimidate, with a proviso that burning a cross in public view was prima facie evidence of an intent to intimidate.

Issue: Does a prohibition on cross burning, but not other forms of intimidation, single out a certain viewpoint for punishment, in violation of the First Amendment?

Rule: (O'Connor, J.) Cross burning is an especially virulent form of threatening speech, and is not necessarily correlated with any particular viewpoint; thus, the statute's prohibition is constitutional.

Dissent: (Souter, J.) The statute singles out expression that historically has represented a particular point of view, and the evidentiary provision makes it likely that ideologically based cross burnings will be punished, in violation of the rule against content- or viewpoint-based speech restrictions.

Ashcroft v. ACLU (S. Ct. 2001)

Facts: The Child Online Protection Act prohibits commercial display of images on the World Wide Web that are patently offensive according to community standards. The lower court found that the statute's reference to "contemporary community standards" made the statute unconstitutionally overbroad.

Issue: Does an Internet decency regulation referencing contemporary community standards violate the First Amendment?

Rule: (Thomas, J.) Such a reference does not render the statute overbroad, since the statute, unlike the Communications Decency Act struck down in *Reno v. ACLU*, reaches a much smaller set of communications, and is generally of a narrower scope. The fact that web postings are necessarily viewable across the nation, and thus subject to the most sensitive communities' tastes, does not render the community standards test facially unconstitutional; juries may be instructed to take a non-geographic understanding of "community," and speakers, if they wish to reach only the most tolerant communities, can choose a more directed medium.

Dissent: (Kennedy, J.) The majority's approach effectively forecloses use of the World Wide Web to speakers whose speech might be considered offensive by small pockets of citizens in different parts of the country.

Ashcroft v. ACLU (S. Ct. 2004)

Facts: The Child Online Protection Act restricts the commercial display of offensive images on the World Wide Web in a way likely to be seen by children, for example, display without a requirement of entry of a credit card number. The lower court entered a preliminary injunction against enforcement of the statute.

Issue: Are such restrictions on speech likely to be unconstitutional?

Rule: (Kennedy, J.) Because this is a content-based restriction the government must show that there are no less speech-restrictive alternatives. Here, the government has not explained how filtering technology, which restricts speech at the receiving end at the behest of particular viewers, and which would filter out foreign and not just U.S.-based web postings, would not be as effective.

Dissent: (Scalia, J.) The type of speech being restricted here could be banned consistent with the Constitution; thus, a lesser restriction of the sort in the statute is necessarily constitutional.

Dissent: (Breyer, J.) While such restrictions should be examined carefully, the statute's restrictions on speech are modest, and filtering software is not an ideal solution, given its inaccuracies and the fact that it is costly.

United States v. Playboy Entertainment Group (S. Ct. 2000)

Facts: Federal law requires cable operators either to fully scramble sexually explicit channels not subscribed to by a viewer or to limit airing of such channels to evening hours when children are not likely to be watching.

Issue: Under what circumstances can a scrambling or time-restricting requirement be upheld?

Rule: (Kennedy, J.) Because this is a content-based restriction of constitutionally protected speech, the government bears the burden of explaining how less speech-restrictive alternatives would not suffice. Here it is possible that an existing statutory provision, requiring full blocking at the behest of individual subscribers, would take care of the problem more effectively, with less of a loss to speech. The government has not explained why this alternative is inadequate.

Dissent: (Scalia, J.) The speech at issue can constitutionally be prohibited; thus, the government may constitutionally take the lesser step of restricting it, as in this statute.

Dissent: (Breyer, J.) While the majority correctly states the standard of review, it applies it too stringently, with the result that the statute is struck down when it should be upheld.

Ashcroft v. Free Speech Coalition (S. Ct. 2002)

Facts: A federal statute prohibited possession of "virtual" child pornography, that is, pornography portrayed as involving children but actually involving youthful looking adult actors or pornography created by use of computer imaging.

Issue: Does the unprotected status of actual child pornography also include virtual child pornography?

Rule: (Kennedy, J.) The statute is unconstitutionally overbroad. The harms of child pornography deal with the method in which it is made, which harms the child models. Virtual child pornography does not cause this harm. Moreover, such speech is constitutionally protected since it is not obscene.

Turner Broadcasting v. FCC (S. Ct. 1994)

Facts: Congress required cable operators to carry certain broadcast signals, in order to ensure the broadcasters' continued financial viability in order in turn to ensure that non–cable subscribers retained access to television.

Issue: Are "must carry" rules content based and therefore presumptively unconstitutional?

Rule: (Kennedy, J.) Such rules are content-neutral, as they are designed to promote over-the-air broadcasting in general, and not a particular viewpoint they may carry. The speech burden on cable operators is not extreme, given the large number of channels cable operators are technologically able to offer and the fact that cable operators are not normally linked to the content of the speech they carry. Intermediate scrutiny is appropriate for such regulations.

Dissent: (O'Connor, J.) The legislative history makes it clear that Congress was manifesting a concern for local content and educational programming when it enacted the "must carry" rules. Thus, these rules are content-based. Strict scrutiny is therefore appropriate.

Bartnicki v. Volper (S. Ct. 2001)

Facts: During a contentious labor negotiation, an individual intercepted a cell phone conversation between union officials and gave the recording to a radio news reporter who played it on the air. The officials sued under a statute criminalizing interception or receipt of such an intercepted conversation knowing it was intercepted.

Issue: Does the public importance of the issues discussed in the conversation immunize under the First Amendment the airing of the conversation?

Rule: (Stevens, J.) Despite the government interest in protecting participants in private conversations, the importance to the public of wide-ranging information and debate on matters of public concern outweighs the privacy concern, and renders the airing of the conversation constitutionally protected.

Dissent: (Rehnquist, C.J.) The majority's rule will actually chill First Amendment expression by rendering all electronic communication less secure from interception and subsequent publication.

City of San Diego v. Roe (S. Ct. 2004)

Facts: A police officer sold sexually explicit videos of himself performing police-type functions in a sexual fantasy setting. When he failed to comply with an order to stop selling the videos he was fired. The officer sued, alleging violation of his speech rights.

Issue: Do the videos constitute speech on a matter of public concern, thus triggering balancing test used to decide speech claims of government employees under *Pickering v. Board of Education* (1968)?

Rule: (per curiam) This type of speech does not touch on matters of public concern; thus the city could discipline the officer without a court considering the officer's First Amendment rights under *Pickering* balancing.

2. The Public Forum Problem

Near v. Minnesota (S. Ct. 1931)

Facts: D, a newspaper, printed articles charging that a "Jewish gangster" was in charge of racketeering in the area, and that law enforcement officials were not doing their jobs. The paper was permanently enjoined from printing any malicious, scandalous, and defamatory material.

Issue: Does the First Amendment proscribe a statute that forbids the publication of material unless it can be proven to be true and non-malicious?

Rule: Under the First Amendment, public speech may not be restricted prior to and unless the author can make a showing of accuracy or proper motive, but may be restricted only after improper motive is established.

Dissent: (Butler, J.) Restrictions on publications which regularly abuse the right to free press and which address only the specific abuse do not amount to previous restraint on publication.

United States v. O'Brien (S. Ct. 1968)

Facts: In knowing violation of a federal statute, D publicly burned his draft card in order to influence others to adopt his antiwar beliefs.

Issue: When "speech" and "non-speech" elements are combined in the same course of conduct, can a sufficiently important governmental interest in regulating the non-speech element justify incidental limitations on First Amendment freedoms?

Rule: (Warren, C.J.) The government may regulate the non-speech element of conduct comprised of both speech and non-speech elements if the regulation is within the constitutional power of the government; if it furthers an important or substantial government interest; if the governmental interest is unrelated to the suppression of free expression; and if the incidental restriction on free expression is no greater than is essential to the furtherance of that interest.

Street v. New York (S. Ct. 1969)

Facts: D, angered that a civil rights leader had been shot, burned, and criticized an American flag on a street corner. D was convicted under a statute that made it a misdemeanor to publicly mutilate, defile, or cast contempt upon, either by words or act, any flag of the United States.

Issue: Is a statute criminalizing defiant or contemptuous verbal expression about a national symbol constitutional?

Rule: (Harlan, J.) A statute that may subject one to criminal sanctions for verbal expression of opinions, merely because they are contrary to the values of the existing order, is contrary to the First Amendment.

Dissent: (Warren, C.J.) An act desecrating the flag should be punished.
Dissent: (Black, J.) When specified conduct is illegal and speech is an integral part of the conduct, a prosecution based on both aspects of the behavior should be permissible.
Dissent: (Fortas, J.) A national symbol should have at least the same restrictions against desecration as personal property, and should be accorded even greater protection, as it has always traditionally been subject to various modes of regulation.

Spence v. Washington (S. Ct. 1974)

Facts: D attached peace symbols made of removable tape to an American flag that he owned, and displayed it on his property. He was convicted under an "improper use" statute.
Issue: Does the First Amendment protect the expression of opinion that is communicated through the manipulation of a copy of a national symbol?
Rule: Absent a significant impairment of a substantial state interest, privately owned national symbols may be used for symbolic communication, particularly where context reveals the act's communicative intent.
Dissent: (Rehnquist, J.) Since a state may impose limitations on speech directly, it would seem to follow *a fortiori* that a state may legislate to protect important state interests, such as the character of a national symbol, even though an incidental limitation on free speech results.

Texas v. Johnson (S. Ct. 1989)

Facts: D was convicted under a statute that made flag burning, with the knowledge that someone likely to observe the action will be seriously offended, a crime.
Issue: Is flag burning a constitutionally protected activity under the First Amendment?
Rule: (Brennan, J.) A flag burning statute designed to prosecute only those acts which are likely to offend an observer is invalid under the First Amendment. A government may not prohibit the expression of an idea simply because society finds the idea itself offensive or disagreeable.
Concurrence: (Kennedy, J.) The flag protects those who hold it in contempt.
Dissent: (Rehnquist, C.J.) The destruction of a national symbol should not be protected, as it forms no essential part of any exposition of ideas protected by the First Amendment, and has a tendency to incite a breach of the peace, which a state has a legitimate governmental interest in trying to avoid.
Dissent: (Stevens, J.) Given its unique value, the same interest that would allow the government to preserve the quality of an important national

asset by, for example, prohibiting spray painting the Lincoln Memorial, should support the prohibition on the desecration of the American flag.

Clark v. Community for Creative Non-Violence (S. Ct. 1984)

Facts: The National Park Service issued a permit to Ps, a group of civil rights protestors, to conduct a demonstration in a park to call attention to the plight of the homeless. The permit allowed erection of two symbolic tent cities. Ps challenged an NPS regulation prohibiting overnight sleeping in national parks.
Issue: May time, place, and manner restrictions be placed constitutionally protected expression?
Rule: (White, J.) The First Amendment guarantee of the right of expression is subject to reasonable time, place, and manner restrictions. Time, place, and manner restrictions are reasonable if they are justified without reference to the content of the regulated speech, are narrowly tailored to serve a significant governmental interest, and leave open ample alternative channels for communication of the information.

Cantwell v. Connecticut (S. Ct. 1940)

Facts: On a public street, D played a record that criticized all organized religions. He was convicted of the common law offense of breach of the peace.
Issue: May communication that does not involve direct personal abuse, but criticism of an institution, be restricted under the First Amendment if it provokes a violent reaction?
Rule: (Roberts, J.) Speech which may be likely to offend, but not likely to cause an actual violent reaction in a reasonable person, is protected by the First Amendment.

Feiner v. New York (S. Ct. 1951)

Facts: D gave a speech inviting people to rise up in arms and to engage in violent activities. The crowd grew excited and subsequently, D was arrested for disorderly conduct.
Issue: May the freedom of speech be suppressed when the purpose of the suppression is to prevent the incitement of a riot?
Rule: (Vinson, J.) When, as a reaction to public expression, a clear and present danger to public safety, peace or order is apparent, the government may prevent or punish the expression.
Concurrence: (Frankfurter, J.) Where there is a substantial need to preserve order, a speaker may not be given immunity from suppression merely because his speech falls within constitutional limits.

Dissent: (Black, J.) The police must first attempt to calm a restless audience without infringing on the speaker's First Amendment rights.

Dissent: (Douglas, J.) The power of the police to prevent a riot as a result of a speaker's exercise of his constitutional rights does not extend to threats against the speaker himself. When that is the case, the police have an obligation to protect the speaker, not to arrest him.

Cox v. Louisiana [Cox I] (S. Ct. 1965)

Facts: D led a demonstration in front of a courthouse to protest the arrests of blacks who sat at a segregated lunch counter. In the presence of a hostile crowd of whites, D exhorted the protestors to also sit at segregated lunch counters. D was convicted of violating the breach of the peace and obstruction of justice.

Issue: Absent a display of violence or violent intent, may public expression be suppressed due to a public official's fear of possible violence?

Rule: (Goldberg, J.) Absent a showing of clear and present danger to order, public expression may not be suppressed. A statute limiting expression must provide clear standards that apply to all members of the public equally, and do not allow enforcement officials unbridled discretion.

Cox v. Louisiana [Cox II] (S. Ct. 1965)

Facts: (Same as above.) Cox was charged and convicted of violating a courthouse picketing statute.

Issue: Is a narrowly drawn statute proscribing precise conduct constitutional when it incidentally infringes on the right to free speech?

Rule: (Goldberg, J.) A statute may proscribe certain conduct if it is drawn clearly enough to provide standards by which the public and enforcement officials may conduct themselves. If the proscribed conduct is used as a form of expression in a certain instance, it may still be constitutionally proscribed under the statute.

Concurrence in *Cox I* and Dissent in *Cox II*: (Black, J.) The First Amendment grants the right to unrestricted freedom of speech, the press, and assembly only in places where people have a right to be for such purposes.

Note: D was acquitted because the sheriff gave apparent sanction to the place of the picketing.

Frisby v. Schulz (S. Ct. 1988)

Facts: An ordinance banned all picketing in front of any private residence or dwelling.

Issue: Is a law prohibiting picketing of residential homes constitutional, when the purpose of the law is to protect residents' right to privacy?

Rule: A state has a substantial and justifiable interest in banning speech directed primarily at those who are presumptively unwilling to receive it. Therefore, a state may inhibit free speech in the form of picketing when it interferes with another constitutional right such as privacy.

Concurrence: (White, J.) An ordinance which forbids all picketing in residential neighborhoods should be void for overbreadth.

Dissent: (Brennan, J.) The ordinance bans significantly more speech than is necessary to achieve the government's substantial and legitimate goal.

Dissent: (Stevens, J.) A statute which limits one's right to expression should be limited to a ban only of conduct that unreasonably interferes with the privacy of the home and does not serve a reasonable communicative purpose.

Adderley v. Florida (S. Ct. 1966)

Facts: Ds, students, went to a jail and protested racial segregation and the previous arrest of other student demonstrators.

Issue: Does a state violate the First Amendment by prohibiting public expression on state property as a means of enforcing a no-trespassing policy?

Rule: Jail grounds are not a public forum. Public expression may be prohibited on government property that is not open to the public as long as such restriction is applied uniformly to all members of the public.

Dissent: (Douglas, J.) Absent a specific law which provides standards for even application, the First Amendment provides a right to public expression in all public places, provided that the legitimate use of the public place is not thereby disrupted and the assembly is peaceful.

Lehman v. Shaker Heights (S. Ct. 1974)

Facts: P, a state assembly candidate, challenged a law that permitted commercial but not political advertisements on city buses.

Issue: Does the First Amendment guarantee a right to public access to publicly owned and controlled areas of communication?

Rule: (Blackmun, J.) The First Amendment does not require that publicly owned areas of communication be open to all types of public use, merely that the restrictions on such use be neither arbitrary, capricious, nor invidious.

Concurrence: (Douglas, J.) The mere fact that a utility or service is publicly owned or operated does not make it a public forum. A public forum is a place whose primary purpose is to be a place for discussion; any place that has a primary purpose which is other than discussion should not subject a captive public to an invasion of privacy by unwanted ideas.

Dissent: (Brennan, J.) Having opened a forum for communication, the city is barred by the First Amendment from discriminating among forum users solely on the basis of message content.

Perry Educ. Ass'n v. Perry Local Educators' Ass'n (S. Ct. 1983)

Facts: P, a teacher's union, was denied access to an interschool mailing system to which the rival, official union was allowed access. Other private non-school groups were also allowed access.
Issue: Is the denial of access to public property that is not by tradition or designation a forum for public communication violative of the First Amendment's protection of speech?
Rule: (White, J.) With respect to public property which is not by tradition or designation a forum for public communication, a state may make distinctions in access on the basis of speaker identity and subject matter as long as the regulation is reasonable in light of the forum's intended use and not an effort to suppress expression merely because it is unpopular, and that a forum has not become public by policy or practice.
Dissent: (Brennan, J.) In focusing on the public forum issue, the Court disregards the First Amendment's central proscription against censorship in the form of viewpoint discrimination in any forum, public or nonpublic.

City Council v. Taxpayers for Vincent (S. Ct. 1984)

Facts: P, a group of supporters of a city council candidate, challenged a municipal ordinance prohibiting the posting of signs on city property contending that the ordinance abridged the freedom of speech.
Issue: May a "viewpoint neutral" regulation that applies equally to all and is not designed to oppress unpopular ideas except those that are deemed to be a public nuisance, withstand the First Amendment?
Rule: (Stevens, J.) Although a legislature may not prohibit a certain type of non-threatening expression across the board, the legislature may restrict conduct which does not amount to direct communication to an audience, but the "throwing of literature into the streets," for anyone who may come across it. This restriction must serve a legitimate government purpose, be nondiscriminatory, and not create an unacceptable risk of suppression of ideas.
Dissent: (Brennan, J.) An interest in eliminating visual clutter is not substantial enough to justify a restriction on First Amendment rights. An aesthetic objective must be especially substantial and there should be no other reasonable means for its accomplishment, in order to overcome the strong presumption against restriction.

Bridges v. California (S. Ct. 1941)

Facts: Appellant was head of a union that was involved in litigation against another union. After a judgment against appellant's union was handed down, appellant published a scathing criticism and a threat to call a strike.

Issue: Are spoken or printed criticisms of courts considered contemptuous, and therefore not constitutionally protected?

Rule: Before out-of-court statements may be punished, the clear and present danger test must be applied, i.e., the substantive evil must be extremely serious and the degree of imminence extremely high.

Dissent: (Frankfurter, J.) A threat to impartial adjudication should not be considered a permissible exercise of free speech. This amounts to an obstruction of justice.

Lovell v. Griffin (S. Ct. 1938)

Facts: A city ordinance required distributors of literature to secure a permit from the city manager to alleviate some of the problems of litter in city streets. D distributed religious material without a permit.

Issue: Is an ordinance that is broad enough to prohibit any form of distribution of any type of literature an unconstitutional infringement of the right to freedom of speech?

Rule: A vague ordinance that allows an official the discretion to prohibit conduct for reasons that do not directly advance the purpose of the ordinance is unconstitutional as a prior restraint on free speech.

Police Dep't of Chicago v. Mosley (S. Ct. 1972)

Facts: A city ordinance prohibited picketing in front of any school building while school was in session, unless the picketing involved a labor dispute.

Issue: Is a law that regulates picketing in terms of its subject matter unconstitutional?

Rule: Under the Equal Protection Clause and the First Amendment, the government may not prohibit others from assembling or speaking on the basis of what they intend to say.

Concurrence: (Burger, C.J.) The First Amendment does not guarantee the right to express any thought one likes, free from government censorship.

Red Lion Broadcasting Co. v. FCC (S. Ct. 1969)

Facts: The FCC, under its fairness doctrine, required that broadcasters allow reply time to the public in cases involving personal attacks or political editorials.

Issue: Does a rule that requires licensed broadcasters to allow reply time to answer personal attacks and political editorials abridge freedom of speech and press?

Rule: (White, J.) Under the First Amendment, licensed broadcasters may be required to allow answers to personal attacks and political editorials. The broadcast media is unique in that broadcasters enjoy a monopoly granted by the government and that the airwaves are finite. This imposes a fiduciary relationship between the broadcaster and the listening or viewing public.

Walker v. City of Birmingham (S. Ct. 1967)

Facts: Ds were cited for contempt of court because they violated a court order forbidding them to participate in certain civil rights marches. However, the ordinance on which the court order was directly based was found to be unconstitutional and thereby made the court order invalid.

Issue: May one disregard a court order if it is based upon an unconstitutional statute?

Rule: A court order must be obeyed until a determination has been made by a court that it is invalid.

Dissent: (Warren, C.J.) An unconstitutional court order should be treated in the same manner as an unconstitutional statute. To treat a court order as valid, even when clearly unconstitutional, is tantamount to saying that the court's power is superior to the Constitution.

Dissent: (Douglas, J.) One should be able to exercise one's right to free expression when the issue is the subject of debate. If one must wait for a court order to be invalidated before one may speak, one may lose the opportunity to participate in the debate.

Shuttlesworth v. City of Birmingham (S. Ct. 1969)

Facts: Ds, civil rights demonstrators, were convicted of participating in a protest march without a permit.

Issue: May one disregard a statute in the hope of having the statute invalidated in a later proceeding?

Rule: A person faced with an unconstitutional statute may disregard it and engage with impunity in the exercise of the right of free expression.

Secretary of State of Maryland v. Joseph H. Munson, Inc. (S. Ct. 1984)

Facts: A local ordinance prohibited the solicitation of contributions by charitable organizations that did not use at least 75% of their receipts for "charitable purposes," those purposes being defined to exclude solicitation expenses, salaries, overhead and other administrative expenses.

Issue: Does the First Amendment proscribe a statute that regulates the solicitation that may be conducted by an organization?

Rule: A statute that regulates the solicitation activity of an organization violates the First Amendment if its legitimate goal may be accomplished by less restrictive means.

Dissent: (Rehnquist, J.) The statute should not be stricken on its face, because the statute only restricts the amount to be spent on non–First Amendment type expenses.

Federal Communications Comm'n v. League of Women Voters (S. Ct. 1984)

Facts: Congress enacted the Public Broadcasting Act to disburse federal funds to noncommercial television and radio stations for station operations and educational programming. The Act forbade any noncommercial educational broadcasting station receiving a grant from the Corporation to engage in editorializing.

Issue: May grants be conditioned on the recipient's restriction of broadcasting?

Rule: A legislature may not condition federal funding on a recipient's restriction of free speech. A broadcast regulation restricting speech will survive a First Amendment challenge only if it is narrowly tailored to further a substantial governmental interest. A broad ban on all editorializing by every station that receives this type of federal funding far exceeds what is necessary to protect against the risk of governmental interference or to prevent the public from assuming that editorials by public broadcasting stations represent the official view of government.

Dissent: (Rehnquist, J.) When the government is simply exercising its power to allocate its own public funds, we need only find that the condition imposed has a rational relationship to Congress' purpose in providing the subsidy and that it is not primarily aimed at the suppression of dangerous ideas.

Tinker v. Des Moines School District (S. Ct. 1969)

Facts: School authorities prohibited students from wearing armbands as a protest against the Vietnam War.

Issue: Is symbolic speech protected by the First Amendment?

Rule: Action that is a silent, passive expression of opinion is symbolic speech protected by the First Amendment.

Concurrence: (Stewart, J.) A child is not necessarily possessed of that full capacity for individual choice which is the presupposition of First Amendment guarantees, and therefore, does not have the same First Amendment rights as an adult.

Concurrence: (White, J.) There is a distinction between communicating by words and communicating by acts or conduct which sufficiently impinge on a valid state interest.

Dissent: (Black, J.) School authorities have the right to issue regulations in order to ensure that the routine of the school day will not be disrupted by a highly emotional issue.

Dissent: (Harlan, J.) School officials should be accorded the widest authority in maintaining discipline and good order in their institutions. Therefore the burden of showing that a school regulation is unconstitutional should be placed on the complainant, something which was not done.

Morse v. Frederick (S. Ct. 2007)

Facts: During a school-sponsored viewing of the Olympic Torch relay on a city street, a student unfurled a banner reading "BONGHiTS4JESUS." Student was disciplined.

Issue: Does punishment of a student for this type of speech violate the First Amendment?

Rule: (Roberts, C.J.) Given the risks drugs pose to students, a school may constitutionally punish a student for making speech that is reasonably viewed as promoting drug use.

Concurrence: (Thomas, J.) We should abandon the idea that the First Amendment protects student speech, which is unsound and has led to an incoherent jurisprudence.

Concurrence: (Alito, J.) I join the majority opinion on the understanding that it goes no further than allowing punishment of pro-drug speech and does not support speech restrictions any time a student speaks out on a controversial social issue.

Partial Concurrence: (Breyer, J.) We should simply hold that the school principal defendant has qualified immunity, and not address the ultimate merits of the First Amendment claim.

Dissent: (Stevens, J.) It is far from clear that the student's speech, which he did merely to attract the attention of television cameras, was speech advocating drug use. The Court's rule against the student therefore restricts too much speech.

Freedman v. Maryland (S. Ct. 1965)

Facts: A local censorship board was authorized to revoke a motion picture distributor's license for the sale or display of obscene materials, and to engage in the prior restraint of allegedly obscene materials.

Issue: What safeguards must be incorporated as part of a film censorship board's procedures in ensuring fairness in its prior restraint actions?

Rule: Although normally prior restraint actions are unconstitutional limitations on First Amendment rights, in obscenity cases involving motion pictures, prior restraint actions may be enforced as long as the following procedural safeguards are followed to avoid arbitrariness, and ensure fairness. A local censorship board

(1) has the burden of proving that the film is obscene;

(2) must defer to a judicial proceeding for the imposition of a valid final restraint on the film;

(3) must either permit the exhibition of the film or go to court for a restraining order; and

(4) must assure a prompt, final judicial decision.

Concurrence: (Douglas, J.) Movies are entitled to the same degree and kind of protection under the First Amendment as other forms of expression. Therefore, no form of censorship is permissible.

International Soc'y for Krishna Consciousness v. Lee (S. Ct. 1992)

Facts: The Port Authority, which owns and operates three airports, adopted regulations forbidding repetitive solicitation of money or distribution of literature within the terminals. The Krishnas wished to distribute religious literature and raise funds in the terminals.

Issue: Is an airport terminal that is operated by a public authority a public forum such that regulations prohibiting solicitation within the terminal violate the First Amendment?

Rule: (Rehnquist, C.J.) Airports are not traditional public fora for speech activity, nor have they been intentionally opened to such activity by their operators. Consequently, regulations prohibiting speech therein need only be reasonable. The solicitation prohibitions are constitutional because they are a reasonable means of preventing fraud and pedestrian congestion.

Times Film Corp. v. Chicago (S. Ct. 1961)

Facts: A city ordinance required submission of all motion pictures for examination prior to their public exhibition.

Issue: Does the First Amendment protection against prior restraint include complete and absolute freedom to exhibit at least once any and every kind of motion picture?

Rule: (Clarke, J.) There is no absolute privilege against prior restraint as applied to motion pictures.

Dissent: (Warren, C.J.) There is no constitutional principle that permits us to hold that the communication of ideas through one medium may be censored while another is immune.

In re Kay (1970)

Facts: A congressman who was giving an address was heckled by a group of protestors who disagreed with his policies. Two weeks later, some of the protestors were charged with willfully disturbing a lawful assembly.

Issue: Is it within a person's First Amendment rights to disrupt a meeting or assembly?

Rule: Audience activities, such as heckling, interrupting, harsh questioning, and booing, even though they may be impolite and discourteous, are protected by the First Amendment. There are some situations, though, where disturbances so inhibit someone else from exercising their right to freedom of speech that a statute criminalizing such behavior would not be unconstitutional.

Schneider v. State (S. Ct. 1939)

Facts: Several city ordinances restricted the distribution of handbills in the streets.

Issue: May the government prohibit the distribution of leaflets in public streets to prevent litter?

Rule: (Roberts, J.) The purpose to keep streets clean and of good appearance is insufficient to justify an ordinance which prohibits a person rightfully on a public street from handing literature to one willing to receive it.

Grayned v. City of Rockford (S. Ct. 1972)

Facts: An ordinance prohibited persons from entering school grounds and making noise that disturbs the operation of classrooms.

Issue: Is a statute that prohibits activities that are disruptive to a school environment constitutional under the First Amendment?

Rule: Reasonable time, place, and manner regulations on First Amendment rights are permitted to further significant governmental interests. A statute that is narrowly tailored to further the compelling state interest in having an undisrupted school session is constitutional.

Dissent: (Douglas, J.): If a speaker is not noisy or boisterous, his conduct should be constitutionally protected. In this case, the disruption did not occur because of the speaker's behavior, but because of the issue.

Schaumburg v. Citizens for a Better Environment (S. Ct. 1980)

Facts: A local ordinance prohibited the solicitation of contributions by charitable organizations that do not use at least 75% of their receipts for "charitable purposes," those purposes being defined to exclude solicitation expenses, salaries, overhead and other administrative expenses.

Issue: Is a statute prohibiting charitable organizations from soliciting contributions if they do not use at least 75% of their receipts for charitable purposes primarily as a prevention of fraud, but which could have been drawn more narrowly so as not to directly limit their First Amendment rights, constitutional?

Rule: A statute prohibiting the solicitation of contributions by charitable organizations that do not use at least 75% of their receipts for charitable purposes, which can effect its primary goal of preventing fraud by being more narrowly drawn so as not to directly limit the organizations' First Amendment rights to spend whatever amount of money on the dissemination of information and their need for solicited contributions, is unconstitutional.

Brown v. Glines (S. Ct. 1980)

Facts: A U.S. Air Force regulation required members of the service to obtain approval from their commanders before circulating petitions on air force bases. The commander could deny permission only if distribution of the material would result in a clear danger to the loyalty, discipline, or morale of servicemen, or a material interference with a military mission.

Issue: Does the requirement for military personnel to obtain permission before circulating a petition on military bases violate the First Amendment?

Rule: The First Amendment rights of military personnel may be limited when reasonably necessary to protect the effectiveness of military operations.

Dissent: (Brennan, J.) The military regulations at issue are prohibited by the First Amendment.

Terminiello v. Chicago (S. Ct. 1945)

Facts: D was convicted for breach of the peace when he addressed a group of people in an auditorium, denouncing Jews and blacks. The address created a rowdy protest in the auditorium.

Issue: Is speech that stirs people to anger, invites dispute, or bring about a condition of unrest protected by the First Amendment?

Rule: Unless the speech is likely to produce a clear and present danger of a serious substantive evil that rises far above public inconvenience, annoyance, or unrest, the freedom of speech is protected against censorship and punishment.

Dissent: (Frankfurter, J.) The Court had no authority to rule on this issue because it was not urged on behalf of the petitioner in the lower courts.

Dissent: (Jackson, J.) In this case the danger of rioting and violence in response to the speech was clear, present and immediate.

Hudgens v. National Labor Relations Board (S. Ct. 1976)

Facts: A group of strikers were prohibited from picketing in a privately owned shopping center.

Issue: Does the First Amendment apply to privately owned areas that are open to the public?

Rule: There is no First Amendment right to expression on private property, even if that property is open to the public.

Concurrence: (White, J.) While the Court's decision is correct as applied to these facts, there is no reason to overrule the standing law.

Dissent: (Marshall, J.) Where a private property owner has eliminated all other channels for a person to effectively communicate his or her ideas, the property owner assumes the responsibility for making forums available for the expression of ideas.

West Virginia State Board of Educ. v. Barnette (S. Ct. 1943)

Facts: A state board of education directed that all public school students and teachers salute the flag as part of regular school activities. P, a Jehovah's Witness, sued on the grounds that it compelled his children to violate a Bible command not to worship a graven image.

Issue: Does a public school's imposition of a compulsory flag salute requirement violate the First Amendment?

Rule: (Jackson, J.) The First Amendment precludes government bodies from requiring symbolic utterances in the absence of a clear and present danger or the essentialness of preclusion to the maintenance of effective and orderly government.

Coates v. Cincinnati (S. Ct. 1971)

Facts: An ordinance made it criminal for three or more persons to assemble on a sidewalk and conduct themselves in a manner annoying to persons passing by.

Issue: Is it constitutional to criminalize conduct that is annoying to others?

Rule: (Stewart, J.) A statute which makes it a crime to annoy others is unconstitutionally vague because it provides no standard by which to determine what type of conduct is prohibited and because it is overbroad in that it also may be interpreted to include conduct which is constitutionally protected.

Dissent: (White, J.) Whether a statute is unconstitutionally vague should be determined on a case-by-case basis. Behavior that is obviously prohibited should not be condoned because the law would be unconstitutional if applied to other behavior.

City of Houston, Tex. v. Hill (S. Ct. 1987)

Facts: A municipal ordinance made it a crime to willfully or intentionally interrupt a policeman during an investigation by verbal challenge.
Issue: Is an ordinance that prohibits verbal interruptions of police officers constitutional?
Rule: (Brennan, J.) An ordinance prohibiting all speech that in any manner interrupts an officer, and is not narrowly tailored to prohibit only disorderly conduct or fighting words, is unconstitutionally overbroad.
Concurrence/Dissent: (Powell, J.) The ordinance is too vague to comport with the First Amendment.
Dissent: (Rehnquist, J.) The ordinance, in the absence of an authoritative construction by the state courts, is not unconstitutional.

Boos v. Barry (S. Ct. 1988)

Facts: A statute prohibited the display of any sign within 500 feet of a foreign embassy that would tend to bring that government into "public disrepute."
Issue: Is a statute that prohibits expression based on the effect of its content on a foreign government's image void for vagueness under the First Amendment?
Rule: A content-based restriction on political speech in a public forum is unconstitutional unless it is necessary to serve a compelling state interest and narrowly drawn to achieve only that end. A statute intended to preserve the dignity of foreign diplomats is overbroad when the state interest would be sufficiently served if the statute was narrowly tailored to prohibit only conduct that intimidated, coerced, threatened, or harassed a foreign official.
Concurrence: (Brennan, J.) A content-based restriction on speech should be strictly scrutinized.
Concurrence/Dissent: (Rehnquist, C.J.) The prohibition against the display of any sign within 500 feet of a foreign embassy which tends to bring that foreign government into "public disrepute" is constitutional.

Pacific Gas and Electric Company v. Public Utilities Comm'n of California (S. Ct. 1986)

Facts: A state utilities commission required a public utility to include communications from a public interest group in its monthly bill.
Issue: Must a non-public forum that is publicly funded provide access for expression?
Rule: (O'Connor, J.) A non-public forum, even one which is publicly funded, may not be required to provide access for the expression of ideas with which it does not agree.

Concurrence: (Burger, C.J.) All that must be decided in this case is whether there is a right to be free from forced association with views with which one disagrees. Such a right clearly exists, based on the weight of authority.

Concurrence: (Marshall, J.) When one has never opened up a forum to the public or when compelled access would hamper one's own ability to speak, there is a First Amendment right for one to bar access.

Dissent: (Rehnquist, J.) Because the interest on which the constitutional protection of corporate speech rests is the societal interest in receiving information and ideas, the constitutional interest of a corporation in not permitting the presentation of other distinct views clearly identified as those of the speaker is *de minimis*.

Dissent: (Stevens, J.) The Commission's requirement differs little from regulations applied daily to variety of commercial communications that have rarely been challenged on First Amendment grounds. This should be especially true of a public utility.

Tashjian v. Republican Party of Connecticut (S. Ct. 1986)

Facts: A Connecticut statute required voters in any party primary to be registered members of that party. The state's Republican Party wished to allow independents to vote in its primary elections.

Issue: May a state regulate participation in party primaries under the First Amendment?

Rule: (Marshall, J.) A statute requiring voters in a party primary to be registered members of that party violates the party's First Amendment right to enter into political association with individuals of its own choosing.

Dissent: (Stevens, J.) The state Republican Party's rules are different for congressional elections than for elections for state legislators. This is plainly in violation of Article I, §2, cl. 1, and the Seventeenth Amendment of the Constitution.

Dissent: (Scalia, J.) The Republican Party's associational interests are not being threatened by the Connecticut law.

Columbia Broadcasting System, Inc. v. Democratic National Committee (S. Ct. 1973)

Facts: Two groups sought to purchase air time on a radio station to discuss controversial issues.

Issue: Is there a constitutional right under the First Amendment to purchase radio time for the presentation of personal views about controversial issues of public importance?

Rule: (Burger, C.J.) The First Amendment does not require the sale of radio or television air time to private groups wishing to discuss controversial issues, even if state action controlling the use of broadcast time is involved. Only when the interests of the public are found to outweigh the private journalistic interests of the broadcasters will government power be asserted on behalf of the public.

Concurrence: (Stewart, J.) The First Amendment prohibits the government from imposing controls on the press. Private broadcasters are members of the press.

Concurrence: (White, J.) Even if state action were found, the right of broadcaster discretion trumps the argument that a state may not infringe on the right to free access to a forum.

Concurrence: (Blackmun, J.) The governmental action issue does not affect the outcome of this case.

Concurrence: (Douglas, J.) A government should not be allowed to control a broadcaster in an effort to allow freer access to the airwaves. This is censorship.

Dissent: (Brennan, J.) The public has strong First Amendment interests in the reception of a full spectrum of views on controversial issues of public importance.

City of Los Angeles v. Preferred Communications, Inc. (S. Ct. 1986)

Facts: A city awarded only one cable television operating franchise when there was clearly physical capacity to accommodate more than one cable television system.

Issue: Must a municipality grant a cable television company the right to use city equipment and property to exercise its First Amendment rights?

Rule: (Rehnquist, J.) A right to use government property is not guaranteed by the First Amendment if that right is to create diversified expression. Where speech and conduct are joined in a single course of action, First Amendment values must be balanced against competing societal interests.

Concurrence: (Blackmun, J.) In assessing First Amendment claims concerning cable access, the Court must determine whether the characteristics of cable television make it sufficiently analogous to another medium to warrant application of an already existing standard or whether those characteristics require a new analysis.

3. Freedom of Expression: Special Contexts

Buckley v. Valeo (S. Ct. 1976)

Facts: P, a senator, challenged the constitutionality of a federal act that set a limit on political campaign contributions and expenditures, required public disclosure of contributions and expenditures above certain levels, and established a system for public funding of presidential campaign activities.

Issue: Do government restrictions on political campaign contributions and expenditures violate the First Amendment?

Rule: (per curiam) Restrictions on campaign expenditures are unconstitutional because they impede protected political expression. However, limitations on contributions in no way infringe on the contributor's freedom to discuss candidates and issues and are therefore constitutional.

Concurrence/Dissent: (Burger, C.J.) Contribution limitations limit exactly the same political activity and suppress communication and political discussion as effectively and to as great an extent as expenditure restrictions.

Concurrence/Dissent: (White, J.) The moral danger attending the risk of unethical use of this money justifies incidental effects that the limitations visit upon First Amendment rights.

Nixon v. Shrink Missouri Government PAC (S. Ct. 2000)

Facts: Political contributors challenged a Missouri law restricting campaign contributions.

Issue: Is *Buckley v. Valeo*, which upheld federal campaign contributions, authority for state law limits on contributions?

Rule: (Souter, J.) There is good reason to think that corruption or the appearance of corruption is a sufficiently grave threat to democracy so as to justify campaign contribution limitations. There is adequate evidence of a concern for the appearance of corruption, and at any rate *Buckley* recognized that the problem was clearly not implausible. Nor does the maximum contribution allowed have to be at least the amount of the contributions allowed in the federal law upheld in *Buckley*; what is required is simply that the restrictions allow candidates to amass sufficient resources to run an effective campaign.

Dissent: (Kennedy, J.) By upholding limits on direct contributions the Court encourages the use of soft money contributions that make it very difficult for outsider candidates to compete, and thus distorts the political process. *Buckley* should be overruled.

Randall v. Sorrell (S. Ct. 2006)

Facts: Vermont enacted stringent limits on campaign expenditures and contributions for state office.

Issue: Do these limits violate the First Amendment rights of speakers and contributors?

Rule: (Breyer, J.) (plurality) They do. Expenditure limits run afoul of *Buckley*, and Vermont does not persuasively distinguish its limits by arguing a different rationale than that used to defend the limits struck down in *Buckley*; namely, that they help candidates avoid spending undue time raising money. The contribution limits also run afoul of *Buckley* because they are too stringent. Among other problems, they make it hard for challengers to run effective campaigns, they impair the rights of political parties by restricting their contributions too severely, and they are not indexed to inflation, thus making the limits more severe in real terms every year. We decline the invitation to overrule *Buckley*.

Concurrence: (Alito, J.) The request to overrule *Buckley* was made only as an afterthought; thus, I would not reach that issue.

Concurrence: (Kennedy, J.) I am skeptical about *Buckley*; therefore I concur only in the judgment.

Concurrence: (Thomas, J.) I concur only in the judgment because I would overrule *Buckley* and accord more protection to the activities regulated by the Vermont law.

Dissent: (Stevens, J.) I have come to believe that *Buckley*'s restrictions on expenditure limits are mistaken; thus, I would overrule that part of *Buckley*.

Dissent: (Souter, J.) I would remand for more development of the First Amendment challenge to the law's expenditure limits to determine how much they mitigate the problem of candidates having to spend undue time raising money. I would also uphold the contribution limits as consistent with *Buckley*, given the facts of how little those limits impair effective campaigning in Vermont.

McConnell v. Federal Elec. Comm'n (S. Ct. 2003)

Facts: Congress passed broad-ranging limitations on campaign contributions, including limits on so-called soft money and issue advertising.

Issue: What types of campaign contribution limits may be imposed consistent with the First Amendment?

Rule: (Stevens, O'Connor, Breyer, JJ.; Rehnquist, C.J.) (1) Bans on use of soft money for federal election activities were constitutional; (2) it was constitutional to require that "soft money" identify a political candidate; (3) it was constitutional to require labor unions and corporations to pay for issue ads from separately segregated funds; and (4) the requirement that broadcasters disclose records of requests for air time for political ads was valid. *Buckley v. Valeo* reaffirmed.

Davis v. Federal Election Comm'n (S. Ct. 2008)

Facts: P, a self-financed political candidate, sued when his self-financing activities had the effect, under federal campaign law, of raising the allowable contribution limits of his opponent, and easing his opponent's ability to coordinate expenditures with the opponent's political party.

Issue: Does the so-called Millionaire's Amendment to federal campaign law violate P's First Amendment rights to spend money on his own campaign?

Rule: (Alito, J.) Yes. The law imposes burdens on P based on P's decision to spend his own money on his election campaign. This burden is not justified by a sufficiently strong government interest.

Dissent: (Stevens, J.) The law does not impose on any burdens on P, who remains free to spend as much as he wants to advocate his own election. The law is an appropriate attempt to equalize the playing field between wealthy and non-wealthy candidates and to diminish the perception that political offices are up for sale to the highest bidder.

Dissent: (Ginsburg, J.) I generally agree with Justice Stevens. However, I see no need to address the soundness of *Buckley v. Valeo*'s constitutional distinction between campaign expenditures and contributions. P should lose even under *Buckley* and I would leave reconsideration of *Buckley* to another day.

Board of Education v. Pico (S. Ct. 1982)

Facts: Ps, teenage students, claimed their First Amendment rights were violated when the local board of education ordered that certain "objectionable" books be removed from district school libraries for board review because they were "anti-American, anti-Christian, anti-Semitic, and just plain filthy."

Issue: May school boards deny access to books because the books contain ideas that conflict with those of the board?

Rule: (Brennan, J.) While school boards have broad discretion in managing school affairs and transmitting community values, boards may not remove books from school library shelves to purposely deny access to an idea because officials disapprove of that idea for political, moral, or social reasons.

Concurrence: (Blackmun, J.) There is a delicate balance between the limited constitutional restrictions imposed by the First Amendment and the necessarily broad state authority to regulate education. This should be achieved by not allowing a state to remove books for the purpose of restricting access to the political ideas or social perspectives discussed in them when that action is motivated simply by the officials' disapproval of the ideas involved.

Dissent: (Burger, C.J.) If schools may legitimately be used as vehicles for inculcating fundamental values, school authorities must have broad discretion to fulfill that obligation. Were federal court review of school board decisions to become law, the Court would risk becoming a "super censor."

Dissent: (Powell, J.) The Court's standard for assessing the constitutionality of school board behavior affords no more than subjective guidance to school boards, their counsel, and to courts that now will be required to decide whether a particular decision was made in a narrowly partisan or political manner.

Dissent: (Rehnquist, J.) As educator, a government is engaged in inculcating social values and knowledge in young people. The idea that students have a right of access in the school to information other than that their educators believe to be necessary is contrary to the nature of inculcative education. The removal of books does not amount to the suppression of ideas any more than a similar filtering process in the initial acquisition of books.

Bethel School District No. 403 v. Fraser (S. Ct. 1986)

Facts: P, a high school student, delivered a speech before a student assembly and used an explicit sexual metaphor in his address. The school administration penalized him for violating the school's rule prohibiting obscenity.

Issue: Does the First Amendment prohibit a school's restricting students' lewd speech?

Rule: (Burger, C.J.) The First Amendment right of free speech does not prohibit schools from penalizing offensive speech delivered in school. The freedom to advocate controversial views in schools must be balanced against society's countervailing interest in teaching students the boundaries of socially appropriate behavior.

Concurrence: (Brennan, J.) The Court's holding concerns only the authority that school officials have to restrict disruptive language uttered before a high school assembly.

Dissent: (Marshall, J.) Where speech is involved, a teacher's assertion that pure speech interfered with education should not be unquestioningly accepted.

Dissent: (Stevens, J.) If a student is to be punished for using offensive speech, he or she is entitled to fair notice of the scope of the prohibition and the consequences of its violation.

Hazelwood School District v. Kuhlmeier (S. Ct. 1988)

Facts: Ps, former high school students, filed a First Amendment suit when their principal deleted two pages from the proofs of a school newspaper that Ps and other students produced as part of a journalism class.

Issue: Does the First Amendment prohibit schools from exercising editorial control over a newspaper produced as part of the curriculum?

Rule: (White, J.) Educators do not offend the First Amendment by exercising editorial control over the style and content of student speech in school-sponsored expressive activities so long as their actions are reasonably related to legitimate pedagogical concerns.

Dissent: (Brennan, J.) Expression's mere incompatibility with a school's pedagogical mission is a constitutionally insufficient justification for suppressing students' speech, particularly where such expression neither prevents a school from pursuing its pedagogical mission nor interferes with a school's orderly operation.

Wood v. Georgia (S. Ct. 1962)

Facts: D, a Georgia sheriff, issued a press release decrying a grand jury investigation of alleged misconduct in local political campaigns. The court, which had ordered the investigation, held D in contempt.

Issue: Is it a violation of First Amendment free speech to penalize criticism of court actions by a non-party who is out of court?

Rule: (Warren, C.J.) Out-of-court expressions are protected by the First Amendment unless they present a clear and present threat to the administration of justice. The threat must be imminent and immediate, not merely likely or remote.

Dissent: (Harlan, J.) The right of free speech is not absolute; when the right to speak conflicts with the rights to an impartial judicial proceeding, an accommodation must be made to preserve the essence of both. Speech creating sufficient danger of an evil that the state may prevent may certainly be punished regardless of whether that evil materializes. Any expression of opinion on the merits of a pending judicial proceeding is likely to affect deliberations.

NAACP v. Alabama (S. Ct. 1958)

Facts: During the course of Alabama's (P) injunction action to prevent NAACP (D) activities in that state, P ordered disclosure of D's membership list.

Issue: Does government violate the freedoms of association and speech by compelling disclosure of a group's membership?

Rule: (Harlan J.) A state may not abridge the right to privacy in association absent a compelling substantial government interest.

NAACP v. Button (S. Ct. 1963)

Facts: The NAACP was convicted of violating a statute prohibiting organizations from retaining lawyers to solicit clients for judicial proceedings in which the organization had no pecuniary right or liability.

Issue: Does the Constitution preclude state regulatory prohibition or the use of litigation to achieve political, rather than personal, redress?

Rule: (Brennan, J.) The First Amendment protects vigorous advocacy through litigation, as a form of political expression and the joining with others to make the advocacy more effective, in order to achieve lawful objectives. A state's interest in the regulation of the legal profession does not justify the limiting of First Amendment rights absent a showing of substantial evils flowing from the exercise of these rights.

Dissent: (Harlan, J.) General regulatory statutes, not intended to control the content of speech but doing so incidentally should be permissible when supported by a permissible government interest.

Shelton v. Tucker (S. Ct. 1960)

Facts: An Arkansas statute required all teachers in state-supported schools or colleges to list every organization to which they belonged or contributed.

Issue: Does the First Amendment permit the requirement that state-employed teachers reveal their group affiliations?

Rule: (Stewart, J.) The First Amendment precludes inquiry by state officials into the group affiliations of its employees.

Dissent: (Frankfurter, J.) In light of the particular kind of restriction upon individual liberty which the regulation entails, it was reasonable for a legislature to choose that form of regulation rather that others less restrictive.

Elfbrandt v. Russell (S. Ct. 1966)

Facts: P sued for declaratory relief after declining to take an oath that was statutorily required of all state employees. The oath promised support of both federal and state constitutions and subjected to perjury and discharge those who knowingly and willfully became or remained affiliated with the Communist Party.

Issue: Does the right to freedom of association and expression proscribe the restriction of membership in an organization that maintains illegal goals?

Rule: (Douglas, J.) The right to freedom of association and speech proscribes states from prohibiting membership in organizations unless the member has the specific intent to share in the purposes and illegal activities of the organization.

Dissent: (White, J.) A state is entitled to condition public employment upon its employees abstaining from knowing membership in organizations advocating the violent overthrow of the government which employs them.

Keyishian v. Board of Regents (S. Ct. 1967)

Facts: Faculty members of the State University of New York refused to sign a certificate, required of New York State employees, that disclaimed association with the Communist Party.

Issue: Are laws violative of First Amendment freedoms of speech and association when they are so broad as to prohibit membership in a group regardless of members' actual advocacy of the group's goals?

Rule: (Brennan, J.) Government regulations affecting First Amendment freedoms of speech and association must be narrowly construed. Vague, overbroad laws touching such freedoms can have a chilling effect on the exercise of those liberties and are therefore unconstitutional. Therefore, legislation that prohibits membership that is unaccompanied by specific intent to further the organization's unlawful goals or that is not active membership violates constitutional limitations.

Dissent: (Clark, J.) The issue here is not freedom of speech or assembly, but whether the state, after a hearing with full judicial review, may disqualify from university teaching those who willfully and deliberately advocate or belong to an organization that advocates the forceful or violent overthrow of our government.

Connick v. Myers (S. Ct. 1983)

Facts: P, an assistant district attorney, was discharged for refusing to accept an intra-office transfer and for circulating among her colleagues a questionnaire regarding morale and level of confidence in superiors.

Issue: Does the First Amendment free speech guaranty apply to a public employee's speech upon matters that are not of public concern?

Rule: (White, J.) When a public employee speaks not as a citizen upon matters of public concern, but upon matters only of personal interest, government employers should enjoy wide latitude in managing their personnel, without First Amendment restrictions. The reasonableness of an employer's response to such speech must be determined in light of the facts of each case.

Dissent: (Brennan, J.) The First Amendment affords special protection to speech that may inform public debate about how our society is to be governed — regardless of whether it actually becomes the subject of public controversy or concern.

Barenblatt v. United States (S. Ct. 1959)

Facts: D, a psychology professor, was convicted for contempt of Congress after refusing to answer certain questions before the Subcommittee of the House Committee on Un-American Activities. D objected to the

Subcommittee's right to inquire into his political and religious beliefs or any "other personal and private affairs" or associations.

Issue: May a witness be compelled to reveal information regarding private relationships?

Rule: (Harlan, J.) Where an investigation is related to a valid legislative purpose and public (particularly national) interests outweigh private concerns, the First Amendment does not permit a witness to resist inquiry into personal associational relationships.

Dissent: (Black, J.) The Court affirms use of the contempt power to enforce questioning in the realm of speech and association. This questioning violates due process, abridges freedom of speech and association, and is not related to Congress' legislative function.

Gibson v. Florida Legislative Committee (S. Ct. 1963)

Facts: D, president of the NAACP's Miami branch, was held in contempt for refusing to bring NAACP membership records to refer to in answering questions before the Investigation Committee.

Issue: Does a legislature's demand for private associational membership information violate the First Amendment?

Rule: (Goldberg, J.) The First Amendment right to privacy of association may not be abridged unless it can be convincingly shown that there is a substantial relation between the private information and a compelling state interest. This is not met when information sought is about someone other than the person being questioned.

Dissent: (Harlan, J.) The Court mistakenly relies on the premise that the governmental interest in investigating Communist infiltration is not sufficient to overcome the countervailing right to freedom of association. It is also difficult to see how this case really presents any serious question as to interference with freedom of association. What we are asked to hold is that Gibson had a constitutional right to give only partial or inaccurate testimony.

New York Times Co. v. United States (S. Ct. 1971)

Facts: The United States (P) sought to enjoin *The New York Times* and *The Washington Post* from publishing the contents of a classified study called "The Pentagon Papers."

Issue: Does the First Amendment prevent the government from exercising prior restraint to prevent the press from publishing sensitive documents?

Rule: (per curiam) There is a heavy presumption against the constitutional validity of a government attempt to exercise prior restraint.

Concurrence: (Black, J.) The First Amendment should be read so that the publication of news may never be enjoined.

Concurrence: (Douglas, J.) The First Amendment leaves no room for governmental restraint on the press. Even the possibility of a serious impact resulting from the publication of sensitive documents is no basis for sanctioning a previous restraint on the press.

Concurrence: (Brennan, J.) The First Amendment tolerates absolutely no prior judicial restraints of the press predicated upon surmise or conjecture that untoward consequences may result. The First Amendment's ban on prior judicial restraint may be overridden only when the nation is at war and national security interests predominate.

Concurrence: (Stewart, J.) The Court is asked, quite simply, to prevent the publication by two newspapers of material that the executive branch insists should not, in the national interest, be published. Though the executive is correct with respect to some of the documents, disclosure of any of them will not necessarily result in direct, immediate, and irreparable damage to our nation or its people.

Concurrence: (White, J.) The United States has not satisfied the very heavy burden which it must meet to warrant an injunction against publication in these cases, at least in the absence of express and appropriately limited congressional authorization for prior restraints in circumstances such as these. That the government mistakenly chose to proceed by injunction does not mean that it could not successfully proceed in another way.

Concurrence: (Marshall, J.) It would be inconsistent with the concept of separation of powers for this court to use its power of contempt to prevent behavior that Congress has specifically declined to prohibit.

Dissent: (Harlan, J.) The Judiciary may not predetermine for itself the probable impact of disclosure on the national security. Executive decisions as to foreign policy are ones for which the Judiciary has neither aptitude, facilities, nor responsibility and which have been held to belong in the domain of political power not subject to judicial intrusion or inquiry.

Dissent: (Blackmun, J.) What is needed here is a weighing of the broad right of the press to print and of the very narrow right of the government to prevent. Even the newspapers concede that there are situations where restraint is in order and is constitutional.

Branzburg v. Hayes (S. Ct. 1972)

Facts: Branzburg and other journalists were held in contempt for refusing to disclose to grand juries all confidential information on organizations and people under criminal investigation by the juries.

Issue: Does the First Amendment proscribe the requirement that journalists divulge confidential information to grand juries?

Rule: (White, J.) Like all citizens, journalists bear the duty of appearing before a grand jury and answering questions relevant to a criminal investigation. The public interest in pursuing and prosecuting crimes reported to the press by informants and in deterring the commission of such crimes outweighs the burden on news gathering that might result from sources' reluctance to reveal information without assured anonymity.

Concurrence: (Powell, J.) If a journalist is asked to give information bearing only a remote and tenuous relationship to the subject of the investigation, he or she can obtain a protective order.

Dissent: (Douglas, J.) Requiring the press to disclose confidentialities will impede the robust dissemination of ideas that the free press fosters.

Dissent: (Stewart, J.) When a journalist is asked to appear before a grand jury and reveal confidences, the government must

(1) show that there is probable cause to believe that the newsman has information clearly relevant to a specific probable violation of law;

(2) demonstrate that the information sought cannot be obtained by alternative means less destructive of First Amendment rights; and

(3) demonstrate a compelling and overriding interest in the information.

Minneapolis Star v. Minnesota Commissioner of Revenue (S. Ct. 1983)

Facts: Minnesota required publishers to pay a use tax on ink and paper. The statute was challenged as a violation of the guarantees of free press and equal protection.

Issue: Is a tax imposed on a method of communication an infringement of First Amendment rights?

Rule: A tax that burdens rights protected by the First Amendment cannot stand unless the burden is necessary to achieve an overriding governmental interest. While the First Amendment does not prohibit economic regulation of the press, regulation that *singles out* the press places a heavy burden of justification on the government.

Concurrence/Dissent: (White, J.) While the Court correctly determined that the tax is invalid, the Court's proposition that the government threatens the First Amendment by favoring the press is questionable. Further, I do not agree that the courts are so incompetent to evaluate the burdens of taxation that we must decline the task in this case.

Dissent: (Rehnquist, J.) A tax scheme that singles out newspapers for "different treatment" has benefited, not burdened, the freedom of speech and of the press. All governmentally created classifications must have some rational basis to be constitutional. The fact that they have been enacted by a presumptively rational legislature, however, arms them with a presumption of rationality.

Nebraska Press Ass'n v. Stuart (S. Ct. 1976)

Facts: An upcoming multiple murder case attracted widespread news coverage and Stuart, a Nebraska state trial court judge, entered a restraining order to preclude the Nebraska Press Association from publishing or broadcasting accounts of confessions or admissions made by the defendant in the case.

Issue: Does the First Amendment permit the restraint of publication of information pertaining to future trials?

Rule: (Burger, J.) Publication of information pertaining to a trial may be restrained only if the proponent for the entry of a prior restraint can establish that the danger is substantial, there is no alternate means to mitigate the danger, and the restraining order would be very effective to prevent the danger.

Concurrence: (Brennan, J.) Publication of information pertaining to future trials should never be banned. There are always more effective ways of assuring a defendant's right to a fair and impartial trial.

United States Civil Serv. Comm'n v. National Ass'n of Letter Carriers (S. Ct. 1973)

Facts: P challenged the constitutionality of the Hatch Act, which prohibited federal employees from taking "an active part in political management or in political campaigns."

Issue: Does a law violate freedom of speech by prohibiting government employees from taking active part in political management or campaigns?

Rule: (White, J.) The government does not abridge freedom of speech by prohibiting federal employees from engaging in political management and political campaigning. The government has a very substantial interest in preventing the development of a corrupt political machine.

Dissent: (Douglas, J.) It is of no concern to government how an employee uses his spare time, unless the activity impairs efficiency or other facets of his job. Government employment may not be denied or penalized on a basis that infringes constitutionally protected interests.

Pickering v. Board of Educ. (S. Ct. 1968)

Facts: The Board of Education dismissed P, a teacher, upon determining that P's published letter, which was critical of board actions in raising revenues for the schools, was "detrimental to the efficient operation and administration of the schools in the district."

Issue: May a school board dismiss an employee for making erroneous statements critical of school operations?

Rule: (Marshall, J.) Critical statements about a government body which are made publicly are protected by the First Amendment unless they can be shown to have impeded the employee's or the government's operations. A government employee has the right guaranteed all citizens to criticize his government, and this right may not be denied even if the statements are false.

Garcetti v. Ceballos (S. Ct. 2006)

Facts: As part of his job duties, P, an attorney with the district attorney's office, wrote a memo recommending the dismissal of a case based on evidence mishandling by the police. The supervisor disciplined the attorney for writing the memo and the attorney sued, alleging violation of his First Amendment rights.

Issue: When an employee speaks as part of his job duties does protection of his First Amendment rights require a court to engage in the balancing of government and individual interests mandated by *Pickering v. Board of Educ.* (1968)?

Rule: (Kennedy, J.) When an employee speaks as part of his job duties he is not speaking as a citizen and thus has no First Amendment rights; thus, *Pickering* balancing does not apply. The First Amendment does not give government employees a right under the First Amendment to perform their jobs as they see fit, free of discipline, to the extent their duties require speech. Employees remain free under the First Amendment to participate in public debate in their capacity as private citizens, but not as employees. This rule does not necessarily extend to government-employed academics, whose job presupposes freedom of inquiry and speech.

Dissent: (Stevens, J.) It is simply wrong to say that there is a categorical difference between an employee's speech made in the course of his job duties and his speech made in his capacity as citizen.

Dissent: (Souter, J.) There is no need for a categorical rule, where many government employees wish to participate in public debate on matters that also happen to relate to their job duties. *Pickering* balancing should continue, though speech made as part of an employee's duties should receive *Pickering* balancing only if it touches on matters of unusual importance and is expressed in responsible ways.

Dissent: (Breyer, J.) *Pickering* should apply to speech made in the course of official duties to the extent that there is increased need for constitutional protection (such as here where the speech is that of a lawyer, who may have constitutional obligations to speak) and where the risk of judicial intrusion into workplace matters is at a minimum.

Elrod v. Burns (S. Ct. 1976)

Facts: D, a newly elected sheriff, dismissed various non-civil service employees of the sheriff's office solely because they were Republicans and had failed to procure the sponsorship of a Democratic Party leader.

Issue: May a local government body dismiss public employees for partisan reasons?

Rule: (Brennan, J.) Public employment may not be denied in the absence of an overriding and substantial policy goal. Political patronage is not such a goal.

Dissent: (Powell, J.) Patronage hiring practices have contributed to American democracy by stimulating political activity and by strengthening parties, thereby helping to make government accountable. It cannot be questioned that these contributions promote important state interests.

Rutan v. Republican Party of Illinois (S. Ct. 1990)

Facts: Governor Thompson of Illinois issued an executive order prohibiting state officials from hiring employees, filling vacancies, creating new positions, etc., without permission of his office. This system was used to limit state employment and related decisions to those who were supported by the Republican Party.

Issue: May promotion, transfer, recall, and hiring decisions involving low-level public employees be constitutionally based on party affiliation and support?

Rule: (Brennan, J.) Patronage-based promotions, transfers, and recalls violate a public employee's First Amendment rights unless party membership is an "appropriate requirement" for that job.

Dissent: (Scalia, J.) Political patronage is an American tradition that provides many benefits, as well as disadvantages, to the operation of government. Therefore, the desirability of a political patronage system is a policy question that should be decided by elected representatives.

Snepp v. United States (S. Ct. 1980)

Facts: Snepp published a book based on his exploits as a CIA agent in violation of an executed agreement in which he promised not to "publish any information or material relating to the Agency, its activities or intelligence activities generally, either during or after the term of his employment without specific prior approval by the Agency." The government brought this suit to enforce the agreement.

Issue: Does a government agency's imposition of a contractual obligation on its employees and former employees not to disclose information about the agency without the agency's prior approval violate the freedom of speech guarantee of the First Amendment?

Rule: (per curiam) When an employee occupies a position of trust in a government agency, the agency may properly require the employee to execute a secrecy agreement, precluding the disclosure of information about the agency without its prior approval. If an employee breaches that agreement, the appropriate remedy is to impose a constructive trust on the profits made from the unapproved disclosure.

Dissent: (Stevens, J.) The imposition of a constructive trust is the appropriate remedy if the breaching party has profited from the result of the breach. If the book had been submitted to the agency for prepublication review, censorship would have been limited to the excision of classified material. As the book contained no classified material, the book would have been cleared for publication in precisely the same form as it now stands. Thus, no profit had been gained as a result of the breach.

Pell v. Procunier (S. Ct. 1974)

Facts: A section of the California Department of Corrections Manual prohibited face-to-face interviews between press representatives and individual inmates.

Issue: Does a state regulation prohibiting face-to-face interviews between journalists and individual inmates in prisons constitute a governmental interference with the free press in violation of the First and Fourteenth Amendments?

Rule: (Stewart, J.) A governmental regulation denying the press access to sources of information available to members of the general public does not abridge the constitutional protections of a free press. The Constitution does not impose upon government an affirmative duty to make available to journalists sources of information not generally available to members of the public.

Dissent: (Douglas, J.) It is not enough to note that the press is denied no more access to the prisons than is denied the public generally. The absolute ban on press interviews with specifically designated inmates is far broader than is necessary to protect any legitimate state interests and is an unconstitutional infringement on the public's right to know.

Richmond Newspapers v. Virginia (S. Ct. 1980)

Facts: A trial judge ordered that the press and public, except witnesses when they testified, be excluded from the proceedings of a murder trial.

Issue: Is the right of the public and the press to attend criminal trials protected under the Constitution?

Rule: (Burger, C.J.) The First Amendment guarantee of speech prohibits the exclusion of the public from criminal trials absent an overriding interest.

Concurrence: (Brennan, J.) The First Amendment right of access should be applied when there is a tradition of public access to the particular type of proceedings, and when such access would further the structural role of the institution involved.

Dissent: (Rehnquist, J.) The Constitution does not require that a state's reasons for denying public access to a trial, where both the prosecutor and the defendant have consented to an order of closure approved by the judge, are subject to any additional constitutional review at our hands.

Indiana v. Glen Theatre, Inc. (S. Ct. 1991)

Facts: Two Indiana establishments wished to provide nude dancing as entertainment. An Indiana statute, however, regulated public nudity by requiring such dancers to wear "pasties" and "G-strings."

Issue: Does the First Amendment protect nude dancing against a state's enforcement of its public indecency law?

Rule: (Rehnquist, C.J.) While nude dancing is expressive conduct within the meaning of the First Amendment, the statute at issue here proscribes not only such dancing but all public nudity. A time, place, and manner restriction such as this can incidentally limit First Amendment freedoms if a sufficiently important governmental interest in regulating the nonspeech element is present. A government regulation is sufficiently justified if it is within the constitutional power of the government; if it furthers an important or substantial governmental interest; if the governmental interest is unrelated to the suppression of free expression; and if the incidental restriction is no greater than necessary.

Concurrence: (Scalia, J.) Since the Indiana statute is a general law regulating conduct and not specifically directed at expression, it is not subject to First Amendment scrutiny at all.

Concurrence: (Souter, J.) This statute may legitimately be applied to nude dancing because such dancing encourages prostitution, increases sexual assaults, and attracts other criminal activity.

Dissent: (White, J.) The purpose of this regulation is to protect the viewers from what the state believes is the harmful message that nude dancing communicates. The prohibition is therefore related to the expressive conduct of the dance, and should only be upheld if narrowly drawn to accomplish a compelling governmental interest.

Zurcher v. Stanford Daily (S. Ct. 1978)

Facts: A district attorney used a warrant obtained from the municipal court to search the offices of a newspaper for photographs of a violent demonstration that had taken place on a college campus. There were no indications that members of the newspaper had participated in the violence.

Issue: Does the Fourth Amendment guarantee against unreasonable search and seizure preclude the issuance of a warrant to search a newspaper premises for evidence of a criminal offense not involving any newspaper personnel?

Rule: (White, J.) When the warrant requested is for the seizure of criminal evidence reasonably believed to be on premises occupied by a newspaper, the preconditions for a warrant, properly administered, should afford sufficient protection to guard against First Amendment violations.

Dissent: (Stewart, J.) It is evident that unannounced police searches of newspaper premises not only disrupt the operation of the newspaper, but more importantly, create the possibility for the disclosure of information received from confidential sources, or of the identity of the sources themselves. Protection of those sources is necessary to ensure that the press can fulfill its constitutionally designated function of informing the public.

Chandler v. Florida (S. Ct. 1981)

Facts: Florida permitted electronic media and photographic coverage of public court proceedings without the parties' consent. Ds moved for a new trial, asserting that television coverage of their case denied them a fair and impartial trial.

Issue: May a state permit broadcast and photographic coverage of a criminal trial, despite a defendant's objections?

Rule: (Burger, C.J.) Photographic and broadcast coverage of certain types of judicial proceedings is constitutional where adequate precautions exist to minimize the prejudicial effect such coverage may have on the jury or on the trial process.

Cole v. Richardson (S. Ct. 1972)

Facts: Richardson, a research sociologist at Boston State Hospital, was dismissed upon refusing to take an oath required of all public employees in Massachusetts.

Issue: May an employee be dismissed from public employment for refusal to take a loyalty oath required of all public employees in a state?

Rule: (Burger, C.J.) A loyalty oath that does not impinge on rights guaranteed under the First and Fourteenth Amendments is a permissible requirement for a state to impose on its public employees.

Dissent: (Douglas, J.) The part of an oath that says "I will oppose the overthrow of the government of the United States of America or of this Commonwealth by force, violence or by any illegal or unconstitutional method" is plainly unconstitutional by our decisions. Advocacy of basic fundamental changes in government, which might popularly be described as "overthrow," is within the protection of the First Amendment even when it is restrictively construed.

Branti v. Finkel (S. Ct. 1980)

Facts: D, a Democrat, was appointed by a Democratic majority in the county legislature to county public defender. Immediately following the appointment, D replaced six of the nine assistant public defenders then in office with Democrats.

Issue: Under the First Amendment, may a public employee be dismissed solely because of political beliefs?

Rule: (per curiam) The First Amendment prohibits the dismissal of a public employee solely because of his private political beliefs unless the hiring authority can demonstrate that partisan affiliation is an appropriate requirement for the effective performance of the public office involved.

Dissent: (Stewart, J.) The judgment in *Elrod v. Burns* does not control the present case because respondents are clearly not "nonconfidential" employees. The respondents are lawyers and the newly appointed public defender was not constitutionally compelled to enter such a close professional and necessarily confidential association if he did not wish to do so.

Roberts v. United States Jaycees (S. Ct. 1984)

Facts: Two local Jaycees began admitting women as regular members in violation of the policy of the national organization. The national organization imposed sanctions.

Issue: Does a state statute prohibiting gender discrimination abridge the constitutionally protected freedom of association right of members of an organization that accepts only men for full voting membership?

Rule: (Brennan, J.) A state may prohibit gender discrimination by a group when the discrimination is not related to the purpose of the group.

Rumsfeld v. Forum for Academic and Institutional Rights (S. Ct. 2006)

Facts: Federal law prohibits financial aid to universities that discriminate against on-campus recruiting by the armed forces. Universities whose non-discrimination policies conflict with the military's ban on gay and lesbian soldiers sued.

Issue: Does the federal funding ban violate the universities' First Amendment rights by forcing them to associate with a discriminatory message with which they disagree?

Rule: (Roberts, C.J.) There would be no First Amendment violation if the recruiting rule were compelled, rather than simply added as a condition of funding; thus, the funding restriction must also be constitutional. The conduct of performing employment recruiting is not inherently expressive such that forcing the schools to associate with it forces them to speak. Nor are schools being forced to associate with that conduct; recruiters are outsiders who come onto campus for a limited purpose, and thus do not become members of the school's expressive association.

Davenport v. Washington Educational Ass'n (S. Ct. 2007)

Facts: State law required that in a unionized workplace non-members who wish to contribute the part of their agency fees allocated to the union's political activity affirmatively consent, rather than presuming consent and requiring them to opt out. The union challenged the rule.

Issue: Does the First Amendment require that unions have the presumptive right to collect these sorts of fees from non-members, if the union wishes to use the money for political expression?

Rule: (Scalia, J.) No. The union has no constitutional right to the political activity-funding part of those fees to begin with; therefore there is no First Amendment problem with requiring non-members to affirmatively consent to providing those amounts to the union.

Concurrence: (Breyer, J.) The Court addresses several arguments the union made for the first time in its appeal to this Court. I would not reach those arguments.

Tennessee Secondary School Athletic Ass'n v. Brentwood Academy (S. Ct. 2007)

Facts: A scholastic athletic conference sanctioned the member school for violating the conference rules about recruiting middle-school students, after providing a hearing to the school.

Issue: Does the sanction violate the school's First Amendment associational rights or its procedural due process rights?

Rule: (Stevens, J.) There are no violations. The school joined the conference voluntarily, and whatever restrictions on its associational rights flowing from the recruiting restrictions are justified by the conference's need to ensure the integrity of its academic competition and prevent pressure on students. The hearing the conference gave the school was adequate, even though the process included an *ex parte* hearing.

Concurrence: (Kennedy, J.) I agree with the result but not with some of the case citations the Court makes in its First Amendment analysis.

Concurrence: (Thomas, J.) I do not believe the conference is a state actor and subject to the Constitution.

Johanns v. Livestock Marketing Ass'n (S. Ct. 2005)

Facts: A federal tax on beef producers finances an advertising campaign urging Americans to consume more beef. P, a beef grower — taxpayer sues, alleging that the tax compels him to subsidize speech with which he disagrees.

Rule: (Souter, J.) The speech is government speech, and thus there is no compelled speech claim. Congress established the basic message and the

Secretary of Agriculture had final control over the details of the advertising.

Concurrence: (Thomas, J.) Compelled advertising speech must always be closely scrutinized. However, since this is the government's speech it is appropriate to reject P's claim.

Concurrence: (Breyer, J.) This kind of program is fundamentally economic regulation and not compelled speech; thus, it should be easily upheld.

Concurrence: (Ginsburg, J.) I resist calling this speech speech by the government. However, because this kind of program is fundamentally economic regulation, the Court's result is correct.

Dissent: (Kennedy, J.) This is not government speech, but private speech. I would reserve for another day whether this kind of program could survive if government also associated itself with the speech.

Dissent: (Souter, J.) This is not government speech. The ads show no sign of government sponsorship, and thus any political check on the government speech is lacking since it is not clear to citizens that in fact it is government doing the talking.

Ysursa v. Pocatello Educ. Ass'n (S. Ct. 2009)

Facts: Idaho law prohibits unions from collecting from non-members fees used for political activities. After litigation both parties agreed that the statute was unconstitutional as applied to private sector unions but constitutional as applied to state employee unions.

Issue: Is the law constitutional as applied to local government unions, such as a teachers' union?

Rule: (Roberts, C.J.) It is constitutional. All the law does is refuse to subsidize political speech by prohibiting the public sector union from extracting resources for political speech from non-consenting non-members. Otherwise the union remains free to speak as much as it wants.

Concurrence: (Ginsburg, J.) This is a narrow issue: given the parties' concessions, the only question is whether local government unions are closer to state employee unions or private sector ones. The Court's decision that they are closer to state employee unions is correct.

Concurrence/Dissent: (Breyer, J.) I might uphold the statute if it were evenhanded, but its singling-out of political speech raises the possibility that it is not.

Dissent: (Stevens, J.) It appears that the statute was aimed at union political activity, and thus is not a viewpoint or even content neutral.

Dissent: (Souter, J.) This case should be dismissed. The union's concession that the statute was valid as applied to state employee unions makes it hard for us to use this case to refine First Amendment doctrine, given the serious constitutional issues we would have to ignore if we simply focused on the statute's applicability to local government unions.

Austin v. Michigan Chamber of Commerce (S. Ct. 1990)

Facts: The Michigan Campaign Finance Act prohibited corporations from using corporate treasury funds for independent expenditures in support of or in opposition to any candidate for state office. Corporations were allowed, however, to make such expenditures from segregated funds used solely for political purposes. Media corporations were exempted from the Act.

Issue 1: May a state require that corporate political expenditures be made only from specifically segregated funds?

Rule 1: (Marshall, J.) The state-granted corporate structure facilitates the amassing of large treasuries, and the state has a compelling interest in preventing corporate wealth from unfairly influencing elections. Therefore, an act requiring that corporations use only specifically segregated funds for political expenditures is constitutional because it is narrowly tailored to eliminate the distortion caused by corporate spending, but still permits corporations to express their political views.

Issue 2: Does exemption of media corporations from the Campaign Finance Act infringe upon equal protection under the Fourteenth Amendment?

Rule 2: It is constitutional to exempt media corporations from the Campaign Finance Act because media corporations differ significantly from other corporations in that their resources are devoted to the collection of information and its dissemination to the public.

Dissent: (Scalia, J.) The state may not exact forfeiture of First Amendment rights in exchange for the special advantages that allow corporations to amass wealth (e.g., limited shareholder liability). Furthermore, the unique role that the press plays in controlling information and educating the public provides especially strong reason to *include*, not exclude, them from the Act.

Barnes v. Glen Theater (S. Ct. 1991)

Facts: An Indiana statute regulating public nudity required that go-go dancers wear pasties and a G-string when they perform.

Issue: Is a statute that prohibits all nudity constitutional, since it also prohibits nude dancing?

Rule: (Rehnquist, C.J.) The statute is constitutional because it satisfies the *O'Brien* test: (1) the statute has a legitimate public purpose of protecting societal order and morality (nudity was a criminal offense at common law); (2) the state interest is unrelated to the suppression of expressive conduct; (3) the state seeks to prevent all public nudity, not just that which is expressive or has an erotic message; and (4) the statute is narrowly tailored in that the requirement that the dancers wear at least pasties and a

G-string is the bare minimum (so to speak) necessary to achieve the state's purpose.

Regan v. Taxation with Representation of Washington (S. Ct. 1983)

Facts: The Internal Revenue Code afforded tax-exempt status to various nonprofit organizations, including veterans' organizations, which engaged in substantial lobbying activity. Another charitable organization was denied tax-exempt status because of its involvement in substantial lobbying activities.

Issue: May a government discriminate in its subsidy of charitable organizations based on the organization's specific activities?

Rule: (Rehnquist, J.) A legislature may determine whether the advantage the public would receive from an activity of a charity is worth the money, and other public costs.

First National Bank of Boston v. Bellotti (S. Ct. 1978)

Facts: Massachusetts enacted a law forbidding the use of corporate funds to publish views about issues having no material effect on the business, property or assets of the corporation.

Issue: May a state regulate speech based on the identity of the speaker?

Rule: (Powell, J.) Under the First Amendment, a legislature is prohibited from dictating the subjects about which persons may speak and the speakers who may address a public issue.

Dissent: (White, J.) The state regulatory interests, in terms of which the alleged curtailment of First Amendment rights must be evaluated, are themselves derived from the First Amendment. The proper question then, is whether the state has struck the best possible balance, i.e., the one which it would have chosen, between competing First Amendment interests.

Houchins v. KQED, Inc. (S. Ct. 1978)

Facts: Upon the suicide of an inmate, allegedly prompted by conditions at a county jail, a television station requested but was refused permission to inspect and photograph that area of the jail.

Issue: Does the First Amendment guarantee of freedom of the press grant the media a constitutional right to greater access than the general public?

Rule: Neither the First nor Fourteenth Amendment mandates a media right of access to government information or sources of information within the government's control.

Dissent: (Stevens, J.) The probable existence of a constitutional violation underscores the special importance of allowing a democratic community access to knowledge about how its servants were treating some of its members who have been committed to their custody.

NAACP v. Claiborne Hardware Co. (S. Ct. 1982)

Facts: The local branch of the NAACP, other civic groups, and individuals (D) led a boycott of white merchants to secure compliance by civic and business leaders with a lengthy list of demands for equality and racial justice.

Issue: Is a political group's use of social pressure and "threats" of social ostracism protected action under the First Amendment?

Rule 1: (Stevens, J.) Speech does not lose its protected character because it may embarrass or coerce people into action. The nonviolent elements of politically motivated boycott activities are entitled to protection of the First Amendment.

Issue 2: May members of an association be held civilly liable for the tortious acts of the association?

Rule 2: Under the First Amendment, civil liability may not be imposed merely because an individual belonged to a group, some members of which committed acts of violence. For liability to be imposed by reason of association alone, it is necessary to establish that the group itself possessed unlawful goals and that the individual held a specific intent to further those illegal aims.

Keller v. State Bar of California (S. Ct. 1990)

Facts: California lawyers are required to join the state bar and pay dues. The state bar used some of the membership dues to finance various ideological or political activities. Twenty-one bar members claimed that the use of their dues to finance activities they were opposed to violated their rights under the First Amendment.

Issue: May a state bar association compel membership if it uses membership dues to finance political and ideological activities?

Rule: (Rehnquist, C.J.) A state bar may compel membership because, as with labor unions, it is inequitable to allow individuals to enjoy the benefits of the organization while avoiding their fair share of the costs. However, a mandatory-membership state bar may only use membership dues to advance goals germane to its purpose, such as regulating the legal profession and improving the quality of legal services. It may not fund activities of an ideological nature that fall outside of these areas (e.g., gun control, environmental protection, etc.).

Legal Services Corp. v. Velasquez (S. Ct. 2001)

Facts: Federal law banned federally funded legal aid organizations from raising certain claims against the federal government.
Issue: Do restrictions on publicly funded lawyers' litigation strategies violate the Free Speech Clause?
Rule: (Kennedy, J.) By intruding into the lawyer-client relationship the rule violates the free speech rights of lawyers. The restriction is not like the one upheld in *Rust v. Sullivan*, as the program in this case funds private speech, which the government cannot attempt to distort without violating the First Amendment.
Dissent: (Scalia, J.) This case is on all fours with *Rust v. Sullivan*, where the Court held that the government can fund speech it wants and defund speech it does not want.

National Endowment for the Arts v. Findley (S. Ct. 1998)

Facts: Federal law funding arts grant program was amended to require the NEA to take into account considerations of decency when making grants.
Issue: Does the decency requirement violate the First Amendment?
Rule: (O'Connor, J.) The statute is not facially unconstitutional. Decency is not a viewpoint-based restriction. For example, education is one of the NEA's missions, and it may be appropriate for an educationally motivated grant to take decency into account when considering the educational suitability of a particular project.
Dissent: (Souter, J.) This is a viewpoint-based statute, which is unconstitutional. The fact that it is a funding program is irrelevant, since governmental favors, as well as burdens, cannot be allocated based on the point of view of the speech made by the target of the burden or benefit.

Dale v. Boy Scouts of America (S. Ct. 2000)

Facts: A Boy Scout troop discharged a scoutmaster and former Eagle Scout once he acknowledged in his college's newspaper that he was gay. P scoutmaster sued under the New Jersey public accommodations law that prohibited discrimination on the basis of sexual orientation, and D Boy Scouts defended on the ground that they had a First Amendment right not to associate with gays.
Issue: To what extent will a court examine an association's assertion that its expression will be impeded through forced association with someone they wish to exclude?
Rule: (Rehnquist, C.J.) A court should accept the assertions of an association that forced association with a particular individual or type of

individual would impede its expression; otherwise courts would be forced into the difficult and inappropriate task of investigating the nature of the group's expression to determine whether forced association would impair the group's First Amendment rights.

Dissent: (Stevens, J.) The majority's rule allows groups such as the Boy Scouts a free pass out of anti-discrimination laws, since they can now simply claim that their expression is inconsistent with forced association with a particular group. On the merits here, there is no evidence that the Boy Scouts' expression ever took the form of opposing gays or homosexuality.

Hurley v. Irish-American Gay, Lesbian and Bisexual Group of Boston (S. Ct. 1995)

Facts: Parade organizers excluded a gay organization from their annual St. Patrick's Day parade. The gay organization sued, claiming a violation of the state's public accommodation law and the organizers defended based on their First Amendment right to associate.

Issue: Is a parade sufficiently expressive such that its organizers can disregard a state's public accommodations law to exclude groups with which the organizers do not wish to associate?

Rule: (Souter, J.) A parade is clearly expressive, as it includes marchers who are making a collective point through symbolic acts as well as speaking through placards and songs. Thus the organizers should be able to control the content of its message by excluding groups with whose message the organizers do not wish to associate.

Madsen v. Women's Health Center (S. Ct. 1995)

Facts: Abortion clinic picketers challenged a court order enjoining them from picketing near an abortion clinic.

Issue: Under what circumstances are abortion clinic injunctions viewpoint-based speech restrictions in violation of the First Amendment?

Rule: (Rehnquist, C.J.) Such restrictions are not content or viewpoint based simply because they happen to target protesters with a particular point of view; injunctions often have this effect simply because they are designed to counteract a particular type of harm. Still, the particularized nature of injunctions carries with them a risk of discriminatory application, and so more searching scrutiny than simple time, place, or manner review is required.

Dissent: (Scalia, J.) Such injunctions should receive strict scrutiny since they are content- and indeed viewpoint-based restrictions on speech, imposed by individual judges rather than by legislatures.

United States v. American Library Ass'n (S. Ct. 2003)

Facts: As a condition of receiving federal funding, libraries were required to limit the access their computers provided to sexually explicit websites.
Issue: Does a funding condition limiting what material libraries may offer to patrons violate the First Amendment rights of libraries?
Rule: (Rehnquist, C.J.) (plurality) Because libraries normally make decisions about which information to offer patrons there is no constitutional violation when the government conditions its funding on the library making such choices.
Concurrence: (Breyer, J.) The protection of children from inappropriate material is a legitimate, and sometimes compelling interest, and the restriction on speech rights is relatively small, since filtering software can be unblocked at a patron's request.
Concurrence: (Kennedy, J.) There is little to the case, given that filtering software can be unblocked at a patron's request.

Eldred v. Ashcroft (S. Ct. 2003)

Facts: In the Copyright Term Extension Act, Congress extended the term of existing and future copyrights by 20 years.
Issue: Did the statute violate either the Copyright Clause's "limited term" provision or the First Amendment rights of those who would otherwise use copyrighted material?
Rule: (Ginsburg, J.) There is no violation of the Copyright Clause; historically Congress has extended the terms of copyrights, and the current term remains finite, even if it might conceivably be extended sometime in the future. Nor is there a violation of First Amendment rights: since copyright protection was a feature of the original Constitution it cannot be understood as creating a First Amendment problem, and at any rate copyright law provides would-be users with a variety of ways to use work still under copyright protection.
Dissent: (Stevens, J.) By allowing retroactive extensions of copyrights the Court sanctions the possibility of perpetual copyrights, which is forbidden by the "limited terms" proviso of the Copyright Clause.

Pleasant Grove City v. Summum (S. Ct. 2009)

Facts: P, a religious organization, asked D city for permission to place in a city park a monument containing the religion's core beliefs. The city, which already had placed in the park, among other things, a monument of the Ten Commandments donated to the city by a private party, declined. The religious organization sued.

Issue: Is the city's placement of a monument in a city park the speech of the private party that donates the monument, in which case the city generally cannot make content- or viewpoint-based restrictions in a public forum like a park, or speech of the government, in which case the government can speak what it wishes as long as it complies with other constitutional commands such as the Establishment Clause?

Rule: (Alito, J.) A city's placement of a monument in its park constitutes government speech. Governments have long used monuments to communicate with the public; a contrary rule would require the government either to remove all monuments or allow private parties to erect their own monuments that speak on other issues or on ways contrary to the viewpoint of existing monuments. These possibilities make clear that public forum doctrine is inappropriate in this context.

Concurrence: (Stevens, J.) While the Court's government speech cases are of questionable validity, here, unlike in the earlier government speech cases, there is no coercion of private speech and no risk that viewers will mistakenly attribute the speech to a private party and thus blur the government's political accountability for its speech.

Concurrence: (Scalia, J.) While the Establishment Clause issue was not decided by the Court, the Court's upholding of a similar Ten Commandments display in *Van Orden v. Perry*, 545 U.S. 677 (2005), means that there is no Establishment Clause problem here.

Concurrence: (Breyer, J.) Labels such as "government speech" and "public forums" cannot be applied rigidly. Here, however, the city's refusal to display the Summum monument does not disproportionately restrict its expression; the religion can still speak in the park through methods more transient than the erection of a monument.

Concurrence: (Souter, J.) There should be no categorical rule that monuments are government speech, for example, religious imagery attached to graves at military cemeteries are not government speech. Moreover, the relationship between the government speech doctrine and the Establishment Clause has yet to be worked out. For example, if a city tries to avoid Establishment Clause problems by adding many secular monuments to its religious monuments, the resulting confusing message may lead an observer to conclude that the monuments reflect private speech, not government speech.

CHAPTER 11

The Constitution and Religion

I. INTRODUCTION

The Religion Clauses of the First Amendment provide that "Congress shall make no law respecting an establishment of religion, or prohibiting the free exercise thereof." The Establishment of Religion and the Free Exercise Clauses apply to the states under the Fourteenth Amendment.

The Establishment of Religion and the Free Exercise Clauses attempt to protect the same fundamental value: the freedom and right of each individual to pursue a religious belief as determined by his conscience without undue governmental interference. However, in some instances, tensions are apparent in the application of the two Clauses. For example, on one hand, public assistance to religiously oriented schools could be a violation of the Establishment of Religion Clause. Yet, the lack of such assistance could violate the Free Exercise Clause because the denial of the funds could be seen as an infringement of the free exercise of the students' religion.

II. THE ESTABLISHMENT CLAUSE

A. *Lemon* Test

The Supreme Court continually applies the three-pronged test, enunciated in *Lemon v. Kurtzman,* 465 U.S. 668 (1984), in evaluating Establishment Clause challenges. The state action must satisfy each of the following conditions to be valid:

MNEMONIC: **PEE**

1. **P**urpose

The state action must have a legitimate secular purpose;

2. Effect

The principal or primary effect must neither advance nor inhibit religion; and

3. Entanglement

There must be no excessive government entanglement with religion.

B. Wall of Separation

The basic purpose of the Establishment Clause is to erect a "wall of separation" between church and state. The Clause clearly forbids the federal government or a state government from:

1. Establishing a church;
2. Passing laws that aid one religion, aid all religions, or prefer one religion over another;
3. Forcing or influencing a person to go to or to remain away from church against his will or forcing a person to profess a belief or disbelief in any religion;
4. Punishing a person for entertaining or professing religious beliefs or disbeliefs, for church attendance or nonattendance;
5. Levying a tax to support religious activities or institutions, to teach or practice religion; and
6. Participating openly or secretly in the affairs of any religious organization or group.

C. Neutrality Principle

The Clause does not forbid every action by government that favors or benefits religion. A general principle governing this area of the law is that the First Amendment requires the state to be neutral in its relations with groups of religious believers and non-believers; it does not require the state to be their adversary. State power is no more to be used to handicap religions than it is to favor them.

1. A state or federal statute granting direct financial assistance to a religiously oriented institution (such as a school or hospital) must be examined under the three-prong test described above. Frequently, such a direct grant violates the Establishment Clause. However, other kinds of benefits and aids (such as transportation subsidies and the loan of secular textbooks) to students attending religiously oriented private schools have been upheld as constitutional.
2. A tax exemption that does not single out a particular church or religious group is considered to be a permissible state accommodation of religion.
3. The grant of a tax deduction for educational expenses of students attending parochial and public schools that predominantly

benefits the parents of parochial school children does not violate the Establishment Clause.

4. The grant of funds to church-related universities and colleges in which the secular functions within the institutions can be easily separated from the religious functions does not violate the Religion Clause.

5. A public school program allowing students "released time" to participate in religious instructions outside the public schools' premises is an accommodation of religion and not a violation of the Religion Clauses of the First Amendment. However, a public school system may not include prayer and Bible reading as part of its daily opening exercises in the classrooms.

D. Religious Displays

The law governing the constitutionality of religious displays such as nativity scenes and the Ten Commandments is very unsettled. At its most general, displays that reveal an intention to endorse a particular religion or religion generally will be constitutionally problematic. However, religious displays that serve a secular purpose, such as noting the nation's religious heritage, are more likely to survive.

III. THE FREE EXERCISE CLAUSE

A. The Free Exercise Clause forbids the outlawing of any religious belief. Note, however, that it is the right to believe that is unconditionally protected. The right to act pursuant to one's beliefs is subject to reasonable regulation designed to protect a compelling state interest. Therefore, a religious practice may be limited, curtailed or restrained to the point of outright prohibition where it involves a clear and present danger to the interests of society.

B. Direct vs. Indirect Burdens on the Free Exercise of Religion

1. Direct Burden

A direct burden on the free exercise of religion occurs when an individual's conduct is made illegal by a statute. The Supreme Court will balance the direct burden on the individual's religious interests against the compelling state interest.

a. A state statute requiring compulsory school attendance for children after the eighth grade was held to violate the Free Exercise Clause as it applied to followers of the Amish faith. *Wisconsin v. Yoder.*

b. A state statute making polygamy illegal was held not to violate the Mormons' right to the free exercise of their religion. *Reynolds v. United States.*

2. Indirect Burden

An indirect burden occurs when a statute makes the free exercise of one's religion more difficult but does not coerce the individual to act contrary to his religious belief. A state need not show compelling state interest to establish the validity of a statute that indirectly burdens the free exercise of religion.

a. A statute that advances a state's secular goals but also indirectly burdens a religious activity does not violate the Free Exercise Clause. *Lyng v. Northwest Indian Cemetery Protective Ass'n.*

b. A state law advancing no strong state interest but that denies someone of an important benefit, such as the award of unemployment compensation benefits for refusal to work on religious grounds, violates the Free Exercise Clause. *Sherbert v. Verner* and *Thomas v. Indiana Employment Security Review Board.* Note, however, that a state statute granting Sabbath observers an absolute and unqualified right not to work on their chosen Sabbath violates the Establishment Clause as the statute had the primary effect of impermissibly advancing a particular religious practice. *Estate of Thornton v. Caldor, Inc.*

CASE CLIPS

Everson v. Board of Educ. (S. Ct. 1947)

Facts: Pursuant to a New Jersey statute, a local school board authorized reimbursement of money spent by parents to transport their children on public buses to private schools. Everson, a local taxpayer, challenged the payments going to parents of Roman Catholic parochial school students as contrary to the First Amendment.

Issue: Does a state's use of tax revenues to subsidize the public transportation cost of students attending parochial schools violate the Establishment of Religion Clause of the First Amendment?

Rule: (Black, J.) The First Amendment's prohibition against the establishment of religion does not bar a state from paying the bus fares of parochial school children as part of a general program under which the state pays the fares of pupils attending public and other schools. The First Amendment requires the state to be neutral in its relations with religious groups, not their adversary.

Dissent: (Rutledge, J.) The First Amendment's prohibition against the establishment of religion is absolute. Undeniably, there is a mixture of religion with secular teaching in all religiously oriented schools, and the funds directed to the parents of students attending such institutions aid and encourage the religious instruction. To obtain public funds for the aid and support of various private religious schools is foreclosed by the Constitution and should not be opened by the Court.

Mueller v. Allen (S. Ct. 1983)

Facts: Minnesota permitted state taxpayers to claim a deduction from gross income for certain expenses incurred in the education of their children at the elementary and secondary school levels. Many of the Minnesota school children attended privately supported, sectarian schools.

Issue: Does a state's allowance of a tax deduction for certain expenses incurred in the elementary and secondary education of children in privately supported, sectarian schools violate the Establishment of Religion Clause of the First Amendment?

Rule: (Rehnquist, J.) To withstand a constitutional challenge to its validity under the Establishment of Religion Clause, a public assistance program must (1) have a secular legislative purpose; (2) neither principally nor primarily advance or inhibit religion; and (3) not foster an excessive government entanglement with religion. A public assistance program which is available to all parents of children attending nonpublic schools, of which parents of children attending sectarian schools predominantly benefit, is constitutional under the foregoing test.

Dissent: (Marshall, J.) A tax deduction has a primary effect that advances religion if it is provided to offset expenditures which are not restricted to the secular activities of parochial schools. The Court, in this instance, has upheld financial support for religious schools without ensuring that the support will be restricted to the secular functions of those schools, and will not be used to fund religious instructions. This result is flatly at odds with the fundamental principle that a state may provide no financial support whatsoever to promote religion.

Zorach v. Clauson (S. Ct. 1952)

Facts: A New York City program permitted its public schools to release certain students during the school day to attend religious centers for religious instruction off the school grounds. The "released time" program did not involve religious instruction in public school classrooms or the expenditure of public funds.

Issue: Does a state-approved public school program setting aside "released time" for students wishing religious instruction off school grounds violate the Establishment of Religion Clause of the First Amendment?

Rule: (Douglas, J.) The Establishment Clause of the First Amendment does not require the government to show callous indifference to religious groups. Therefore, when a state encourages religious instruction by adjusting the schedule of public events to accommodate a program of outside religious instructions, such action reflects the long religious history of the Nation and does not violate the Establishment Clause of the First Amendment.

Dissent: (Black, J.) Under the state's "released time" program, some of the students are released on the condition that they attend the religious classes, get reports on whether they attend, and the other children are held in school until the religious hour is over. The state is manipulating its compulsory education laws to help religious sects get pupils. This is not separation but combination of church and state.

Wallace v. Jaffree (S. Ct. 1985)

Facts: Ishmael Jaffree alleged that, pursuant to the Alabama law authorizing a period of silence for "meditation or voluntary prayer," teachers in the public school system subjected two of his minor children to various acts of religious indoctrination, in violation of the First Amendment.

Issue: Does a state law authorizing a period of silence for "meditation and voluntary prayer" violate the constitutional prohibition against the establishment of religion?

Rule: (Stevens, J.) A statute enacted primarily to endorse and promote religion with no secular purpose in mind violates the established, constitutional principle that government must pursue a course of complete neutrality toward the establishment of religion.

Dissent: (Burger, C.J.) To suggest that a moment-of-silence statute that includes the word "prayer" unconstitutionally endorses religion, while one that simply provides for a moment of silence does not, manifests not neutrality but hostility toward religion. The statute in question does not remotely threaten religious liberty; it affirmatively furthers the values of religious freedom and tolerance that the Establishment Clause was designed to protect.

Edwards v. Aguillard (S. Ct. 1987)

Facts: Louisiana's Creationism Act forbade the teaching of the theory of evolution in public schools unless accompanied by instruction in "creation science." Aguillard and others challenged the Act as violative of the Establishment Clause of the First Amendment.

Issue: Does a state law authorizing equal treatment for creation science and evolution science in public schools violate the Establishment Clause of the First Amendment?

Rule: (Brennan, J.) Creation science is a religious belief and it may be taught in public schools only if it furthers an identifiable secular purpose. The secular goals of fairness and academic freedom are insufficient to validate an act which endorses religion in violation of the First Amendment.

Dissent: (Scalia, J.) The record is inadequate from which to conclude that the state legislators were motivated primarily by the desire to advance a religious belief. The statute does manifest a secular purpose in its attempt to protect academic freedom.

Lynch v. Donnelly (S. Ct. 1984)

Facts: The City of Pawtucket, Rhode Island erected a Christmas display as part of its observances of the Christmas holiday season. The Christmas display included a crèche, which was deemed in violation of the Establishment Clause of the First Amendment.

Issue: Does the inclusion of a religious symbol in a Christmas display erected and maintained by a city government violate the Establishment Clause of the First Amendment?

Rule: (Burger, C.J.) When there is no evidence that the inclusion of a religious symbol in a Christmas display is a purposeful effort to express subtle governmental advocacy of a particular religious message, and when there exists a legitimate secular purpose in erecting the display, such governmental action does not offend the Constitution.

Dissent: (Brennan, J.) The Court's less than vigorous application of the established three-prong *Lemon* test suggests that its commitment to those standards may only be superficial. The city's maintenance and display at public expense of a symbol as distinctively sectarian as a crèche simply cannot be squared with controlling precedent. It is contrary to the purposes and values of the Establishment Clause to pretend, as the Court does, that the otherwise secular setting of the nativity scene dilutes in some fashion the crèche's singular religiosity.

Sherbert v. Verner (S. Ct. 1963)

Facts: Sherbert's refusal to work on Saturday, the Sabbath Day of her faith, caused her to be discharged from employment and prevented her from obtaining new employment. Her claim for South Carolina state unemployment compensation benefits was refused because the law barred benefits to workers who without good cause failed to accept "suitable work when offered."

Issue: Does a state eligibility provision for the receipt of unemployment compensation benefits, requiring a worker to accept suitable work when offered, impermissibly burden the free exercise of a religion, which commands the observance of a specific day of rest?

Rule: (Brennan, J.) A state may not constitutionally apply an eligibility provision for the receipt of state unemployment compensation benefits so as to constrain a worker to abandon his religious convictions respecting the observance of the day of rest.

Dissent: (Harlan, J.) The meaning of the Court's holding is that a state must single out for financial assistance those whose behavior is religiously motivated, even though it denies such assistance to others whose identical behavior is not religiously motivated. Under the circumstances of this case, it would be a permissible accommodation of religion for a state, if it chose to do so, to create an exception to its eligibility requirements. However, to compel a state to do so is inappropriate in light of the indirect, remote and insubstantial effect lack of accommodation would have on the free exercise of religion.

Employment Div. Oregon Dep't of Human Res. v. Smith (S. Ct. 1990)

Facts: Oregon law prohibited the religious use of peyote. Oregon law also denied unemployment benefits to employees discharged for violation of state statutes. Smith was fired from his job for ingesting peyote at a religious ceremony and denied unemployment compensation.

Issue: Is Oregon's prohibition on the religious use of peyote permissible under the Free Exercise Clause of the Constitution, such that the state may deny unemployment benefits to persons fired from their jobs for such drug use?

Rule: (Scalia, J.) Prohibiting the exercise of religion, where it is merely the incidental effect of a generally applicable and otherwise valid statute, is permissible under the Free Exercise Clause. An individual's religious beliefs do not excuse him from compliance with an otherwise neutral, valid law prohibiting conduct that the state is free to regulate.

Concurrence: (O'Connor, J.) Oregon's uniform law prohibiting peyote is essential to accomplish its overriding governmental interest in preventing physical harm caused by drug use.

Dissent: (Blackmun, J.) The Free Exercise Clause should be interpreted more broadly. A law that prohibits certain conduct, which happens to be an act of worship for someone, manifestly does prohibit that person's free exercise of religion.

Wisconsin v. Yoder (S. Ct. 1972)

Facts: Wisconsin's compulsory attendance law required children under the age of 16 to attend public or private schools. Yoder and others (D), members of the Old Order Amish Religion, declined to continue to send their children to school after they had completed the eighth grade. D believed that continued education of the children would endanger their own salvation and that of their children.

Issue: May a state impose a compulsory attendance law requiring school-age children to attend school beyond the eighth grade if the law interferes with the legitimate beliefs and practices of a religious group?

Rule: (Burger, C.J.) A state law interfering with religious beliefs and practices is valid only if (1) it does not deny the free exercise of religious belief or (2) the state interest furthered by application of the law is of sufficient magnitude to override the interest claiming protection under the Free Exercise Clause. The enforcement of a state's requirement of compulsory formal education after the eighth grade denies the free exercise of religious beliefs because the requirement would gravely endanger or destroy a group's religious way of life.

Dissent: (Douglas, J.) Children have constitutionally protectible interests and if a child desires to attend high school, and is mature enough to have that desire respected, the state may well be able to override the parents' religiously motivated objections. Children should be given an opportunity to be heard before the state grants the exemption which the Court honors in this instance.

Walz v. Tax Comm'n of City of New York (S. Ct. 1970)

Facts: The New York Constitution authorized property tax exemptions to religious organizations for properties used solely for religious worship.

Issue: Does the grant of a property tax exemption to religious organizations constitute a state sponsorship of religion in violation of the First Amendment's prohibition against the establishment of religion?

Rule: (Burger, C.J.) The grant of a tax exemption to religious organizations does not constitute the establishment of religion because the state does not transfer part of its revenue to churches but simply abstains from demanding that the church support the state. Additionally, the grant of the exemption is a valid exercise of state authority because of the secular purpose behind the exemption and the effect of the exemption is to create only a minimal and remote involvement between church and state.

Dissent: (Douglas, J.) Subsidies, either through direct grant or tax exemption for sectarian causes, whether carried on by church qua church or by church qua welfare agency must be treated in a suspect manner lest in time church qua church is allowed to be on the public payroll.

Committee for Pub. Educ. and Religious Liberty v. Regan (S. Ct. 1980)

Facts: The New York legislature appropriated public funds to reimburse both church-sponsored and secular nonpublic schools for performing various services mandated by the state. The services included the "administration, grading and the compiling and reporting of the results of tests and examinations," including both state-prepared and teacher-prepared tests.

Issue: Does a state's appropriation of funds to reimburse religiously oriented schools and their staff for rendering some educational-related services violate the First Amendment's prohibition against the establishment of religion?

Rule: (White, J.) A state's legislative provision does not contravene the Establishment Clause if (1) it has a secular legislative purpose; (2) its principal or primary effect neither advances nor inhibits religion; and (3) it does not foster an excessive government entanglement with religion. The services for which the religiously oriented schools and staff would be reimbursed are discrete and easily identifiable and suggest no excessive entanglement with the religion of the schools.

Dissent: (Blackmun, J.) The Court's holding is not compelled by precedent as our decisions in this area cannot be plotted along a straight line. The authorization of direct financial assistance to religiously oriented schools violates the Religion Clauses of the Constitution.

Roemer v. Board of Public Works of Maryland (S. Ct. 1976)

Facts: Maryland, through a grant program, provided funding for any accredited private institution of higher learning. The aid took the form of an annual fiscal year subsidy to qualifying colleges and universities. A grant recipient could use the funds in whatever fashion, except that none of the money could be used for "sectarian" purposes.

Issue: May a state provide funding for church-affiliated post-secondary institutions without violating the Establishment Clause of the First Amendment?

Rule: (Blackmun, J.) State funding of church-related post-secondary institutions is constitutionally permissible if the secular activities can be separated from the sectarian ones, and only the separable secular activities receive state funds.

Dissent: (Brennan, J.) The payment of general subsidies to religious institutions constitutes impermissible state involvement with religion.

School District of Abington Township v. Schempp (S. Ct. 1963)

Facts: Public schools allowed the reading of the Bible (without commentary) and the recitation of the Lord's Prayer.

Issue: Do public school opening exercises that include Bible reading and recitation of prayers violate the Establishment Clause of the First Amendment?

Rule: (Clark, J.) Bible reading and recitation of prayers are religious exercises and the public schools' inclusion of these exercises in their daily opening sessions violates the Establishment Clause of the First Amendment.

Epperson v. Arkansas (S. Ct. 1968)

Facts: The State of Arkansas prohibited teaching evolution in its public schools.

Issue: Does a state law that prohibits teaching evolution in the public schools violate the Religion Clauses of the First Amendment?

Rule: (Fortas, J.) A state's right to prescribe the curriculum for its public schools does not allow it to prohibit the teaching of a scientific theory or doctrine because it conflicts with a particular religious doctrine. Such a law is contrary to the Religion Clauses of the First Amendment.

McGowan v. Maryland (S. Ct. 1961)

Facts: A Maryland statute prohibited the Sunday sale of most merchandise.

Issue: Does a state law prohibiting the sale of merchandise on Sunday, the Sabbath of the predominant Christian sects, violate the guarantee of separation of church and state under the First Amendment?

Rule: (Warren, C.J.) State laws prohibiting the Sunday sale of merchandise have a secular purpose in establishing a uniform day of rest and recreation for the community. Upon a finding of a secular purpose and effect of a statute, the Court defers to the state legislature's determination that the enactment of the statute is not to aid religion.

Dissent: (Douglas, J.) Sunday is a word heavily overlaid with religious connotations emanating from the Christian roots of our civilization. The Establishment Clause protects citizens against any law which selects any religious custom, practice, or ritual, puts the force of government behind it, and penalizes a person for not observing it.

Braunfeld v. Brown (S. Ct. 1961)

Facts: A Pennsylvania criminal statute proscribed the Sunday retail sale of certain enumerated commodities. Braunfeld and other Jewish merchants contended that the compulsory closing of their businesses on Sunday severely disadvantaged them because their religion already required them to abstain from all manner of work from nightfall Fridays until nightfall Saturdays.

Issue: Does a state's criminal statute prohibiting the retail sale of certain items on Sunday interfere with the free exercise of a religious faith that requires its adherents to abstain from work from Friday afternoon to Saturday afternoon?

Rule: (Warren, C.J.) A state law prohibiting Sunday retail sales does not criminalize any religious practice, it merely imposes an indirect burden on the observance of a particular religious faith. A state law, the purpose and effect of which is to advance the state's secular goals but which imposes indirect burdens on religious observances, is valid unless the state may accomplish its purpose by means which do not impose such a burden.

Estate of Thornton v. Caldor, Inc. (S. Ct. 1985)

Facts: Caldor (D), a chain of retail stores, required its managerial employees to work every third or fourth Sunday. Thornton, a manager with D, refused to work on Sundays and invoked in his defense a Connecticut statute that provided that "no person who states that a particular day of the week is observed as his Sabbath may be required by his employer to work on such a day. An employee's refusal to work on his Sabbath shall not constitute grounds for his dismissal."

Issue: Does a state statute providing employees with the absolute right not to work on their chosen Sabbath violate the Establishment Clause of the First Amendment?

Rule: (Burger, C.J.) A state law bestowing an absolute and unqualified right on Sabbath observers, regardless of all other interests, not to work on their chosen Sabbath has a primary effect of impermissibly advancing a particular religious practice in contravention of the Establishment Clause of the First Amendment.

Lemon v. Kurtzman (S. Ct. 1971)

Facts: The Rhode Island Salary Supplement Act of 1969 supplemented the salaries of nonpublic elementary school teachers. The Act provided that any teacher applying for the salary supplement must first agree in writing, "not to teach a course in religion for such time as he or she receives any salary supplements." The Pennsylvania Nonpublic Elementary and Secondary Education Act directly reimbursed nonpublic schools solely for their actual expenditure for teachers' salaries, textbooks and instructional materials. However, the Act prohibited reimbursement for any course that contained "any subject matter expressing religious teaching, or the morals or forms of worship of any sect."

Issue: Does a state statute providing financial assistance to nonpublic elementary schools with a primarily religious orientation violate the Establishment Clause of the First Amendment?

Rule: The validity of a state statute challenged under the Establishment Clause of the First Amendment is established by determining if the statute (1) has a secular legislative purpose; (2) neither principally nor primarily advances or inhibits religion; and (3) does not foster "an excessive government entanglement with religion." A state aid program requiring teachers of nonpublic schools to make a total separation between secular teaching and the religious doctrines of the institutions of which they are a part presents grave potential for excessive government entanglement in the religious character of religiously oriented nonpublic schools.

Tilton v. Richardson (S. Ct. 1971)

Facts: Title I of the Higher Education Facilities Act of 1963 provided federal construction grants for buildings and facilities used exclusively for secular educational purposes. Several church-related institutions received federal construction grants.

Issue: Does the granting of federal funds to church-related educational institutions for the construction of post-secondary facilities have the primary effect of advancing religion in violation of the Establishment Clause of the First Amendment?

Rule: A federal construction grant to otherwise eligible church-related institutions does not primarily advance religion if there is no evidence of religion in the use of the constructed, post-secondary facilities. Further, the potential for entanglement between church and state is minimal because of the non-sectarian nature of post-secondary courses and the lower risk of government aid being used for religious purposes.

Dissent: (Brennan, J.) A sectarian university is an educational institution in which the propagation and advancement of a particular religion is a primary function of the institution. Such an institution is dedicated to two goals, secular education and religious instruction. When aid flows directly to the institution, both functions benefit.

Grand Rapids School District v. Ball (S. Ct. 1985)

Facts: Two publicly financed educational programs were adopted. Under the Shared Time Program, certain remedial programs were taught during the regular school day by public school teachers with educational materials provided at public expense. Under the Community Education Program, classes for adults and children were taught after the regular school day. Both programs were conducted in parochial school classrooms, "rented" by the school district for that purpose.

Issue: Does a publicly financed educational program conducted on parochial school premises leased for that purpose have the primary effect of advancing religion in violation of the Establishment Clause of the First Amendment?

Rule: (Brennan, J.) A publicly financed educational program conducted on religious school premises presents a substantial and unacceptable risk that the state-sponsored instructional personnel might overtly or subtly advance the religious message of the church-related schools in which they serve.

Larson v. Valente (S. Ct. 1982)

Facts: A state statute provided that only those religious organizations that received more than half of their total contributions from members of affiliated organizations would remain tax exempt.

Issue: Does a state tax law granting denominational preference violate the Free Exercise Clause of the First Amendment?

Rule: A state tax law granting denominational preference is highly suspect and strict scrutiny is applied in adjudging its constitutionality. Such a law is valid only if it is justified by a compelling governmental interest and the law must be closely fitted to further that interest. The state interest in protecting its citizens from abusive solicitation practices is insufficient to justify the imposition of burdens on selective religious denominations.

Dissent: (White, J.) The 50% rule is not a deliberate and explicit legislative preference for some religious denominations over others. Some religions will qualify for the exemption and some will not, but this depends on the source of their contributions, not on their brand of religion. Therefore, deference should be shown to the state legislature's judgment that the risk of fraud is greater from religious organizations receiving most of their funds through public solicitation.

Committee for Pub. Educ. and Liberty v. NYQUIST (S. Ct. 1973)

Facts: New York established three financial aid programs for private elementary and secondary schools. First, the state gave direct money grants to qualifying schools for the maintenance of school property and equipment. Second, tuition grants were made available to children of lower-income families. Finally, parents who had incomes too high for the tuition reimbursement program were eligible for tax deductions.

Issue: Does governmental aid to private schools violate the Establishment Clause?

Rule: (Powell, J.) To pass muster under the Establishment Clause the law in question must reflect a clearly secular legislative purpose, must have a primary effect that neither advances nor inhibits religions, and must avoid excessive government entanglement with religion. While these aid packages serve the secular purpose of preserving a healthy and safe educational environment for all school children, they have the effect of subsidizing and advancing the religious mission of sectarian schools by distributing public funds without limitations on their use.

Dissent: (Burger, C.J.) The balance between the policies of free exercise and establishment of religion tips in favor of the former when the legislation moves away from direct aid to religious institutions and takes on the character of general aid to individual families.

Dissent: (Rehnquist, J.) By providing benefits here, New York has merely recognized that parents who are sending their children to nonpublic schools are rendering the state a service by decreasing the costs of public education and by physically relieving an already overburdened public school system.

Dissent: (White, J.) The state could constitutionally give parents the amount of money it would have cost to educate the child in a public school. With these programs, New York is merely seeking to prevent the demise of the nonpublic school system — an educational resource that delivers quality education at a cost to the public substantially below the per-pupil cost of the public schools.

Hobbie v. Unemployment Appeals Comm'n (S. Ct. 1987)

Facts: Hobbie's employer discharged her when she refused to work certain scheduled hours because of sincerely held religious convictions adopted after beginning employment. She was subsequently denied unemployment benefits by the state.

Issue: May a state deny unemployment benefits where the unemployment stems from the applicant's religious beliefs?

Rule: (Brennan, J.) Where the state conditions receipt of an important benefit upon conduct proscribed by a religious faith, or where it denies such a benefit because of conduct mandated by religious belief, thereby putting substantial pressure on an adherent to modify his behavior and to violate his beliefs, a burden upon religion exists. Such a burden must be subjected to strict scrutiny and could be justified only by proof by the state of a compelling interest.

Dissent: (Rehnquist, C.J.) Denial of unemployment benefits in this instance does not make unlawful the applicant's religious practices; it just makes them more expensive.

Corporation of the Presiding Bishop of the Church of Jesus Christ of Latter-Day Saints v. Amos (S. Ct. 1987)

Facts: Section 702 of the Civil Rights Act of 1964 exempted religious organizations from Title VII's prohibition against discrimination in employment on the basis of religion. Mayson worked at the Deseret Gymnasium in Salt Lake City for 16 years, but was discharged in 1981 because he failed to obtain a certificate proving that he was a member of the Mormon Church. He asserted that Section 702 was unconstitutional when applied to secular positions within the religious organization.

Issue: May the government allow religious employers to discriminate on religious grounds consistently with the Establishment Clause?

Rule: (White, J.) Under the *Lemon* analysis, it is a permissible legislative purpose to alleviate significant governmental interference with the ability of religious organizations to define and carry out their religious missions. Furthermore, a law is not unconstitutional simply because it allows churches to advance religion, which is their very purpose. A law only has forbidden "effects" under *Lemon* if the government itself has advanced religion through its own activities and influence.

Concurrence: (Brennan, J.) Ideally, religious organizations should be able to discriminate on the basis of religion only with respect to religious activities. However, the application of a religious-secular distinction is difficult because the character of an activity is not self-evident. The best way to accommodate this concern is to grant a categorical exemption for such non-profit religious enterprises.

Concurrence: (O'Connor, J.) Almost any government benefit to religion could be recharacterized as simply "allowing" a religion to better advance itself. The test under the Establishment Clause should be whether the government's purpose is to endorse religion and whether the statute actually conveys a message of endorsement.

Engel v. Vitale (S. Ct. 1962)

Facts: A New York school district, pursuant to the state board of regents' recommendation, required the daily recitation of a prayer in classrooms within its district.

Issue: May a state use its public schools' classrooms to encourage the daily recitation of prescribed prayers without violating the Establishment Clause of the First Amendment?

Rule: A daily invocation of a prescribed prayer is a religious activity and its use thereof in public classrooms breaches the constitutional wall of separation between church and state in violation of the Establishment Clause of the First Amendment.

Dissent: (Stewart, J.) The Court in this instance has misapplied a great constitutional principle. It is difficult to see how an "official religion" is established by allowing those who want to say a prayer to do so. On the contrary, to deny the wish of those school children to join in reciting the prayer is to deny them the opportunity of sharing in the spiritual heritage of our Nation.

Murray v. Curlett (S. Ct. 1963)

Facts: The Baltimore School Board instituted the practice of Bible reading in its public schools. Madalyn Murray, a professed atheist, challenged the practice as violative of the Establishment Clause of the First Amendment.

Issue: May public schools include Bible reading exercises and the recitation of prayer in their daily opening exercises without violating the Religion Clauses of the First Amendment?

Rule: Bible reading and the recitation of the Lord's Prayer are religious exercises and the public schools' inclusion of these exercises in their daily opening sessions violates the Establishment Clause of the First Amendment.

Board of Educ. v. Allen (S. Ct. 1968)

Facts: A New York law required school districts to purchase and loan textbooks upon request for use by all students attending parochial, other private, and public schools.

Issue: Does a state law requiring public school authorities to loan secular textbooks to students in parochial and other private schools violate the Establishment Clause of the First Amendment?

Rule: A state law requiring secular textbooks to be loaned free of charge to all students in specified grades has a secular, legislative purpose, the furtherance of educational opportunities available to the young, and does not have the primary effect of advancing religion. The Establishment Clause does not prevent a state from extending certain benefits to its citizens regardless of their religious affiliation.

Dissent: (Black, J.) The law in question is a flagrant and open violation of the First and Fourteenth Amendments. Tax revenues cannot constitutionally be used to support religious schools. The First Amendment's prohibition against governmental establishment of religion was written on the assumption that state aid to religion and religious schools generates disharmony, discord, hatred and strife among people. The wall of separation between church and state should remain high and impregnable.

Thomas v. Indiana Employment Security Review Board (S. Ct. 1981)

Facts: Thomas (P), a Jehovah's Witness, quit his job upon being transferred to the armaments production department of his company. P alleged that assisting in the production of weapons violated his religious beliefs. The State of Indiana refused to grant unemployment compensation benefits after determining that P's termination of his employment was not for "good cause arising in connection with his work."

Issue: Does a state's denial of unemployment compensation benefits to an individual who terminated his employment because his religious beliefs forbade participation in the production of weaponry violate the First Amendment right to the free exercise of religion?

Rule: When a state conditions receipt of an important benefit upon conduct proscribed by a religious faith, or when it denies such a benefit because of conduct mandated by religious beliefs, thereby placing substantial pressure on an adherent to modify his behavior and to violate his beliefs, a burden upon religion exists. Such burden on religion is permissible only upon a showing that it is the least restrictive means of achieving some compelling state interest.

Dissent: (Rehnquist, J.) The Court reads the Free Exercise Clause more broadly than is warranted. In this case it cannot be said that the state has discriminated against this individual on the basis of his religious beliefs or that he was denied benefits because of his religion. The state has enacted a general statute, the purpose and effect of which is to advance the state's secular goals. The Free Exercise Clause does not require the state to conform that statute to the dictates of the religious conscience of any group.

State ex rel. Swann v. Pack (1975)

Facts: Swann, pursuant to a state statute forbidding the handling or exhibition of poisonous snakes "in such a manner as to endanger the life and health of any person," brought suit against Pack, pastor of The

Holiness Church of God in Jesus Name, to force the discontinuance of a religious practice that involved the handling of poisonous snakes.

Issue: May a state enjoin a religious group from handling poisonous snakes as a part of its religious service and in accordance with its articles of faith, on the basis that such action constitutes a public nuisance?

Rule: Although the right to believe is absolute, the right to act is subject to reasonable regulation designed to protect a compelling state interest. Therefore, a religious practice may be limited, curtailed or restrained to the point of outright prohibition, where it involves a clear and present danger to the interests of society.

Lee v. Weisman (S. Ct. 1992)

Facts: At the invitation of the Providence school system, a rabbi offered nondenominational invocation and benediction prayers at a public middle school graduation.

Issue: Is the Establishment Clause of the First Amendment violated by permitting clergy to offer nondenominational prayers at graduation ceremonies of public schools?

Rule: (Kennedy, J.) Clergy may not offer prayers at public school graduations. This constitutes pervasive government involvement with religious activity; the second prong of the *Lemon* test provides that a governmental practice must have a primary effect that neither aids nor inhibits religion.

Dissent: (Scalia, J.) Constitutional interpretation cannot rest upon the Justices' changing philosophy, but must have deep foundations in historic practices. The longstanding tradition of prayer at official ceremonies makes it clear that the Establishment Clause does not forbid the government from accommodating it.

Aguilar v. Felton (S. Ct. 1985)

Facts: The City of New York, pursuant to a state statute authorizing the Secretary of Education to financially assist local educational institutions to meet the needs of educationally deprived children from low-income families, provided instructional services to parochial school students on the premises of parochial schools, including private, church-affiliated schools.

Issue: May a city use public funds to finance instructional programs for students on the premises of private, parochial schools?

Rule: A city instructional program for students conducted on parochial schools' premises necessarily demands continuous supervision by the city. Continuous city supervision inevitably results in excessive entanglement of church and state in violation of the Establishment Clause of the First Amendment.

Dissent: (Rehnquist, J.) The Court strikes down nondiscriminatory, nonsectarian aid to educationally deprived children from low-income families through the "Catch 22" paradox of its own creation – that is, aid must be supervised to ensure no entanglement but the supervision itself is held to cause an entanglement. We have traveled far afield from the concerns which prompted the adoption of the First Amendment when we rely on gossamer abstractions to invalidate a law which obviously meets an entirely secular need.

Bowen v. Kendrick (S. Ct. 1988)

Facts: A federal grant program provided funding to institutions, including religiously affiliated organizations, that rendered services relating to adolescent sexuality and pregnancy.

Issue: Does a federally funded program allowing religiously affiliated organizations to participate in providing educational and counseling services to adolescents violate the Establishment of Religion Clause of the First Amendment?

Rule: Religiously affiliated organizations not "pervasively sectarian" may participate in federally funded social programs if (1) the program has a secular purpose; (2) the organization's participation does not have the primary effect of advancing its religious doctrines; and (3) the necessary monitoring functions of the state do not result in excessive entanglement between church and state.

Dissent: (Blackmun, J.) The risk of advancing religion at public expense, and of creating an appearance that the government is endorsing the medium and the message, is great when the religious organization is directly engaged in pedagogy. While it is evident that the federal statute does not pass muster under *Lemon*'s "effects" prong, the unconstitutionality of the statute becomes even more apparent when one discerns the degree of entanglement between church and state that would be required to prevent subsidizing the advancement of religion through federal funds.

Allegheny County v. ACLU (S. Ct. 1989)

Facts: The City of Pittsburgh constructed two holiday displays on public property. A crèche was placed on the Grand Staircase of the Allegheny County Courthouse, and a Chanukah menorah was placed just outside the City-County Building, next to a Christmas tree and a sign saluting liberty. The Court of Appeals ruled that each display violated the Establishment Clause.

Issue: May the government display objects with religious significance on public grounds?

Rule: (Blackmun, J.) As noted in Justice O'Connor's *Lynch* concurrence, the government's use of an object with religious meaning is unconstitutional if it has the effect of endorsing religion. The effect of the display depends upon the message that the government's practice communicates; that inquiry turns upon the context in which the contested object appears. In this case, the crèche stands alone on the most beautiful part of the county building — nothing in the context of the display detracts from its religious message, and therefore it impermissibly expresses the government's endorsement of Christianity. The display of the Chanukah menorah, however, is accompanied by larger, secular symbols of the winter season. Thus, it is not "sufficiently likely" that residents of Pittsburgh will perceive the combined display of the tree, the sign, and the menorah as an endorsement or "disapproval of their individual religious choices."
Concurrence: (Kennedy, J.) There is no suggestion here that the government's power to coerce has been used to further the interests of Christianity or Judaism in any way. No one was compelled to observe or participate in any religious ceremony or activity. There is no realistic risk, therefore, that the crèche or the menorah represent an effort to proselytize or are otherwise the first step down the road to an establishment of religion.
Concurrence: (O'Connor, J.) An Establishment Clause standard that prohibits only "coercive" practices or overt efforts at government proselytization fails to take account of the numerous more subtle ways that government can show favoritism to particular beliefs. Religious liberty is better protected through the "endorsement" test, which depends on a sensitivity to the unique circumstances and context of a particular challenged practice.
Dissent: (Brennan, J.) The display of an object that retains a specifically Christian or other religious meaning is incompatible with the separation of church and state demanded by our Constitution.
Dissent: (Stevens, J.) The Establishment Clause should be construed to create a strong presumption against the display of religious symbols on public property.

Lyng v. Northwest Indian Cemetery Protective Ass'n (S. Ct. 1988)

Facts: The federal government wished to permit timber harvesting in, or construct a road through, a section of the National Forest in northwest California that three American Indian tribes had traditionally used for religious purposes.
Issue: May the federal government, consistent with the Free Exercise Clause of the First Amendment, pursue a land-use program that would have severe adverse effects on a portion of the land used by a group of American Indians for religious purposes?

Rule: (Stevens, J.) A federal program making it more difficult to practice certain religions but which does not coerce individuals into acting contrary to their religious belief is valid without a showing of compelling justification for the program. Therefore, government is not precluded from pursuing certain programs because it renders the practice of a religion much more difficult.

Dissent: (Brennan, J.) When proposed government action poses a "substantial and realistic threat of frustrating . . . religious practices," the government bears the burden of "coming forward with a compelling state interest sufficient to justify the infringement of those practices."

Zobrest v. Catalina Foothills Dist. (S. Ct. 1993)

Facts: Parents of a deaf child sued when the state refused to provide a sign language interpreter to their child who was a student in a religious school, when a statute generally provided such services to students.

Issue: Is the Establishment Clause violated when the state provides a sign language interpreter to a religious school student as part of its overall provision of such interpreters to deaf students?

Rule: (Rehnquist, C.J.) There is no Establishment Clause violation in such a case, given the evenhandedness of the state assistance and the attenuated link between that assistance and benefits accruing to the religious school itself.

Dissent: (Blackmun, J.) Provision of this assistance places the government in a religious classroom, transmitting religious doctrine.

Board of Education Kiryas Joel Village Sch. Dist. v. Grumet (S. Ct. 1994)

Facts: New York created a new school district including only members of a particular Hasidic Jewish sect, in order to accommodate the sect's particular requirements with regard to education.

Issue: Does the New York law merely accommodate religious expression, or become a religious establishment?

Rule: (Souter, J.) By carving out a district for one religious group New York has established a religion. There is no way for a court to know whether other groups will receive similar treatment, or indeed whether religion in general will be favored over non-religion.

Dissent: (Scalia, J.) The Court confuses accommodation of a small religious sect with establishment.

Agostini v. Felton (S. Ct. 1997)

Facts: New York program sending remedial education instructors into parochial schools was deemed unconstitutional and enjoined; after intervening case law the state sought to escape from the injunction, arguing that the program was now constitutional under the new case law.

Issue: May a state send instructors into parochial schools to instruct on non-sectarian topics?

Rule: (O'Connor, J.) Subsequent case law makes clear that such programs are constitutional, since they are evenhanded as between religious and non-religious education; as long as the program includes mechanisms for ensuring that the state teachers do not entangle themselves in religious education there is no Establishment Clause violation.

Dissent: (Souter, J.) The Court's decision legitimizes massive government aid to religious schools, and therefore violates the Establishment Clause.

Rosenberger v. Rectors of the Univ. of Virginia (S. Ct. 1995)

Facts: A state university refused to allocate funds to a student group that ran a religious publication, citing the Establishment Clause.

Issue: Does a refusal to fund a student religious group violate the First Amendment, and if so, is such violation necessary in order to comply with the Establishment Clause?

Rule: (Kennedy, J.) There is a First Amendment violation as here the school has created a forum but then engaged in viewpoint discrimination within that forum. Nor is the violation excused by the need to comply with the Establishment Clause: because the student program money would be handed out evenhandedly, there is no unconstitutional government promotion of religion.

Locke v. Davey (S. Ct. 2004)

Facts: Washington state gives scholarships to eligible college students, but, because of a state constitutional provision against aid to religious schools, does not provide scholarships for students pursuing degrees in theology.

Issue: Does the state violate the Free Exercise Clause by not distinguishing between religious studies and all others when providing scholarship assistance?

Rule: (Rehnquist, C.J.) If there is any room between the requirements of the Free Exercise and Establishment Clauses, these facts fall within that room. The state must be free to honor its non-Establishment principle in this way. The state has simply chosen not to fund religious instruction.

Dissent: (Scalia, J.) This is discrimination against religion and thus runs afoul of the Free Exercise Clause.

City of Boerne v. Flores (S. Ct. 1997)

Facts: P, a Catholic archdiocese, sued D city alleging that the city's failure to allow it to expand a church in a historic district violated the federal Religious Freedom Restoration Act, which required that states imposing restrictions that affected religious practice show that the restriction was narrowly tailored in order to serve a compelling government interest.

Rule: (Kennedy, J.) Congress' power to enforce the Fourteenth Amendment does not give it the power to reinterpret the Fourteenth Amendment, and there was an insufficient factual showing to convince the Court that the statute was "congruent and proportional" to the Fourteenth Amendment rights the statute sought to protect.

Zelman v. Simmons-Harris (S. Ct. 2002)

Facts: Ohio provided Cleveland school students with vouchers that they could use in a variety of different public school settings, or in any private school, including a religious school, as long as the private school did not teach hatred of other religions.

Issue: Do voucher programs violate the Establishment Clause by giving aid to students who can take the aid to parochial schools?

Rule: (Rehnquist, C.J.) Such programs do not violate the Constitution as the vouchers can be used either at public or private school; most students choose to stay in public schools, so there is not a favoritism shown for religious education.

Dissent: (Souter, J.) This program allows significant aid to religious schools. Most students who took vouchers for private education used them at private schools, and indeed the amount of the vouchers was close to the average cost of education in Catholic schools, where many students took their vouchers. The requirement that the schools not teach hatred will enmesh state officials in making judgments about religious doctrine.

Lamb's Chapel v. Center Moriches Sch. Dist. (S. Ct. 1993)

Facts: A school district made its facilities available to local community groups, but prohibited religious groups from use when they wanted to use the facilities to discuss family and childrearing from a religious perspective.

Issue: Is the exclusion of religious groups a violation of the Free Speech Clause?

Rule: (White, J.) The district's action constitutes viewpoint discrimination, as other discussions of family and childrearing from a nonreligious perspective were allowed. Nor would allowing the group access violate the Establishment Clause, as it would be clear that the discussions were not school sponsored and would not lead anyone to think that their religious viewpoint was endorsed by the district.

Good News Club v. Milford Central School (S. Ct. 2001)

Facts: A school allowed use of its facilities for certain purposes, but denied use to a religious group that wished to engage in religious speech.
Issue: Does denial of a religious group's request to use facilities, otherwise open for community groups, to engage in religious speech violate the group's free speech rights?
Rule: (Thomas, J.) This case is indistinguishable from *Lamb's Chapel*; there is no significant difference in the fact that in *Lamb's Chapel* the group wanted to speak on a secular topic from a religious perspective, while here it wants to engage in religious speech. As in *Lamb's Chapel*, allowing the group to speak would not have violated the Establishment Clause, given that the activities took place after school hours and would not have been perceived as endorsed by the school.
Dissent: (Souter, J.) The group seeks to use the facility for religious purposes, not to speak on secular topics from a religious perspective; thus, the case is distinguishable from *Lamb's Chapel*.

Church of the Lukumi Babalu Aye v. Hialeah (S. Ct. 1993)

Facts: The city banned the ritual sacrifice of animals and otherwise banned killing animals, but with exceptions that left ritual sacrifice the only major activity banned. A religious group that engaged in ritual sacrifices sued, claiming a violation of their Free Exercise Clause rights.
Issue: May a city, in pursuit of a desire to protect against animal cruelty, ban animal sacrifices?
Rule: (Kennedy, J.) The ordinance targets religious conduct and hence is subject to strict scrutiny. The ordinance is not narrowly tailored to carry out its humane goals and thus violates the Free Exercise Clause.

McCreary County v. ACLU (S. Ct. 2005)

Facts: A Kentucky county posted large copies of the Ten Commandments in its courtrooms. After litigation began the county added smaller copies of several other historical documents containing religious elements. After a court enjoined the display, the county again changed the display to include equal-sized displays of a variety of documents including the Ten Commandments, and text explaining their relevance to American law and history.
Issue: Does the final version of the display violate the Establishment Clause, in light of the history of the county's action?

Rule: (Souter, J.) Considered in light of the history of the litigation, the county had an intent to emphasize the religious message of the commandments, rather than their secular nature as legal rules. The county's final display was unaccompanied by any resolution from the county suggesting a different purpose than the religious one underlying the first two displays. Thus, the preliminary injunction against the display was proper.

Concurrence: (O'Connor, J.) The county's display conveys to the reasonable observer a message of endorsement of a particular religion and thus violates the Establishment Clause.

Dissent: (Scalia, J.) Given federal officials' conduct early in the nation's history, the Establishment Clause must be understood to allow government to favor religion over irreligion, or even monotheistic religions over polytheistic ones.

Van Orden v. Perry (S. Ct. 2005)

Fact: The Fraternal Order of Eagles donated two large tablets of the Ten Commandments to the State of Texas, which displayed them on the state capitol grounds along with other sculptures reflecting various aspects of Texas history and the cultures of the people making up Texas. An individual using the state law library sued, alleging the display of the tablets violated the Establishment Clause.

Issue: Is the Establishment Clause violated by a display of the Ten Commandments among a larger display of sculptures reflecting secular themes?

Plurality Rule: (Rehnquist, C.J.) The test from *Lemon v. Kurtzman*, 403 U.S. 602 (1971) is not appropriate to judge the type of passive monument at issue here. Historically governments in the United States have acknowledged the role of religion in American life; this monument is similar to those historical examples. Moreover, the Ten Commandments have been recognized for their role in America's heritage.

Concurrence: (Scalia, J.) Government can favor religion over non-religion and can also, in a non-proselytizing way, venerate the Ten Commandments.

Concurrence: (Thomas, J.) It may be that the Establishment Clause should not be incorporated so as to apply against the states. But even if it does the proper test is state coercion of religious belief, which is absent here.

Concurrence in the Judgment: (Breyer, J.) This is a close call that cannot be answered by abstract tests. Here, it appears that the display, which was unchallenged for 40 years, conveyed a predominantly secular message.

Dissent: (Stevens, J.) In displaying the tablets Texas endorses the moral code of the Judeo-Christian God, in violation of the Establishment Clause.

Dissent: (O'Connor, J.) I agree with Justice Souter's dissent.

Dissent: (Souter, J.) An observer on the state capitol grounds would believe that Texas is speaking a religious, not a secular, message by presenting the tablets, given the lettering of the monument and the lack of a unifying, secular theme of all the other sculptures on the capitol grounds.

Cutter v. Wilkinson (S. Ct. 2005)

Facts: State prisoners sued prison officials alleging violation of their rights under the Religious Land Use and Institutionalized Persons Act (RLUIPA), which, *inter alia*, provides that government "shall not impose a substantial burden on the religious exercise of a person residing in or confined to an institution" unless the burden furthers "a compelling government interest" and does so by "the least restrictive means." Officials responded that the statute violated the Establishment Clause by giving religious exercise rights greater protection than other constitutional rights.
Issue: Does RLUIPA violate the Establishment Clause?
Rule: (Ginsburg, J.) It does not. The statute alleviates exceptional government-created burdens on religious exercise caused by commitment of the individual to a government institution. The statute requires that accommodations take into account the effect they have on non-believers, requires neutrality between religions, and allows government to take account of legitimate security concerns. If accommodations requested under the statute become unduly burdensome then officials may challenge the statute as applied to such overly onerous accommodation requests.
Concurrence: (Thomas, J.) The historical understanding of the Establishment Clause leads to the same conclusion as the majority's, since that understanding shows that the Clause does not prohibit the federal government from legislating on matters of religion.